Encyclopedia of

Travel Literature

Encyclopedia of

Travel Literature

Christopher K. Brown

ABC-CLIO

Santa Barbara, California
Denver, Colorado
Oxford, England

Library of Congress Cataloging-in-Publication Data
Brown, Christopher K. (Christopher Kevin), 1967–
Encyclopedia of travel literature / Christopher K. Brown.
    p. cm.
Includes bibliographical references and index.
  ISBN 0-87436-940-1 (hardcover : alk. paper)
  1. Travelers' writings—Encyclopedias. 2. Travel in
literature—Encyclopedias. I. Title.
G465.B765   2000
910'.2—dc21   00-009591

06 05 04 03 02 01 00   10 9 8 7 6 5 4 3 2 1

ABC-CLIO, Inc.
130 Cremona Drive, P.O. Box 1911
Santa Barbara, California 93116-1911

Typesetting by Pro Production, Mahwah, New Jersey

This book is printed on acid-free paper ⊗.
Manufactured in the United States of America.

CONTENTS

Introduction, vii

Encyclopedia of Travel Literature

v

INTRODUCTION

When I tell people that I wrote the *Encyclopedia of Travel Literature,* they usually smile and look confused. Some think it is about hotel listings, train schedules, and tourist attractions. Others think it is a compendium of trip journals and voyage accounts, an anthology misnamed *encyclopedia.* Most just respond by asking, "What *is* travel literature?"

Of course, as with any really good question, the answer is complex. To more clearly explain what it is that this book is about, we have to recognize the two distinct components of the term: *travel* and *literature.*

On the one hand, we have *travel,* which evokes images of a voyage, of a journey, or of going from one place to another. In spite of the way the word *travel* is sometimes colloquially used—"Travel time on the inbound expressway is 20 minutes" or "French wine does not travel well"—I want to employ the word to suggest its fullest and traditional sense. *Travel* as a modern English word grew out of the Middle English *travailen* (to toil or to make a toilsome journey), which comes from the Old French *travaillier* (to labor or to work at strenuous physical or mental activities). The same root grew into the contemporary *travail* with its simultaneous connotations of grueling labor and misadventure. Thus travel, at its core, may not be as we think of it—a vacation—but rather a serious activity that is filled with adversity, difficulty, and discomfort: in short, travel is a sort of work.

One aspect of the work of travel lies in recording the journey, the experiences, and the learning gained from them. In many world cultures the idea of a pilgrimage, religious or otherwise, is central to the narrative history of a people. Whether it be an Islamic pilgrimage to Mecca, or one made by early Anglo-Christians to Canterbury (as seen, for example, in Geoffrey Chaucer's *Canterbury Tales*), or other types of pilgrimages in countless other traditions, the journey is imagined to be educational and worthy of recounting in narrative form.

We must also recall that travel literature can never be objective. These texts are always a representation of a perception, and as such, there is a significant element of subjectivity contained within them. As hard as some of these stories try to be documentary-style reports, they can never succeed in fully capturing the objective phenomena. In reading these texts we must resist the temptation to view them as anything more than an individual's take on a very complex world.

Moreover, given that the majority of human history occurred before the advent of the photographic camera, a written record served as proof of having actually been somewhere. As William Bligh, captain of the *Bounty,* noted in a letter to his colleague, "I am indebted for securing my journals and commission, with some material ship papers. Without these I had nothing to certify what I had done and my honour and character might have been suspected, without my possessing a proper document to have defended them" (Rugoff 437). The text provides material evidence, albeit highly subjective, of a particular travel.

Toward this end, the authors discussed in this volume have written about their own travels, either in first-person accounts or in mediated fictional disguise (or somewhere in between). While it may be possible to imagine a place one has never actually visited, it seems to me that there is a spark of energy and verisimilitude that shines out of personal experience recalled. We often understand life as a journey; to invert the metaphor suggests that the travels of life function to teach us profound and personal lessons.

It is at this point that we have to consider the second term: *literature*. What makes a text literary or not remains a vexing question that still arouses great debates among scholars. Yet it is clear to me that not everything written constitutes literature. To be sure, a text may have specific components of interest or great value in a certain context, but it may be all but unreadable to a general audience. For the purpose of this book, I will use a very conservative and somewhat traditional measuring stick: literature names texts that transcend their own era to ring true or to be valuable to subsequent generations. Texts that can still teach us about curiosity and wonder, about courage, about determination, about those abstract traits that may be called the "human spirit" are to my mind literature. In addition, the authors covered in this volume have a general appeal based both on the quality of their writing style and on their plots. Without a doubt, almost every text is of some interest to some specialist for some reason, but literature is interesting to a broad community of people for a variety of reasons.

Hence *travel literature* designates those texts that recount the journey of a person from one place to a significantly different place and that have enduring qualities—be they formal or content-based—that resonate with readers from different eras with different interests and backgrounds.

Using these qualifications as selection criteria would yield a book 10 times as large as the one you hold in your hands. Just wander into a good antiquarian bookstore and browse the shelves and shelves of travel tales, many with provocative titles but little name recognition. Many of these texts, though perhaps travel literature, have not been integrated into the canon, that is, the sanctioned or generally accepted body of related works. As scholars and students investigate additional primary texts and formulate more inclusive definitions of travel literature, surely some of these works will be resuscitated and included in the canon. To further refine the topic, let me limit the scope of this project to travel literature of several particular variants.

For this volume, I am restricting coverage to include only Western European culture, including the United States. There are many great and magnificent examples of travel literature from many different traditions; I shall leave them for subsequent volumes. Not only are the authors discussed in this book from the Western tradition, they must also be widely available in a modern English edition or translation. There exists a wealth of untranslated Dutch travelogues, a host of out-of-print nineteenth-century travel novels, endless rare travel poems, and so forth. These too, unfortunately, must be omitted from this collection. Finally, I have attempted to select the most famous travelers—many of whom are famous for other accomplishments—and the most well-known accounts of travel, exploration, and adventure. In other words, you will notice a preponderance of canonical literary figures who you might be surprised to learn were avid travelers who wrote astoundingly vivid tales of their journeys.

Beyond biographical and historical fact, the authors covered in this encyclopedia share another common characteristic: they all employ travel either as the engine of the plot or as the motivation for writing the book. In other words, the main event of the plot has to be travel, as in Jules Verne's *Around the World in Eighty Days*, or travel has to be the reason for writing the text, as in Christopher Columbus's diaries. To be sure, there are a vast number of texts that deal in part with travel or contain instances of travel. Almost every novel ever written has some moment of travel or transition. Although the principles employed in this book and outlined in this introduction surely apply to these situations in other texts, for the sake of a manageable project, this volume contains only texts in which travel is both primary as a theme and central as an event.

Furthermore, I have selected the Age of Exploration (roughly the fifteenth century) as a chronological starting point. It is no coincidence that this period corresponds to the Renaissance and the rise of print culture facilitated by the invention of the printing press. As European states became more stable and wealthier, people began to range far and wide abroad. Concurrently, emerging print technologies allowed an exchange of written ideas in unprecedented quantities. Writing about journeys was a way to learn about far-flung and wondrous places without risking the danger, hardship, and expense of the voyage.

I do not mean to discount the glorious and educational travel literature of the Greeks, Romans, and early Christians. Certainly, to name only the most famous, *The Odyssey, The Aeneid,* and the Bible remain archetypal travelers' tales that define the genre. Oral tales and folklore as well contain vast quantities of what must surely be called travel literature. Such texts are, alas, not to be found in this volume. However, some of them are discussed in detail in other ABC-CLIO books such as *The Encyclopedia of Traditional Epics* and *Travel Legend and Lore.*

When limiting the scope of this project, I consciously sought an array of different forms. I have tried to balance the number of travelogues, fictional travel novels, travel poems, and adventure logs. To achieve roughly proportional coverage, I have had to pass over some decent and worthy texts in each category.

Now that we have some precise parameters, let me note a consistent thematic component that marks the texts in this study. The best sort of travel literature tells two stories:

the story of looking at difference, of seeing other peoples, other places, other ideas; and the story of what such looking tells us about the looker. In fact, this combination has made the genre of travel literature a current academic "hot topic" that great numbers of scholars are pursuing and analyzing.

Through reading these stories of travel, exploration, and adventure, we not only get to see many foreign peoples and places, but we also come to see how the narrator/author responds to difference. The academic terms for these positions are the *self* and the *other.* As asserted by many theoretical schools from psychoanalysis to postcolonialism, humans must recognize the other in order to know the self. The process by which this recognition occurs hinges upon knowing and accepting often profound and irreconcilable differences among individuals, cultures, or any number of ideological camps. By extension, reading these texts suggests to us strategies to accommodate an array of unfamiliar others found at every turn in daily life. Said another way, reading these texts can teach us quite a lot about ourselves.

It is through comparison and contrast that we know most certainly who we are as individuals and as members of a larger culture. In infancy, each one of us had to identify a differentiated self that is distinct from the other that is the mother. As social creatures, we form various groups—from families to communities to nations—in order to define ourselves as insiders among outsiders. Although often in subtle ways, humans notice and respond to difference every day. Only by recognizing what we *are not* can we fully understand what we *are.* When we leave our homes, when we step outside the familiar, we begin to see that which we have taken for granted. Traveling to a new city invariably leads to comparison: "This sure isn't like New York" or even "This reminds me of Berlin"—the implication of the latter being that the city one is in and Berlin are alike in being very different from, say, Bangkok. Thus travel and narrative accounts thereof serve as allegories of larger issues of personal growth and cultural exchange.

Notions of difference exist down to the fundamental nature of language. As structuralists and deconstructionists argue, linguistic communication depends upon differentiation and distinction to carry meaning. Therefore, in the writing of the journey there are many levels of recognizing difference.

Accounts of prolonged travel often starkly differentiate home from elsewhere. Nothing encourages homesickness and patriotism more than a year or so abroad. It fascinates me to see how we remember our own culture after an extended absence. That which normally goes unnoticed can become an obsession when we are far away from home. How many British travelers yearn for the landscapes of England, of which they heretofore thought nothing—or even bemoaned? Most of the travelers' tales included in this book share the common thread of noting difference; they use the familiar notions of home as a sort of canvas on which to paint an image of the foreign. To use Dorothy's famous line from *The Wizard of Oz:* "Toto, I don't think we're in Kansas anymore." Obviously, Oz differs greatly from home. Consciously or subconsciously, the traveler always sets the foreign in comparison to home.

Embedded in travel literature is a link to a larger discussion of colonialism. Implicit within most cultural comparisons lurks a judgmental hierarchy: "We do it this way, they do it that way" may sound neutral but may also contain a subtext of superiority and inferiority. Noting difference may be benign, but seeking to eradicate those differences, especially on a selective basis, has led to some of the worst atrocities of modern civilization. Throughout the various entries in this encyclopedia, I provide examples of particularly provocative incidents of imperialism, but for the most part discussions of colonialism require a greater level of historical context and textual detail than I can provide in the space of this volume. Certainly many of the texts examined in this work can be discussed in terms of their colonialist tendencies, but I leave such precise applications to the reader.

Finally, I wish to acknowledge the rich metaphoric tradition of travel. Life is often figured as a sort of journey and reading as a voyage into another world. To borrow John Keats's famous line about reading a translation of Homer, "Much have I travell'd in realms of gold." To read is a form of travel, and travel literature functions as more than armchair recreation. We might think of travel as one of the primary experiences of human existence, against which everything else is compared. I invite you, then, to join me in an adventure through texts and the worlds they describe. What we can learn about ourselves and a variety of others is almost limitless.

Bon voyage!

Encyclopedia of

Travel Literature

ADAMS, DOUGLAS

According to Douglas Adams (English, 1952–), the idea for *The Hitchhiker's Guide to the Galaxy* "first cropped up while I was lying drunk in a field in Innsbruck, Austria, in 1971" (Adams vi). He had been wandering widely through Europe when the idea struck. In the last 25 years, Adams has adapted his satiric parody of travel literature for many media: a BBC radio series, television and film versions, comic books, and, of course, a bewildering collection of texts. The series has enjoyed astounding success, with worldwide sales of the books alone estimated at over 14 million copies! For the sake of this study, I will restrict my commentary to the collected stories published by Wings Books as *The Ultimate Hitchhiker's Guide* (1996). This edition contains an introductory essay by Adams and all six novels: *The Hitchhiker's Guide to the Galaxy; The Restaurant at the End of the Universe; Life, the Universe, and Everything; So Long, and Thanks for All the Fish; Young Zaphod Plays It Safe;* and *Mostly Harmless.* Of course, all of these texts have been published separately and in various combinations.

The premise for all of these stories is the desire for cheap travel and aimless adventure, going not to get anywhere in particular, but simply to go; yet instead of limiting the scope to Earth, Adams depicts the random wanderings of his characters through the wide universe. Yet again and again, travel throughout the universe resembles nothing so much as wandering around Europe.

The principal personalities in all six novels are Arthur Dent, a bumbling Englishman who stumbles into and out of all manner of remarkable situations; Ford Prefect, a plucky intergalactic travel writer who befriends Arthur; Zaphod Beeblebrox, onetime president of the universe turned renegade turned hero; and Trillian, the Earthling love interest of, at various times, all three.

As neophytes to a richly inhabited universe, readers identify with Arthur, to whom all of this is strange, new, and mostly incomprehensible. He quickly learns, however, that the key to intergalactic travel is the ability to hitchhike on passing interstellar ships and that the only invaluable tool in the universe, for the cosmic vagabond at least, is a computerized "book" called *The Hitchhiker's Guide to the Galaxy.* This book contains all he needs to know about the infinite universe (!): its people, its places, and its quirks. Using this guide, Arthur and Ford gallivant in many directions through time and space.

As travel literature, Adams's work functions by repeatedly using the oddness of the universe to set the familiar, Earthly equivalents in relief. In other words, by experiencing difference, Arthur—and, by association, the reader—reflects upon his own home.

The physical difficulties of traveling provide one example of Arthur finding that some components of a journey are indeed universal. To depict the fatigue and discomfort of intergalactic travel is to inflate the familiar woes of Earthly voyages. Along the way, Adams inserts his own wry and biting critique of modernity. Arthur muses:

> The trouble with most forms of transport . . . is basically that not one of them is worth all the bother. On Earth—when there had been an Earth, before it was demolished to make way for a new hyperspace bypass—the problem had been with cars. The disadvantages involved in pulling lots of black sticky slime from out of the ground where it had been

safely hidden out of harm's way, turning it into tar to cover the land with, smoke to fill the air with and pouring the rest into the sea, all seemed to outweigh the advantages of being able to get more quickly from one place to another—particularly when the place you arrived at had probably become, as a result of this, very similar to the place you had left, i.e., covered with tar, full of smoke and short of fish. (257)

On another occasion, Arthur likens the development of time travel to the homogenization of the modern world. Backward time travel has the curious, if not paradoxical, ability to make the past more like the future: "Just as easy travel eroded the differences between one country and another, and between one world and another, so time travel is now eroding the differences between one age and another. 'The past,' they say, 'is now truly like a foreign country. They do things exactly the same there'" (390). Much as the early modern travelers found that venturing forth to foreign cultures could shed light upon their beloved homelands, so too does Adams propose that space and time travel can teach valuable lessons. As readers of this series, we may find it uncanny to imagine a universe that is at once very different but also so similar to what we already know, as though affirming our hope that some characteristics and ideas are universal. Cynically, Adams seems to posit greed, lust, and egomania as the traits that we Earthlings share with our cosmic cousins.

Nonetheless, travel teaches Arthur and changes his perspective. Upon his return to Earth (he has to go back in time to get there), after having seen the universe, Arthur views his familiar home very differently: "They were not the same eyes with which he had last looked out at this particular scene, and the brain which interpreted the images the eyes resolved was not the same brain. There had been no surgery involved, just the continual wrenching of experience" (506). This passage might serve as an encapsulated summary of the entire history of travel literature: expanding one's horizons changes everything. Having seen difference changes the entire perceptive process; we do indeed see with new eyes.

Arthur continues with this idea in the next book: "He had long ago realized that a lot of things that he had thought of as natural, like buying people presents at Christmas, stopping at red lights or falling at a rate of 32 feet per second, were just the habits of his own world and didn't necessarily work the same way anywhere else" (709). It seems an easy leap to apply the same logic to Earthly travel between different cultures: seeing the foreign makes us aware of the familiar. That which we take for granted may be entirely culture specific—or worse yet, completely arbitrary. Seeing the other can cause us to view our homes in a new light.

The *Hitchhiker's Guide* series goes a long way toward demonstrating and highlighting the principles of travel and the lessons of travel literature; indeed, as readers we do not need to hitchhike far and wide to learn what Arthur can teach us.

References: Adams 1996

ADDISON, JOSEPH

One of the touted literary lions of the eighteenth century, Joseph Addison (English, 1672–1719) has any number of great accomplishments to his credit. Famous in his own lifetime, he published widely in popular journals like *Tatler, The Guardian,* and *The Spectator.* Sometime teacher, translator of Roman classics, statesman, poet, opera librettist, and traveler, Addison's curiosity had vast resources.

Well educated and socially well connected, Addison quickly made a name for himself as a promising young man of letters. To facilitate his further cultural development, the government gave him financial support to continue his studies—of language, history, art, and culture—on the Continent. For four years,

1700–1704, the Crown liberally funded Addison's pursuit of whatsoever he desired to learn. He chose to spend his time in France and Italy. The result was a small and mostly overlooked text called *Remarks on Several Parts of Italy . . . in the Years 1701, 1702, 1703.* Hardly a title for a best-seller, yet this rich little text provides a fine example of travel literature.

Though it will perhaps seem dry and long-winded to contemporary readers, in style and structure it is pure eighteenth-century essay. Addison's aim seems to be to capture a history of what he learned and how he learned it while on tour, and as such, his writing is a series of attempts at understanding cultural difference, noting historical continuity, and explaining the world around him. Like a boundlessly curious child, Addison relates his experiments and efforts to comprehend both France and Italy more fully. One of the joys of reading this work is to see how Addison's keen analytical powers take simple observations and place them in a highly sophisticated larger context.

A wide range of topics receives Addison's attention in this text. Regional linguistic quirks, geographic wonders, historic literary places, art, music, and many more subjects make up this eclectic collection. He muses on the popularity of snow—rather than ice—to chill drinks in Naples; he contrasts court manners in different cities; he tracks down references from Virgil's *Aeneid;* he describes the nuances of Italian opera; he experiments with the poisonous vapors of the *grotto del Cani* (near Naples); and he comments upon dozens of other otherwise unrelated subjects. In its scattered logic his text embodies the pure essay, literally an attempt or trial at suggesting ideas and evoking images.

Among the most interesting anecdotes are Addison's insightful characterizations of the French and the Italians in general: while they have some decided distinctions, it becomes clear that they, with the English, share a common cultural legacy and are more similar than different. Instead of confirming a disassociation, Addison suggests a unity: having seen the foreign, he places Britain, Italy, and France in a larger cultural and historical context—namely, Europe.

With its elegant style and exuberant focus, Addison's account remains one of the more lucid examples of the grand educational tour that teaches in so many different ways. By providing him with a larger circle of experience and exposure, the tour encouraged Addison to think in broader terms—the result of which is obvious in his subsequent works. It is through travel that this great and curious mind was encouraged to look at its home culture and to see both the strengths and weaknesses of England.

See also: Grand Tour
References: Adams 1988; Addison 1726; Fussell 1987

AKENSIDE, MARK

Mark Akenside (English, 1721–1770) was, like so many of the travel writers of the eighteenth century, noteworthy primarily in another field: he was the official physician to King George III in 1761. In this capacity he traveled throughout Europe. Besides his official function, Akenside was also an innovative poet whose subject matter was often travel. His book *The Pleasures of Imagination* was not published until 1774, four years after his death.

The Pleasures of Imagination is interesting for a number of reasons. For the sake of this study, Akenside's book of blank verse serves to blend, as the title suggests, the world of imagination and the world of travel into one singular experience. Pondering and musing become forms of travel; to wander in the mind is the same process, for Akenside, as to wander in exotic lands.

In addition, Akenside takes to heart the sentiment that "the past is a foreign place." Thus throughout his book, the narrator is voyaging into classical Greek ideals as much as he is traveling to eighteenth-century Greece. His physical journey corresponds with his imaginative voyage back to the Golden Age.

Stylistically, *The Pleasures of Imagination* brims with enthusiasm, energy, and vigor. Akenside possesses a vivid imagination and an impassioned sense of wording. His highly metaphoric language and innovative use of abstract comparisons make him fascinating to read. Even within the rather rigid confines of blank verse's iambic pentameter lines, he is able to express an energy and vitality that make the poem thrill.

As an example of Akenside's writing, let us look at a section about Greece. The narrator, awed by the legacy of the place, invokes the glorious and idolized past as a way to understand the country that he currently visits:

. . . From the blooming store
Of these auspicious fields, may I unblamed
Transplant some living blossoms to adorn
My native clime: while far above the flight
Of fancy's plume aspiring, I unlock
The springs of ancient wisdom; while I join
Thy name, thrice honoured! with
     th'immortal praise

Of nature; while to my compatriot youth
I point the high example of thy sons,
And tune to Attic themes the British lyre.
(Crossley-Holland 135)

Not only does he presume that the reason to travel is to learn lessons that can be taken home ("may I unblamed / Transplant some living blossoms to adorn / My native clime"), but he also sets his praise of Greece against the backdrop of Britain ("And tune to Attic themes the British lyre"). To do so reinforces one of the central themes of this volume: as much as we travel to learn of a foreign culture, we almost always come away learning something about our own culture. Indeed, Akenside seems to be mining Greece for ways to make eighteenth-century Britain a better place.

References: Crossley-Holland 1986

ARMAND, LOUIS, BARON DE LAHONTAN

See Lahontan, Louis-Armand de Lom d'Arce, Baron de

B

examples that range from silly snobbism to horrific racism. Travelers are assumed to have had a classical education—early versions do not even bother to translate Latin inscriptions—and to have plenty of money to spend. Sexism abounds in the very format of these books, for there are special sections with advice for women travelers; generally these sections recommend absurd modesty, paranoid precautions, and minimal exertion.

These fascinating documents go a long way toward describing what it must have been like to be a traveler more than 100 years ago. To analyze them is to delve into the nature of elite anglophone travelers' expectations. To my knowledge, there exists no major scholarly study of these travel guides.

BAEDEKER'S

Baedeker's is the name of one of the most widely used and well respected of all travel guidebook series. In the 1830s, German printer Karl Baedeker (1801–1859) began the series that continued to set the standard for independent travel guides until the 1920s. While the name was resuscitated in the latter part of the twentieth century, the new *Baedeker's* guides bear little resemblance to the originals of old.

Literary references to *Baedeker's France* and *Baedeker's Italy* are innumerable in turn-of-the-century novels; it seems everyone who traveled toted a *Baedeker's*. Beyond the standard Continental destinations, the series expanded to include parts of North Africa and Central Asia.

Generally meticulously researched and containing amazingly accurate maps, these old volumes can still occasionally be found at antiquarian bookstores. Each volume provides a comprehensive—if conservative— historical background of the region it covers as well as an enormous supply of literary and artistic references. From experience, I can say that to this day they are still a valuable travel resource (although the restaurant listings leave something to be desired!).

Nineteenth-century guidebooks are quite worthy of study; what they presume tells us much about the sort of person who traveled. By reading these guides, we can see what sorts of things mattered to the nineteenth-century traveler. Every volume brims with

BAINES, THOMAS

See Lord, W. B., and Thomas Baines

BARTRAM, WILLIAM

Although a minor travel writer, William Bartram (American, 1739–1823) serves as an excellent example of an American colonist traveling in the wilds of North America. Particularly noteworthy are his attitudes toward natural phenomena and Native Americans.

The son of a prominent Pennsylvania Quaker, Bartram grew up with substantial opportunities. His father took him on several lengthy and arduous journeys while he was still a child, and these formative experiences clearly made a great impression on Bartram. Though trained as a botanist, he was well versed in the arts, noted as a painter, and spoke a number of languages. His book, humbly titled *Travels* (1791), met with wide success both in America and in Great Britain. It chronicles his extensive voyage around North America, particularly the Southwest and the Wild West.

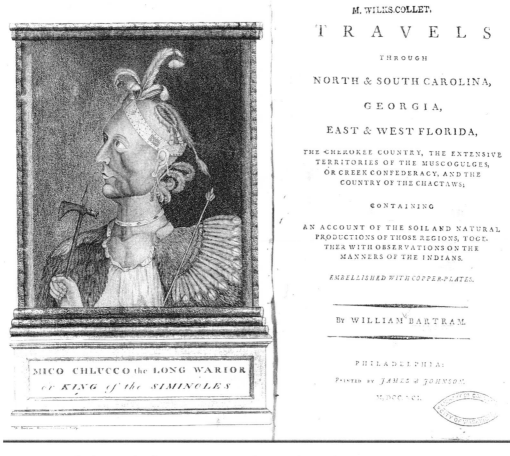

M. WILKS.COLLET.

T R A V E L S

THROUGH

NORTH & SOUTH CAROLINA,

G E O R G I A,

EAST & WEST FLORIDA,

THE CHEROKEE COUNTRY, THE EXTENSIVE
TERRITORIES OF THE MUSCOGULGES,
OR CREEK CONFEDERACY, AND THE
COUNTRY OF THE CHACTAWS;

CONTAINING

AN ACCOUNT OF THE SOIL AND NATURAL
PRODUCTIONS OF THOSE REGIONS, TOGE-
THER WITH OBSERVATIONS ON THE
MANNERS OF THE INDIANS.

EMBELLISHED WITH COPPER-PLATES.

By WILLIAM BARTRAM.

PHILADELPHIA:
PRINTED BY JAMES & JOHNSON.
M,DCC,XCI.

MICO CHLUCCO the LONG WARIOR
or KING of the SIMINOLES

Frontispiece and title page of William Bartram's Travels through North and South Carolina . . .
(Philadelphia: James and Johnson, 1791) (Library of Congress)

Bartram was most interested in undeveloped and unpopulated tracts of land; the "natural world" was his domain.

His writing is at times obsessed with taxonomy, but amid his copious and accurate detail are moments of extreme beauty. His enthusiasm may strike the modern reader as sticky sweet, but in his day such an emotional response to nature was indeed praiseworthy. In fact, Bartram's work appears to have influenced the subsequent generation of poets and essayists significantly: Thomas Carlyle and Ralph Waldo Emerson each praise Bartram, while both Samuel Taylor Coleridge and William Wordsworth appear to have borrowed imagery from him (Adams 423).

In a long section from *Travels* that details his exploration of the St. Johns River in Florida, we see Bartram calmly narrating a harrowing night in the swamps. Alone in his canoe, he camps for the night on a small isthmus. With painstaking detail, he describes his encounters with alligators, bears, and wolves. His long and tranquil paragraphs rarely show fear, but instead express awe at the brute force of these predators. He describes the scene:

The alligators were in such incredible numbers, and so close together from shore to shore, that it would have been easy to have walked across on their heads. . . . I have seen an alligator take up out of the water several great fish at a time, and just squeeze them betwixt his jaws, while the tail of the great trout flapped about his eyes and lip, ere he had swallowed them. The horrid noise of their closing jaws . . . the floods of water and blood rushing out of their mouths, and the cloud of vapour issuing from their wide nostrils, were truly frightful. (Adams 427)

Methodically, Bartram secures his belongings and fends off a variety of wild beasts for the night. In most cases, he depicts the natural world as the opposite of the civilized world whence he came. This binary relationship contains the seeds of the notion that the raw, brute forces of nature are in need of being harnessed by man.

In another instance, Bartram observes the profound abundance of nature again, but this time it is replete with Cherokee Indians. Adhering to eighteenth-century attitudes, he regards the Cherokee as part of nature, not unlike the flora and fauna, and thereby something to be studied and recorded. Instead of writing the Native Americans as bloodthirsty killers, as so many of his contemporaries did, Bartram envisions them as *noble savages*—a term that denotes peoples thought of as naturally simple and virtuous on the basis of not having yet been corrupted by Western civilization. As such, the Cherokee are prelapsarian; they have neither fallen nor been evicted from Eden and are thus innocent and joyous. Bartram writes breathlessly of

a vast expanse of green meadows and strawberry fields; a meandering river gliding through, saluting in its various turning . . . flocks of turkies strolling about them; herds of deer prancing in the meads or bounding over the hills; companies of young, innocent Cherokee virgins, some busy gathering the rich fragrant fruit, others . . . lay reclined under the shade of [an array of flowering trees], disclosing their beauties to the fluttering breeze, and bathing their limbs in cool fleeting streams; whilst other parties, more gay and libertine, were yet collecting strawberries, or wantonly chasing their companions, tantalising

them, staining their lips and cheeks with the rich fruit. (Adams 431)

Paradise found indeed!

It is precisely the emotion in his writing that makes Bartram interesting to study. By carefully reading his texts, we may begin to understand more about the author and the society that made him. Bartram's representations provide a clear example of a traveler who overlooks the rugged hardships of the land and instead lauds the vast and untouched—and highly idealized—realm of nature. In his era nature served as antidote to the maladies of civilization. Though he treats us to numerous tales of nature and beauty in the wilderness, his writing also provides an insight into the ideology of his age. Once again, this is one of the primary joys of travel literature: beyond the pleasure of the tale we are afforded insight into the narrator and his culture.

References: Adams 1988

BAUDRILLARD, JEAN

Jean Baudrillard (French, 1929–) is one of the leading philosophers of postmodernism. He has written a number of highly theoretical works as well as his 1986 travel essay called *America*. Following in the tradition of Alexis de Tocqueville and other French travelers to the United States, Baudrillard finds modern America a place at once mysteriously beautiful and unthinkably horrible. The commonplace events of his journey are spun into deeply telling symbols of America's fundamental identity.

Baudrillard's text is not in a diary or a journal format; rather, he gives us unconnected observations and snippets from his trip across the United States. It is almost as if his anecdotes are postcards: each one is tiny and self-contained, yet each captures minuscule details and startlingly astute observations. What he notes often seems random, but when framed in his (sometimes convoluted) interpretation, the objects become clearly meaningful. California, Salt Lake City, and New York unfold under Baudrillard's scrutiny.

The text functions as provocative postmodern travel literature in that it transforms the routine into something noteworthy by seeing it from a different—in this case foreign, specifically French—perspective. That which we might ordinarily not notice about our own homeland strikes the outsider's eye as bizarre or poetic or magnificent. When talking about New York, for instance, he observes:

> The number of people here who think alone, sing alone, and eat and talk alone in the streets is mind-boggling. . . . Why do people live in New York? There is no relationship between them. Except for an inner electricity which results from the simple fact of their being crowded together. A magical sensation of contiguity and attraction for an artificial centrality. . . . There is no human reason to be here, except for the sheer ecstasy of being crowded together. (Baudrillard 15)

Indeed, such observations shift us necessarily into seeing through the philosopher's eyes rather than through the eyes of a student pursuing a degree, a parent earning her living, or a tourist in town for a Broadway show. By seeing alternatively, the hope is that we might begin to be more conscious of the decisions and actions of our lives.

At times he is biting in his observations; at other times he is full of admiration. Perhaps it is this ambivalence that makes Baudrillard so interesting to read but at the same time makes him very difficult to pin down. We have come an enormous distance from the early explorers of the sixteenth century, with their clear sense of the European Christian as superior and the native as inferior. Indeed, as an example of travel literature for the present, perhaps this is one of the most sophisticated exercises. From highway signs to supermarkets, from architecture to advertising, from politics to commerce, Baudrillard addresses a remarkable array of American elements. As a highly trained thinker, he is able to unmask aspects of contemporary society to display their underlying meaning. It is by borrowing the traveler's perspective that we are able to learn from this text about ourselves.

See also: Tocqueville, Alexis de
References: Baudrillard 1988

BELL, GERTRUDE

A tireless and intrepid traveler, Gertrude Bell (English, 1868–1926) plunged boldly into the Islamic world. Her skills were many; she has been noted as a mountaineer, as an archeologist, and even as a British spy. While it is possible to call her a writer, her book is a difficult-to-find collection of her letters. Perhaps its unassuming title, *The Letters of Gertrude Bell* (1911), dissuades some readers. Nonetheless, her writing is indeed fine travel literature, for it is vivid, daring, and insightful.

Beginning in the early 1890s, Bell embarked upon a series of journeys to the Near and Middle East. Her route—if it can be called such—circled near and far throughout Persia, Syria, and Anatolia. All told, her voyages lasted almost 20 years!

One particular anecdote illustrates her character quite well. After surviving two weeks of crossing the harsh Syrian desert, she emerged full of vigor. The dumbfounded Arab chief who was to serve as her host is said to have exclaimed with trepidation, "And if this is one of their women! Allah, what must their men be like!" (Newby 271). Sexism aside, the anecdote reflects positively on Bell's tenacity and determination.

More than simply demonstrating that women could and would do what men did, Bell writes with great delight and kindness on the oft-criticized Islamic world. Upon reaching an oasis in Persia in June of 1892, Bell found herself regaled by the "prince."

Out of a sense of duty and hospitality, he treated Bell magnificently. Astonished, she remarked, with her peculiar second-person voice, "And all the time your host was probably a perfect stranger into whose privacy you had forced yourself in this unblushing way. Ah, we have no hospitality in the west and no manners" (Newby 272). Such open comparisons of Persia to England—to the favor of Persia—occur throughout Bell's writing and highlight her learning process: she learned both of the Arab cultures and of herself.

Bell's prose is extremely accessible, but it is not without subtle nuances. Her tales move quickly, but they are punctuated with tidbits of cultural observations, geographic notes, and her own exuberant emotions. Unlike many of the epistolary travelogues—be they real letters or a formal convention—Bell's rings with genuine excitement and unpretentious desires.

The harsh climate of the desert functions as an elaborate metaphor throughout Bell's writing. The constant struggle for water and shelter seems a distillation of the more complex adversities of life. When there is no water or shelter to be found, little else is important; continuing the trek becomes a matter of survival rather than a simple pleasure. At this moment, travel and life become one. Yet the lessons learned under extreme deprivation can easily be applied to more mundane situations.

Even with death a real and immediate possibility, Bell does not despair but continues to note the beauty of the landscape, the cheer of her companions, and her own excitement. When things are bleakest, she writes before bed, without a hint of irony, "If you could see the western sky with the evening star burning in it, you would give thanks—as I do" (D'Oyley 291). Perhaps this optimism is one the greatest lessons to be found in her writing.

References: D'Oyley 1932; Newby 1985

BIGNOLD, THOMAS FRANK

Thomas Frank Bignold (English, 1839–1888) served in Her Majesty's Bengal Civil Service during the British occupation of India. As a civil servant, Bignold's journey to India was not so much a choice as a duty. Yet his book of verse, *Leviora: Being the Rhyme of a Successful Competitor* (1888), serves as a good illustration of how some colonialist writing can exist as a subset of travel literature. Bignold's book has numerous worthy examples that can indeed help us see how this subspecies of travel literature works. Other than this single, fairly rare volume, it seems nothing else has marked Bignold to be remembered by history.

Most of Bignold's poems are autobiographical: they relate stories of a first-person narrator and his family in India. Let us use for our example his poem "The Holiday" (Crossley-Holland 308). Imagine the narrator as a bureaucrat during a particularly troubled and violent period of the Raj. The poem begins with a classical trope (or figurative expression)—the apostrophe (or phrase addressed directly to the audience or a god) of "Embalm, O Muse"—and then quickly shifts to something much less poetic: his desire for a vacation from the rigors of work ("The worn Civilian's well-earned holiday"). Already displaced and living in a foreign culture, the narrator posits travel as a means of escape.

In spite of starting in an exotic locale, in this case Calcutta, Bignold scarcely notes his surroundings. The foreign land has become a sort of home, hence it is, to a degree, invisible. But all the human senses are to be piqued by the tonic of travel. The narrator chooses a sea passage, with the mystery and potential vastness of the water to excite him:

> A trip to sea! but whither, gentle Muse?
> The waves are all before us, where to choose;
> Bound for what port, of all the ports that are?

It is the process of being in motion that constitutes the excitement in this case. It matters less where he is bound than that he is going.

Bignold also notes that traveling does not begin and end with the trip; rather, it precedes departure and lingers considerably after return. The formulation of plans, the arrangement of necessities, the preparations many and various comprise a portion of the traveler's joy. Said otherwise, the narrator recognizes travel as considerably more than physically going from one place to another.

Bignold's account of the actual journey shifts quickly to a light and playful style that contrasts with the stern and worried tone of the poem's first 30 lines. He jests, perhaps, at the things, attendants, and baggage he and his family needs when he says, "And I with wife and children will embark / A band two short of Noah's in the ark." Stress and worry have departed before the ship has left.

As they set out to sea, Bignold provides a lengthy account of the penal colony that they pass. He speaks compassionately of the prisoners, as though they are but plying a different trade than he is. Much suggests that this section symbolically represents the constraints of his own life as a civil servant. Bignold's escape, however, is easy, and so the journey begins.

Once at sea, the narrator delights in his isolation. The captain becomes a substitute king and their ship a microcosm of society. Says the narrator of the captain,

> Here in his sea-grit realm, mid balmy gales,
> Teased by no wire and only monthly mails
> High in his tree-clad seat above the wave
> He holds such court as crowned king might
>   crave.

The captain is thus contrasted to the very real monarch whom Bignold serves, and life at sea sets his bureaucratic life into stark relief.

The journey continues but briefly, as the holiday is quickly over. Remember, this is a working fellow, not an aristocrat on a Grand Tour. They return, tired but refreshed, to the chaotic violence of India under the Raj.

Though the actual travel is done, its effects are not. The stories remain to be told, the poems to be read, and the experience to be relived. True to its form as travel literature, "The Holiday" ends with the narrator having benefited from his journey and brimming with enthusiasm for sharing his account (and sending it to his publisher, "the Englishman"). The final stanza reads:

> So to Port Blair once more. Nay, do not
>   pout!
> My Muse, like you, fair reader, is tired out;
> I will but note the kindness and good-will
> That all untiring lighted on us still
> And urge on all who need a change of air
> The round,—Rangoon, Camorta, and Port
>   Blair;
> And to that end as swiftly as I can
> Shall take this copy to the 'Englishman'.

Travel, literature, work, and life melt into a single item in this poem, and as such, it remains an exemplary work.

See also: Grand Tour; Raj
References: Crossley-Holland 1986

BIRD, ISABELLA

Not to be confused with the similarly named Elizabeth Bishop, Isabella Bird (later Bishop by marriage; English, 1831–1904) was a proper but intrepid Victorian lady. After a rather unpromising start, she developed into one of the greatest travelers of all time. Her numerous volumes display a gift for storytelling and an exquisitely unpretentious expressive manner. For Bird, travel meant life and freedom; she ventured near and far to learn of geographies, of cultures, and, perhaps most importantly, of the universal traits that all humans share.

As the daughter of a prominent clergyman, she led a fairly sheltered early life. Shy and sickly, she fought a number of illnesses in her childhood. As an adolescent, things hardly improved; it was only when the family doctor recommended travel as a tonic that

The Author's First Ride in Perak; *frontispiece illustration in* The Golden Chersonese and the Way Thither *by Isabella Bird (New York: G. P. Putnam's Sons, 1883) (Library of Congress)*

Bird began a full recovery. Her father allowed her a modest sum that she could use to travel as she saw fit. She shrewdly succeeded in making that gift go a very long way. This journey seemed to flow into many others, and when all was said and done, she had circled the globe many times and written a multitude of very fine travel books. They are: *The Englishwoman in America* (1856), *Six Months in the Sandwich Islands* (1875), *A Lady's Life in the Rocky Mountains* (1879), *Unbeaten Tracks in Japan* (1880), *The Golden Chersonese and the Way Thither* (1883), *Journeys in Persia and Kurdistan* (1891), and *The Yangtze Valley and Beyond: An Account of Journeys in China* (1899).

In 1854, Bird set off to visit relatives in Canada. The voyage over seemed to have a remarkable effect: both the freedom and the fresh air of the Atlantic worked wonders on her illness (Stefoff 30). Thrilled with her newfound independence, she stayed only briefly with her cousin and ventured off for a three-month tour of eastern Canada and the Great Lakes region of the United States. Awed by the vast landscape and the often-rustic trains and coaches, Bird sent copious letters back to her family in Great Britain.

These letters were later compiled into her first book, *The Englishwoman in America*. Genially observational and certainly the product of a novice voyager, the text is pleasant mostly for its youthful exuberance and levity. Bird rarely minds being the butt of the joke, playfully acknowledging her own misconceptions and mistakes. As her first work, it sets the tone for her subsequent journeys and accounts thereof.

After this jaunt, she returned home, where her health deteriorated again. For a number of years she languished, writing occasionally for magazines and newspapers. What she seemed most to want was material for a new text, but she found little at hand in Britain. Returning to his original remedy, her doctor advised another journey; this medicine Bird happily took. So off she went in the opposite direction in 1872, to see the South Pacific.

As with her earlier trip, the voyage itself proved restorative. Tellingly, her letters from the passage outshine her accounts of the places she visited. Australia and New Zealand proved disappointing; Bird thought them dull and nasty. She quickly changed her plans and caught a freighter bound for San Francisco.

Magically, her spirits rebounded, eventually reaching a sort of bliss when the ship was caught in a raging storm. Clearly, the journey itself was what most thrilled Bird. At one point she rhapsodizes, "At last I am in love. And the old sea-god has so stolen my soul that hereafter though I must be elsewhere in body, I shall be with him in spirit" (Stefoff 31). This obsession with the sea would drive her for many years.

After the storm, they stopped off in the Sandwich Islands (modern Hawaii). Captivated, she disembarked and spent more than six months traversing the islands independently and capriciously. Her account of these excursions, like her first book, is comprised of letters she sent home, published as *Six Months in the Sandwich Islands.*

Enchanted with the natives and delighted with the climate—which was warm enough that she could shed the many stiff layers a Victorian woman was expected to wear—her energy and excitement propel the text effortlessly. She traveled freely and often solo, camping, climbing, riding horses, and wearing trousers. She writes of her unencumbered lifestyle: "This is the height of enjoyment in travelling. I have just camped under a *lauhaula* tree, with my saddle inverted for a pillow, my horse tied by a long lariat to a guava bush, my gear, saddle-bags, and rations for two days lying about, and my saddle blanket drying in the sun. . . . The novelty is that I am alone, my conveyance my own horse; no luggage to look after, for it is all in my saddle-bags; no guide to bother, hurry, or hinder me" (Stefoff 32). Notably, this was the antithesis of Victorian travel for women, and it

thus caused something of a scandal upon publication of the text.

After the islands, she continued to North America, again forsaking the established cities for a taste of the wilderness. Using her skills at horsemanship (perhaps we should say "horsewomanship"), she set out to explore the mountains that stretch from California to Colorado. This journey lasted some two years, with one entire winter spent stranded snowbound in a mountain cabin. Her diary and letters of this adventure were compiled and published as *A Lady's Life in the Rocky Mountains.*

This text is written in a more sophisticated voice, perhaps partly as a result of her having spent long periods of relative idleness. She waxes poetic about the natural beauty of her surroundings and spends considerable time developing the characters of those whom she meets. Most prominent in this book, aside from Bird herself, is a love interest named, aptly, Mountain Joe Nugget. While there is clearly a great attraction and mutual interest between the two, Bird eventually decides that marriage would curtail her wanderlust and freedom. So she returned to Britain alone and published her tale, which was met with considerable success.

Shortly after her return, Bird met Dr. John Bishop, who promptly fell in love with her. Still scornful of a marital encumbrance, Bird rejected his proposals and set off for Japan. For half a year she roamed the small villages and mountain hamlets of Japan, learning much about the country people and old traditions. Seeking remote and untraveled cites, Bird was probably one of the first Europeans to visit the isolated Japanese island of Hokkaido. With the success of her last book ensuring publication of her next, she sought to increase the danger factor of her travels and elevate the style of her accounts. Her two-volume account, called *Unbeaten Tracks in Japan,* proved that Bird had attained the status she desired: she had become a major and influential travel writer.

Branching off into poetic inclusion and elaborate literary references, and seeking geographic firsts, Bird's tales of Japan are remarkably good. Her voice as an author has a serene and knowing tone, unlike her earlier work that relied on her autobiographical naïveté. Such confidence, however, is not without risks: she seems obsessed with the lack of Christianity among the Japanese, and thus she veers occasionally toward proselytizing. Nonetheless, Bird retains a genuine interest in travel as an opportunity to learn. In one situation in Japan, she has just witnessed a frightful construction accident. She recounts, "Four policemen then appeared and demanded my passport, as if I were responsible for the accident. . . .They asked me what I was travelling for and on being told 'to learn about the country,' they asked if I was making a map!" (Newby 359). Indeed, we can see the gentle tone with which Bird relates the tale; she knows the value of travel, but she kindly overlooks the fact that this makes little sense to some people.

Bird abandoned her former procedure of returning to England with a text in favor of sending it to her publisher. In so doing, she could remain in Asia and begin yet another project. She had stumbled upon a passage on a steamer bound for the Malay Peninsula—an opportunity that Bird readily embraced. Her route sent her to Hong Kong, and to various ports in southern China, Vietnam, and Singapore; each of these places is detailed lavishly in *The Golden Chersonese and the Way Thither*. Perhaps more hurried than her previous books, the entries are often slightly disjointed and clipped. Yet Bird remains vivid and endearing in this text as well, sharing jovially her adventures in a radically exotic land. Rather than delving into details of the indigenous cultures, however, in this book Bird seems content to relate her daily adventures, from riding elephants to eating fiery-hot foods to donning native garb.

Even a traveler as hearty as Bird can suffer from exhaustion. After Malaysia, she returned to Scotland. Settling in to her safe life again proved depressing to Bird; the death of her dear sister dismayed her even further. Sensing the time was right, Dr. Bishop renewed his proposal, this time meeting with success. In 1881, they were married—Bird was then 50 years old. Dr. Bishop, sadly, died less than five years into the marriage. A period of frantic domestic activity followed, but Bird found these activities only minimally satisfying. As a means of recovering from the loss, Isabella Bird Bishop went on the road again, notebook in hand.

For years she had been obsessed with Central Asia. In 1888, she set out to wander the region indefinitely. She spent more than two years exploring and adventuring in India, Pakistan, Tibet, and the Middle East. This trip proved to be the most physically harrowing of all, with rugged terrain, frigid temperatures, and generally misogynistic people at every turn. Again she endured, and she succeeded in writing a patient yet gripping account published in two volumes as *Journeys in Persia and Kurdistan*.

By this point in her career, Bird Bishop was famous both for her daring deeds and for her eloquent tales. In 1892, she became the first woman ever to be invited as a distinguished guest speaker for London's Royal Geographic Society (Stefoff 38). She was subsequently elected to full membership of the same society, again the first woman to achieve the distinction.

Astoundingly, Bird Bishop continued to travel. Her Central Asian trip, which she had suggested would be her last, was followed by yet another journey: three years in China (1894–1897). Of course, she continued to write and publish the details of her travels, this time as *The Yangtze Valley and Beyond: An Account of Journeys in China*. On this junket, she met with some of the most dangerous situations of her career.

Due to the political climate, China was generally considered hostile toward European travelers. In spite of numerous warnings, Bird

Bishop insisted on making the trip and venturing into many isolated and provincial locales. Armed with a revolver and her iron will, she found herself attacked, harassed, and hounded repeatedly. Remarkably, she was neither seriously injured nor provoked into shooting any of her attackers. In her text she exhibits an extraordinary amount of grace and goodwill; she forgives and even sympathizes with her assailants. She lightly brushes off particularly rough treatment in one village by saying, in retrospect, "I was half inclined to return to Wan, but, in fact, though there was much clamour and hooting in several places, I was only actually attacked once again, and am very glad that I persevered with my journey" (Robinson 299).

Though fearless, Bird Bishop was not stupid. She quietly traveled along the river westward into Tibet. She was always at home in the mountains, so her accounts of the months she spent with villagers in the Himalayas are some of the most jovial she ever wrote. One can only imagine the shock and delight of Tibetan yak herders at the sight of a 65-year-old Englishwoman riding alone out of China! By this time, Bird Bishop had become legendary in Britain; her books were eagerly awaited, and each caused a sensation upon release.

She returned home yet again, only to find idleness depressing. Aged 70 years, she packed a modest bag and set off yet again for an epic adventure: this time she chose the mountains of North Africa. She rode a full 1,000 miles on horseback through the Atlas Mountains (in Morocco) but found that her energy was flagging. Indeed, this is the one trip that does not have a polished and published account. She returned to Scotland somewhat saddened at having had to cut the trip slightly short.

In her final years, Bird Bishop shifted her focus to philanthropy and social welfare, founding hospitals and orchestrating relief work. She died in 1904, a beloved celebrity.

Perhaps Isabella Bird Bishop was one of the greatest travelers—male or female—of all time. For her boundless wit and creativity, her expansive and passionate interests, and her tireless pursuit of the foreign, she deserves great praise. In her extensive oeuvre, or body of work, we can see her own philosophies of travel develop and expand: what begins as wonder grows into a worldview. Her staunch refusal to behave like a fragile lady certainly inspired many women travelers of her own and subsequent eras to go forth simply for the pleasure of going. Through it all, she took the time to write, to share, to teach, and to express the myriad of joys that flow from a life of motion and adventure.

References: Newby 1985; Robinson 1994; Stefoff 1992

BISHOP, ELIZABETH

A free-spirited and feisty character, Elizabeth Bishop (American, 1911–1979) seemed preoccupied with two things: travel and writing. Her poems, like her life, seem edgy and unsettled. Among her fine works of travel verse are *North and South* (1946), *Questions of Travel* (1965), *Geography III* (1976), and *Complete Poems, 1927–1979* (published posthumously in 1983). In 1956, she won the Pulitzer Prize for *Poems: North and South: A Cold Spring,* which revised and added 17 poems to the 1946 edition.

Born in Massachusetts and strictly raised by her grandparents in Canada, Bishop learned to be tough at a very young age. The early death of her father and mental collapse of her mother could easily have thwarted a less driven young woman. After her education at Vassar, she traveled widely and finally settled in South America. These peregrinations served as rich source material for her poetry.

Many of Bishop's travel poems at first glance seem impressionistic, with their evocative descriptions and visual emphasis, yet this style is balanced with extremely subtle semantics and complex thematic arrangements. They often contain multiple voices that seem to struggle in a series of points and counter-points. In this respect, Bishop aspires to capture the mental ambivalence that often arises during travel. On the one hand, the adventure is glorious; on the other, it is often unpleasant or taxing.

One example can serve to illustrate Bishop's travel poetry. "Questions of Travel" begins with a series of rapidly flowing, observational lines describing waterfalls:

> There are too many waterfalls here; the
>   crowded streams
> hurry too rapidly down to the sea,
> and the pressure of so many clouds on the
>   mountaintops
> makes them spill over the sides in slow-
>   motion,
> turning to waterfalls under our very
>   eyes.
> (Craig 433)

The narrator seems dissatisfied with the sight, and she continues by wondering if she ought to have made the trip at all. Deeply questioning the idea behind travel, she wonders if dreams of far-off places are not better left in imagination.

The first stanza closes with doubt, but the next rises with certainty:

> But surely it would have been a pity
> not to have seen the trees along the road,
> really exaggerated in their beauty,
> not to have seen them gesturing
> like noble pantomimists, robed in pink.
> (434)

As a counterpoint, the narrator realizes that often the most precious aspect of the journey is not the end result—the destination—but the process of getting there.

The poem continues on this positive note, listing a sequence of things it would have been a pity not to have seen or done. Just when the momentum of this sort of description becomes convincing, however, the original, skeptical voice returns. In the "sudden golden silence . . . the traveller takes a notebook" and writes:

> Is it lack of imagination that makes us come
> to imagined places, not just stay at home?
> Or could Pascal have been not entirely right
> about just sitting quietly in one's room?
>
> Continent, city, country, society:
> the choice is never wide and never free.
> And here, or there . . . No. Should we have
>   stayed at home,
> wherever that may be?
> (434)

Not only do we have the conflation of writing and travel—indeed, travel provides the opportunity and inspiration for the narrator's commentary—but also we have the quintessential traveler's question asked in this stanza: What is the use of travel? In response to that question, the narrator demonstrates rather than states the benefit: to learn. She has begun to question the Cartesian logic of Pascal that anchors existence in the mere act of thinking. She has learned of experience and action in the process of traveling.

Such lessons, metaphysical as well as cultural, are the material for Bishop's travel poetry. Throughout, she alternates between a voice that questions the worth of travel and a voice that gushes at the thrill of new places. For this sophisticated reckoning of opposites, Bishop's poetry deserves mention as a form of travel literature.

References: Craig 1996

BISHOP, ISABELLA BIRD

See Bird, Isabella

BLIGH, WILLIAM

Captain William Bligh (English, 1754–1817) was both hero and author of one of the more dramatic examples of travel literature. His adventure is chronicled in his own *Narrative of*

Scene from the film version of Mutiny on the *Bounty (Photofest)*

the Mutiny on the Bounty (1788), as well as in Lord Byron's *The Island* and in Charles Nordhoff and Norman Hall's novelistic treatment also called *Mutiny on the* Bounty.

The story in all cases is relatively simple: a driven and severe Captain Bligh pushes his crew to the point of mutiny. Bligh is set adrift on a small open boat in which he navigates thousands of miles of the South Pacific. *Narrative of the Mutiny on the* Bounty is a classic example of travelogue that becomes fictionalized; the characters are almost too perfectly cast to be strictly historically credible. The result is a continuous literary and cinematic reworking of the story to the point where the historic and fictional aspects are intertwined.

Bligh's autobiographical tale indicates that he was a master mariner and a dedicated—even obsessed—explorer. Having served on Captain James Cook's second voyage, Bligh was recruited to take HMS *Bounty* to the Pacific island of Tahiti to gather breadfruit plants for transplantation to the West Indies. After a prolonged stay in Tahiti—Bligh even suggests that an ardent desire for the magnificent climate and beautiful native women must have been the cause—the *Bounty* set out for the Friendly Islands (also called Tonga Islands). Seemingly out of the blue, first mate Fletcher Christian and a rowdy portion of the crew mutinied, setting the captain and 18 men adrift in an open boat. Bligh rose to the occasion by mastering his new craft and commanding what remained of his crew. Against all odds and in the face of extreme difficulties, the small boat survived an estimated 4,000 miles, finally landing on Timor. From there, Bligh returned with his loyal sailors to England, where they received a hero's welcome.

Undaunted, Bligh attempted the same voyage again, this time succeeding in transplanting the breadfruit trees. His own story continues through numerous adventures and twists and turns of his career. For our purposes, however, it is the *Narrative of the Mutiny on the* Bounty that is significant. His subse-

quent accounts are extremely rare, and his later adventures never rival his early feats.

The story is interesting—and dramatic—principally because Bligh seems unaware that his men are restless. His own sense of discipline is mighty, but he cannot see that his crew might perceive him as tyrannical. The result is that we have a narrator who is at once protagonist and antagonist. With remarkable calm, Bligh tells of his undoing: "I demanded what their intention was in giving this order [to cast us adrift], and endeavoured to persuade the people near me not to persist in such acts of violence; but it was to no effect" (Rugoff 436). The mutineers seem torn in their resolve; they oust the captain but provide him with provisions and even swords. One of the leaders of the rebellion, a fellow named Christian, seems particularly ambivalent. His character is much developed in the fictional accounts but only superficially noted in Bligh's own retelling.

Bligh maintains a positive attitude and writes a remarkable series of reassessments of his own history. In exile, he reviews and revises his own story; the full text is thus an account of the events leading up to the climactic mutiny, then a review and embellishment of the same story. The result is a magnificent look at narrative and memory; as readers, we can see how Bligh's story changes. Perhaps the journey helps him to see differently.

Yet another noteworthy aspect of the story is Bligh's encounters with the natives. The contrast between the kindness of the islanders and the cruelty of the ship's mutineers causes Bligh some remorse; his own men behaved in a far less "Christian" (note the irony of the chief mutineer's name) manner than the natives. Yet eventually they too turn against him and attack the open boat with stones. This leads Bligh to avoid further contact with native peoples, hence he and his crew suffer long weeks at sea, buffeted by the rains and with little to eat. Through it all, Bligh retains control and order on his ship; such extreme discipline was probably the only reason they survived.

The *Narrative of the Mutiny on the* Bounty endures because it contains all the elements of a good novel: desire, confrontation, the unexpected, a struggle for power, character growth, and an exotic setting. Although ostensibly written from Bligh's own ship log, the tale succeeds in stimulating the armchair literary traveler to a satisfying degree. In the end, we might describe the text as the story of a traveler with an unquenchable desire to fulfill his duty: on one level, he is duty bound to complete his mission, but on another, Bligh seems to feel that travel and exploration are also his greatest pleasures.

References: Rugoff 1960

BLY, NELLIE

Nellie Bly, pen name of Elizabeth Cochrane Seaman (American, 1867–1922), has become something of a legend. Her accomplishments—as an activist, as a reporter, and as a writer of travel literature—would alone have merited her fame, but her name-recognition has indubitably benefited from the wildly popular Steven Foster song ("Nellie Bly") that sings her praises. Energetic and intrepid, she delighted readers with her commentary on American life, politics, corruption, and women's rights. Her newspaper sent her to Mexico, where she filed comparative reports on life in another country; this excursion seems to have piqued her appetite for travel. Following this journey, she had herself committed to a mental ward in order to document the treatment of mental patients. Her account of life in an insane asylum (*Ten Days in a Madhouse,* 1888) increased both her popularity and her credibility as a serious author. Perhaps her crowning achievement was her well-publicized dash around the globe, the account of which she published as *Nellie Bly's Book: Around the World in Seventy-two Days* (1890). It remains a classic of travel writing.

As a young journalist, Bly thrilled readers of several American newspapers and magazines

Journalist Nellie Bly with traveling bag; 1890 photograph (Bettmann/Corbis)

with her daring frankness and impassioned tone. She insisted upon uncovering the heart of a story regardless of the danger involved and thus became one of the pioneers of hard-hitting investigative journalism. After her book on madness, she set out to literally conquer the world: with the support of the *New York World* (newspaper), Bly embarked on a whirlwind circumnavigation of the globe. Jules Verne's fictional account *Around the World in Eighty Days* (1873) had been a smash success; Bly sought not only to circle the globe for real but to beat Phineas T. Fogg's (Verne's protagonist) time.

She succeeded in managing such an arduous trip, and with her reports filed en route she charmed American and European readers, who watched her journey with excitement. Upon her celebrated return, she compiled her reports and journals into a substantial and delightful account: *Nellie Bly's Book: Around the World in Seventy-two Days.* Such a feat drew praise on many accounts. She had taken the stuff of legend and made it real; to travel the entire globe in one swift route was nothing short of an awesome display of the modern marvel of travel. Beyond this, true to her feminist spirit, she had done it as a woman, proving that her gender could be tough, brave, and pioneering. To top it all off, her book is beautifully written and full of drama as well as humor.

Her account balances the natural splendor of the astoundingly diverse landscapes she crossed—from oceans to mountains; from scorching heat to bitter cold—with excited reflection on the similarity of the world's people. Indeed, Bly is delighted by the warmth and encouragement she finds at every turn; her trip demonstrates that though people around the world may look different and speak different languages, there is a human essence that unifies them all. In spite of her frantic and exhausting pace, Bly's energy never flagged. In this one journey she covered the globe and, through her writing, brought thousands of readers along with her. Upon her return, she was lauded as a hero, an adventurer, and an ambassador of peace and goodwill.

After this epic adventure, she shifted her focus away from travel and literature, preferring the world of business. After she married Robert Seaman in 1895, Bly's activism focused upon growing successful companies that believed in quality products and humane treatment of workers. Again she proved wildly successful, in terms of both profitability and social conscience.

Her travels later in life included a trip to Europe, where she found herself stranded by the outbreak of World War I. Seizing the day, she returned to journalism and filed numerous stories about the war and its human consequences. Though fine in quality, these writings do not fall under the scope of this project.

Bly's life and travels remain a testament to the bravery of women struggling to prove their equality. She was often the voice of the powerless and the poor—both men and women—and assuredly countless followers lived vicariously through her bold journey around the world.

See also: Verne, Jules
References: Hart 1965; Stefoff 1992

BÖLL, HEINRICH

A great and lauded novelist, Heinrich Böll (German, 1917–1985) was awarded the Nobel Prize for literature in 1972. To be sure, his contribution to literature has been vast, but in terms of travel literature he wrote but a single volume, *Irish Journal,* although travel figures prominently in many of his works. Though a lone example of the genre in his oeuvre, the text is significant for its structure, its style, and its content.

In the 1950s, Böll made a journey to Ireland, and in the process of wandering he kept a detailed journal of his experiences. He resists the urge to judge overtly; instead, he adopts a style that can best be described as subtle self-effacement. Rarely does he note himself, his opinions, or his emotions. His accounts feel genuine and authentic, more cinematic than literary. In reading Böll, I find the illusion of "really having been there" quite sustainable.

True to Böll's mastery of the novelistic form, *Irish Journal* reads like a novel: characters develop evenly and meaningfully, the dialogue feels natural, and the descriptive details are credibly random. As a study in form, this work is a great example of autobiography that blends seamlessly into novelistic fiction.

Full of literary references, Böll's text defines Ireland by the art created there, most particularly its rich literary heritage. Böll seems to want to make a connection between the geography—winds, rain, sea, green hills—and Irish literary production. On an excursion to William Butler Yeats's tomb, for example, the cab driver and the climate become more important than Yeats. Böll's descriptions of the village and its inhabitants are more vividly colored than his account of the actual grave site. Yet there is an incredible respect and tenderness with which the scene is rendered:

> Rooks flew up from the old gravestones, circled cawing around the old church tower. Yeats' grave was wet, the stone was cold, and the lines which Yeats had had inscribed on his gravestone were as cold as the ice needles that had been shot at me from Swift's tomb. . . . The ferns lay flat on the surrounding hills, beaten down by the rain, rust-colored and withered. I felt cold. . . . Rocks in the mist, the lonely church, encircled by fluttering rooks, and three thousand miles of water beyond Yeats' grave. Not a swan to be seen. (Newby 246)

Böll's is a modern variant of travel literature, influenced by everyone from James Boswell to Johann Wolfgang von Goethe to Sir Richard Burton. He seems happy to acknowledge the influences on his writing. In this regard, *Irish Journal* is a lesson in the history of travel literature; to read it is to see tributes to many of the classically great accounts of travel and exploration.

Yet his journal is most interesting because it is so beautifully written and because its subject is so objectively seen. If we think that Böll's trip occurs hard on the heels of World War II and yet is so tenderly, respectfully, and lovingly told, we can begin to see the joy of this text. In spite of bearing political animosities, Böll is able to see a foreign culture and recognize that it has things it can teach him. With that frame of mind, Böll's travels are an education in understanding a

commonality among all humans, regardless of nationality.

References: Newby 1985

BORROW, GEORGE

Victorian writer George Borrow (English, 1803–1881) defies easy categorization. His personal travels were wide and diverse, and his writing reflects this range. Part journal, part reportage, and part literary essay, his books were well received and continue to be endearing. Many of his books reside on the fringes of travel literature in that they contain significant incidents of travel and adventure but are not primarily driven by a journey or voyage. Several of his titles, however, do focus primarily on travel. *The Bible in Spain* (1843), *Wild Wales* (1862), and *Ballads of All Nations* (1874?) are usually considered Borrow's contributions to the genre.

Borrow trained as a lawyer and worked as a missionary in his early years. His travels in Europe, Russia, and the Far East were wide and protracted. He had an extraordinary ear for languages and a passion for cultural difference; as a result, Borrow found travel a delight. Enthusiastic, full of energy, and fearless, Borrow set out to travel and to write as a way of life. His voyages seem to have been pure travel in that he rarely had a fixed itinerary; rather, he let one place lead to another according to the people he met or the tales he heard that recommended new places.

His writing generally appeals with its picaresque pace and vivid characters. Exotic settings and strange adventures lend excitement to his tales. Often spiced with gypsies, rogues, tricksters, and con artists, Borrow's tales reside in a hybrid space somewhere between fiction and autobiography. Even in his travelogue *Wild Wales,* Borrow relies on extensive passages of dialogue to tell his story.

The British Bible Society commissioned Borrow to translate the New Testament into several languages. Later, pleased with his work, they sent him on a five-year mission to circulate the Anglican Bible in Catholic Spain. His tale *The Bible in Spain* tells of his adventures on this trip, including his imprisonment. Spain was in the midst of a civil war, thus Borrow found himself in numerous scrapes and close situations. While his mission was ostensibly religious, his text focuses almost exclusively on travel rather than spirituality. Along the way, he encounters a quirky and almost unbelievable set of characters, some of whom aid him while others impede him.

In typically exuberant form, Borrow spent four months of 1854 in Wales tramping about on foot. He walked hundreds of miles, wandering wherever the roads happened to lead. He tells his stories of this journey in *Wild Wales.* Borrow comes across as an unpretentious, old-fashioned traveler: impervious to weather, delighted with the countryside, and always eager to have a pint and a chat at the pub. He visits historic and literary sites as well as random places that simply catch his curious eye. Instead of finding Wales hopelessly agrarian, Borrow appears to find genuine pleasure in slow-paced country life. In contrast to London's urban life, rural Wales provides a delightful change.

In all of his books, Borrow notes the differences between his destination and his familiar England. The comparisons nearly always reflect a lesson learned—and then transmitted to the reader. Indeed, even in nearby Wales, Borrow finds considerable and noteworthy difference. In a scene from *Wild Wales* labeled "Dialogue with a Crusty Countryman," Borrow writes:

Strolling along . . . I was overtaken by an old fellow with a stick in his hand, walking very briskly. He had a crusty and rather conceited look. I spoke to him in Welsh, and he answered in English, saying that I need not trouble myself by speaking Welsh, as he had plenty of English. . . . I asked about Rhys Goch and his chair [a local legend]. He told me that he knew nothing of either, and began to talk of Her Majesty's ministers and the fine sights of London. I asked him about a stream [nearby]. . . . He told me he did not know and asked me the name of the Queen's eldest daughter. I told him I did not know, and remarked that it was very odd that he could not tell me the name of a stream in his own vale. He replied that it was not a bit more odd than that I could not tell him the name of the eldest daughter of the Queen of England; I told him that when I was in Wales I wanted to talk about Welsh matters, and he told me that when he was with the English he wanted to talk about English matters. (Rugoff 588–589)

Indeed, the rustic has taught Borrow a valuable lesson about perspectives.

Ballads of All Nations is an interesting collection of verse about many of the exotic countries Borrow visited. His disjointed poems lack a singular narrative thread; instead, they stand alone as excerpts from a life of travel. Over the years, Borrow had journeyed to numerous countries, including Russia, China, and most of those in Europe and in the Far East. Though often heavily laden with proselytizing and religious rhetoric, the poems resulting from these trips nonetheless capture much of the glory and excitement of encountering foreign people and places. As with his other works, Borrow's poems brim with the joy of new experiences and unfamiliar ways.

References: Harvey 1967; Newby 1985; Rugoff 1960

BOSWELL, JAMES

The biography of James Boswell (Scottish, 1740–1795) underwent a remarkable revision in the twentieth century with the discovery of his lifelong journal. This vast record of his complicated and interesting life has spurred Boswell scholarship enormously. His literary contributions are many, including two fine volumes of travel literature: *An Account of Corsica: The Journal of a Tour to That Island* (1768) and *A Journal of the Tour to the Hebrides with Samuel Johnson, LL. D.* (1785).

Born into an unhappy family, Boswell managed to escape into a halfhearted pursuit of law. This first taste of freedom from his troubled family inspired subsequent journeys, first to Utrecht, ostensibly to continue his legal studies, and later throughout Europe on a Grand Tour of Italy, Germany, Switzerland, and France. His initial departure from London inspired in Boswell considerable ambivalence: "I set out upon my travels with a kind of gloom upon my mind. My enthusiastic love of London made me leave it with a heavy heart" (Newby 133). Yet soon enough he discovered the joys of travel, although throughout his works he repeatedly longs for the familiar comforts of London.

Dissatisfied with his legal studies, he set off in 1764 to see Europe and to engage as many different ideas as possible. His encounters with the intellectuals of the Continent, including Jean-Jacques Rousseau and Voltaire, inspired him. On Rousseau's recommendation, Boswell, full of zeal and excitement, ventured to Corsica. His true interest resided in writing, and his record of his early travels, *An Account of Corsica,* launched his literary career. The book brought him a modest degree of fame and (perhaps an immodest degree of) confidence.

Boswell opens his narrative with rather more enthusiasm than he showed for his trip to Utrecht:

> Having resolved to pass some years abroad for my instruction and entertainment, I conceived a design of visiting the island of Corsica. I wished for something more than just the common course of what is called the tour of Europe, and Corsica occurred to me as a place which nobody else had seen, and where I should find what was to be seen nowhere else, a people actually fighting for liberty and forming themselves from a poor, inconsiderable, oppressed nation into a flourishing and independent state. (Fussell 181–182)

Indeed, Boswell's Corsican text delves into history, politics, and local customs. His style brims with youthful enthusiasm and brash idealism. It is also rich with sarcasm and his characteristic moments of melancholia.

Throughout the text, Boswell focuses on what can be learned from the Corsicans. He writes as though he feels an obligation to share their struggle with his English readers; his tone suggests a considerable empathy with their oppressed plight. Whenever possible, he relates the Corsican situation to other, perhaps less severe, struggles in England.

Upon his return to London, Boswell found that fame and success suited him very well. He tried his hand at politics as well as literary projects, failing in the former and succeeding in the latter. His friendship with Samuel Johnson, among other intellectuals, ensured his position in the world of the London literati.

In 1773, Boswell and Johnson set off for their famous tour of Scotland. Johnson published his account of the journey in 1775, whereas Boswell's account, *A Journal of the Tour to the Hebrides,* was published only after Johnson's death. It is a fascinating and rich moment in literary history: two superior writers have left accounts of the identical trip. To read them together affords us the opportunity to observe how differently two individuals observe the same objective phenomena around them.

Boswell's text focuses heavily on Johnson's process of observation. As a Scotsman, Boswell finds less about Scotland noteworthy: to him, it was fairly familiar. Instead, he provides a wonderful narrative of his friend's travel discoveries. Peppered with affectionate and amusing quotes from Johnson, Boswell's text is anchored in a character rather than a place. Proud and pleased to be in the company of such an illustrious figure, the younger Boswell beams about their adventures. Whereas Johnson indulges in details, Boswell evokes the mood of travel via the excitement of seeing partly through his friend's eyes.

In my mind, these two texts are inseparable: alone they are simply good examples of travel writing, but together they are masterful. Happy to play the jester to Johnson's straight man, Boswell delightfully recounts a vast series of amusing anecdotes. Yet learning always lurks as his subtext. Indeed, Johnson teaches the younger Boswell how to learn from travel; in experience resides wisdom. In sharing his version of the story, we begin to see just how subjective travel literature can be.

See also: Grand Tour; Johnson, Samuel
References: Drabble 1998; Fussell 1987; Newby 1985

BOUGAINVILLE, LOUIS-ANTOINE DE

A man of extraordinary learning, Louis-Antoine de Bougainville (French, 1729–1811) came from a privileged background but distinguished himself by his own superior accomplishments. Having studied law, sailed in the French navy, written a treatise on calculus, served as ambassador to England, and masterminded the colonization of the Falkland Islands, Bougainville at age 38 decided he wanted to circumnavigate the globe.

His two-year journey (1767–1769) was an overwhelming success, closely watched by both the French and the English press. His two ships, the *Boudeuse* and the *Etoile,* mastered the Strait of Magellan and then explored numerous Pacific islands, including Tahiti. Through it all, Bougainville wrote spirited and detailed accounts, focusing on a wide range of subjects, including native cultures, geography, life aboard the ship, languages, and his own process of self-discovery.

His Tahitian entries are some of the most interesting stories in the two volumes of his account. He named Tahiti "New Cythera," a reference to a Greek mythological island that was associated with Aphrodite (Venus), the goddess of love. In one particularly classical passage, Bougainville notes that his hosts not only offered food, but also sexual access to young women: "the hut was immediately filled with a curious crowd of men and women, who made a circle round the guest, and the young victim of hospitality. The ground was spread with leaves and flowers, and their musicians sung an hymeneal song to the tune of their flutes. Here Venus is the goddess of hospitality, her worship does not admit any mysteries, and every tribute paid to her is a feast for the whole nation" (Adams 300). To be sure, Bougainville's accounts of the unspoiled "savages" of the islands and their alleged sexual freedom became famous, not to mention controversial, throughout Europe.

Denis Diderot wrote his famous *Supplément au voyage de Bougainville* (Supplement to Bougainville's Voyage) immediately after reading Bougainville's account in 1772. Diderot, unlike Bougainville, never visited the South Pacific; his tales are pure imaginative extensions of the original journey. Bougainville's stories seemed to prove some of Jean-Jacques Rousseau's theories about "natural man" (the idea that although men are not naturally equal, it is the development of societies from primitive to advanced civilizations that spawns artificial, politically enforced inequalities that can lead to ruin) and the Tahitians to be an example of "noble savages" (natives deemed noble and virtuous on the basis of nonexposure to the influence of Western civilization). From Bougainville's accounts, it is easy to see why Tahiti evoked visions of an Eden-like paradise; yet, as with most travel literature, what Bougainville sees tells us as much about European mores and fantasies as it tells us about Tahitian culture. On the islands, he found a culture that seemed to demonstrate that the Christian, European doctrine of monogamy is only one possible dogma. The ramifications are vast; it is to Bougainville's credit that he attempts to describe what he sees with honesty and accuracy.

Sexual freedom causes the greatest conundrum for Bougainville (and, he claims, for his men): "our customs do not admit these public proceedings. . . . [In fact,] every one of our men had found it impossible to conquer his repugnance, and [now] conform[s] to the customs of the country" (Adams 300). Indeed, when his men were faced with the temptation of sex outside of marriage—a practice deemed unacceptable in European society but which is considered socially acceptable by the natives—they all succumb to the practice. Travel causes these men to re-evaluate their notions of propriety.

Bougainville's account constantly compares the native culture to European culture. His men and the natives play music for each other, share food, and compare behavior; in every instance, there is a contrast between the self and the other. The result is a text that speaks as much about his home culture as it does about a shockingly foreign culture. Seeing a radical difference definitely causes Bougainville, and his readers, to observe the familiar more carefully.

After returning from his circumnavigation and finding his writings highly successful, Bougainville refused to rest. He made a number of subsequent journeys and continued to provide dutiful service to the French government. Although the literary output from these travels was published, Bougainville's later tales never capture the same wide-eyed wonder, excitement, and stylistic coherence of his first work.

See also: Circumnavigation
References: Adams 1988

BOUGRENET, JACQUES LOUIS DE

Jacques Louis de Bougrenet, Chevalier de la Tocnaye (French, ?–1798), in spite of his elaborately elegant name, strikes me as one of the more unassuming of the well-to-do eighteenth-century travelers. A French cavalry officer by trade, Bougrenet fled to England in 1792 when the Revolution in France turned against the king. He made his home in Britain for several years but happily remained

an outsider looking upon his adopted home with the eyes of a foreigner. When the political situation in France calmed down, Bougrenet returned; because of his years abroad, however, he was then able to look upon his original home with the same detached traveler's perspective.

Obviously a man of considerable independent means, he spent six years walking across Great Britain and then Ireland. The fruits of these endeavors are two quirky travel books, *Promenade dans La Grand Bretagne* (published in translation as *A Walk through Great Britain,* 1795) and *A Frenchman's Walk through Ireland* (1798). Unlike many eighteenth-century travelers who claim to have made walking tours but took carriages between many towns, Bougrenet evidently did walk the whole way.

Under the necessity of traveling lightly, he carried all of his belongings in several small silk bundles that he slung over his shoulders. Although this description makes him sound like a tramp, he was able to engage both the lower and the upper classes, thus making him a social wanderer as well as a traveler. Bougrenet succeeded in being one of the lightest packers ever. He claims:

> Although my baggage was inconsiderable, I wanted for nothing, and had the means of appearing in society as well dressed as others.
>
> For the information of future travellers on foot, it is my pleasure to give details of my complete equipment.
>
> A powder bag made out of a woman's glove.
>
> A razor.
>
> Thread.
>
> Needles.
>
> Scissors.
>
> A comb, carried in one of a pair of dress shoes.
>
> A pair of silk stockings.
>
> Breeches, fine enough to be, when folded, not bigger than a fist.
>
> Two very fine shirts.
>
> Three cravats.
>
> Three handkerchiefs.

The clothes in which I travelled.
(Newby 220)

His writing ranges from lively and anecdotal to horribly dull. The slower passages, however, have value in that they are rigorously accurate notes of places and their characteristics. Never one to shun the smaller villages, Bougrenet offers unique descriptions of country folk and their lifestyle.

Above all, Bougrenet writes with a humble earnestness that is endearing. He seems genuinely excited to see—and to write about—even the most banal occurrences. Thus, while his prose and his structure may not be the most scintillating, to try to make sense of a man who would spend six years walking and noting all things British and Irish is a fascinating exercise.

References: Newby 1985

BROWNE, EDWARD GRANVILLE

A minor late-Victorian figure, Edward Granville Browne (English, 1862–1926) was both a scholar and a traveler. His ardent pursuit of multiple Persian dialects led him to live among various peoples of the Middle East from 1887 to 1888. His account of this experience, *A Year among the Persians* (1893), is a highly regarded classic of travel literature.

While his tale is thrilling and well told, Browne rarely escapes his Anglocentric bias. His colonialist bent often seems absurdly arrogant to contemporary readers. Invariably, the Persians come across as bumbling and foolish; they serve as comic impediments to his "noble quest" for understanding and documenting the structure of the Persian language.

Browne's obsession with language is telling and significant. He intuitively recognizes that knowing a language precisely can inform one of how a culture thinks. Words are not only a tool for knowing, but they are valuable in themselves. His struggles to comprehend linguistic details thus stand in for his larger cultural curiosity.

In addition, we can praise Browne for being one of a dying breed: he is a traveler who journeys in the name of scholarly knowledge. His goal was to be the definitive expert on Persian dialects; toward that end, he risked all manner of dangers and difficulties. His tone reflects a typical British "stiff upper lip" in the face of adversity. This same tone makes him a sort of caricature.

Finally, his adventures are often amusing. Persia of the nineteenth century captured the fantasy of many Europeans; the Orientalist movement in art and literature testifies clearly to that. Browne is almost giddy when the actual Persia he is visiting lives up to his exotic fantasies of the Levant. For example, having injured his eye, desperate for some relief, Browne allows his friend Ustá Akbar to apply a poultice of egg whites and hollyhock leaves. The cure turns out to be worse than the disease, irritating his eye intolerably. Apologetically, Akbar recommends a second "cure": a pipe of opium. Browne's response:

Opium! There was something fascinating about the idea. The action on the mental functions exercised by narcotic drugs had always possessed for me a special interest. . . . I signified my willingness to try Ustá Akbar's new cure; and ten minutes later my whole being was permeated with that glow of tranquil beatitude, conscious of itself, nay, almost exultant in its own peaceful serenity, which constitutes the fatal charm of what the Persians call *par excellence* 'the Antidote' (*tiryák*). (Newby 268)

Note how cultural understanding, linguistics, and new experiences all blend together in this passage.

Though his journey ostensibly sought to study language, it is clear that Browne was also studying himself. In writing his account, he attempted to catalog his progress and to teach his readers of his gains. In the process, he produced a text that intrigues as well as entertains.

See also: Levant
References: Newby 1985

BROWNING, ROBERT

Robert Browning (English, 1812–1889) figures prominently in the history of British literature. His poetic production was vast and often stunningly fine. Although he is not noted as a travel writer, his many years abroad influenced a number of his poems to varying degrees. For the sake of this volume, we can look at one example, "Home Thoughts from Abroad," though there are many others from which to choose.

Despite the fact that Browning was minimally educated and from a modest family, he caught the eye of some of the era's major literary and political figures very early in his life. Just over 20 years of age, he published his first work, *Pauline,* in 1833; it sold fairly well and helped to fund Browning's trip to Italy, Greece, and Turkey in 1834, but later in his career Browning distanced himself from this early, somewhat melodramatic poem. His next major work, *Paraclesus* (1835), was inspired by his journey. It tells the tale of a historical figure and is set in Italy, Constantinople, and Switzerland—all places that he had visited. This work captured the attention of such literary greats as Thomas Carlyle and William Wordsworth, who subsequently helped to make Browning's career.

Continuously writing and publishing his works, Browning became a well-known poet. Many of his poems rely on Greek and Roman history as well as classical allusions to these cultures; in these works the details are surely drawn in part from his own travels. When he married Elizabeth Barrett in 1846, the literary couple moved to Italy and traveled widely in southern Europe and the Near East. When she died in 1861, Browning returned to London, although he continued to travel occasionally. In these many years abroad, Browning found himself feeling deeply ambivalent: while the history, climate, and excitement of Italy suited, it never felt like home, thus he exhibited a tendency toward nostalgia and idealization of England.

"Home Thoughts, from Abroad" demonstrates an interesting feature of travel literature: being abroad seems to inspire detailed recollections that are ordinarily not noted. The poem's opening, "Oh, to be in England / Now that April's there," locates the narrator somewhere abroad, probably Italy, as he reminisces longingly about his home. His recollections are elaborate and precise: from the songs of the finch and the thrush to elm leaves, pear blossoms, and buttercups, he notes extraordinary details and fondly weaves these details into his poem. The implication of this sort of representation is that when one is abroad, both the natural and social worlds are different; we can assume that wherever the narrator is, he has not found it to be the same as England. In the face of such unfamiliarity, the narrator is inspired to recall minute and often very personal details. Were these details ever present, they might continue to be unnoticed; but because they are absent, the memory of them must serve as replacement.

Evoking his erstwhile life in England, Browning indulges in a form of nostalgia and contrast. Perhaps as symbolic of his childhood innocence, the idealized English spring stands in contrast to his own accumulation of years and experiences. As travel literature, the poem marks the differences between home and anywhere else while at the same time portraying these differences as learning experiences.

Only in the final line of the poem do we escape from the realm of memory to get a glimpse of the present foreign land: the narrator proclaims the flowers of England "Far brighter than this gaudy melon-flower!" Although the poem ends perhaps regrettably in the present and in the foreign, we must note

Portrait of Robert Browning at the age of 46 (Bettmann/Corbis)

that it is being abroad that has caused both the memories and the poem itself.

References: Crossley-Holland 1986; Harvey 1967

BRUCE, JAMES

In spite of their fabulous and flamboyant content, the books of James Bruce (Scottish, 1730–1794) have not been in print for more than a century. Only in the late twentieth century did Bruce's work see a resurgence in anthologies and in scholarly analysis. A lifelong traveler, explorer, and adventurer, Bruce spent the early part of his career tracking down Roman ruins scattered from Central Asia to North Africa to the Mediterranean islands. As a result of his ease with languages and comfort with cultural differences—and a robustly gregarious personality—Bruce was posted as the British consul to Algiers in 1763.

His greatest adventure, however, occurred from 1768 to 1773, when he set out to explore the Red Sea, eventually landing in Gonder, the capital of Abyssinia (present-day Ethiopia). Although he returned to Great Britain in 1773 with vast quantities of notes, drawings, artifacts, and observations, it took until 1790 for Bruce to compile his story into an elaborate five-volume work titled Travels to Discover the Source of the Nile.

Although the work was long in coming, Bruce himself was something of a legendary sensation in Britain. His stories had circulated via word of mouth from his own repeated and animated renditions. Equal parts braggadocio, fact, and humor, his stories caused great controversies. Allegations of exaggeration—if not outright fabrication—swarmed around the tales. Doggedly, Bruce maintained that his tales were true, defending his honor and his word against a variety of satiric attacks. Powerful, egoistic, and easily excited, Bruce remained a celebrated target for jests and jibes. Regardless of the truth of some of his more dubious stories, Bruce's Travels contains a wealth of both unique observations and thrilling adventures.

Whether he is telling of cultural practices of the Abyssinians or the geographic quirks of the Nile, Bruce is easily readable. He has a decided knack for blending dry observations with stories of danger and daring. In this regard, his work can be considered literary; his structure and prose style are far more novelistic than most travelogues. One of his more famous tales describes in great detail the (alleged) Abyssinian practice of eating beef sliced from a live cow. This story was too much for British audiences to stomach, and its veracity remained constantly suspect. Nonetheless, the level of detail is extremely valuable. Bruce carefully notes gender roles, table rituals, and the like, and he even makes an attempt at proposing recipes. As a result, Bruce provides a superior model for observing another culture.

When Bruce openly challenges other explorers who claimed to have found the source of the Nile, he is not only serving his own glory, but putting himself within the long tradition of travel and exploration writing. He seems to have an insatiable desire for competition, for besting and setting straight those who preceded him. Thus, when talking of the Nile—and Father Jerónimo Lobo's observations of its source—Bruce slides into his own brand of sarcastic dismissal.

Overall, we must acknowledge Bruce's efforts as extreme and his storytelling as superb. His tales rank with some of the most vivid of all time; be they true or exaggerated, they are nothing if not fun to read.

References: Adams 1988

BRYDONE, PATRICK

Patrick Brydone (Scottish, 1736–1818) is a minor figure in both history and literature. Educated and moderately prominent—he attained the titles comptroller of the Stamp

Office and fellow of the Royal Society—Brydone made a single contribution to travel literature: a two-volume work called *A Tour through Sicily and Malta in a Series of Letters to William Beckford, Esq.* (1773). The book was extremely successful in his lifetime, selling out seven editions, but in modern times it has not been reissued, nor is it often noted by scholars or in classrooms.

As a travel tale, the text is noteworthy because of Brydone's incessant comparison of different cultures contained therein. At times he compares Sicily to mainland Italy; at times he compares the whole of Mediterranean culture to British culture. These oppositions allow the reader to observe Brydone learning and changing his ideas. Indeed, after all is said and done, he has learned more about himself than of the Italians, Sicilians, or Maltese.

The epistolary structure is a literary device in this case; the letters comprising the text were not sent (so far as scholars can tell), but rather written from Brydone's travel notes and journals after his return. Unfortunately, the original notes are not available for us to study. Nonetheless, structuring his accounts as if they were letters neatly divides the book into independent essays of sort and eliminates the need for completely seamless transitions. In other words, his structure marshals the factual details, which otherwise may have been dry and dull, into a literary narrative.

The book contains numerous amusing and highly detailed anecdotes; generally, Brydone is an astute observer and a graceful writer. His focus repeatedly returns to women and their situation in Italy, and for this reason, the story has numerous applications for gender studies. He visits a convent as well as aristocratic houses; he interacts with the poor as well as the well-to-do. In addition, his enthusiasm is endearing and contagious. Sicily and Malta seem seductive, alluring, and exotic.

For a taste of Brydone, we might visit a passage that describes an aristocratic party:

We were joyfully admitted of this chearful little circle, where we amused ourselves very well for several hours.—I only mention this, to shew you the different system of behaviour here [in Sicily] and in Italy [as a whole], where no such familiar intercourse is allowed amongst young people before marriage. The young ladies here are easy, affable, and unaffected; and, not (as on the continent) perpetually stuck up by the sides of their mothers, who bring them into company, not for their amusement, but rather to offer them to sale; and seem mightily afraid lest every one should steal them, or that they themselves should make an elopement; which indeed I should think there was some danger of, considering the restraint under which they are kept. (Adams 398)

His enthusiasm is clear from his gushing sentences, and his interest may be more than simply objective musings. Throughout the text, Brydone follows his incisive observations with witty commentary and playful asides that serve to frame the passages. The result is a text that is ripe for analysis as well as fun to read.

References: Adams 1962

BUCCANEER

Beginning in the seventeenth century, England, France, and Holland equipped captains with "letters of Marque," allowing them to prey upon Spanish, Portuguese, and occasionally other nations' ships. Says David Marley in his *Pirates and Privateers of the Americas,* these buccaneers were "a distinct class of mercenary . . . who made seaborne descents against their enemies under any flag of convenience, motivated principally by greed and a thirst for violent reprisal" (Marley ix).

The word *buccaneer* comes from the Native American *boucan,* which is a sort of smokehouse or barbecue. While it would be nice to imagine the name suggesting that the

Buccaneers; *painting by Frederick Judd Waugh, c. 1910 (Library of Congress)*

buccaneers roasted their prisoners, the name was given to these ship-bound rogues because they roasted their meat on board ship—a dangerous maneuver on a wooden vessel.

The Spanish called them *corsarios* after the sort of ship the English favored, the *Corsair,* while the Dutch called them *vrijbuiter* (and the French *flibustiers*), literally "freebooters." As rovers and swashbucklers, the buccaneers often figure prominently in travel literature. At times they are fearsome, as seen in many of the eighteenth-century travelogues, and at times they are romantic, heroic wanderers, as seen in a number of travel novels.

Officially sanctioning privateers continued in Europe until 1856, when such practices were banned by a treaty signed in Paris by the major European powers, the Declaration of Paris.

References: Marley 1994; OED

BURCHELL, WILLIAM J.

William J. Burchell (English, 1782–1863) remains a minor figure in history but an author worth reading. His chief claim to fame is that he "discovered" a new type of zebra and lent it his name. Although he has several natural history books to his credit, his single travel writing is the little-known *Travels in the Interior of South Africa* (1822).

Burchell was sent to South Africa as a royal botanist in 1810. Plans were made for him to establish himself, then for his fiancée to follow shortly thereafter. She made it as far as the ship but evidently fell in love with the captain, whom she married. Enraged and despondent, Burchell set out for the deepest, darkest wilds of Africa. From 1811 to 1812, he traveled, fearlessly and tirelessly.

Not only did Burchell's exploration provide him with literary material, but his expedition collected some 60,000 items ranging from artifacts to plants to species of animals. His logs and records are meticulous, if vast.

The rest of his life was spent writing his travelogue, cataloging his finds, and discussing his collection. It is as though the two years he spent in the interior were the only time he was truly alive. When he found that this material had become exhausted—when he was aged 82 years—he killed himself.

Travels in the Interior of South Africa is considerably more exciting to read than Burchell's natural history books. In this text he tells many harrowing tales of savages, wild beasts, and a relentless climate. But beyond being a simple tale of the wilderness—there are many, many of those—Burchell's account reveals his fascination with the other white colonists whom he encountered. He spends a disproportionate amount of energy describing the Dutch farmers in extraordinary detail. The scientist in him seems to be drawn to study these characters who are more like him than the natives but who are still wholly foreign. Fortunately for us, his scientific inquisitiveness was matched by a gift for writing: his story is both dramatic and written with a literary flair.

Burchell's text is thus notable as a strange mix: on the one hand, he uses travel and exploration as an escape from the hurt of having been jilted; on the other, he seems genuinely surprised at how others—be they Dutch or native or anything in between—live. It is exactly this enthusiastic wonder running through Burchell's text that makes it interesting.

References: Newby 1985

BURCKHARDT, JOHANN LUDWIG

Surely one of the most fascinating and bold of all travelers, Johann Ludwig Burckhardt (Swiss, 1784–1817) experienced adventures that leave readers delighted with wonder. A master of disguises and languages, Burckhardt recounts his forays into Africa and the Middle East, filling them with daring deeds and narrow escapes. His two rather famous books, *Travels in Nubia* (1819) and *Travels in Syria and the Holy Land* (1822), vividly tell his tales.

In 1812, he readied a disguise and plunged into the Nubian desert (present-day Sudan) with a camel caravan. His intention was to reach the slave markets of Shendi—a trading crossroads along the Nile River—and from there to Jidda, a coastal town on the Red Sea. From Jidda, he believed, he could blend in with throngs of pilgrims on their way to Mecca, the most holy—and forbidden to outsiders—of the Muslim mosques. His return route was equally elaborate and exotic; unfortunately, he died halfway through his return, in Cairo, where he was buried, still disguised as a Muslim, with the name Ibrāhīm ibn 'Abd Allāh.

Burckhardt's exploits along the way set one's head spinning. He was the first European to set eyes on the city of Petra, an ancient and holy stone city in present-day Jordan. He is credited with discovering the great rock temple in Egypt that belonged to Ramses II (at Abu Simbel). And of course he succeeded in visiting Mecca. Before reaching his destination, from a small town outside of Mecca called Taif, Burckhardt found his cover blown. While he was in fear for his life, and almost certainly thwarted in his bid to access Mecca, a most peculiar event occurred: the viceroy of Egypt, Mehemet Ali, who knew Burckhardt by reputation alone, pronounced him a devout and knowledgeable Muslim, which was certainly stretching the facts a bit. Such an honor was—and still is—unheard of. Ali's motivation has never been revealed. This enabled Burckhardt to attain his goal, perhaps the only European non-Muslim to openly and safely visit Mecca.

Burckhardt's books are both easily accessible and full of glorious tales. Written as first-person travelogues, they sway from the quotidian (meals, customs, provisions, geography, and climate) to the exceptional (disguised skulking in the night, brash deception, harrowing escapes). While he lacked an especial knack for storytelling, his tales nevertheless survive on the basis of their sheer fearlessness. Nonchalant understatements substitute for stylistic drama, but the texts still thrill.

In the final analysis, Burckhardt was a great traveler and a passable author. His work is a fascinating study into a passion for travel and for seeing—if not imitating—the cultural other. True to the genre of travel literature, the act of writing his tales was, for Burckhardt, inseparable from the act of traveling. One almost gets the feeling that Burckhardt calculated some of his adventures and risks simply to provide a more spectacular story. To him, travel, tales, and living were one in the same.

References: Newby 1985

BURTON, SIR RICHARD FRANCIS

Sir Richard Francis Burton (English, 1821–1890) must be considered one of the darlings of travel literature. His life and his enormous body of writing form one seamless whole. Over the years, he has become a legend of travel and literary production, beloved equally for his daring deeds, his stirring prose, and his charismatic manner. Although he is the author of nearly 80 books, his most famous tale remains his *Pilgrimage to Al-Medinah and Mecca* (1855–1856). His other travels took him far and wide through India, Africa, the Americas, and, of course, Islamic regions.

Burton dropped out of Trinity College, Oxford, to join the Indian army in 1842. He quickly demonstrated outstanding skills as a leader, swordsman, and strategist; these same abilities would serve him handily throughout his career. The pattern of his life appears cyclical in retrospect: he would spend several years adventuring and compiling experience and notes, then he would return to England to publish his work, and then he would launch again into some ever more daring or exotic adventure.

In addition to his vast body of travel literature, Burton also translated many foreign classics into English. An astoundingly gifted linguist, his translations of *1001 Arabian Nights* (1885–1888), *The Kama Sutra* (1883), and *The Perfumed Garden* (1886) were smashing successes. Once he passed 50 years, he slowed down slightly, serving as a British diplomat first at Damascus and then at Trieste.

For the sake of space, I will concentrate on only a few of his texts, although they are universally of high quality, extreme interest, and substantial merit. All entirely autobiographical, they combine to paint a stunning picture of perhaps the most crafty, impetuous, suave, and adept of all travelers. He early acquired the nickname "Ruffian Dick" and certainly lived up to the moniker. Intellectually voracious, a master of disguises, astoundingly widely read, a frightful womanizer, a ferocious warrior, a master storyteller, and infinitely adaptable to obscure or extreme situations, Burton towers above all other travelers.

Sometime in the early 1850s, Burton began to scheme about penetrating the holy city of Mecca. As a Christian, he was strictly forbidden to enter the heavily guarded and sacred space of the city. He might have been able to convert to Islam, but he shunned the idea in favor of accepting a challenge. He would go as a Christian in disguise, and thus his Afghan Muslim alter ego was born. Had he been caught at such a ruse, he would have been summarily executed, but such dangers only excited him further. To expand his journey into an even more impressive gambit, he set out to reach not only Mecca but Medina (burial place of the prophet Muhammad) as well.

Of course, he succeeded brilliantly. And although his risks were monumental, he returned with an affected air of nonchalance.

Studio portrait of Sir Richard Francis Burton (Bettmann/Corbis)

His conclusion is pure Burton: having accomplished two incredible feats of bravery, daring, and adventure, he writes, "Those who find danger the salt of pleasure may visit Meccah; but if asked whether the results justify the risk, I should reply in the negative" (Newby 264). Indeed, for Burton, it appears that the journey itself is the object of the exercise; the rewards are the return home, the glory, and the story rather than the actual arrival at the destination.

Not only is achieving the goal important, but so is the style with which it is achieved, at least in Burton's world. To be sure, he accomplished his mission in grand form. The tale is related boisterously in his *Personal Narrative of a Pilgrimage to Al-Madinah and Mecca*. Although the book is often derided as arrogant, it is also sardonically funny and filled with a wealth of tangential stories and historical asides that delight in their own right. As a portrait of a traveler rather than of a place, this is fine literature indeed.

After this journey, he set off for East Africa to try his luck at infiltrating a different culture's forbidden city. Again he succeeded: he was the first white man to enter and return from the closed city of Harar. This account is published as *First Footsteps in Eastern Africa* (1856).

On his next journey he returned to Africa again to do geographic exploration. The race to find the source of the Nile River was in full swing, and Burton wanted badly to have the distinction. Teaming up with explorer John Speke, we see Burton as frightfully competitive and perhaps rather abrasive. Together they explored 900 miles of East Africa. Through great adversity and hardship they slogged on, injured and often ill. A disagreement parted them briefly as each followed his own hunch. Burton is usually credited with discovering Lake Tanganyika while Speke was off discovering Lake Victoria, thereby earning the honor of discovering the Nile's headwaters. Burton was furious with Speke as a result. Burton's account is found in *The Lake Districts of Africa* (1860).

Changing pace altogether in 1860, Burton visited the United States. He was particularly fascinated with the Mormon settlement in Utah, probably because of their curious codes of behavior and secretive ways. Access to the central temple is forbidden to non-Mormons, and this probably challenged Burton. Again he adapts himself in order to be accepted by the local community, and as an intimate outsider, he reflects at length on their culture. The story is told in his *City of the Saints* (1861). The latter portion of the text recounts his overland trip from Utah to California.

Wanderings in West Africa describes Burton's long journey and fascinating further exploits in Africa. He makes detailed observations of the lives and customs of native tribes dwelling along the West African coast. Anthropologists have long held invaluable his descriptions. In this volume he describes tribal rituals concerning birth, marriage, and death, tribal fetishism, ritual murder, cannibalism, and exotic sexual practices. Recently, however, many of the accounts from this text have come under scrutiny as exaggerated or embellished.

Other Burton texts include *Goa, and the Blue Mountain; or, Six Months of Six Leave* (India), *The Gold-Mines of Midian* (Arabian Peninsula), *Sindh and the Races That Inhabit the Valley of the Indus* (India), *Two Trips to Gorilla Land and the Cataracts of the Congo* (Africa), *The Erotic Traveler* (sex customs and practices), *A Mission to Gelele* (Amazon basin), and *Vikram and the Vampire; or, Tales of Hindu Devilry* (sorcery in India).

Burton led an amazing life filled with travels and prolific literary production. His contribution to the field has been enormous. For his smug attitudes and cultural insensitivity we might criticize him, but we must also marvel at his accomplishments. To amass such a quantity of excursions and noteworthy exploits is rare indeed; to capture them with flair, literary style, and excitement is rarer still.

See also: Speke, John Hanning
References: Benét 1965; Newby 1985; Rice 1991

BUTLER, SAMUEL

A curious figure, Samuel Butler (English, 1835–1902) exists on the fringes of travel literature. He was an eminently learned man who was both an important literary scholar and a notable biologist. *Erewhon* (1872), perhaps his most famous novel, is as much a tale of adventure as of travel. Butler did, however, write a series of letters and journal entries that were collected and compiled by his father under the title *A First Year in Canterbury Settlement* (1863). These letters document Butler's breach with his family in 1859: they wanted him to enter the clergy (his grandfather had been a bishop and his father a clergyman); he refused and fled to New Zealand to try his hand at farming.

Butler's letters are a harsh look at a culture and lifestyle that did not suit him. He returned to England in 1864, to work on his scholarly and literary pursuits. Because of his critical eye, *A First Year in Canterbury Settlement* can be called rather good travel literature. Butler's constant opposition between here, New Zealand, and there, England, demonstrates his keen need to compare these two lifestyles. He also seems to mock the tidy taxonomies of many a naturalist travel writer with his cynical observations. For example, when speaking of plant and insect life, Butler states, "The insects are insignificant and ugly, and, like the plant, devoid of general interest. There is one rather pretty butterfly, like our English tortoise shell. There is a sprinkling of beetle, a few ants, and a detestable sandfly" (Newby 522). Compare this to the elaborate and precise descriptions of plant and insect life we find in other explorers' accounts!

What makes Butler amusing is his dry wit. He wryly relates stories that betray an ironic detachment that marks him as a true traveler. To exist in the strangeness of another land, one must have a sense of humor and detachment. And, besides, he has an obvious love for stories, however silly and improbable. We can see both traits in a brief passage that begins by describing the lack of fish but the overwhelming presence of (only barely edible) eels. Relates Butler, "the servants, getting up, found an eel chasing a cat round about the room. I believe this story. The eel was in a bucket of water and doomed to die upon the morrow. Doubtless the cat had attempted to take liberties with him; on which a sudden thought struck the eel that he might as well eat the cat as the cat eat him; and he was preparing to suit the action to the word when he was discovered" (Newby 522). Humorous, detached, literary, and critical all at once, Butler constantly forces his readers to examine their opinions and beliefs.

I should discuss his novelistic work briefly. *Erewhon,* probably his masterpiece, is an anagram for *nowhere.* The novel is framed as a traveler's tale, but then it mutates into something else. The plot begins as a shepherd sets out to cross a mountain range and bumbles into a utopian community that satirizes the harshness of Victorian London. In this strange land, culture, beauty, truth, and honesty are valued above all. Peace and equality reign supreme in Erewhon; scorn and harsh criticism are directed at places like England. At the heart of Butler's satire is a bold critique of the practice of religion. Although some aspects of this novel resemble pure travel literature, it would be best to categorize this tale as utopian satire that uses travel as a device for escape.

As an expatriate first in New Zealand and later in Canada, Butler's life was comprised of a sequence of experiences in foreign lands. While he clearly states that England did not suit him, it seems that neither did his adopted homes. As acerbic as he can be toward Britain, there remains some degree of nostalgia for his home. The result is a sort of critique that demonstrates some real emotions for his birthplace. Rarely, if ever, does Butler escape the perspectives and expectations instilled in him by his native England. For this reason, his writing can function as travel literature; his vantage is almost always comparative in nature and reveals an ongoing struggle to reconcile an ideal vision of home with the flawed reality.

References: Newby 1985

BYRON, LORD

The story of George Gordon (English, 1788–1824), better known as Lord Byron, defies simple analysis. Capable of magnificent poetry and brilliant vision, Byron also made his share of idiotic decisions and stupid gestures. As a result of this enigma, Lord Byron plays a large part in the legends of British literature: many regard his life as the model for his famous "Byronic hero." With his life and some of his poetic output, Byron demonstrates, among many other things, a traveler's sensibilities.

Byron grew up in a troubled, if wealthy and influential, family. He came into his title, and the opportunities contained therein, at the young age of 10. After completing his education at Harrow and Cambridge, he published *Hours of Idleness* (1807) amid controversy and mixed reviews. This early work demonstrated Byron's great potential, but also his dangerous tendencies toward self-indulgence and arrogance. It bombed with the critics, and this stung Byron's pride; so began his lifelong battle with critics and the press. He proceeded to satirize reviewers and critics in his next work; it also met with a tepid reception. This sent Byron packing: he made a Grand Tour of Europe and the Near East from 1809 to 1811, where he gained both maturity and experience. This voyage seems to have made all the difference, for his subsequent writing bubbles with an energy and excitement, not to mention exotic characters and backdrops.

He published his fictionalized poetic account of the tour as *Childe Harold's Pilgrimage* (1812, 1816, 1817). The poem tells of a disillusioned young traveler who sets out to gain knowledge of the world and to experience the places he has learned of at school. As a result, the poem is both wonderfully descriptive and full of literary and historical references. Wherever the narrator goes, the place conjures up some famous account or occurrence from history; as such, the poem is a wonderful source of references to other famous travel accounts. Over the course of the poem, Childe Harold narrates visits to Portugal, Spain, Greece, Albania, Belgium, (what is now) Germany, and the Alps.

Childe Harold's Pilgrimage is an interesting and challenging account of places, but people are conspicuously lacking in the poem. Byron seems to have been vastly more enchanted with geography, history, and art than with local cultures. The only exception is with beautiful women: "Harold" notes them and pursues them with romantic fervor. This same theme is, of course, expanded upon considerably in *Don Juan,* the story of a wandering rake (picaro) whose travels are a series of seductions.

Byron returned to England, took his seat in the House of Lords, and wrote numerous poems that feature details from his travels. Many of these works are experiments with classicism rather than pure travel verse, but they mark Byron as a cultural and historical traveler of great potential.

After a failed marriage and continued battles with a generally conservative culture, Byron again left his home for the Continent. For a time, he lived at Lake Geneva, Switzerland, with Percy Bysshe and Mary Shelley. The rest of his life was spent abroad, nearly in constant motion. His travels, at times with the Shelleys, ranged over much of Italy, Switzerland, Greece, and Turkey. His lifelong immersion in foreign cultures influenced much of his great poetry. The urge to travel compelled Byron until the end; that same wanderlust appears as a dominant motif—or central recurring theme—in much of his later writing. He moved to Venice and later set out for Greece, where he died.

While his literary production, culminating in the unfinished masterpiece *Don Juan,* earns him a place among the greatest authors, Byron is not especially noted as a travel writer. Yet his own wandering adventures unquestionably influenced his writing to the point that whatever else it might be, it leans toward travel literature. Byron's breathless excitement and delight with travel function as more than just enthusiasm: travel often effects changes in his characters and inspires them to pursue ever-loftier ideals and dreams.

In addition to his more famous poetry, Byron also left a quantity of interesting correspondence, which has been collected and published as *Letters.* Because of his many years of travel, these letters cover a wide array of places and experiences. Often they are more candid and observational than his emotion-filled poetry. Yet the Byronic enthusiasm often shines through in the letters as well.

All told, Byron can be considered a contributor to travel literature in several regards. Primarily, his poetry is rich with factual details and references. Second, the spirit of travel drove his life and his writing; we can see this in his form as well as in his content. His verse often wanders between ideas and places, much as a traveler wanders for the thrill of the journey rather than to reach a precise destination. And finally, his journeys abroad taught him—and his writings reflect this learning—of the foolishness of his familiar, stifling, upper-class England.

See also: Grand Tour; Picaro
References: Crossley-Holland 1986; Harvey 1967; Newby 1985

BYRON, ROBERT

Robert Byron (English, 1905–1941), though perhaps less famous than his distant relative Lord (George Gordon) Byron, appears on almost any must-read list of travel literature. Although his life was cut short when he was killed in the line of intelligence duty in Persia during World War II, his contributions to the field remain great and praiseworthy.

A brilliant scholar who crackled with energy, wit, and curiosity, he began to distinguish himself shortly after taking his degree at Oxford University. His early pursuits included a celebrated account of Byzantine aesthetics titled *The Station: Athos, Treasures, and Men* (1928). This he followed with the equally fine *The Byzantine Achievement* (1929) and then an even more ambitious book titled *The Birth of Western Painting* (1930). His scholarship was a balanced mixture of the theoretical and the practical: he devoted enormous energy to finding examples of art and architecture not previously incorporated into the collection of artistic works accepted by the European establishment as classical and then weaving them into a rigorous though theoretical framework.

He then turned to pure travel literature with his account of the Soviet Union and Central Asia in *The Road to Oxiana* (1937). Lauded for inventing a new form of travel literature, Byron applied modernist techniques to the genre: his narrative is expressionistic, fragmented, destabilizing, and intentionally obtuse. The text must be read and studied, for it changes, kaleidoscope-like, over subsequent readings. He blends objective experience with subjective associations; facts tangle with emotions; the form of the tale competes with the plot for primacy. His work is a montage of material history, official documents, anecdotes, analysis, dialogues, asides—a veritable scrapbook from his journeys stitched loosely together with his narration. Doubtless, Byron's work has influenced all travel literature that has followed it.

The plot is fairly simple: in search of architecture, Byron and a friend, Christopher Sykes, depart from England in 1933 to Persia, Afghanistan, and the Islamic portions of the USSR. The name *Oxiana* refers to the Oxus River that runs along the northern border of Afghanistan. Ostensibly, Byron and Sykes are seeking a single work: an eleventh-century burial column called Gumbad-i-Kabus. But getting there is another matter entirely. They choose an overland route that takes them through Russia and then south to the Middle East. While they have a precise objective, the process of getting there soon eclipses the importance of their primary goal. Indeed, this is a celebration of travel, loosely guided by a singular end.

Early in the book, Byron makes his rather famous proclamation that travel is a forgotten liberal art: "The *pleasures* of travel need no re-iteration. But when the impulse is so imperious that it amounts to a spiritual necessity, then travel must rank with the more serious forms of endeavour" (Fussell 528). His accounts are clear and incisive, ranging from cultural critique to aesthetic interpretation. His attention to detail is not at all codified or predictable; instead, like the modernist fiction of James Joyce or Virginia Woolf, his language runs wild to evoke the tale. Selecting an example to embody this work is nearly impossible; nearly every page is dense and richly textured. Perhaps this excerpt will demonstrate. Byron is in his second day in Moscow and finds this capital to be thrilling and strange. He writes of the Red Square:

> And then as the lights came out and the snowflakes, long imminent, began to wander down in front of them, the scene became alive. As I reached the turn to the bridge, a company of soldiers came marching up the opposite street; the Red Army! visible agent of proletarian power and hardly less fantastic to my eyes than its fortress over the river. In their grey serge dressing-gowns swinging right down to the feet, and their grey serge helmet with pointed Tartar crowns, they looked like so many goblins on an infernal errand. Tramp! tramp! swung the grey serge skirts; but not a footfall sounded. . . . Behind the chanting goblins the Kremlin rose aglow with electricity, like some ghostly back-cloth to the hurrying city, tower upon tower, dome upon dome, piling up from the rose-red ramparts and the snowy eminence within them, to the last gigantic onion of Ivan Veliki, 450 feet above the black river. (Byron 86)

The small details, deeply colored by Byron's own subjectivity, carry the narrative and make it vivid.

For Byron, travel changes the way we see history and, by extension, the way we see ourselves in history. His experience is captured in his mind's eye, and it travels with him evermore, influencing all subsequent visions and experiences. He concludes in the chapter about Moscow, "The vision was over. I had exchanged the experience of a moment for a memory that will support me till I die. I shall never see Moscow again as I saw it on that afternoon" (86). Memory, and the written account that tries to represent that memory, is the prize of travel.

The political situation was tense, and travel through the Middle East caused them endless difficulties. Governments were extremely sensitive to Western critique and were worried—perhaps rightfully so—of spies. At every turn, visas and customs requirements challenged Byron and Sykes. But, of course, our heroes prevail and find that once beyond any border they have delights aplenty. From haggling to exploring to the daily adventure of a meal, Byron exuberantly relates his tale.

Plucky and daft, the twosome proceed to have great fun at each stop. For example, in Azerbaijan they are both commanded to produce five identification photographs for customs (an absurd quantity); they protest by staging a sort of sit-in at the customs house, ordering in tea and refusing to provide even one photo. Not wanting to be bothered, the agent allows them to pass with only one photo. When told to fill out a lengthy form—which Byron includes completed in his book—they have great fun mocking it. Claiming themselves to be a painter and a philosopher, they declare that they are accompanied by "a genie and a book by Henry James" (Fussell 542). Byron seems self-aware, even performative, in his behavior, as though simultaneously acknowledging and mocking the fact that his travels are largely designed to be represented in literature.

Byron's depictions of the characters they meet are equal parts caricature and random detail. They poke fun at absolutely everyone and everything. Yet their jests are of a fairly good-natured sort; the accounts seem at worst snobbish, at best hilarious.

Again and again their adventures thrill; from arrests to adverse weather to archeological wonders, Byron's tale is packed full of glorious experiences. His entries are made daily, but they vary widely: some days receive a scant paragraph, while others merit dozens of pages.

When they finally reach their destination, the stunning Gumbad-i-Kabus, the account takes but a few pages. It is the ostensible end they were seeking, but when they arrive we feel nothing by way of closure. Rather, we begin to see that the process of travel, the simple daily adventures of obtaining food, water, and shelter, that was the unspoken objective all along. It is this joy in the process of travel—and the unflagging desire to capture the accounts on paper and in memory—that makes this a great work of travel literature.

References: Byron 1982; Fussell 1987; Newby 1985

C

CABEZA DE VACA, ALVAR NÚÑEZ

Alvar Núñez Cabeza de Vaca (Spanish, 1490?–1557?) wrote two very popular accounts of travel; as a sixteenth-century explorer and writer, Cabeza de Vaca can be said to have been one of the earliest successful travel writers. His traveler's tales were widely circulated, although they did not get translated into English until the nineteenth century. The English translations are titled *The Journey of Alvar Núñez Cabeza de Vaca and His Companions from Florida to the Pacific* (1537) and *Cabeza de Vaca's Adventures in the Unknown Interior of America* (1545?).

His first book tells of his journey to the Gulf of Mexico (1528–1536), while his second recounts his subsequent journey to South America. In his first journey he set out to find gold and treasure in the New World. What he found instead was extreme hostility: of some 600 men, Cabeza de Vaca survived with only 3 others to wander from tribe to tribe throughout what is now the American Southwest. It is precisely this wandering that gave him a reputation as an expert on the New World. His accounts are often exaggerated, yet he must be given credit for writing the first European account of a buffalo and for having spent time living with several of the native tribes. Perhaps it is this intimate understanding of indigenous cultures that later got him in trouble.

Against all odds, Cabeza de Vaca made it back to Europe and was promptly given charge of another expedition to the New World. Upon arrival, he made it very clear that he believed in mercy and kindness to the native peoples. He joined intellectual forces with several of the high-ranking missionaries to promote American Indian rights. His second travelogue tells of his fight to help the natives while persuading his fellow colonialists that these people were not beasts.

Cabeza de Vaca writes sympathetically and powerfully from his adopted native perspective. He is the European who has become the other and who writes about it from the inside. After an extended stay in the wilds, he encounters some fellow Spanish explorers; he describes the meeting: "I overtook four of them on horseback. . . . [They were] astonished at the sight of me, so strangely habited as I was, and in the company with Indians. They stood staring at me a length of time, so confounded that they neither hailed me nor drew near to make an inquiry. I bade them take me to their chief: accordingly we went together half a league to the place where was Diego de Alcaraz, their captain" (Adams 86). Notice how even his language—he calls the leader a "chief"—suggests his identification with the Native Americans. Simultaneously, Cabeza de Vaca is an insider and an outsider. He has seen through the eyes of the native, but he cannot ever escape who he actually is. As such, Cabeza de Vaca seems constantly to struggle between following his orders to explore South America and doing what he believes is best for the natives.

References: Adams 1988; Rugoff 1960

CALDERÓN DE LA BARCA, FRANCES

Though born Frances Erskine Inglis (Scottish, 1804–1882), when she married Don Angel Calderón de la Barca in 1838 both her name and her life changed. He was soon appointed Spanish minister to Mexico, and so they sailed to Veracruz by way of Cuba. Over the course of several years, Calderón wrote lively letters that were subsequently published as *Life in Mexico* (1843). As a foreigner in a prominent role, one might expect Calderón to be rather prim and proper: not so. Her letters demonstrate a great sense of humor and a wonderfully unpretentious character.

Her stories often paint life in Mexico as nasty, grimy, and difficult, but there is little judgment attached to these descriptions. Instead, Calderón is rather offhand about the travail of her journeys. Having been crammed into a coach, for example, she "groans" adieu to her friends and then begins to describe her coach mates. One lady gets the brunt of her acerbic wit: "[She is] a horrible, long, lean, bird-like female, with immense red goggle-eyes, coal-black teeth, fingers like claws, a great goitre, and drinking brandy at intervals [!]" (Newby 470).

Or again, this diplomatic lady displays her unassuming honesty when relating a story of seeing a robber's severed head displayed in a forest as an example to vagabonds:

An object really in keeping with the wild scenery, was the head of the celebrated robber *Maldonado,* nailed to the pine-tree beneath which he committed his last murder. It is now quite black, and grins there, a warning to his comrades and an encouragement to travellers. . . . That grinning skull was once the head of a man, and an ugly one too, they say; but stranger still it is to think that this man was once a baby, and sat on his mother's knee, and that his mother may have been pleased to see him cut his *first tooth.* If she could but see his teeth now! (Newby 471)

In another famous account, she is invited to an elaborate ceremony committing a young girl to a convent. Sensitive to different customs, but disturbed nonetheless, Calderón is critical of this procedure in which "a child

can thus be dragged from the mother who bore and bred her, and immured in a cloister for life, amongst strangers, to whom she has no tie, and towards whom she owe no duty. . . . Let the young take their chance of sunshine or story; the calm and shady retreat is for helpless and unprotected old age" (Robinson 414–415). Though appalled, she refrains from making a scene, well aware that she is an outsider who can do nothing more than observe and learn.

As a modest, female voice of a traveler in Mexico, Calderón's writing is noteworthy. She has clearly calculated her letters to resound with as much shock value as she can muster, but in a fairly unpretentious manner. In addition, she provides a valuable insight into the daily life of a diplomat's wife in nineteenth-century Mexico. Finally, she paints a rare picture of the customs and behavior of the well-to-do class of locals. Her letters are interesting reading, for she has a true openness to the adventures of experiencing a foreign culture.

References: Newby 1985; Robinson 1994

CALVERLEY, CHARLES STUART

Charles Stuart Calverley (English, 1831–1884) was a lighthearted fellow, known principally for his parodies and light verses. He was also a translator of classics. His publications, the titles of which are rather uninspired, include *Verses and Translations* (1862), *Theocritus Translated into English Verse* (1869), and *Fly Leaves* (1872). As a man of letters, Calverley made a number of trips to the Continent and often wrote poems to tell of his journeys. Within this oeuvre, or body of work, are a number of fine pieces of travel verse.

One example of his travel verse is a poem called "Dover to Munich." The poem is written in Calverley's usual light and playful style and concentrates on the sensations that travel causes in him. Each mode of transportation is noted and commented upon: from ferry to coach to riverboat, Calverley compares the merits of each vehicle. The normal traveler's gripes arise whimsically from the poem: from slovenly passengers to tiny benches to atrocious food, he complains but also enjoys the adventure (and perhaps the cathartic relief of griping).

The people whom Calverley encounters seem to warrant his focused poetic attention. On the riverboat he describes his cabin mates:

> We've a nun here (called Thérèse),
> Two couriers out of place,
> One Yankee with a face
>   Like a ferret's:
> And three youths in scarlet caps
> Drinking chocolate and schnapps—
> A diet which perhaps
>   Has its merits.
> (Crossley-Holland 16)

Beyond descriptions Calverley does not go; he is as a recording machine, noting sights and those around him without engaging them (at least in the poem). Travel seems to inspire his senses: sights, sounds, smells all receive loving descriptions.

Later in the poem, Calverley provides us with a fine example of the scholar-traveler who seeks out art. When the narrator finally reaches Munich, the city rates several stanzas, but the art gallery rates nearly a dozen. He describes and reacts to paintings with transports of joy and excitement:

> And all purest, loveliest fancies
>   That in poets' souls may dwell
> Started into shape and substance
>   At the touch of Raphael.
> (Crossley-Holland 17)

Thus travel provides the narrator with a heightened awareness, exposure to art, and a subject upon which to write. In this regard, travel functions as a type of muse that inspires Calverley's poetry.

References: Crossley-Holland 1986

CAPE HORN

Cape Horn is the promontory at the southernmost point of South America. Sailing this treacherous route follows the contours of the islands comprising Tierra del Fuego. Ferdinand Magellan, in an effort to avoid this harrowing passage, discovered a narrow strait—still called the Strait of Magellan—to the northwest of Tierra Del Fuego, thus avoiding Cape Horn. Many travelers have written of the horror of Cape Horn, among them Captain James Cook and Jacob Roggeveen.

References: Oxford Atlas of Exploration 1997

CAPE OF GOOD HOPE

The southernmost (although located at the southwest tip) promontory of Africa still bears the name Cape of Good Hope. It remains a dangerously rough passage in spite of its mild-sounding name. Notorious for its storms, massive swells, and gale-force winds, it remains a challenging and dangerous passage. Early conquerors include Pedro Álvars Cabral, Bartolomeu Dias, and Ferdinand Magellan.

References: Oxford Atlas of Exploration 1997

CARERI, GIOVANNI FRANCISCO GEMELLI

Unfortunately, Giovanni Francisco Gemelli Careri (1668?–1705?) has mostly vanished from the annals of history. We know precious little about his life, and his six-volume *Trip around the World* (1700) is a very rare book. His writing is, however, reprinted in brief excerpts in a number of travel anthologies.

A wealthy and educated Italian, Careri set out to travel around the globe from 1693 to 1699. He refused to couch his expedition in scientific terms—he simply wanted to see and experience a myriad of places. The resulting

The coastline of the Cape of Good Hope, South Africa, c. 1984 (O. Alamany and E. Vicens/Corbis)

account of the journey is thus personal and unpretentious.

What an adventure Careri had! Magnificently well rounded, Careri shows as much interest in architecture as geology; he is as thrilled to hunt as he is to talk politics; he seems as pleased to encounter indigenous peoples as to be entertained by expatriate Europeans. His voyage took him first to Africa (both North and South), then off to the Far East, and finally to Central and South America. Employing every imaginable form of transport, Careri finds himself on a Spanish galleon; on camels, mules, and horses; in canoes; in a sedan chair; and, of course, on foot.

The value of Careri's work is twofold. First, he strives for as much objectivity as he can muster. His accounts try to be unbiased and nonjudgmental with regard to the huge array of wondrous things he sees. As a historical, cultural record, his book has great value. Second, he ranges widely and (relatively) quickly but from a consistent perspective. We can thus compare, say, Careri's account of Africa with his own account of South America without having to factor in a different writer's perspective. In addition, his account represents a great cross section of the globe over the course of a few decades; this quick survey allows us to compare diverse cultures from a single perspective over a relatively brief period of time instead of comparing accounts that are separated by a greater span of time. In other words, Careri's observations help us to form a more accurate sociological opinion.

Formally, Careri's account is rather lax. While he attempts to make daily entries, many days seem to have vanished entirely. While some entries are copious and thorough, others are but a few lines of vague description: "Thursday 25th, I went shooting among the vineyards, where there are abundance of thrushes, and woodcocks" (Adams 270). Nonetheless, the quality of his more ambitious passages sheds amusing and fact-filled light upon his subject as well as upon his presumptions. What Careri finds noteworthy is itself an important detail; indirectly, we can begin to piece together an example of an early-eighteenth-century worldview.

As the journey proceeds, the simple objective of seeing the world fuses with Careri's desire to write about what he sees. Indeed, these goals are inextricably bound. In one instance, Careri is having grave difficulty with the law in Smyrna: he has been mistaken for a known criminal and finds himself before a magistrate. For a time, things look grim, but eventually he is cleared. Instead of rage, the good-natured Careri displays gratitude toward his accusers: "You give me such a subject to insert into my Manuscripts, as has not happened to me in all my Travels, nor perhaps has any other Traveller met with the like" (Adams 271).

In short, Careri is a consummate gentleman traveler who seeks experience both to learn from it and to write of it. His passion for seeing other cultures—lots of other cultures—is extraordinary, and his calm, rational voice is refreshing. For these reasons, Careri's work—if you can find it—is exemplary.

References: Adams 1988

CARR, SIR JOHN

A nominally prominent eighteenth-century figure, Sir John Carr (English, 1732–1807) wrote essays, plays, and a satire of travel literature called *The Life and Opinions of Tristram Shandy, Gentleman, Volume 3* (1760), a parody of Laurence Sterne's picaresque travel story *Tristram Shandy*. As a parody, this volume puts

an interesting spin on the genre, but it cannot technically be regarded as travel literature itself. Carr also composed a number of interesting poems, many of which qualify as travel literature. His simply titled *Poems* (1809) was published after his death.

Carr's travels appear to have been mostly in Europe; a number of letters and other correspondence refer to his journeys to Scandinavia, the Mediterranean basin, and France. Generally, Carr seems to have traveled as an escape from the diversions of his life in England and as an excuse to write poetry and personal essays. While he was not obsessed with travel, his excursions abroad seem to have made a considerable impact upon his thinking and provided him with interesting material.

For the sake of this encyclopedia, Carr's "Sonnet upon a Swedish Cottage, Written on the Road, within a Few Miles of Stockholm" serves as a fine example of travel verse that describes cultural exchange and the desire to incorporate the foreign into the homeland.

Here, far from all the pomp ambition seeks,
  Much sought, but only whilst untasted
    praised,
Content and innocence, with rosy cheeks,
  Enjoy the simple shed their hands have
    raised.

On a grey rock it stands, whose fretted base
  The distant cat'ract's murm'ring waters
    lave,
Whilst o'er its mossy roof, with varying
    grace,
  The slender branches of the white birch
    wave.

Around the forest-fir is heard to sigh,
  On which the pensive ear delights to
    dwell,
Whilst, as the gazing trav'ller passes by,
  The grey goat, starting, sounds his tinkling
    bell.
Oh! in my native land, ere life's decline,
May such a spot, so wild, so sweet, be mine!
(Crossley-Holland 223)

To the narrator of this poem, the solitude of traveling allows him to appreciate the simplicity and humility of a small cottage. He infers a happily rustic and innocent life associated with that vision. The cabin and grounds are described in language usually reserved for major architectural or historical landmarks; clearly, the narrator has idealized this place.

Through the quartet of the third stanza, his praise increases: the scene begins even to seem pastoral. Yet, as this is a sonnet, Carr uses the final couplet to mark a transition in tone and meaning. In these final two lines, linked by their rhyme, he shifts out of the present and into the future and leaps from Sweden to Britain: he wants to reproduce this cozy cottage in his own homeland.

Implicitly, these lines contain a comparison between home and elsewhere. Such a desire to capture the foreign—much as we take photographs (or memories)—and to bring it home marks a major theme of travel literature. Borrowing, adopting, and adapting that which is discovered on the road is a common response to travel; the desire to absorb the foreign—a form of learning about the other—remains one of the driving forces behind travel and travel literature.

See also: Sterne, Laurence
References: Crossley-Holland 1986

CARRE, ABBÉ

Little record remains of Abbé Carre (French, 1633?–1699?) save his three-volume travelogue from 1699 that records his journey from France to the Middle East and then to India. While these volumes may have been insufficient to earn him a permanent place as a major figure in history, they do engagingly capture the early moments of European imperialism in Asia. He records his adventures, his observations, and, most of all, his opinions. By noting what Carre chooses to record and how he describes it, we can gain insight into the man as well as the European culture that produced him.

We must remember that Carre's travels correspond with an important period of European political history. France, England, Portugal, and the Netherlands were all vying for trade routes to the Far East, and this rivalry often escalated into full-scale wars. Louis XIV had just sent part of his fleet to secure France's trade channels, and there is some evidence to suggest that Abbé Carre was sent to see from the inside if the French East India Company was indeed loyal. (Carre, introduction to vol. 1). Thus large portions of Carre's journals detail trade and commercial practices.

Yet interspersed with these banal accounts are some wonderful examples of travel writing. His style of writing is vivacious: he tells stories with nearly certain exaggeration, and his tone suggests a sort of arrogant swagger. I get the feeling he had no desire for "objectivity," but rather wanted simply to tell a good story. He also has a love for seemingly gratuitous detail; he randomly digresses and speculates about all manner of things. One of my favorite asides is a lengthy comparison between the state of happiness of a French nun and a concubine in a harem (vol. 1, 251ff.). Both are hypothetical characters that serve to illustrate Carre's vivid imagination. The scene is in some ways a distillation of his whole project: by comparing the East with his European homeland, Carre provides significant details about both cultures.

In other accounts he uses his quick wit and nimble thinking to get himself out of serious trouble. Evidently quite an accomplished linguist and actor, Carre tells of several situations where he has passed himself off as Dutch or Portuguese. Note that this suggests a European affinity, a sort of "us against them" scenario. The so-called white races appear as interchangeable, in spite of their political squabbles.

Carre claims in his dedication that his work is "a stainless mirror, in which I show clearly the most hidden and secret things that have occurred in the administration of your [Minister Colbert's] trade in these distant Eastern lands" (vol. 1, 1). Yet in practice he tends toward exaggeration at almost every turn. As a historical document, his writings are suspect, but as travel literature, they are excellent.

First and foremost, Carre is concerned about writing his story. He suggests that unless he can record it, the events will be somehow lost and thus the journey not worth having been made. One vivid yarn relates a chase wherein he finally decides to stand and fight against the band of robbers that has pursued him. Finding himself severely outnumbered, he tries to negotiate a deal: "I told them that if they would not touch my papers and letters [i.e., the travelogue we are discussing] I would gladly give them my clothes and all my belongings, and that otherwise I was resolved to die and to kill five or six of them" (vol. 1, 71). They agree, rob him of everything, and leave him horseless and in a coarse shirt with his papers. He seems, in the text, unconcerned with his misfortune, although he admits to some uneasiness at the sound of nearby lions roaring.

Such a story lends a sense of worth to the text; it was "bought" at such extreme hardship, hence it must be precious. We may share his excitement and anxiety, but like the plot of most any novel, we assume that he will make it through: after all, there are still two more volumes ahead of us. In this way, Carre has blended genres to combine a picaresque novel with a travelogue. As such, he has made himself into something of a literary character, a roguish picaro who deals nonchalantly with adversity because he knows he will survive at least until the end of the book.

Carre is also significant because of his attitude toward the cultures he passes through: to him, Asia is not a culture or a place, but rather a commodity to be bought and sold. Such a commodification of the other is the trademark of high colonialism, and Carre reflects his culture's extreme mercantile desires.

What can be had in Asia are things to sell, be they spices, tea, or stories of adventure and exotic others. After returning to France with the first volume of his work, Carre declared that he must travel again in order to write the next two volumes. In this case, writing about the journey serves as the driving force behind travel: Carre goes in order to live that which he can subsequently reduce to narrative.

See also: Picaresque; Picaro
References: Carre 1947

CATHAY

The archaic name, though still used in poetry or as an archaism, for China. The term derives from the Tatar (i.e., the Turkic and Mongol tribes that dominated the Middle East, China, and Eastern Europe in the Middle Ages) name for China. This origin is significant because it marks Cathay as a name imposed upon China by an outside, invading force; as such, it has colonialist or imperialist undertones.

References: OED

CÉLINE, LOUIS-FERDINAND

Louis-Ferdinand Céline (French, 1894–1961) is the pen name of Louis-Ferdinand Destouches. Céline was a troubled French novelist best known for his absurdly misanthropic books *Journey to the End of Night* (1932) and *Death on the Installment Plan* (1936). Both of these books, while fiction, draw heavily on Céline's own voyages and travels. After becoming a communist, Céline made a journey to Russia and quickly renounced his position in his treatise *Mea Culpa* (1937). These three early works are on the fringes of travel literature in that they contain considerable episodes of travel and exploration but are not expressly about travel itself. I have included them because travel is the engine that drives the plot of these tales;

the characters develop directly as a result of their being in motion. In addition, Céline's protagonists employ travel as an escape from all that is wrong with the modern world: to them, voyaging abroad is a way of being reborn into a different context. Céline's later works are mostly political in nature and thus outside the scope of this encyclopedia.

As a dissatisfied and cynical French citizen, Céline spent much of his life moving. Long stints in Denmark, East Africa, and a variety of French cities were punctuated by significant voyages to Russia, East Asia, the United States, and several nations in Africa. Always skeptical of French politics, Céline proposed that moving abroad was a political act. From his foreign perspective, he argued, he could be a more incisive critic of his homeland; in principle, this is one of the fundamental aspirations of all travel literature.

Perhaps the best illustration of Céline's work as travel writing is *Journey to the End of Night*. The novel is a more or less autobiographical account of a cynical drifter named Ferdinand Bardamu in the aftermath of World War I. Bardamu's journeys range wide and far; his fundamental alienation makes him a traveler wherever he goes, from his "home" in France to colonial Africa to the United States. Of course, Bardamu's journey is not only a physical state: his bodily wanderings correspond to his psychological growth and mental adventures. Just as he tries to understand the radical difference between himself and the natives in Africa, he tries to understand an equally radical difference between himself and his fellow Europeans. The story is thus about seeking differences and learning from them.

Written in a vivid and modern style, the story is haunting and memorable. Bardamu's endless pessimism charges every observation he makes with a deep and cutting irony. After a stint in a mental hospital, Bardamu hits upon the notion to head for Africa: "The further away I go, the better. . . . Personally I only wanted to get away, but as one ought always to look useful if one isn't rich and as, anyway, my studies didn't seem to be getting me anywhere, it couldn't very well last. . . . So 'Africa has it,' I said, and I let myself be hounded towards the tropics where I was told you only had not to drink too much and to behave fairly well to make your way at once" (Céline 108). Certainly not the most inspired traveler! With that glib assertion, he launches himself into a new world.

His enthusiasm goes from bad to worse as he details the horrors of Africa. But in spite of his endless carping, Bardamu learns numerous lessons from both natives and his fellow colonists. In good cynical fashion, however, they are not wise lessons, but lessons in how to deceive, trick, and manipulate. Nonetheless, it is the process of being in motion—and being able to flee—that facilitates Bardamu's learning.

From Africa, he heads to the United States. In the slums of New York or the factories of Detroit, Bardamu finds humiliation and unpleasantness on par with what he found in deepest Africa. But once again, it is the exposure to the foreign and having the perspective of an outsider that allow him to learn. The details of Céline's own life and travels seem to resemble the grumbling voyages of his protagonist in nearly every situation.

Throughout his misadventures, Bardamu remains in motion: it is all he has. As a political statement, his rootlessness enables him to ally himself not with a country or a flag, but with the larger population of international workers. This socialist sentiment made the book something of a scandal originally. For our purposes, let it be said that Céline's story uses travel as a sustained metaphor for life; indeed, the traveler in motion is a free man. If there is any solace at all to be found, for Bardamu at least, it is in the occasional solidarity that he finds in meeting wayward cynics like himself on the road.

References: Céline 1960; France 1995

CERVANTES, MIGUEL DE

One of the most praised and studied stories in Western literature is *Don Quixote* (1605 and 1615) by Miguel de Cervantes (Spanish, 1547–1616). While not primarily a work of travel literature, this novel has had sufficient influence on travel writing to merit a brief entry in this encyclopedia.

Cervantes was something of a traveler himself. Coming from a wealthy family, he had the opportunity to wander widely through the Mediterranean region and in North Africa. He was imprisoned in Algeria for several years, eventually to be ransomed. Such travel adventures seem to have influenced him considerably. His literary reputation is almost wholly contingent upon *Don Quixote.* While he wrote in many forms, he rarely—if ever—approached the greatness of this early work. In this text Cervantes toys with notions of perception and perspective: Quixote is a wanderer perceiving the strange world very differently from those around him. In many ways, Quixote is the archetypal traveler.

Very briefly, the story tells of an unsettled country gentleman who reads himself crazy enough to believe that he is really an errant knight named Don Quixote de la Mancha. The story is thus a satire of chivalric romances and of courtly tales of love and bravery. Quixote and his comic sidekick, Sancho Panza, set off to follow a peasant girl who is mistakenly believed to be the lovely Lady Dulcinea. The adventure leads them far and wide, through a series of comic misadventures, including the famous scene wherein Quixote mistakes windmills for dragons and sheep for armies. Throughout, our hero's overly active imagination causes him to misperceive the commonplace; in so doing, Cervantes has made Quixote a foreign traveler in his own land.

The influence of this book on Western fiction has been enormous. As one of the earliest examples of a European novel, its form alone is significant. Shunning the more traditional verse in favor of prose allowed Cervantes to write in a descriptive and rather uninhibited manner. As prose became the dominant form of travel writing, we must acknowledge some debt to this early prose account of adventures on the road. Indeed, it is what Quixote randomly encounters on his journey that drives the tale.

In addition, *Don Quixote* is a prime example of the picaresque novel. In this form of writing, a wandering, likable rogue figures at the center of the story; his adventures, usually great difficulties and miraculous recoveries, form the nucleus of the plot. As such, Quixote represents a very early picaro. His troubles are excessive to the point of comedy, and his solutions are endearing and innovative. The picaresque novel became a significant category of travel writing, especially in the eighteenth century; clearly, later writers in this category owe some debt to Cervantes.

Another major theme in *Don Quixote* is the notion of a quest. Often interpreted as a reformation of the search for the Holy Grail, the Grail Quest was an abundant trope—that is, a symbol used to figuratively represent something else—in medieval and early Renaissance literature. With the beginning of the Enlightenment, Cervantes refigured the Grail Quest by satirizing and mocking it. Instead of a journey to search for the key to salvation, Quixote's quests after an illusion. Where the Grail Quest is noble, gallant, and chivalrous, Quixote's quest is farcical, boorish, and selfish. As quests necessarily involve travel and adventure, there is often a residue of the Grail Quest—or a mockery of the same—in almost all travel literature.

Finally, *Don Quixote* must be considered travel literature because it is through the hero's adventures that he learns. His travels teach him many lessons, the least of which is not to read too many chivalric romances! By encountering different and unfamiliar people and places, Quixote is able to learn of himself

Don Quixote and Sancho Setting Out; *engraving by Gustav Doré, 1863, from* Don Quixote *by Miguel de Cervantes (Chris Hellier/CORBIS)*

and his own shortcomings. And by traveling, he is able to overcome his madness. Who could ask for anything more from a journey?

See also: Grail Quest; Picaresque; Picaro

CHAMPLAIN, SAMUEL DE

Samuel de Champlain (French, 1567–1635) has given us a very detailed account of his numerous travels from Europe to North America. His first voyage was to the West Indies, where he distinguished himself as a brave sailor and a keen observer. His journals from the first voyage betray his ardent enthusiasm and his bold dreams. His next voyage was to Canada in 1603 to trade furs. The mix of commerce with exploration suited Champlain well; his travels could be financially self-sustaining, thus more independent.

Over the next 20 years, Champlain explored Canada and left us an exquisitely detailed record of its geography and its native peoples. In addition to being a historic record, his tales are endearing. His stories often display considerable narrative talent and dramatic excitement. Early in his travels he befriended the Huron tribe and over the years dealt with them fairly and humanely. He eventually helped the Huron to defeat the Iroquois, thereby making the Iroquois a sworn enemy of France. By trading with the Huron, Champlain sincerely believed that he could "civilize" them. Regardless of how we now view this colonialist ambition, the benefits of trading with the Europeans allowed the Huron opportunities that other tribes did not have.

As well as producing one of the earliest records of the Huron ways, Champlain was one of the first to map the Great Lakes. Ever excited to be the first European to see a particular place, Champlain's list of "firsts" is astounding: he was the first European to see much of the interior of North America. His accomplishments were not, however, limited to the geographic; Champlain was to become the first governor of Quebec (1620).

Illustration depicting "four Native American Indians of New France," from Voyages et descouvertures faites en la Nouvelle France, depuis l'année 1615 *by Samuel de Champlain (Paris, 1619) (Library of Congress)*

His writing is no less prolific than his deeds. Every one of his voyages has an elaborate published journal as a record. Furthermore, numerous volumes of collected tales and excerpts have been published in different combinations. For the English reader, the authoritative edition is the Champlain Society's six-volume set of translated journals (Champlain 1927).

Like most explorers of his era, Champlain cannot help seeing with European eyes; implicit in any of his observations is a comparison that sets Native Americans and Europeans in opposition. Repeatedly, Champlain compares the two cultures, as in this description of the Huron lifestyle from *Voyages and Discoveries in New France from 1615 to 1618:* "Their life is a miserable one in comparison with our own; but they are happy among themselves, not having experienced anything better, and not imagining that anything more excellent is to be found" (Rugoff 792).

While reading Champlain as a source of information about the New World, we can also read him backward and, in so doing, learn something about European attitudes. Indeed, while we learn about the Huron, we simultaneously learn about the Europeans who observed them and sought to conquer them. In this mode, we might read Champlain as the epitome of the early European explorer: he felt it his duty to spread European ways to those "less fortunate." But as we see from his life and writing, the "savages" also taught Champlain quite a lot. Perhaps this concurrent give-and-take is one of the finest results of travel and exploration.

References: Adams 1988; Champlain 1927; Rugoff 1960

CIRCUMNAVIGATION

The process of sailing (or flying) around the entire earth. The goal of circling the globe presumes an understanding of a round earth, thus the desire to achieve this end arose in the late fifteenth century in the Age of Exploration. Early attempts to circumnavigate the globe were driven as much by a sense of adventure as by a desire for trade routes to the East Indies. The first successful around-the-world journey is usually attributed to Ferdinand Magellan; although he died before the trip was complete, his crew fulfilled the mission. To this day there is still allure to the notion of circling the entire planet, as seen by the many advertisements for travel "around the world."

Interestingly, the notion of circumnavigation shifts the emphasis of the voyage from the reaching of the destination to the process of transportation. In this regard, circumnavigation is an abstract notion that implicitly recognizes the value of travel itself.

CLAUDE MIRROR

The Claude Mirror, also known as the Claude Lorraine Glass, was a type of mirror used mostly by eighteenth-century travelers to help frame their views of landscapes. The mirror was handheld, convex, and often tinted; the effect was to focus a wide-angle view into a smaller, bordered image. The tinted glass served to more dramatically highlight the contrasts between light and dark and to cut down on glare (in an era before sunglasses). The traveler stood with his back to the vista and held the mirror to reflect the scene.

The Claude Mirror was named after the French painter Claude Lorraine (1600–1682), who popularized the "classical landscape" among the upper classes of Europe in the seventeenth century. This genre of painting often idealized the ancient Roman countryside as an idyllic and harmonious place where nature and culture peacefully coexisted. Stylistically, Lorraine's paintings concentrate wide-angle views onto a canvas, often employing a dramatic light-to-dark contrast (chiaroscuro). Characters are usually small and minimal compared to the vastness of the landscape, which is often balanced with a staunch classical structure. The novelty and popularity of both the theme and the style enjoyed considerable success for nearly a century.

Use of the Claude Mirror is interesting in that the device mediates the view of nature through a mechanical device: nature is thus made to look like a painting rather than the other way around. For the eighteenth-century traveler, who would most likely have been wealthy and educated, making the foreign scenes look more like the more familiar

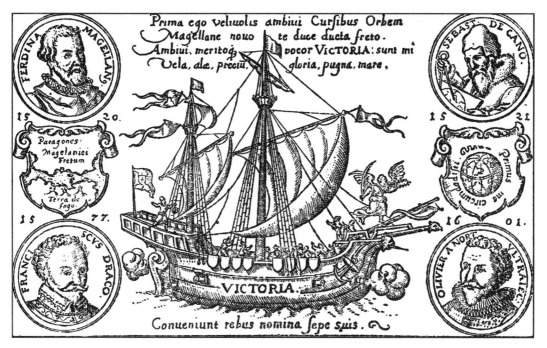

Ferdinand Magellan's ship Victoria, *which completed the first circumnavigation of the world, with portraits of Magellan and Francis Drake (Bettmann/Corbis)*

painted images was desirable. Perhaps we may see the Claude Mirror as a precursor to the photographic camera, which often functions in a similar manner.

References: OED

CLEMENS, SAMUEL LANGHORNE

See Twain, Mark

COLERIDGE, SAMUEL TAYLOR

One of the great poets of the romantic period, Samuel Taylor Coleridge (English, 1772–1834) wrote a vast number of poems, essays, and plays. As he was the son of a vicar, it was always assumed he would devote his life to the church. But his success at school, combined with the death of his father, impelled Coleridge to pursue literature. Although his early life was spent in England, he eventually discovered the allure of travel, and it seems to have made a great impression on him. Part of

his education was spent in Germany (1798–1799), and he later lived in Malta (1804–1806) and Italy (1807). His travels around England and Ireland were also vast and frequent. As a famous, if notorious, figure, he had ample opportunities to visit many of the capitals of Europe.

Coleridge's energetic poetry proclaims in jubilant terms the virtues of travel. As a major force in English romantic poetry, his prolific literary production has had wide-ranging influence; likewise, his relatively few travel poems are often regarded as highly influential to later nineteenth-century poets. While he is not noted particularly as a travel poet, much of his famous work contains elements of travel literature. "Kubla Khan" and "The Rime of the Ancient Mariner" both utilize travel and exotic backgrounds as major components, but in neither one is travel the main point of the work. As such, these poems might be called fringe travel literature.

There are, however, a number of examples of Coleridge's poetry that function more purely as travel verse. One example will suffice to demonstrate Coleridge's travel sensibilities. "The Delinquent Travellers" is a substantial sample that contains many of the elements of pure travel literature. It begins:

> Some are home-sick—some two or three,
> They're third year on the Arctic Sea—
> . . . But O, what scores are sick of Home,
> Agog for Paris or for Rome!
> (Crossley-Holland 9)

The desire for travel seems universal and unquenchable: only a tiny few are homesick, and only after lonely years at sea. Travel functions in this poem as inspiration, to poets and wanderers alike.

Coleridge goes on to compare stability and motionlessness to humiliating confinement; in other words, motion equals freedom. He urges,

> Keep moving! Steam, or Gas, or Stage,
> Hold, cabin, steerage, hencoop's cage—
> Tour, Journey, Voyage, Lounge, Ride, Walk,
> Skim, Sketch, Excursion, Travel-talk—
> For move you must! 'Tis now the rage,
> The law and fashion of the Age.
> (10)

In the name of glory and adventure, one ought to feel compelled toward motion.

In the less manic middle section of the poem, the narrator does acknowledge the dangers and the cost of such journeys. In romantic fashion, Coleridge weighs both sides of the equation, and his emotions swing against travel. This sentiment is quick to fade, however, as he concludes that one must do anything necessary to make a journey. Like the traveler who oscillates between feeling glum at the rigors of travel and feeling exultant at the joys, so too does the poem wildly bounce between emotional poles.

In the end, the narrator insists that the rewards of travel are great, both to individual and to country:

> Who ramble East, West, North and South,
> With leaky purse and open mouth,
> In search of varieties exotic
> The usefullest and most patriotic,
> And merriest, too, believe me, Sirs!
> Are your Delinquent Travellers!
> (12)

This exuberant ode to travels of all sorts suggests that travel is a kind of rite of passage for all who would be good fathers, patriots, and gentlemen. As such, travel serves as an integral part of a citizen's education and maturation.

In this poem, as well as in numerous others, Coleridge emotionally debates the costs and benefits of travel. With his keen interest in perspective and vantage points, Coleridge needs the jolting effects of travel to encourage him to look at the constant natural world and human condition from different angles. In his life, his letters, and his poetry, he returns to this theme and allows himself to be taught by his travels.

References: Crossley-Holland 1986; Harvey 1967

COLUMBUS, CHRISTOPHER

A famous name in exploration, to be sure, Christopher Columbus (Italian born, later Portuguese, 1451–1506) may not in fact live up to the myth that usually surrounds him. Often erroneously credited with "discovering" America, Columbus was but the first European to stumble onto the Americas and to publish his account. Nordic seafaring peoples had reached the same destination long before. Nonetheless, Columbus was an intrepid traveler with a bold, even stubborn, vision.

His story is often told: repeatedly ridiculed for his notion that the earth was round, he struggled to find a patron to support his voyages. After a number of less ambitious expeditions, he believed that he had sufficient experience to seek the Far East—Cathay (China)

Christopher Columbus Leaving Spain to Go to America; *from* America, Part 4, *by Theodor de Bry, 1528–1598 (Library of Congress)*

and Cipango or Cipangu (Japan) as described by Marco Polo—by traveling westward. Monarchs from Portugal, then England, then France refused to support this venture. At last the Spanish monarchs Ferdinand and Isabella somewhat reluctantly pledged three ships and their crews to the expedition. And off went Columbus on his famous 1492 voyage.

While Columbus did not write a travel diary as such, it was standard practice for the captain of an expedition to keep a "ship's log." Columbus was particularly enthusiastic about his logbook. After his successful return, he presented his journal to Ferdinand and Isabella, who treasured it. A single copy was made and returned to Columbus. Unfortunately, both

copies have been lost. What we do have is a third-person journal written by Bishop Bartolomé de Las Casas, who lived in the New World starting in 1502. He obviously had spent considerable time talking with Columbus and reading, even quoting, his ship's log.

After his initial discovery, Columbus made several return trips exploring what is now Cuba, the Bahamas, numerous Caribbean islands, and the northern coast of South America. His logs of these journeys, parts of which still exist, have lost the thrill and excitement that seem to have been present on his first journey. In addition, Columbus's later voyages were fraught with discipline problems and personal strife; it turns out that Columbus

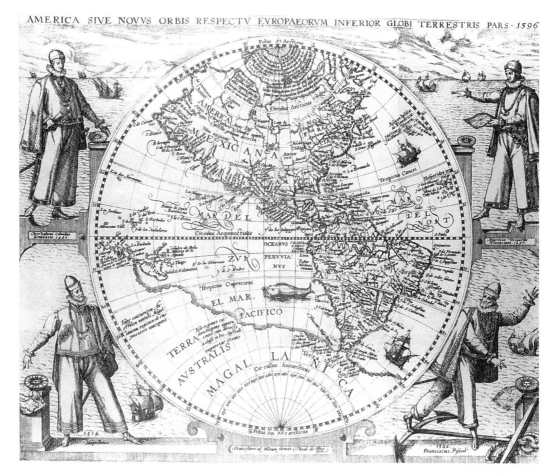

Map of the Americas with portraits of Christopher Columbus, Amerigo Vespucci, Ferdinand Magellan, and Francisco Pizarro; from America by Theodor de Bry, 1600 (Library of Congress)

was a rather better visionary than an administrator of Spanish colonial interests.

Thus Columbus, while a great explorer, cannot be considered a major author of travel literature. Yet because of his fame and importance, he rates a place in this study. For the sake of purity, we can look at Las Casas's transcription—he claims verbatim—of Columbus's initial days in the Bahamas.

On this voyage, we see Columbus amazed at his discovery. He is ambivalent toward the natives: on the one hand, he repeatedly tries to befriend them; on the other, he keeps a number of them by force aboard his ship. While he seems very interested in the discovery of other "islands" (which will turn

out to be Cuba), his desire is not in the name of geographic discovery, but rather in search of gold.

Columbus's description of his first encounter with the natives is telling indeed. He writes (allegedly):

I knew that they were a people to be delivered and converted to our holy faith rather by love than by force. [We] gave to some among them some red caps and some glass beads, which they hung round their necks, and many other thing of little value. At this they were greatly pleased and entirely our friends that it was a wonder to see. Afterwards they . . . brought us parrot and cotton thread in balls, and spears and many other things. . . . In fact, they took all and gave all, such as they had, with good will, but it seemed to me that they were a people very deficient in everything. They also go naked as their mothers bore them. (Adams 55)

We can see his missionary tendencies, his colonialist urges, and his Eurocentric attitudes quite clearly in this passage. Yet as a first encounter, his writings are sure to fascinate and to illuminate a culture that had been unrecorded previously.

Much of Columbus's logbook is technical—navigational headings, wind characteristics, climate—but frequently he falls into reveries about the vast potential for gold in these uncharted and abundant islands. It should be noted that Columbus thought he had reached the Far East; he had no idea he had discovered an entire vast continent between Europe and Asia. Although disappointed at not finding gold immediately, Columbus nonetheless seems to view the New World as a sort of paradise found, if a slightly deficient paradise with no gold. He compares it to his favorite places in Europe:

The plain of Cordova [did] not come near [the quality of these lands], the difference being as great as between night and day. [The natives] said that all these lands were cultivated, and that a wide and large river passed through the center of the valley. . . . All the trees were green and full of fruit, and the plants tall and covered with flowers. The roads were broad and good. The climate was like April in Castille; the nightingale and other birds sang as they do in Spain . . . and it was the most pleasant place in the world. Some birds sang sweetly at night. The crickets and frogs are heard a good deal. The fish are like those of Spain. . . . Gold was not found, and it is not wonderful that it should not have been found in so short a time. (Rugoff 695)

One of the main characteristics of Columbus's writings is a wide-eyed wonder that may well make his accounts slightly suspect. Yet if we compare his earlier visions with the infinitely less enthusiastic logs of his subsequent voyages, we can begin to form a larger picture of Columbus.

Without a doubt, his idealism faded quickly. The joy and excitement of his initial discoveries gave way to disgust at the endless greed and cruelty on the part of his men and the early colonists. While Columbus appears to have resisted a wholesale pillage of the New World, he was guilty of numerous transgressions and abuses himself. Eventually he was reprimanded by the Crown and recalled to Europe, where he lived out his days in poverty and scorn.

References: Adams 1988; Fussell 1987; *Oxford Atlas of Exploration* 1997; Rugoff 1960

THE CONTINENT

Although technically a geographic term that describes any one of the major land masses of the earth—Asia, Antarctica, Australia, Europe, North America, South America—many travel writers use "the Continent" to refer to continental Europe (as opposed to Great Britain). Hence an English traveler (or an American) might refer to "an impending visit to *the continent*" meaning a trip to mainland Europe. This phrasing is particularly common in accounts that describe the Grand Tours that were popular in the eighteenth and nineteenth centuries.

See also: Grand Tour

COOK, CAPTAIN JAMES

Captain James Cook (English, 1728–1779) is another of the legendary adventurers of the European tradition. Perhaps the defining feature of Cook as a man was his insatiable yearning for exploration: in his introduction to *Captain Cook's Journal during His First Voyage round the World . . . 1768–1771,* he writes that he feels driven "not only to go farther than any man had ever been before, but as far as possible for a man to go" (Rugoff 419). Beyond his urgent need to surpass any previous explorers, Cook had deep desires to serve scientific inquiry and to treat native peoples humanely. His writings display this rare combination: he is scientific, orderly, and precise while also being humane, compassionate, and honest.

As a young man, he made his name as a superior seaman, surveyor, and cartographer. In 1768, Cook was given command of an expedition to the legendary "Southern Continent" (what we now know as Antarctica); it was the break he needed. The expedition, funded lavishly by the British monarchy, seemed simple to begin with, but Cook took the opportunity to make a few side trips. Along the way, he explored Tahiti, discovered the Society Islands, revealed that New Zealand was an island, and mapped 1,000 miles of Australia's coast. Clearly, Cook was a man driven by many ambitions. After reaching Antarctica, he found that his timing was bad, for the ice floes blocked further progress. He returned to great praise, but in his own mind he seems to have felt his journey a failure.

As a remedy, he made a second voyage (1772–1775) to Antarctica. He sailed as far as the ice fields and then began to circumnavigate the entire of Antarctica! Surviving in such extreme conditions for over a year represents a great testament to his fortitude, not to mention his skills as a leader. To prevent a mutiny under such conditions required a creative blend of iron discipline and fierce loyalty. After circling the continent, he concluded that there were no habitable latitudes in Antarctica. He returned to a second round of great praise in England.

In 1776, Cook set out for the other Pole in search of an Arctic passage from the Pacific to the Atlantic above North America (a backward Northwest Passage). Curiously, he first sailed the South Pacific—discovering the Hawaiian Islands along the way—and then up the coast of North America and around Alaska. His maps of this coastline were some of the first and best. Above the Bering Strait, however, Cook found his passage thwarted, so he returned to warmer climes. Unfortunately, he was killed by natives in Hawaii.

Remarkably, in a little more than a decade of travels, Cook made a dozen major contributions to geographic exploration. His journals show him to be a man of deep conviction with a keen sense of justice. These texts are some of the finest and earliest examples of writing that neither romanticizes native peoples nor assumes that all things European are superior. Describing the Australian Aborigines, Cook writes:

> They may appear to some to be the most wretched people upon earth; but in reality they are far more happier than we Europeans, being wholly unacquainted not only with the superfluous but the necessary conveniences so much sought after in Europe; they are happy in not knowing the use of them. . . . They covet not magnificent houses, household stuff, etc. . . . In short, they seemed to set no value upon anything we gave them, nor would they ever part with anything of their own for any one article we could offer them. (Rugoff 426–427)

It is this enlightened and open-minded perspective that makes Cook's journals so enjoyable and so interesting. His writings demonstrate that while Cook was a consummate explorer—indeed, he went simply for the sake of going—he was also an explorer of the ideas of culture and civilization. Implicit behind the above passage is a comparison between himself (the European) and the native. The result of the comparison is that Cook seems to question his own cultural values: the native appears "wretched" but is in fact "happier than we Europeans." Cook is able to see that there is a variety of perspectives on such a broad notion as happiness, and he seems to

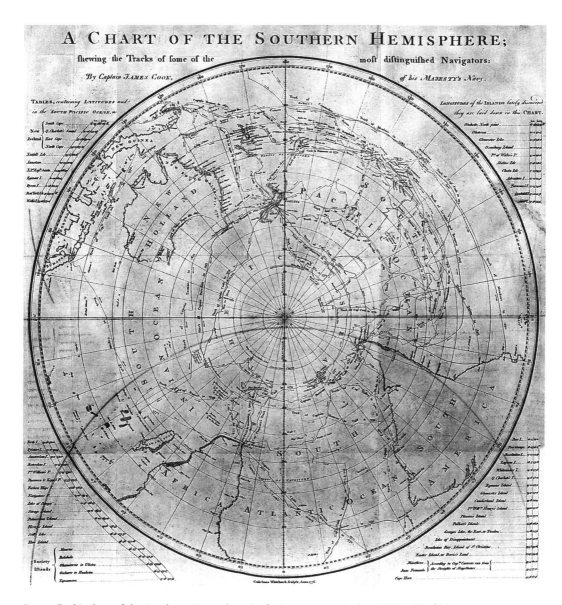

James Cook's chart of the Southern Hemisphere (with Antarctica missing), c. 1770s (Corbis)

realize that his perspective is not necessarily the best one.

References: Rugoff 1960

COOPER, JAMES FENIMORE

James Fenimore Cooper (American, 1789–1851) has left his mark on several learned fields. Author of more than 50 books, Cooper wrote fiction, political theory, a guide to manners and etiquette, social criticism, and travel literature. Although most famous for his so-named Leatherstocking series—five tales featuring the protagonist Natty Bumppo—Cooper's travel literature is extraordinary in its own right.

The son of a wealthy Federalist politician, Cooper was educated thoroughly and intensively as a child. At age 13 he was sent to Yale, only to be expelled after three years, much to the dismay of his father. In rebellion, Cooper took to the sea for a number of years. While at sea he came to love the excitement of the voyage and realized that adventures abroad can be a grand opportunity for learning. Although he clearly made notes while abroad, it was not until his return from sea that he began to compose these notes and stories as novels. By 1811, he had returned to New England, married, and established himself as a gentleman farmer. It was only at age 30 that he began to write seriously and for publication. Some accounts contend that his first book, *Precaution* (1820), was written on a challenge from his wife (Hart 182).

His early books—*The Spy* (1821), *The Pilot* (1823), and *The Pioneers* (1823)—met with enough critical success to encourage Cooper to continue writing. His later fiction is usually considered one of the foundations of American literature and includes the classic *The Last of the Mohicans* (1826).

Perhaps as a response to his father's vocal federalism, Cooper displayed a continual fascination with politics and social class. Among his works are book-length studies of democracy, class structure, and America. His eloquent comparisons between the United States and the great European nations relentlessly contrast the differences in cultures. As a result, Cooper was one of the earliest American writers to be taken seriously in Europe. To continue his research and writing, he lived and traveled in the Old World from 1826 to 1833. In these years he wrote, among other works, five superior books of travel literature.

In general, these tales tell of European culture from an American perspective and are thus great examples of the learning that takes place during travel. Cooper makes decidedly American observations: he is critical but respectful of European politics, class dynamics, and power. As he says, "I have no idea of boring mankind with statistics, and dry essays on Politics, but to give only, rapid sketches of

what I shall see, with *American* eyes" (Cooper 258). In addition, they are beautifully written.

Over his seven years in Europe, Cooper published accounts of England, France, Germany, Switzerland, and Italy. As with his sea tales, it took some years to craft his notes into publishable works: he returned to the States in 1833 but did not publish his accounts until several years later. The time was well spent, however, for it is obvious that he took considerable care with his writing and structure. The majority of all five volumes of *Gleanings in Europe* is made up of letters sent to a wide range of people both in the United States and in Europe. For this reason, there is no linear chronology or plot in these books, save Cooper's own edification and development. Yet his letters are elaborate enough to be engaging. Because each letter is more or less self-contained, Cooper can change tones, styles, and subjects very quickly and with little fanfare; this tends to quicken the pace of his work in that he need not make transitions.

His books were published both in the United States and in Europe simultaneously. There is some variation in the titles of the American versus the British first editions, but for our purposes, I have used the title of the American editions. *Sketches in Switzerland* (1836), *Sketches in Switzerland: Part the Second* (1836, which included Germany), and *Gleanings in Europe* (1837–1838, with one volume each on England, France, and Italy) remain some of the better accounts of European culture in the eighteenth century.

Although his reputation by this time was sufficiently established, his travel literature did not sell well at all. It may be that Cooper was too critical—of both America and Europe—to make these books commercial successes. It was also the case that Cooper was extremely antagonistic toward the press, and thus he had plenty of enemies among reporters and reviewers. Finally, the market was glutted with accounts of travel and exploration of Europe; readers were more inclined to buy the wild tales of African or Asian exploration with their nude natives, cannibals, and unthinkable beasts. Nonetheless, in retrospect, these five books are exemplary.

Throughout, Cooper concentrates on the higher reaches of polite society, but he does so with particularly American style. He states repeatedly—if proudly—that although he has all sorts of letters of introduction to the "right people," he absolutely refuses to use them. Therefore, instead of imposing himself as an obligation upon others, he seeks to win his friends by his wit and charm. This has the benefit of allowing him a traveler's freedom: he must make his own way and trust fate to show him the way. In addition, this process feeds his ego: he knows he is appreciated and welcomed into European society on his own merits rather than because of his fame.

To be sure, he found great hospitality. Doors opened to him as if by magic, and the best people embraced him warmly. These years seem filled with elegant dinners, cultural performances, and lively discourses. At every turn, he makes comparisons—usually triangular comparisons among America, England, and wherever he happens to be. For example, in Paris, a city he particularly adored, Cooper observes:

> It is, moreover, a great mistake to imagine that the French are not hospitable, and that they do not entertain as freely, and as often as any other people. The only difference between them and the English, in this respect, or between them and ourselves, is in the better taste and ease which regulate their intercourse of this nature. While there is a great deal of true elegance, there is no fuss, at a French entertainment. . . . Society is divided into *castes,* in Paris . . . and the degrees of elegance and refinement increase as one ascends, as a matter of course, but there is less of effort, in every class, than is usual with us. (Adams 457)

Among his encounters are numerous minor nobles, cultural figures, and politicians. These brushes with fame seem to thrill Cooper. He often seems innocently awed

when he meets them, and he takes great pains to quote them exactly. Several times he relates his conversations with Sir Walter Scott, including Scott's own reflections on Cooper's work: "I'll tell you what I most like . . . and it is the manner in which you maintain the ascendancy of your own country on all proper occasions, without descending to vulgar abuse of ours" (Cooper 150). Yet in spite of this compliment, Cooper is not afraid to be critical of Scott, to his readers at least, a few pages down. He complains first of Scott's handwriting, then of his manners: "I was much surprised . . . for it denoted a want of familiarity with the world, that one would not have expected in a man who had been so very much and so long courted by the great. But, after all, his life had been provincial" (Cooper 153). This honesty is often what makes Cooper so interesting to read: he rarely pulls his punches.

In his accounts of Italy, as is to be expected, Cooper rhapsodizes over the classical ruins, although with a lesser scholarly and historical knowledge than other famous travelers of the era. This may imply a bit of snobbery toward Italy in that its social sphere rates lower than its ruins. A similar thing happens in Switzerland: he adopts a romantic tone with regard to the natural splendor. It is an interesting struggle to watch. Cooper wrangles with the emotions—irrational and uncontrollable—evoked by this grandeur as conflicting with his sense of order and reason.

Particularly in his Swiss gleanings, as well as in his sea tales, Cooper is famous for his opposition of nature and culture. This theme runs throughout his work. Nature, wilderness, and the "uncivilized" are not relegated to the beastly in Cooper; rather, they are attractive and powerful, if dangerous. Speaking generally, we might summarize that Cooper sought to import lessons learned from wild nature into the civilized world in which he most often lived.

Upon returning to America, Cooper continued his prolific production and turned out a bewildering array of texts. A number of them are part travel literature and must be noted as such. *Homeward Bound* (1838) and *Home as Found* (1838) are both fictional accounts of social ideals set against a return from abroad. He expounds elaborately upon the influence home has on men of "good spirit": home is at the core of patriotism, which is for Cooper a noble virtue. Several years later he returned to the theme of travel in his factual account of Christopher Columbus's first expedition called *Mercedes of Castile* (1840). This seems to have led him to revisit the sailing themes so dear to him in his early works, for he subsequently wrote a history of the British navy (*The Two Admirals,* 1842), a historical novel about privateers (*Wing-and-Wing,* 1842), a story of a sailor (*Ned Meyers,* 1843), and two mostly autobiographical tales of his own days at sea (*Afloat and Ashore,* 1844, and *Miles Wallingford,* 1844).

In sum, Cooper's was an extraordinary career full of adventures in both nature and society. His books have been influential in many arenas, and his travel literature provides us with a detailed and rich history of the European upper classes, as well as a picture of Cooper's own struggle to carve out a distinctly American identity. For Cooper, travel seems to have been a way to learn about politics and society. In visiting Europe, he found that his own beloved America had something valuable to contribute.

References: Adams 1988; Cooper 1983; Hart 1965

CORYATE, THOMAS

A fascinating character, Thomas Coryate (English, 1577–1617) started his career as a court jester under James I. Although Oxford educated, he was a true comic fool: everything about him seems to have been steeped in mirth. The history is unclear, but for whatever reason, he set out on a monumental journey that eventually took him 2,000 miles on foot to nearly 50 cities! True to form, he titled his book about this experience—which was one of the first traveler's guides—*Coryats Crudities: Hastily Gobled Up in Five Moneths Travells in France, Savoy, Italy, Rhetia Commonly Called the Grisons Country, Helvetia Alias Switzerland, Some Parts of High Germany, and the Netherlands; Newly Digested in the Hungry Aire of Odcombe in the County of Somerset, and Now Dispersed to the Nourishment of the Travelling Members of This Kingdome* (1608)! Upon his return, his shoes were made a relic of sorts and hung in a local church; they remained there for 200 years.

Not content with one epic journey, Coryate set out on a second voyage—again on foot—in 1612 to Greece, Turkey, Asia Minor, North Africa, the Middle East, and India. His account of this travel is fragmentary; he never made it home, but some letters and notebooks did. These pieces were compiled into a book called *Thomas Coryate Traveller* (1616).

Coryats Crudities is a simple account of travel, part commentary, part useful guidebook. For both aspects, it is a remarkable document that sheds an odd light upon many different places, customs, and peoples. In addition, Coryate's work can be used as an insight into what was considered commonplace: he states that his purpose is to note the extraordinary, thus we can deduce that if he notes something, it was uncommon at the English court. Finally, as we might expect, Coryate's text is rich with humor of all sorts and is thus a marvelously amusing read.

At the end of *Coryats Crudities,* Coryate states gleefully: "Of all the pleasures in the world travell is (in my opinion) the sweetest and most delightful" (Adams 216). This joy overflows from his text. No effort is too great to bear for this pleasure; he often tells happily of cold nights spent sleeping in a ditch or his great rigors in learning a language. Even the most extreme situations seem not to astound this brash and hardy traveler. He nonchalantly notes all manner of strange cultural differences with little or no judgment.

A single example of many should suffice to illustrate Coryate's style. When passing a vineyard near the town of Wormes, Germany, he plucks a bunch of grapes. The farmer, furious, brandishing a weapon, "in a great fury pulled off very violently my hat from my head . . . looked very fiercely upon me with eyes sparkling fire in a manner, and with his Almanne wordes which I understood not, swaggered most insolently with me, holding up his halbert in that threatening manner at me, that I continually expected a blow, and was in deadly feare lest he would have made me a prey for the wormes before I should ever put my foote in the gallant City of Wormes" (Adams 223). Perpetually jovial, observant, and faithful to his duty of recording his journey, Coryate delights his readers with his tales. He is truly one of the fathers of travel literature.

References: Adams 1988; Newby 1985; Rugoff 1960

DALLAM, THOMAS

The story of Thomas Dallam (English, fl. 1600) is both charming and fascinating. As Queen Elizabeth's master organ maker, Dallam was sent to Turkey to present Sultan Mehmed III with a gift from Her Majesty. Constantinople was a bustling trade city, and Elizabethan merchants were hungry for new markets; but the sultan had a ferocious reputation. To flatter him, Elizabeth had Dallam build an exquisite instrument and then accompany it to Turkey. Aware that his moment of glory had begun, Dallam kept a delightful diary of his yearlong adventure and published *The Diary of Thomas Dallam* (1600) upon his return.

Very little is known of Dallam, but one thing is certain: he was an extraordinary craftsman. To be sure to impress the sultan, Elizabeth spared no expense on constructing the organ. From Dallam's own descriptions, we learn that the instrument could be played manually or allowed to play five-part songs by itself. In addition, the contraption had mechanical musicians that blew horns, carved birds that flapped and twittered, a glockenspiel, and any number of other moving ornamental components. Because of its complexity, Dallam was the only one who could be trusted to assemble the organ—and to repair any damage that occurred in shipping. The story, then, is of a craftsman turned diplomat.

The first portion of Dallam's account is rather dull in that he dwells with a novice's eye on the ship and the journey. Although not exciting, this section is a valuable description of life on an Elizabethan sailing vessel. When he arrives in Constantinople, however, the tale becomes much more interesting.

The organ proves to be a smashing success with the sultan, who finds it a most amazing device. Dallam's delight is compounded by the dreamlike grandeur of the sultan's palace. In the grand hall where the gift is presented, the sultan is "alone" with his staff of 200 dazzling pages and courtiers and another 200 bodyguards and eunuchs clad in lavish Oriental garb. The sultan commands that Dallam play for him; with great trepidation, for even the mildest breach of etiquette would cost him his life, Dallam performs, with roaring success.

Emboldened by his intimacy with the sultan and a purse full of gold, Dallam risks a peek at the harem, another capital offense. His description is one of the few from the era, and he was able to recall as well as describe the girls' attire with great detail. But his guide tolerated only a brief glimpse before putting an end to Dallam's excessive gawking. The guide, "made a wry mouth and stamped with his foot to make me give over looking, which I was very loath to do, for that sight did please me wondrous well" (Rugoff 173).

One of the most interesting aspects of Dallam's book is his innocent perspective. Travel scholar Milton Rugoff writes of Dallam, "although [his journey] was relatively uneventful, seeing it through his naïve eyes makes it seem like a visit to Wonderland. Its culmination . . . [is] one of the most quaint and beguiling descriptions in Elizabethan writing" (169). Indeed, as a traveler's account of a radically different world, Dallam's book is a delight. For its details, for its boyish tone, and for its straightforward presentation, this story remains a great work of travel literature.

References: Brent 1893; Newby 1985; Rugoff 1960

DALLAS, SIR GEORGE

Sir George Dallas (English, 1758–1833) may not be a household name, nor indeed is there much written about him, but he did write a singularly fine book of travel verse called *The India Guide; or, Journal of a Voyage to the East Indies in the Year MDCCLXXX* (1785). In this book Dallas dwells upon the passage itself; that is, he harps upon the journey rather than the destination. Such a focus is significant in that it calls attention to the nature of travel: motion, adversity, and unpleasantness all receive detailed descriptions, and they are to be respected for their power to teach.

Dallas set out for India as a colonist in 1780, as the title indicates, but it took five years for him to publish the account. Instead of a simple travelogue, Dallas's account became an elaborately wrought literary work. He establishes a literary device to mediate his own complaints: his book is purportedly the record of a probably fictitious Miss Emily Brittle. Ostensibly, *The India Guide* represents her letters to her mother. Using a woman as a mouthpiece, Dallas is able to fully voice dismay and displeasure with the journey and eventually to make fun of frail travelers. The text also raises some interesting gender issues: as a male, his complaints would have made him seem weak, whereas hidden in a female voice, he can bemoan the difficulties of travel with impunity.

The narrator very quickly wishes not to have embarked upon the journey: " . . . 'tis too late to repent I left home, / 'Tis not so to grieve that I ventured to roam" (Crossley-Holland 6). The tumultuous seas, the rough accommodations, the terror of the unknown are "her" chief complaints. What some travelers revel in, this narrator loathes.

Yet Dallas's voice shines through eventually, making Miss Brittle—her name a description of her character—something of a joke. She complains of the pitching of the ship and some unfortunate, if comic, consequences:

Not many weeks since, I had only to scoop
From my lap the contents of a tureen of
    soup;
And when with my clean clothes I again had
    sat down,
A vile leg of mutton fell right on my gown.
Sometimes I was soiled from my head to my
    toe
With nasty pork chops, or greasy pilau.
(Crossley-Holland 8)

Her troubles become almost unbearable as the six-week voyage progresses. Misadventures abound, from the escape of the ship's livestock to the perpetual profanity she has to endure. In her outrage we cannot help finding a bit of humor.

Perhaps Dallas employed this device as a way to make light of travel while at the same time expressing a deep respect for the power of travel to teach toughness. Over the course of the many poetic letters of the book, Miss Brittle does learn quite a bit and does become considerably more durable. At its core, then, Dallas's book is about the power of travel to effect personal growth and about the engrossing nature of the voyage itself. In the end, it is not arriving that is important, but the process of getting there.

References: Crossley-Holland 1986

DAMPIER, WILLIAM

One of the great eighteenth-century influences on later travel literature surely must be William Dampier (English, 1652–1715). His writing has been called influential to everyone from Samuel Taylor Coleridge to Daniel Defoe. His several travel books were widely praised for their form, style, and content.

A traveler from his early years, Dampier started as a solider in the Caribbean, which led to a career as a privateer. In search of treasure to pillage and unvisited lands to discover, his journey took him all through Central and South America, and eventually he circumnavigated the globe. His account, *A New Voyage round the World* (1697), made him famous and influential. This fame earned him official recognition and royal sponsorship that, in turn, led to a major expedition to the Pacific and another book: *Voyage to New Holland* (1703). All told, he has three circumnavigations to his credit, and he was the first Englishman to see quite a number of places.

In addition to his status as an author, he was a talented artist and a collector of artifacts as well as biological samples and specimens. His drawings of harbors were said to be very valuable to cartographers seeking to map potential colonial outposts. His accomplishments were many: he was the pilot with Woodes Rogers when they captured a Spanish galleon laden with treasure, he helped rescue Alexander Selkirk (the model for the character Robinson Crusoe), he was one of the first Englishmen to see Australia, he was presented to Queen Anne's court, he was friends with the famous diarist Samuel Pepys, and he was an eminent member of the Royal Society. His books have seen continual popularity and have inspired dreams and adventures for more than two centuries.

A brave and fiercely disciplined man, Dampier ran a tight ship and never passed up a chance for glory. True to his buccaneering beginnings, he also saw his share of violent scraps with a variety of indigenous peoples and with his Spanish foes. In the name of England and commerce, Dampier was considered one of the most aggressive explorer-colonists of the early eighteenth century.

His narratives are fact filled and nonchalant; he describes life-threatening encounters in the same tone as he relates the weather. But due to the sheer volume of adversity he encountered and bested, his tales are exciting. While contemporary readers may view Dampier as cruel to the natives that he meets, he justified his behavior in the name of Christianizing and civilizing the heathen world. What to our sensibilities is a rough imposition of ideas was to him a noble and laudable task. In his own era his exploits were considered wildly heroic.

One of the interesting aspects of Dampier's writing is how carefully he notes the pains he took to preserve his journals and notebooks. For example, while trudging through the jungles of South America, with a restless following of semihostile natives whom he constantly bribed, he notes: "Foreseeing a Necessity of wading through Rivers frequently in our Landmarch, I took care before I left the ship to provide my self a large Joint of Bambo, which I stopt at both Ends, closing it with Wax, so as to keep out any Water. In this I preserved my Journal and other Writings from being wet, tho' I was often forced to swim" (Adams 245–246). For many days he toted this contraption, often more worried about his writing than his crew. Such devotion to the record of the journey is a fine example of Dampier's attitude: the trip and the story of the trip are inseparable. The work of the journey is as much the writing about it as the actual effort of exploration.

Another value in Dampier's works is that he illustrates the fierce competition among the colonial powers—England, Spain, Portugal, and the Netherlands—to "claim" rights to their discoveries. He was keenly aware of the progress being made by his rivals. In one instance, he and his men steal a package of mail to see what the Spanish are up to and what they know of his own progress. It is with no small amount of pride that he relates the contents of one such letter: "That there would be English Privateers that Year in the West-Indies, who would make such great Discoveries, as to open a Door into the South-Seas; which they supposed was the fastest shut: And the Letters were accordingly full of Cautions to their Friends to be very watchful and careful of their Coasts" (Adams 250). These intrigues add considerably to Dampier's tales; not only is he an explorer, but a sort of spy as well.

In his writings about the Pacific, Dampier balances geological/geographical observations with descriptions of indigenous cultures with notes as to the potential for commerce and colonization. It is remarkable how similar are his experiences in both the Pacific and the West Indies; he employs precisely the same tactics of bribery and goodwill backed up with the brutal force of his musket in both cases. And again in the East Indies, he seems almost obsessed with discovering lucrative goods to bring back to Europe with him.

In the final analysis, Dampier's books are fascinating documents that describe his incredible explorations. But perhaps most interesting is to read them as an insight into this eminent, if cryptic, character. Rarely does he give us any clue as to what drives him to press ever onward; rarely does he stray from a kind of obsessive professionalism. We know little or nothing about his own emotions, desires, or personal attributes. In some respects, he effaces himself to such a degree that Dampier the man dissolves in front of his avowedly "objective" descriptions of his adventures. Perhaps this is what makes the stories such great travel literature: the written tales stand in for and replace the actual man and his journeys.

See also: Buccaneer
References: Adams 1988

DANA, RICHARD HENRY

Richard Henry Dana's (American, 1815–1882) story is an interesting one. Although he was a member of a literary family, Dana's most important inspiration came not from the world of high culture, but from his own great adventures at sea. The result is the beloved *Two Years before the Mast* (1840), a classic of travel literature.

The product of a cultured and well-off Massachusetts family, Dana led an uneventful life until his third year at Harvard, when problems with his vision forced him to withdraw from the university (1834). To facilitate a recovery, he set out on a challenging sea voyage—some medicine! Despite his wealthy and distinguished upbringing, Dana impetuously chose a working passage on the merchant brig. One ship led to another, and for two years, Dana traveled. After this one extended episode, Dana curtailed his wandering. His vision improved during the journey, and he went on to become a lawyer with considerable sympathy for sailors. He later became an expert on naval law and the technical aspects of naval protocol. His literary fire was never rekindled.

While he made several other major journeys in his later life—to Europe, to the Caribbean, and around the United States—he published but one other travel book, *To Cuba and Back* (1859). Unfortunately, it lacks the vivid and endearing qualities of his first book.

Perhaps because the high literary set of his day included his father, Dana anonymously published his sensational and dramatic account of his initial journey, *Two Years before the Mast*. The tale recounts the adventures arising on a voyage from Boston to San Francisco via Cape Horn. Dana wrote his account in elaborate journal entries that contain complex psychological portraits of his fellow sailors, details about his labor as a deckhand, and an ongoing narrative of his own maturation.

Dana's story includes lengthy and lyrical passages about the beauty of the sea set beside quick-paced jaunts to the port grog hall. Repeatedly, Dana describes in painful detail the mistreatment of sailors: whippings, vindictive orders, psychotic captains, and grueling labor. There is little doubt that Dana loved the physical mechanisms of the ship—he lovingly includes them on nearly every page. Although Dana originally intended his book as an exposé on the terrible conditions for sailors at sea (Adams 526), his cheerful, upbeat writing style and enthusiastic tales make this an enjoyable book rather than a somber undercover report.

Whenever on land, Dana is quick to note characteristics of local people and places. His details are rich and deep but not overwhelmingly thick; he seems to have an instinctive sense of how much is enough. Because his shipmates remain the same for long periods, Dana is able to develop his characters as he comes to know his fellow travelers. Such character development makes his travelogue feel like a novel, full of drama and suspense.

Throughout it all, however, Dana repeatedly plays the role of outsider. His class status and his education lend him a removed perspective. While he participates in the "sailor's lifestyle," he can never be a true insider. After observing two of his mates endure a savage whipping by the captain, Dana fumes, "A few rapid thoughts, I don't know what—our situation [as sailors], a resolution to see the captain punished when we got home—crossed my mind; but the falling of the blows and the cries of the men called me back once more" (Adams 530–531). He imagines using his social status and knowledge of the law to bring charges against the cruel, megalomaniacal captain. His distanced vantage point means that he is both traveling as a sailor and traveling between social classes by slumming with the common seamen. These combined travels work profound changes on Dana's character; indeed, he learns much about himself and his former lifestyle from his journeys.

Whether he is comparing shipboard food to the luxurious meals he remembers from home or contrasting the characteristics of light and rain in South America to those in Boston, Dana clearly demonstrates that observing difference necessitates looking carefully at the familiar. The bonds among men at sea—laboring, living, and in some cases dying together—teaches him of honor and loyalty; the tyranny of various captains teaches him of justice and right. Many complex lessons spill off the pages of Dana's book, perhaps none so important as his recognition that the acts of writing and traveling are the stuff of life.

See also: Picaro
References: Adams 1988; Benét 1965; Hart 1965

DARWIN, CHARLES

Although famous for his theory of evolution via natural selection, Charles Darwin (English, 1809–1882) may be considered a superior travel writer as well. His *Voyage of the Beagle* (1839, revised 1845 and 1860) interests both as scientific treatise and as travel literature. Perhaps because Darwin's naturalistic work, particularly his theory of evolution, has been so overwhelmingly influential to modern science, we often pass over his tales of adventure and exploration. It is a shame to do so: they are particularly fine.

Educated roundly—in medicine, theology, and natural science—at Edinburgh and Cambridge, he set off in 1831 on a five-year journey to South America and Australia to study zoology. His first book, *Voyage of the Beagle*, tells the story of his first major exploration and the astounding things he saw. Upon his return, he was made an officer of the Geological Society, which put Darwin in contact with many noted scientists of the day. He steadily developed his ideas, in spite of considerable resistance from the scientific community. Finally he published *Origin of Species* (1859); it made an immediate splash and generated a tempest of controversy that in some communities is still raging today. Five more scientific works followed, each one addressing criticism of his original themes and providing additional examples as evidence.

Yet it is his first book, *Voyage of the* Beagle, that is the finest example of travel literature. Impressionable and indefatigable as a young man, Darwin reveled in the excitement of seeing so many exotic and different places. It was in fact precisely these differences that led him to his theory of evolution: in seeing other communities—in this case not human, but zoological—he was able to learn new lessons about that which was familiar to him.

As the ship's naturalist, he was to concentrate on botany and zoology, but analysis of native peoples unofficially fell under Darwin's

Illustration of H.M.S. Beagle *carrying Charles Darwin's expedition in the Straits of Magellan (Bettmann/Corbis)*

jurisdiction as well. He spent considerable time documenting behavior of various indigenous tribes. From noting rituals to physiology to apparel, Darwin's powers of observation astound. Modern readers may find his accounts rather bristling with Anglocentrism, but if we can filter out his own bias, we are treated to an incredibly astute and interesting set of descriptions.

Beyond a keen look at South America and Australia, Darwin offers us a wonderfully thoughtful and literary account. While the work is written in daily entries, he often digresses into vivid and humanistic descriptions. For example, on February 20, 1835, he writes of a major earthquake he experienced in Chile:

This day has been memorable in the annals of Valdivia, for the most severe earthquake experience by the oldest inhabitant. . . . There was no difficulty in standing upright, but the motion made me almost giddy: it was something like the movement of a vessel in a little cross-ripple, or still more like that felt by a person skating over thin ice, which bends under the weight of his body.

A bad earthquake at once destroys our oldest associations: the earth, the very emblem of solidity, has moved beneath our feet like a thin crust over a fluid;—one second of time has created in the mind a strange idea of insecurity, which hours of reflection would not have produced. (Darwin 212)

His encounters and interactions with locals express Darwin's obvious desire to compare perspectives on the world. He quizzes some natives of Maldonado (in present-day Uruguay) to find that "the greater number of the inhabitants had an indistinct idea that England, London, and North America, were different names for the same place; but the better informed well knew that London and North America were separate countries close together, and that England was a large town in London!" (Fussell 349).

Not only is this an interesting reflection of what was known by the natives, but we can also see Darwin's own character through the questions he asks. Indeed, it strikes him as shocking that the whole world does not know precisely the relationship between England and London..

His conclusion to *Voyage of the* Beagle is a classic passage of travel literature. Darwin spends a dozen pages discussing the costs and benefits of travel in minute detail. What is beautiful, what is terrible; privations and boons; joys and sorrows; gains and consequences are all discussed in this marvelous essay. He concludes:

> It has been said that the love of the chase is an inherent delight in man—a relic of an instinctive passion. If so, I am sure the pleasure of living in the open air, with the sky for a roof and the ground for a table, is part of the same feeling; it is the savage returning to his wild and native habits. I always look back to our boat cruises, and my land journeys, when through unfrequented countries, with an extreme delight, which no scenes of civilization could have created. I do not doubt that every traveller must remember the glowing sense of happiness that he experienced when he first breathed in a foreign clime, where the civilized man had seldom or never trod. (Fussell 361)

Travel, Darwin goes on to say, teaches a man of the world and of himself. Through seeing distant lands and foreign peoples, the traveler learns, best of all, "how many truly kind-hearted people there are, with whom he never before had, or ever again will have any further communication, who yet are ready to offer him the most disinterested assistance" (Fussell 362).

Cheerful, good-natured, curious to the extreme, Darwin exhibits some of the finest traits of a good traveler. His commitment to his diary testifies to his insistence that travel and writing are fused together. Lastly, it is fascinating to watch the generation of a great idea; from his early journals to the much later *Fall of Man,* Darwin's notions grow and shift with awe-inspiring subtlety and precision. It is through experience of the foreign—through seeing difference—that he was able to produce his monumental hypothesis.

References: Adams 1988; Darwin 1906; Fussell 1987; Newby 1985

DAVIDSON, ROBYN

One of the quirkiest of the contemporary travel writers, Robyn Davidson (Australian, 1950–) has made a career out of her toughness. Sometimes called "the camel woman," she has a poetic appreciation for the subtleties of the desert and the lessons that desolation can teach. Her two books of travel literature, *Tracks* (1980) and *Desert Places* (1996), tell of her epic adventures in two different deserts.

Tracks recounts her 1,700-mile solo trek across the western half of Australia. With her dog and four camels, she walked from one isolated settlement to another through some of the harshest and most barren landscape in the world. Marshaling four stubborn pack animals, enduring scorching heat, defending herself against animal and male predators, and providing her readers with a lively narrative—it's all in a day's work for Davidson.

With a dauntless spirit and an endless sense of humor, Davidson cooked up the idea of this trip as a way to test her self-reliance. Indeed, the journey itself is the heart of the project; reaching her destination simply meant that the trip was done. Along the way, she found that the challenges, the silence, and the beauty of the wilderness affect her deeply. Davidson's journey is as much about self-discovery and self-understanding as it is about finding something heretofore undiscovered in the Australian desert.

Similarly, *Desert Places* tells of a journey through a barren land, although this time Davidson's desert is in northwest India. Seeking to utilize her skills and travel wisdom, in 1992 Davidson joined a nomadic people called the Rabari. She spent a full year living with this tribe, wandering, trading, and tending livestock as one of them. Highly sensitive to the tenuous existence of these people, Davidson came to love, trust, and be accepted by her hosts. Through all imaginable difficulties—from illness to language barriers, from natural disasters to malnutrition—Davidson did more than endure: she thrived. *Desert Places* is thus at once a story of determined, extreme cultural immersion and a tale that tells the world of a way of life that teeters on the brink of extinction. As with her first book, the result of the journey is a newfound appreciation for life and for her own abilities.

Writes Davidson at the end of *Tracks,*

> As I look back on the trip now, as I try to sort out fact from fiction, try to remember how I felt at that particular time, or during that particular incident, try to relive those memories that have been buried so deep, and distorted so ruthlessly, there is one clear fact that emerges from the quagmire. The trip was easy. It was no more dangerous than crossing the street, or driving to the beach, or eating peanuts. The two important things that I did learn were that you are as powerful and as strong as you allow yourself to be, and that the most difficult part of any endeavour is taking the first step. . . . Camel trips, as I suspected all along, and as I was about to have confirmed, do not begin or end, they merely change form. (Davidson 254)

The fact and the fiction of travel have merged for Davidson, and her written words are entirely tangled with her memories. Her journeys and her life blend together to become one; said otherwise, daily life functions as a sort of journey. And every journey teaches us something. These are the traditional themes of travel literature that appear in both of Davidson's fine works.

References: Davidson 1995

DAY-LEWIS, CECIL

Irish-born Englishman Cecil Day-Lewis (1904–1972) is a notable poet and author in several genres. He wrote mysteries under the pseudonym Nicholas Blake and was a Marxist poet in the 1930s with such notables as W. H. Auden and Stephen Spender. Not usually noted as a travel writer—although he did write a verse translation of Virgil's archetypal travel tale *The Aeneid* in 1952—Day-Lewis does have one very fine book of travel poems. After a journey to Italy in 1952 with the British novelist Rosamond Lehmann, Day-Lewis published an entire book of travel verse titled *An Italian Visit* (1953).

An example from this work, the poem "The Tourists," will suffice to display the caliber of Day-Lewis's travel writing. In this poem we can see the complexity of his notions of travel and tourism. Along the way, we can also get a feel for Day-Lewis's evocative metrics and staccato phrasing.

> Arriving was their passion.
> Into the new place out of the blue
> Flying, sailing, driving—
> How well these veteran tourists knew
> Each fashion of arriving.
>
> Leaving a place behind them,
> There was no sense of loss: they fed
> Upon the act of leaving—
> So hot their hearts for the land ahead—
> As a kind of pre-conceiving.
>
> Arrival has stern laws, though,
> Condemning men to lose their eyes
> If they have treated travel
> As a brief necessary disease,
> A pause before arrival.
>
> And merciless the fate is
> Of him who leaves nothing behind,
> No hostage, no reversion:
> He travels on, not only blind
> But a stateless person.
>
> Fleeing from love and hate,
> Pursuing change, consumed by motion,
> Such arrivistes, unseeing,

Forfeit through endless self-evasion
The estate of simple being.
(Crossley-Holland 25)

These five rather complex stanzas suggest some of the dominant aspects of travel and travel writing. As though mimicking the ceaseless coming and going of the poem's subjects, stanza one treats arriving, two departing, three arriving, four leaving, and five fleeing, as though the whole process is subsumed under this final, larger heading.

Day-Lewis is addressing the notion of travel simply for travel's sake. How many travelers go simply to be able to say, "I've been there"? Quite a few, it seems to me. They arrive, again and again, though in different places, equating all arrivals as the same, regardless of the specifics of the destination.

When they leave, "There was no sense of loss: they fed / Upon the act of leaving—" to concentrate not on what they had seen or done, but on what new arrival is forthcoming. Such travel mania firmly establishes travel as the end rather than the means to some form of learning. In an era that glamorized travel (the 1950s), Day-Lewis asks us to dive beneath the glittering surface and to have human and emotional interactions with a place.

Day-Lewis concludes that "merciless the fate is / Of him who leaves nothing behind." We can read these lines in two equally plausible ways. How empty is a departure where one has not given of oneself to the visited spot, and how shallow not to leave behind a written account—be it poem, letter, or journal—to solidify the experience into text. Without souvenirs, without taking something away from the trip—best perhaps a lesson—the traveler is doomed to blindness and to statelessness, which we might stretch to suggest lacking in identity. We know who we are from our memories, yet who of us have not found memory infinitely fallible?

In the final stanza Day-Lewis really turns up the heat: by frantically fleeing, those "consumed by motion" deny themselves in a process of "self-evasion" so that they become like T. S. Eliot's famous "Hollow Men." Furthermore, they forfeit "The estate of simple being," which we might read to mean they doom themselves to live not in the present moment—glorious or tragic, but always real—but in the perpetually deferred and just-around-the-corner illusion of tomorrow.

Perhaps we can summarize this poem by saying that it asks us to imagine engaging the moment and place—the time and the space—we inhabit presently. Often travel is a way to force that awareness; but for some, the lesson is wholly missed.

References: Crossley-Holland 1986

DEFOE, DANIEL

The accomplishments and contributions to history of Daniel Defoe (English, 1660?–1731) are many. Political activist, merchant, traveler, and writer, Defoe appears to have been astoundingly diverse. His early writings are mostly journalistic; they range from a political satire to discussions of trade and exploration. Among his vast oeuvre, or body of work—more than 500 books!—are many famous titles, a number of which are outstanding examples of travel literature. His travel novels include *Robinson Crusoe* (1719), *A New Voyage round the World* (1725), and *The Four Years' Voyage of Captain George Roberts* (1726). His most significant nonfiction travel title is *Tour thro' the Whole Island of Great Britain* (1724–1726).

Throughout his life, Defoe felt drawn to foreign lands. His early voyages included substantial visits to France, Spain, the Low Countries, Italy, and Germany. For a time he found himself entangled in English politics, but after some years he set out to travel in even wider circles. His journeys, whether around the British Isles or far abroad, continued up to the point of his death.

Generally credited with being one of the first true English novels, *Robinson Crusoe* is a mainstay of English literature and literary

Title page for Robinson Crusoe *by Daniel Defoe;*
English eighteenth-century woodcut (Bettmann/Corbis)

tion. Crusoe's successes are many: he domesticates goats, he continuously improves his living space, he builds a serviceable boat, he shuns the cannibalistic natives, he rescues his eventual companion Friday, and he generally finds peace. This micro-utopia, of course, stands in for a stripped-down but idealized version of the Europe he remembers. At every step, the reader, and occasionally Crusoe himself, can see a reflection—or a projection—of the familiar on the foreign island.

In addition, Crusoe undergoes profound psychological and philosophical changes in response to his solitude. He reflects upon the ways of Europe and realizes the foolishness and myopia of that society. Crusoe has learned volumes about himself and his familiar culture by having to recreate it from the ground up. An opportunity to test his newfound lessons arises when an English ship appears. With the crew in a state of mutiny, Crusoe must play the hero and make peace on the ship. He quells their fierce passions and is taken back to England.

With its wealth of details and inherent credibility, *Robinson Crusoe* is both entertaining and provocative. Contrasts always feature prominently in travel literature, and in Defoe's novel it is the contrast between England and an isolated island that drives the text. Observing difference, and consequently reflecting upon the standards of the familiar, seems formulaic to modern readers, but in Defoe's era this process was rarely represented in literature. As such, *Robinson Crusoe* stands as one of the original travel novels.

Defoe's earlier novels, *The Four Years' Voyage of Captain George Roberts* and *A New Voyage round the World,* both presented themselves as travelogues. Using existing histories and his copious imagination, Defoe was able to write these (mostly) fictional tales that were calculated to captivate readers; many presumed that they were true stories. As novels, they feel like romances, and as travel literature, they espouse the lessons and benefits of experiencing difference. These adventures bring out the best and the worst in men. It is

history. It has significant elements of travel literature and must be noted as one of the earliest English examples of fictional adventure prose. Defoe based his vivid tale on the marooning of Alexander Selkirk in the South Seas (probably as told by William Dampier and/or Woodes Rogers). Rather than retelling a somewhat familiar tale, Defoe made it into a dramatic romance novel of adventure and personal growth by significantly embellishing and altering the story. Nonetheless, he presented the novel as a true account, and it therefore became all the more thrilling to its readership.

The plot of *Robinson Crusoe* is fairly simple. Shipwrecked, Crusoe has to construct a tolerable life in solitude and utter self-reliance. With precise detail, Defoe describes how his hero fashions the physical space of the island into something resembling civiliza-

as if travel provides access to a person's core identity.

As a novelist, Defoe met with considerable success, but his nonfiction travel writing remarkably met with an even greater popularity. Of course, in the present era we have mostly forgotten Defoe's travelogues in favor of his novels. Nonetheless, the charm of his firsthand travel accounts is unmistakable.

Tour thro' the Whole Island of Great Britain (in three volumes) met with rave reviews and went through numerous editions and printings. Some used it as a travel guide, others as a way to remember places they had seen, and still others were simply captivated by its vivid descriptions and thorough coverage. It is usually considered one of the first best-seller travel guides.

Defoe's *Tour* is remarkable in that it deftly blends history with firsthand experience. Drawing upon a wealth of materials, including earlier travel guides, pure history, local fables, and his own observations, Defoe writes a travelogue that feels more like a novel than anything else. Balancing the rural and the urban, *Tour* wanders from major hubs out to small villages. Cutting across class lines, Defoe interviews and describes both dignitaries and farmers, and a range of folks in between.

Masterfully, Defoe draws his reader into the tale. Unlike many travelogues, Defoe's *Tour* does not rely upon an overwhelming first-person vantage point. Indeed, it is written in the first person, perhaps from Defoe's perspective, but it is modestly so. The effect is reassuring: we feel that we are reading something very objective and precisely real. The narrator almost seems to efface himself to leave the glorious subject—Great Britain—as the primary focal point. And unlike so many travelers, Defoe's narrator is easygoing and willing to find himself in a vast array of different—and difficult—situations and places. To be sure, he is willing to criticize general aspects of the culture and its actions, but only in an abstract and removed manner.

This is not to suggest that Defoe is solely theoretical. Much of this narrative revolves around the mundane and quotidian. Food is duly noted with detail; the differences between one town's dishes and another's are carefully elaborated. Commercial ventures also receive considerable mention in this text, as though Defoe were fascinated with the fact that London received so much from so many different places. It is a testament to Defoe's shrewd eye that this mercantile magic intrigued him, for at the time Britain was only beginning to shift from an agrarian society to an industrial society. He found the transition fascinating and worthy of sustained commentary.

Throughout all three volumes, Defoe engages in a series of comparisons. At every juncture, he notes difference: this town drives its geese to market differently than that town; these farmers behave differently than Londoners; this village's architecture is different from that town's. In this manner, Defoe's *Tour* is true travel literature. He is comparing what is most familiar to him—the big city, politics, refinement—with what he sees on his tour. The comparison teaches him not only about the other regions of Britain, but of himself; he learns of his own presumptions, his own nationalism, and his own expectations.

Down to the very language he uses, Defoe is traveling in the foreignness of his homeland. He comments: "It cannot pass my observation here, that when we are come this length from London, the dialect of the English tongue, or the country way of expressing themselves is not easily understood, it is so strangely altered" (Adams 331). It is fascinating to him to note difference so close to home, as though the familiar were somehow made foreign.

After the successful *Tour,* Defoe composed several other travel-related titles. He wrote a *History of Discovery,* which compiled summaries of exploration and adventure. He then continued writing novels, many of which, like *Robinson Crusoe,* describe travel and a wandering spirit. *Memoirs of a Cavalier* is a story about a young picaro and his journeys. *Of Captain Mission* tells the adventures of a mild-mannered pirate (privateer). In almost all of his works we can find elements of travel literature and a permeability between fact and fiction.

Perhaps it is the composite nature of Defoe's writing—part fact, part fiction—that makes him one of the greats of both literature and travel literature. He is believable and vivid in every case; as readers, we are invited to believe what is make-believe and to fictionalize true history. Without a doubt, all subsequent travel literature owes a debt to Defoe for making the genre a form of popular—and commercial—entertainment.

See also: Buccaneer; Dampier, William; Picaresque; Picaro
References: Adams 1988; Harvey 1967

DESTOUCHES, LOUIS-FERDINAND

See Céline, Louis-Ferdinand

DICKENS, CHARLES

Often regarded as the greatest novelist of the nineteenth century, Charles Dickens (English, 1812–1870) remains a popular literary lion. His vast body of work still interests everyone from scholars to beach-holiday readers to film directors. Perhaps because his novels are so well loved—and so lengthy—his two works of travel literature are most sorely neglected. Yet they are beautiful and amusing, if less dramatic than his novels. *American Notes* (1842) and *Pictures from Italy* (1846) detail his extended journeys. Part diary, part newspaper-style reportage, part novelistic sketches, these two books are amusing as well as informative.

Dickens raised himself above his family's poverty by hard work. His legendary energy and desire to succeed propelled him from his earliest days as child worker in a warehouse to a junior clerk at a law firm. This eventually led him to journalism, which in turn encouraged him to write fiction. Most of his novels were published serially in a variety of newspapers or literary magazines.

As a famous and successful author, Dickens traveled to America in 1842 and published his account as *American Notes* very soon after returning to England. The text addresses numerous issues: slavery, manners, politics, copyright law, and morals all receive attention. Many of Dickens's opinions were controversial, either in the United States or in England. It seems that almost everyone took issue with some aspect of the text, but this is exactly its strength: Dickens was one of the first major figures to write of America and England as brothers who agree to be different. Instead of reflexively lamenting the United States as a son gone awry, Dickens alternates between critiquing and praising the former British colony.

True to his novelistic style, Dickens relates his experiences in vivid terms, often with considerable humor. For example, when describing the sights in Washington, D.C., Dickens notes the figure of Justice in the Capitol building. He reads in his guidebook that prudish American taste would not allow for a nude Justice, as she appears in most traditional representations. Dickens describes the clothed figure: "Poor Justice! She has been made to wear much stranger garments in America than those she pines in, in the Capitol. Let us hope that she has changed her dress-maker since they were fashioned, and that the public sentiment of the country did not cut out the clothes she hides her lovely figure in" (Fussell 314–315). Such playful chiding is an effective way of contrasting the taste of England to that of America. Fundamentally, *American Notes* is an elaborate comparison wherein Dickens observes the European roots, and the strange new flowers, of the United States.

Four years later, Dickens journeyed to Italy and wrote a different sort of travel book. *Pictures from Italy* is true to its name: the text unfolds as a series of tourist vignettes and

Photograph of Charles Dickens at his writing desk by J. S. Gurney, 1867 (Library of Congress)

wonderfully descriptive accounts of everything Dickens saw. Much less political and more historical than his earlier travelogue *American Notes,* Dickens's tales of Italy feel more like fiction than cultural commentary. He gushes with enthusiasm and excitement for even such simple pleasures as a meal at a stagecoach stop. Throughout the book, Dickens promotes and enjoys the grand history and contemporaneous charm of Italy.

Both texts share the masterful, descriptive craftsmanship for which Dickens is justly famous. In addition, both books have historical value in that they portray their subject nations with painstaking detail. In the end, these works seek to teach of foreign places and of the need to experience a variety of cultures.

References: Fussell 1987

DOUGHTY, CHARLES MONTAGU

Charles Montagu Doughty (English, 1843–1926) was a late-Victorian travel writer with an obsession for language. His most famous book is a noted and massive work of travel literature called *Arabia Deserta* (1888). In addition, he wrote a fairly popular book of verse: *The Dawn of Britain* (1906). He set out to live a great travel adventure and to write a great work of literature that described it: on both accounts, he succeeded brilliantly.

Arabia Deserta tells of Doughty's two years of wandering around Arabia. He set out in the autumn of 1876 with the intent of joining a caravan from Damascus to Mecca. Eventually, Doughty left the caravan in favor of roaming, boldly, on his own. He nonetheless did make it to Mecca. Mostly on foot and dressed as a pilgrim, Doughty chose to call himself a Christian, which subjected him to various abuses at the hands of several tribes. European colonialism of the Middle East was going full steam at the time, thus there was considerable animosity toward Europeans. But Doughty, through his painstaking acquisition of various

languages and his understanding of cultural manners, found his way safely among otherwise hostile peoples.

One of his most vivid accounts is of life among the nomadic Bedouins. Written in a series of vignettes, the account bounces between topics. Constantly in danger—from rival tribes, from harsh elements, from treachery—Doughty displays admirable courage and fortitude. In one of my favorite passages he describes the scene around him:

> The sun, entering as a tyrant upon the waste landscape, darts upon us a torment of firey beams. . . . Grave is that giddy heat upon the crown of the head; the ears tingle with a flickering shrillness, a subtle crepitation it seems, in the glassiness of this sun-stricken nature: the hot sand blinks in the eyes, there is little refreshment to find in the tent's shelter. . . . Mountains looming like dry bones through the thin air, stand far around about us. . . . Herds of weak nomad camels waver dispersedly, seeking pasture in the midst of this hollow fainting country, where but lately the swarming locusts have fretted every green thing. (Newby 265)

What a lovely place for a holiday! It is this intimate honesty that characterizes Doughty: he refuses to romanticize or idealize what he sees.

Doughty's style reflects his interests. His English is peppered with Arabic expressions, words, and literal translations (that he often goes on to explain). Modern readers may find his classically educated, even archaic, prose a bit dense. Yet it is this anachronistic and elaborately wrought phrasing that is often splendidly telling. His care and subtlety of language masterfully sculpt his details into one of the most vivid and memorable works of travel literature written in the nineteenth century.

When asked why he made his arduous journey, he allegedly replied that he traveled in order to "redeem the English language from the slough into which it had fallen since the time of Spencer" (Fussell 16). In so saying, he identified travel as his muse; to travel is to be inspired to write. Indeed, Doughty is a textbook example of the educated gentleman adventure writer for whom travel and literary production are inseparable.

References: Fussell 1987; Newby 1985; Rugoff 1960

DRAKE, SIR FRANCIS

The name Sir Francis Drake (English, 1540?–1596) invariably conjures up images of heroic adventures. Indeed, he was the first Englishman to circumnavigate the globe. But curiously, his status as hero is rather dubious: to the Spanish, Drake is a villain of the highest magnitude. His expedition to South America is the stuff of which legends are made. After landing in Panama, he waylaid 30 tons of silver from the Spaniards. With his loot, he proceeded south to the Strait of Magellan, brutally suppressing a mutiny along the way. Attrition took its toll on his five ships: two were abandoned, one sank in a storm, and another fled home. Drake remained on the *Golden Hind,* looting and pirating any town, ship, or caravan that he encountered. He worked his way as far as the Pacific Northwest and then continued west to the Philippines. His plundering and

thieving decreased as he made his way to Asia and then around Cape Horn. When he returned to England, he was knighted by Queen Elizabeth (and vilified by Spain).

His second voyage began almost immediately thereafter. He led a fleet to the Atlantic coast of North America and the Gulf of Mexico. Accounts of his battle prowess approach mythic proportions: he apparently sank 30 Spanish ships in the Bay of Cádiz. As Spain and England fought for territory, Drake may safely be said to have been a major factor.

Unfortunately, most of Drake's own writings have been lost. We have numerous accounts collected from his contemporaries and a transcribed oral history by his nephew (who also bore the name and title Sir Francis Drake). Thus what appears to be a firsthand telling of (the elder) Drake's adventures is in fact written secondhand by a relation. The stories vary in quality; what redeems them is the extreme courage—and pluck—of Drake as a heroic vagabond.

References: Adams 1988; Penzer 1926

DUDEVANT, AMANDINE-AURORE-LUCILE DUPIN

See Sand, George

E

ELDORADO (OR EL DORADO)

This legendary city of the New World was said to be ruled by El Dorado (literally, "the gilded one"). The city is also known as Manoa. Some versions have El Dorado the king as covered in oil and gold dust, while others suggest a sort of cloth of gold. The legend appears to have come from the Spaniards, although the story of a golden ruler is not uncommon in Incan lore. Most explorers believed that the city was located in what is now Colombia.

Many conflicting notions circulated about this city and its gold-clad ruler, but one trait is universal: the city was believed to have unimaginable wealth from gold and jewels. This fact led to numerous organized attempts to find the city. Sir Walter Raleigh organized two expeditions (1595 and 1617) expressly to find and pilfer the city; he failed on both occasions. Voltaire, writing much later (1759), has his character Candide stumble upon Eldorado.

In later usage, the term is used for any place of spectacular wealth and grandeur.

References: OED; Voltaire 1966

EMPIRE

Literally, *empire* denotes a state of supreme rule by an emperor. The notion of empire has a long history. The word is of Latin origin and referred initially to the lands ruled by the Roman emperors (beginning with Augustus Caesar in 27 B.C.E.). Subsequently, the term was applied to the Holy Roman Empire. In the early nineteenth century, Napoleon I adopted the term (as did Napoleons II and III). The British began to use the term *Indian Empire* in 1876 when Victoria was named empress of India. These are but a few of the many uses of the word.

Empire is important to travel literature because it is the root of the idea of imperialism. Not only does imperialism name the system of government under an emperor, but it also suggests the systematic and premeditated goal of dominating an underdeveloped or weaker nation. Most often, imperialism works by draining materials and labor of the colony to the markets of the imperial power. While the colony provides the product, the imperial power reaps the lion's share of the profits.

Imperialism—commercial, political, or cultural—has often driven travelers first to trade with, then to colonize, a variety of cultures around the world. From the zeal of the early spice traders, to the great race to claim the Indies, to the colonization of Africa and the Americas, to European domination of the world, the history of imperialism is inextricably linked to the history of travel literature.

References: Harvey 1967; OED

EMPSON, SIR WILLIAM

Although not usually associated with travel literature, Sir William Empson (English, 1906–1984) was a modern man of letters. He was author of numerous books of verse, essays, and criticism, including *Poems* (1935), *The Gathering Storm* (1940), *The Structure of Complex Words* (1951), and *Milton's God* (1962). His works are often characterized by tempering rational scientific discourses with wit, creativity, and philosophy.

As a prominent scholar, he held teaching posts in Great Britain and later in both Japan and China. His travels beyond these extended stays were mostly touristic in nature. None-theless, his letters and poems reflect the influ-ence these visits had on an already complex character.

One of his poems in particular is very well suited to this study. Titled simply "China" (from *Complete Poems,* 1949), it is an account of a small trip that he made while living in China. Empson usually writes in a very clas-sically constrained verse, yet the experience of travel in this case changes his style. He learns from the experience, and as the poem progresses he adopts a different tone. It is a very good example of travel as a catalyst for new forms, styles, or images.

Empson's rendering of travel is deeply po-etic and shrouded in metaphor. What begins as a series of laments about the hardship of travel—the odd food, the jarring sensation of motion, the raw climate—rapidly gives way to a comparison of cultures. In the fifth stanza, he writes:

> The serious music strains to squeeze—
>   The angel coolies sing like us
> —Duties, and literature, and fees
>   To lift an under-roaded bus
> (Crossley-Holland 331)

Chinese culture, radically different from Emp-son's own, "strains" and confuses. Seeing the difference "squeezes" or tests notions of obli-gations (and taxes!), art, expectations. Yet what have these lofty and theoretical notions to do with the common difficulties of travel? Emp-son's "under-roaded bus" refers to the bus he was riding becoming repeatedly bogged in the mud. The daily events of travel mix and blend with the higher cultural comparisons that Empson wants to make.

In the final two stanzas, Empson is at his most abstract. He concludes the poem:

> The paddy fields are wings of bees
>   The great Wall as a dragon crawls
> To one who flies or one who sees
>   The twisted contour of their walls
>
> A liver fluke of sheep agrees
>   Most rightly proud of her complacencies
> With snail so well they make one piece
>   Most wrecked and longest of all histories.
> (332)

The natural world (bees, field, sheep, snails) and the man-made world (the wall) coalesce into one composite experience by the end of the poem. Empson has been changed by his experience of the foreign; his response to the trip is to feel a new respect for China as a re-sult of its vast and ancient heritage. Along the way, he seems to gain an aspect of humility, a trait not usually associated with Empson. In other words, history and poetry, and travel and writing, show themselves to be insepara-ble from each other.

References: Crossley-Holland 1986

a literary device than a reflection of a real journey. Often, as we see in Fielding's novels, regardless of where one travels, the same greed, violence, lust, and instability exist. This is in contrast to true travel literature where the foreign is noteworthy particularly because it is different from home.

While Fielding's novels often read like some of the great accounts of travel and adventure, they mark themselves as different in that they are wildly fictitious—even sarcastic—in their exaggeration of normalcy. Moreover, Fielding's texts figure love of a woman as the driving force behind the adventures rather than love of travel. Finally, while the travel novel and the picaresque novel both encourage travel for travel's sake—that is, the object of travel is not necessarily to get somewhere—in the travel novel foreign lands and peoples teach the protagonist his/her lessons, whereas in the picaresque novel the hero learns of him/herself from coincidence and often from a sudden revelation by one of the other characters. In *Joseph Andrews,* for example, Joseph learns from Lady Booby that he is not the son of a farmer, but the son of a nobleman; his edification comes not from an event or from voyaging, but from being told of his importance.

Unlike the novels, however, Fielding's *Journal of a Voyage to Lisbon* must be considered fine travel literature. With his health failing, Fielding sought the warm climate of Portugal. Accompanied by an entourage of his wife, his daughter and her friend, and their various servants, they set out for a sea passage. Diligently, Fielding kept his journal and even edited it and arranged for its publication before his health failed utterly and he died in Lisbon.

His journal reflects his enormous erudition: it is full of literary and artistic references, classical maxims, and historical correlatives. In addition, the text is lighthearted, at times gently ironic, at other times flavored with slapstick. Always a master of characterization,

FIELDING, HENRY

Famous for two great novels—*Joseph Andrews* and *Tom Jones*—Henry Fielding (English, 1707–1754) also wrote a travel book: *Journal of a Voyage to Lisbon* (1755). While his novels incorporate many incidents of travel and adventure, they are not, strictly speaking, travel literature. Rather, they are considered picaresque novels, which is to say that wandering and travel adventures are central to the plot, but it is unimportant where the characters travel. Travel in the picaresque novel functions to drive the story forward, yet it is more

Engraving of Henry Fielding, by J. C. Butte, c. 1850 (Library of Congress)

Fielding describes the various people he meets while on the voyage in a vivid and complex manner. From fashionable traveling aristocracy to working-class merchants, Fielding draws them all with masterful precision and wit. In spite of his debilitating illness—which often confined him to bed—he keeps up a cheerful tone, almost as though to assure himself that he is not gravely ill.

In his preface Fielding adeptly positions his book in relation to the history of travel literature, a subject about which he had considerable knowledge. In this regard, Fielding's work anchors the genre by acknowledging and responding to the entire history. For Fielding, it is not enough simply to travel: one must learn along the way, and beyond that, one must write about the process. He advises aspiring travel writers to have "good sense enough to apply their peregrinations to a proper use, so as to acquire from them a real and valuable knowledge of men and things, both which are best known by comparison. If the customs and manners of men were everywhere the same, there would be no office so dull as that of a traveler. . . . Surely it would give him very little opportunity of communicating any kind of entertainment or improvement to others" (Adams 334). For Fielding, and for this encyclopedia, the value of travel and travel writing is both entertainment and education. Traveling, as Fielding said, "either in books or ships" (Adams 336), is a similar endeavor: both going abroad and reading about it improve perspective and increase wisdom.

Fielding's accounts are novelistic in their dialogue and endearing in their levity. From the depictions of his encounters with provincial innkeepers to those with miserly sea captains and daring coachmen, this *Journal* reads much like fiction, although Fielding insists that he is merely recording his days faithfully. Gently he makes fun of himself and, by extension, of standard English behavior, by contrasting his desires—for food, lodging, decorum, and so forth—to what he receives while traveling. The differences in Portugal highlight what might be taken for granted in London. Along the way, we laugh and enjoy; the *Journal* indeed is both educational and entertaining.

See also: Picaresque
References: Adams 1988

FLAUBERT, GUSTAVE

Gustave Flaubert (French, 1821–1880) achieved great fame as a novelist; indeed, he is usually considered one of the finest and most influential writers of the nineteenth century. His most celebrated novels, including *Madame Bovary, A Sentimental Education,* and *Salammbô,* cannot be considered travel literature. But in his letters and journals he succeeded in capturing his own travels with astounding grace and excitement. After Flaubert's death, some of his travel writing was collected and published as *Correspondence* (1881). It is this work that I will consider Flaubert's contribution to the genre of travel literature.

A master of phraseology and subtle usage of language, Flaubert produced writing that is at once lyrical and vivid. He was obsessed with finding the perfect word and the perfect sentence to convey his idea, often in colorful visual metaphors. Flaubert also believed in the doctrine of "art for art's sake"; in other words, art has an intrinsic value that is not influenced by outside factors like public reception. For this reason, Flaubert pioneered a number of new techniques and stylistic turns. He was convinced that he could refine his writing to perfection and beauty, regardless of literary convention or tradition. It was an easy leap for Flaubert to substitute "travel" for "art," resulting in "travel for travel's sake."

In 1849, already a notable author, Flaubert sought experience and adventure in "the Orient" (what we would now call the Near East and the Middle East). His zeal for experimentation and social interaction remains legendary: he was more concerned with exotic encounters than with ancient history. That which was different from France seemed to intrigue him most, including opium, harems, and Muslim rituals.

Much of his account of the Orient is highly charged with eroticism. Even subject matter that is not overtly sexual is made somewhat sensual or sexy. When this penchant is combined with his sensitive eye for detail and his incredibly precise word choices, Flaubert's writing is nothing short of dizzying. For example, here we see his description of a dancer in Egypt (which he would later echo in *Salammbô*):

> [She] is a tall, splendid creature, lighter in colouring than an Arab . . . her skin, particularly on her body, is slightly coffee-coloured. When she bends, her flesh ripples into bronze ridges. Her eyes are dark and enormous, her eyebrows black, her nostrils open and wide; heavy shoulders, full, apple-shaped breasts. She wore a large tarboosh [conical hat], ornamented on the top with a convex gold disk, in the middle of which was a small green stone imitating an emerald. (Newby 74)

In all of his accounts Flaubert is keen to capture his experiences in words; for this, he can be deemed a travel writer. Rather than seeking to flaunt his fame abroad, Flaubert sought humbly to learn. Said he, "Traveling makes one modest. You see what a tiny place you occupy in the world" (Fussell 14). It is the spirit of the unexpected and the wholly different that thrills Flaubert. By living those moments, he was able to write of them, in a somewhat subdued and mediated form, in his novels.

References: Fussell 1987; Newby 1985

FORSTER, E. M.

E. M. Forster (English, 1879–1970) often ranks as one of the major literary figures of the twentieth century. His literary production is vast and widely varied: it includes a number of famous novels (many of which have been made into films), volumes of literary criticism and essays, and a marvelous selection of short stories. Forster's work is difficult to classify simply as travel literature because his texts are complex and multidimensional. Nonetheless, many of his stories use travel and exotic adventure as much more than an amusing backdrop. In Forster, travel is often one of several driving forces behind the plot and the growth of his characters.

Well-to-do and meticulously educated at Cambridge University, Forster refused to let his social advantages lead him to sloth. Rather, he began writing while at the university and continued with astounding energy for the next 20-odd years. Even his earliest stories are well crafted and provocative; he began to publish them immediately after graduation in a number of journals and newspapers. With his meteoric rise to fame came additional privileges and responsibilities: he felt that his work had to improve, so he sought details by traveling to the remote locations that serve as settings for his stories. Widely traveled in Europe, Forster also lived in Alexandria (Egypt) and in India for a time.

Two of Forster's early novels, *Where Angels Fear to Tread* (1905) and *A Room with a View* (1908), followed his extensive stay in Italy; not coincidentally, both books are set there. *Where Angels Fear to Tread* follows a group of upper-middle-class English tourists exploring Italy. Throughout, the characters take great note of the cultural, historical, and geographic differences between England and Italy; in so doing, they begin to learn of themselves and how silly their class mores actually are. As in many of Forster's tales, travel leads to romance and transformations of various sorts.

This same theme appears again in *A Room with a View*. The well-bred Lucy Honeychurch is allowed to visit Italy under the strict supervision of her guardian. Upon arrival at the hotel, she laments vociferously

Still from the movie version of A Passage to India *(Photofest)*

that her room has no view, so lower-middle-class George Emerson, a fellow traveler, gallantly offers to swap rooms with her. Slowly, amid the adventure, excitement, and disorientation of travel, Lucy and George fall in love. When compared to her stolid suitor in England, George is the very picture of passion. It is travel and being abroad that allow Lucy to see her true desires; on her voyage she finds herself.

Even *Howards End* (1910), not a work of travel literature at all, contains strong elements of a traveler's ethos. Ostensibly a story of two British families—the rich Wilcox clan and the poor but well-reared Schlegel sisters—the novel revolves around a core message: "only connect," as Forster said of his novel's topic. By this he meant that different people, be they different classes, races, nationalities, or genders, should find a way to connect with one another. Through this affinity of informed comparison, one might find

creativity, self-knowledge, and even passion. While set only in England, the theory underlying the story is the stuff of pure travel literature: through knowing the other we can better know ourselves.

Perhaps Forster's most travel-oriented novel is *A Passage to India* (1924). Again, due to the complexity of the story and its structure, it is not, strictly speaking, pure travel literature. But several elements of the book mark it as a textbook example of great travel writing. Set in India during the time of the Raj, the novel poignantly contrasts the English colonists to the Hindu locals.

The plot is complex: Adela Quested travels to India to visit her fiancé, Ronny Heaslop. While visiting Marabar Caves, Adela has a misguided hallucination that her Hindu friend Dr. Aziz has taken advantage of her. This leads to a sort of racial hysteria in the community that destroys friendships and trust. Over the course of this cultural comparison, the underlying racism and cruelty of the British rule over India is unveiled. With the help of Ronny's mother, Adela comes to know Dr. Aziz, Indian culture, and some of its unsettling mysticism. In the end, Adela retracts her accusation, thereby asserting a truth that flies in the face of racist expectations.

Once again, travel and cross-cultural exposure lead to learning and transformation. Only through acquiring a more thorough knowledge of the Indian culture is Adela able to see the truth. Her travels have radically altered her life: socially, spiritually, and intellectually, she finds herself changed by the journey.

For these novels, as well as for many of his short stories that contain similar elements, E. M. Forster must be allowed the designation of travel writer. His tales figure travel and exposure to foreign cultures at the core of learning; being disoriented in a foreign land often is the catalyst to a major psychological or developmental transition. And lastly, his stories of travel urge us to take time to reflect deeply on our desires, our prejudices, and ourselves. What better way to do this than to take a voyage?

FOX, CAPTAIN LUKE

Like many other explorers, Captain Luke Fox (English, 1586–1635) ardently sought the legendary Northwest Passage. In 1631, he departed England with a crew of 22. Less than a year later, his crew ill and his mission failed, Fox returned. His account of the voyage, *Fox from the North-west Passage* (1635), makes the best of an unsuccessful endeavor.

Fox's writing deserves note for two reasons. By standards of the day, Fox, aged 45 when be began his voyage, was among the older of the sea captains exploring North America. Perhaps this gave him a more mature perspective; indeed, the youthful and idealistic euphoria of some of the younger captains does not color Fox's writing. Second, as a classically educated fellow, Fox peppered his

book with classical references and a wry sense of humor. In fact, when Fox published his journal, he added two essays written after his return to England: one argues the probability of the existence of the Northwest Passage, the other explains his decision to return to England. In the end, we remember Fox more for his writing than for his travels, the former being superior, the latter being relatively dull.

References: Adams 1988

FRASER, G. S.

George Sutherland Fraser (Scottish, 1915–1980) is a minor intellectual figure. Mostly associated with the New Apocalypse movement, he was a poet, essayist, and critic. His most famous work is *Vision and Rhetoric* (1960), although for a time he was a fairly noteworthy scholar of Dylan Thomas and Ezra Pound. Buried in his work are a couple of fascinating travel poems, probably autobiographical in nature.

For the sake of this book, I would like to talk about only one of these poems, "The Traveller Has Regrets." In this work Fraser highlights several key aspects of travel literature; for this, he serves as a good example of a writer who has helped define the genre.

The traveller has regrets
For the receding shore
That with its many nets
Has caught, not to restore,
The white lights in the bay,
The blue lights on the hill,
Though night with many stars
May travel with him still,
But night has nought to say,
Only a colour and shape
Changing like cloth shaking,
A dancer with a cape
Whose dance is heart-breaking,
Night with its many stars
Can warn travellers
There's only time to kill

And nothing much to say:
But the blue lights on the hill,
The white lights in the bay
Told us the meal was laid
And that the bed was made
And that we could not stay.
(Crossley-Holland 27)

This poem is a particularly good example of several of the themes that define travel literature. Immediately, Fraser establishes as issues the ephemeral nature of experience and the unstoppable passage of time. His narrator laments the departure ("receding shore") and the impossible return to that moment ("not to restore"). His journey to that particular place—unnamed in the poem, thus any place—has ended, and although he may return to that physical location, it will never be precisely the same. Indeed, experiences depend on both space and time, thus to return to any place can satisfy only half of the desire. Perhaps we might think of time as like the water flowing in a riverbed: one can return to the same banks of the river, but technically speaking, it is not the same river in that the water has flowed onward, irretrievably.

He continues this theme in a larger context. While the night sky "May travel with him still," it will always be a new and different experience that occurs under that sky. Just being in a given place—in this case under those particular stars—does not make the experience whole. In the same way, being in a particular town does not ensure that the same grand times had there before will be had again.

Clearly, the narrator laments his departure. From the "heart-breaking dance" to the message that "we could not stay," sadness at leaving has overwhelmed him. Yet there is an energy and a beauty to his lines that suggest that travel, like life, must continue: no one can stay fixed in a pure and perfect moment for long. Hence when the night sky warns the traveler that "There's only time to kill / And nothing much to say," we realize that we must sail on the sea of days that swells before us.

The narrator appears to have learned from travel a lesson about life and has shared that lesson in writing. Whether we be travelers on the high seas or through cyberspace, or anywhere in between, we must continue to move. Our consolation can be only that there are blue and white lights of other harbors waiting to greet us elsewhere.

References: Crossley-Holland 1986

FULLER, MARGARET

One of the great female intellectuals and social critics of her day, Margaret Fuller, Marchioness Ossoli (American, 1810–1850), also wrote some particularly fine travel literature. *Summer on the Lakes* (1844) was her first attempt at travel writing. Her success with this first book led to numerous letters, essays, and journalistic pieces. Many of these smaller pieces were collected and published posthumously as *At Home and Abroad; or, Things and Thoughts in America and Europe* (1856). The rest of her travel writing can be found amid political, social, and philosophical work published as *Writings* (1941).

Well-to-do and part of a highly educated Harvard University family, Fuller demonstrated her intellectual capacities as a young girl. With a gift for languages and literary studies, she completed a rigorous and broadly classical education. Using these mental tools, she became a scholar, lecturer, and writer. Friendly with Ralph Waldo Emerson and a number of the transcendentalists, she is noted as a philosopher. Applying her theoretical frame to the world around her, she also wrote and lectured on women's rights, the evils of slavery, and the shameful federal policies toward Native Americans. A voice of the underprivileged and abused, Fuller argued vociferously for social change.

Summer on the Lakes chronicles her voyage to the Great Lakes. Partly to observe the social differences between the East Coast and the Midwest, and partly to experience life among the American Indian tribes, the trip was not tourism, but rather a chance to learn. From the outset, Fuller's intention was to write a book on these subjects. In this respect, traveling facilitated her writing; the two actions were inseparable to Fuller. The text met with critical success despite its progressive political tone.

One success led to another, and Fuller was offered a job as a correspondent in Europe for the *New York Times*. Her letters and columns did a splendid job evoking the excitement of Europe without succumbing to automatic praise. Gracefully, tactfully, but incisively, Fuller compared Europe to America, not always to the Old World's credit. Highlighting the cultural differences served as a very effective vehicle for Fuller to encourage both American and European self-reflection. As she says in one of her letters, "The American in Europe, if a thinking mind, can only become more American" (Adams 477).

From England, France, and Italy, Fuller wrote on a wide range of topics. Her pet topics—women's rights and the rights of the poor—continued to appear with regularity, but more sophisticated analyses of the legal and political systems, class structures, and the value (and cost) of a long history became recurrent themes as well. She married an Italian nobleman, Marchese Ossoli, and continued to write both for the American press and for Italian publication. In 1850, Margaret, her husband, and their child boarded a vessel bound for America; unfortunately, their ship sank in a storm and the family drowned.

In spite of her short career, Margaret Fuller's travel writing is significant for its style as well as for its content. With its breezy reportage tone, her writing is genial and casual. But her issues are often deceptively thorny. Her kindness and willingness to take up unpopular and unglamorous causes shade her writing with a warming generosity. As an American female voice, she addresses different issues and has different perspectives from many of her contemporaries. And her expressive exuberance for travel and adventure confirms her status as a true traveler who learned from her excursions and insisted upon teaching her readers what she had learned.

, *References:* Adams 1988

GAGE, THOMAS

The story of Thomas Gage (English, 1600–1656) is an elaborate tangle of cultures and ideas. In his travelogue *The English American, His Travels by Sea and Land; or, A New Survey of the West Indies* (1648) are all the elements of a gothic novel: religion, spite, passion, deception, and a series of exotic locations. These novelistic elements blend beautifully with Gage's focus on travel and adventure. While the text feels like fiction, it is in fact a polished representation of Gage's voyages.

Gage turned to the Roman Catholic Church fairly early in his life. He believed that he could best serve God by working as a missionary in the New World. His convictions took him to Central America (1625–1637) and later to Jamaica and the islands of the Caribbean. His writing is an odd combination of styles and forms: although structured as a travelogue, the text includes significant character development and lengthy passages that read more like essays. Throughout, Gage appears as the central character; over the course of the book, we observe his personal growth and spiritual difficulties in the face of many troubling and challenging experiences. In this fashion, Gage is a product of his adventures.

The plot of the story is roughly as follows. Due to the English hostility to Roman Catholicism, young Gage went to Spain to become a Dominican. Requesting and receiving a posting in the Philippines, Gage departed Europe for East Asia via the New World. In a demonstration of resistance and uneasiness with colonization, Gage remained in Mexico, against the orders of his clerical superiors. For more than a decade, Gage wandered Central America, increasing his personal fortune and railing upon the cruelty of his former church brothers. His faith continued to slip, until he eventually renounced Catholicism to adopt Puritanism. He writes himself as a legendary figure to be feared for his words and for his honesty.

For the era, his words are often shockingly progressive. For example, Gage upbraids the entire colonial venture, loosely disguised as missionary work:

> Thus in religion they [the natives] are superstitiously led on and blinded in the observance of what they have been taught more for the good and profit of their priest than for any good of their souls, not perceiving that their religion is a policy to enrich their teachers. But not only do the friars and priests live by them and eat the sweat of their brows, but also all the Spaniards, who not only with their work and service (being themselves many given to idleness) grow wealthy and rich, but with needless offices and authority are still fleecing them, and taking from them that little which they gain with much hardness and severity. (Adams 190)

It is no wonder that Gage's book sold well in Britain and that the Spanish vilified him!

As a renegade, and as an observer on the fringes of nationalism and religion, Gage must be noted as having a unique perspective. He brashly dares to describe many sorts of ethical, spiritual, and moral transgressions by the Spaniards and the Catholic Church. Very literally, he was always simultaneously an insider and an outsider. As one of the first non-Spaniards intimate with Spanish colonial policies, and as a lapsed Catholic familiar with church machinations, Gage has much insight to offer us. In this particular case, traveling to the colonies was an exercise not in observing the indigenous peoples, but in observing the colonizers. To learn more fully of his religion and his European culture, Gage took to travel; what he saw shook his beliefs to the core.

References: Adams 1988

GALTON, SIR FRANCIS

Books that provide advice to travelers constitute a subset of travel literature. Sir Francis Galton (English, 1822–1911) wrote one of the finest examples of this subgenre. *The Art of Travel* (1860) is the result of his own rather extensive travels, and it is an interesting guide to what Victorian travelers were expected to know.

Galton's fame came from many endeavors. A gentleman of diverse learning, he published books of many sorts. He wrote on genetics, meteorology, mathematics, psychology, memory, cartography, and criminology, as well as travel theory. In addition, he was a cousin of Charles Darwin.

In the early 1850s, he braved the wilds of southwestern Africa, and from this experience he composed *The Art of Travel*. It contains a myriad of data: practical advice, field medicine, transcultural communication tips, navigation techniques, and what can only be called a primer of positive travel attitudes.

While mostly confined to factual information, as opposed to narratives of adventure, Galton's book is nonetheless written with numerous practical examples that serve as illustrations of his points. The introduction remains particularly interesting in that it propounds several reasons for adventure travel: to learn, to test oneself, to do one's duty, and to capture the unexplored in writing. Galton takes great pains to make much of the dry material interesting by referring to a bewildering array of travel advice gleaned from wide-ranging sources. In this regard, the book is a fascinating compendium of thoughts and tips on how to cope with common and

uncommon circumstances. It is also a rich source of references—however brief—to travel writing throughout the ages.

Furthermore, Galton's work stands out for its honest acknowledgment of the many and various adversities and difficulties that were expected components of nineteenth-century travel. For those of us accustomed to plush and leisurely vacations, Galton's book helps to highlight the arduous nature of premodern adventures in Africa (or elsewhere). Reading the text in this manner, we begin to understand the courage and devotion that the great adventure travelers possessed. That they managed to write such eloquent and literary accounts under such circumstances is sure to cause us to wonder.

References: Newby 1985

GAMA, VASCO DA

Along with Ferdinand Magellan and Christopher Columbus, Vasco da Gama (Portuguese, 1469?–1524) must be recognized as a pioneer of exploration. The record of his journey, published in English by the Hakluyt Society in 1898, is called *A Journal of the First Voyage of Vasco da Gama*. It recounts his quest to find a trade route to India that went to the south of Africa. Despite encountering difficulties like hurricanes and mutinies, da Gama reached Calicut after nearly a year. Faced with an extremely hostile ruler, da Gama had to fight his way out of the harbor, suffering considerable losses. He returned to Portugal and was knighted by King Emanuel for his great discovery. As exploration, the voyage was a resounding success.

In his account of his first journey it becomes clear that, for da Gama, the point is going rather than arriving. The voyage itself is the important subject of da Gama's journal. From the trivial daily routines on the ship to the first European description of the natives of southern Africa, da Gama's texts are an exercise in discipline. He relates the ordinary

Vasco da Gama delivers the letter of King Manuel of Portugal to the Samorim of Calicut; *photomechanical print, c. 1905 (Library of Congress)*

and the extraordinary with the same tone and in the same factual manner: "We remained five days at this place enjoying ourselves, and reposing from the hardships endured during a passage in the course of which all of us had been face to face with death" (Adams 69). As a study in order and bravery, da Gama's journals are magnificent. What he lacks, however, is any sort of drama or flair for storytelling.

As a foundation for the Portuguese colonial empire, da Gama's journal describes how the trading outposts in the Indian Ocean were established. In subsequent voyages, da Gama led a military convoy back to Calicut to establish a factory. This show of force enabled Portugal to secure a stronghold in India, thereby ensuring a supply of such valuable commodities as cinnamon, cloves, ginger, pepper, and precious stones. In the history of colonialism, da Gama's journals are significant because they describe the first moments of the veritable conquest of the East. What

began as the spirit of exploration for da Gama transforms into the spirit of mercantilism for his successors.

References: Adams 1988

GOETHE, JOHANN WOLFGANG VON

Often evoked as the best nineteenth-century example of a universal genius, Goethe (German, 1749–1832) distinguished himself in an astounding array of fields. Although famous for his plays, poems, and novels, Goethe also wrote a wholly successful and exquisite travel book translated as *Travels in Italy* (1813). From his notes, journal entries, and actual letters, Goethe compiled the volume, which met with immediate favor throughout Europe. While the text is ostensibly epistolary in form, it is generally agreed that these letters are more of a literary device than actual missives.

Portrait of Vasco da Gama; woodcut, 1572
(Bettmann/Corbis)

By and large, the letters recount a variety of sights and deeds, all of them framed by Goethe's incisive mind and rich writing style. As befits a man of Goethe's diverse abilities, *Travels in Italy* describes all social levels, from the upper classes to artists to servants. He remarks on art and architecture as well as on clothing and conversation styles, and on very much in between. In addition, Goethe's reputation as a womanizer made him very attractive in some social circles; openly, he describes—so much as nineteenth-century decorum allows—his flirtations and dalliances. In almost every situation, Goethe seems to be extremely frank and forthright; it is for this reason that the story is often called an autobiographical sketch. By extension, this

also makes it great travel literature, for we are learning not only of the foreign place, but of the author as well.

Charm, wit, keen perception, and unpretentiousness are only a few of the vast number of characteristics that Goethe displays in this work. Throughout, Goethe seems never to forget that traveling is about learning of and recognizing new perspectives. In a scene set in Malesine (near Venice), for example, Goethe is drawing an old battlement tower in the morning light. Curious onlookers gather, and one bold fellow accuses Goethe of being a spy—the tower being an ancient fortification now in disuse. As the local authorities arrive, a friendly debate ensues; instead of maddening, Goethe finds the scene wholly amusing. He tries to convince his accusers that he is simply looking at the ruins, but to the constabulary they are not ruins, but the infrastructure of the city. The townsfolk cannot see the beauty of the tower because it is familiar and plays a specific role for them; but to Goethe's foreign eyes, it is something different. Reconciling those two distinct positions proves impossible, and Goethe's drawing is torn in half. Yet the story is told with relish, not with pique; in so doing, Goethe affirms himself as willing to learn all sorts of lessons, including some that he had not expected to encounter.

In another incident, similar in theme, Goethe muses:

My old gift of seeing the world with eyes of that artist, whose pictures have most recently made an impression on me, has occasioned [in] me some peculiar reflections. It is evident that the eye forms itself by the objects, which, from youth up, it is accustomed to look upon, and so the Venetian artist must see all things in a clearer and brighter light than other men. We, whose eye when out of doors, falls on a dingy soil, which, when not muddy, is dusty,—and which, always colourless . . . can never attain to such a cheerful view of nature. (Newby 137)

Goethe in the Campagna, *by J. H. W. Tischbein, c. 1848 (Kavaler/Art Resource, NY, NY)*

Once again, perception is deemed wholly subjective, thus the same object might appear distinctly different from two perspectives. Learning to accept the possibility—and prevalence—of different perspectives is at the heart of travel literature.

Relatively early in the sequence of letters (March 9, 1787), Goethe provides a lucid summary of the joy of travel and the power of travel writing: "This is the pleasant part of travelling, that even ordinary matters, by their novelty and unexpectedness, often acquire the appearance of an adventure" (Adams 373). To be sure, Goethe takes the quotidian moments of his journey and crafts them into stories that teach monumental lessons. In the final analysis, *Travels in Italy* thrills and teaches simultaneously, and as a result, it must be considered among the finest of travel writings in our tradition.

References: Adams 1988; Newby 1985

GOLDSMITH, OLIVER

As with many of the great eighteenth-century writers, Oliver Goldsmith (Irish-born, English, 1730?–1774) made a Grand Tour of Europe as a part of his cultural education. He had studied medicine, and before settling into a practice, he spent two years wandering on the cheap. Usually broke but always ready for adventure, Goldsmith funded his tour by gambling, "busking" (playing music on the streets for donations), and engaging in an array of petty swindles and cons. Perhaps his most successful venture was transposing his adventures into a poem called "The Traveller" (1756), which he sold with considerable success. Upon returning to Great Britain, he turned his attention to small-scale writing and publishing, working with the novelist Samuel Richardson and making the acquaintance of Samuel Johnson.

A copy of "The Traveller" made it into the hands of the powerful Literary Club, and so began a successful writing career. Goldsmith took his notes and expanded them into *An Enquiry into the Present State of Polite Learning in Europe* (1759). This sociological study of manners and cultural behavior is a cousin to travel literature and interesting in its own right. It compares the social behavior of England with that of the other great European powers. Goldsmith went on to publish widely and to earn himself a place in the history of literature with such great novels as *The Vicar of Wakefield* (1766) and his spoof of Charles Montesquieu's *Persian Letters* called *The Citizen of the World* (1762), as well as his caricature of the literary wits of his age titled *Retaliation* (1774). But for our purposes, it is his first, early poem that is noteworthy.

"The Traveller" is a curious poem that attempts to teach—if a little heavy-handedly—Goldsmith's readers about the various cultures of Europe. Particularly, he is concerned with how different peoples have very different modes of being happy. His style is overblown and sophomoric, but his insights are provocative and often compelling. Partly because he was on a very limited budget, Goldsmith encountered a large smattering of lower-class locals. While many eighteenth-century travelers kept to their own social milieu, Goldsmith, perhaps out of necessity, often engaged with peasants and laborers. His observations of them are not simply snobbish descriptions; rather, he gently and humbly suggests that the rich might learn something from the poor. Thus when describing a farmer's humble evening, Goldsmith writes:

At night returning, every labour sped,
He sits him down the monarch of a shed;
Smiles by his cheerful fire, and round surveys
His children's looks, that brighten at the
    blaze;
While his loved partner, boastful of her
    hoard,
Displays her cleanly platter on the board:
And haply too some pilgrim, thither led,
With many a tale repays the nightly bed.
(Crossley-Holland 188)

To be sure, Goldsmith is idealizing the peasant life, and clearly his presence alters their behavior. Nonetheless, that he characterizes a rustic, laboring family in positive and friendly terms is notable.

In addition, we can see the value of narrative in the above passage: the narrator repays his room and board by telling tales. It is a subtle reminder, but a recurrent theme in this didactic poem, that travel and stories go hand in hand. So not only is Goldsmith the traveler writing a poem about his travels, but he is the character in the poem who uses his tales as currency. As the traveler encounters novelty, he learns; as he learns, he writes to teach others. In one neat package, Goldsmith gives the thrills of adventure, the insights learned from encountering a variety of foreign cultures, and the well-crafted literary account.

See also: Grand Tour; Montesquieu, Charles
References: Crossley-Holland 1986; Fussell 1987

GRAIL QUEST

The Grail Quest is a frequently found theme in many medieval writings. The common idea is that a long and arduous journey or quest is made in search of a powerful talisman, the Grail (also know as the Holy Grail, or Sangreal or Sangraal). During the course of this travail, the seeker often learns about himself.

The myth of the Grail features prominently in many European literary traditions, perhaps most famously in Arthurian legend (as seen in

The Round Table and the Holy Grail; *miniature from the* Roman de Tristan, *late fifteenth century (Giraudon/Art Resource, NY)*

Sir Thomas Malory's *Morte d'Arthur*). In this variant of the legend, the Holy Grail has a Christian lineage: it is said to have been Jesus Christ's cup at the Last Supper. The Grail provides a variety of powers, including peace, power, and blessedness. Without the Grail, King Arthur's reign deteriorates; desperate, he sends his knights on a mighty quest that takes them far and wide in search of the talisman.

Other variants of the myth trace the Grail to a pagan symbol of female sexuality—with-out the Grail, fertility suffers. In Celtic lore, the Grail bestows warrior courage and strength in battle. Regardless, it is something that is to be sought on an epic pilgrimage, thus Grail Quest stories are an early form of travel literature.

While most of the original legends were written (or otherwise imagined) before the fifteenth century—the starting point of the scope of this encyclopedia—numerous subse-quent travel tales evoke the myth of the Grail

Quest. In its distilled form, the Grail Quest therefore signifies any journey through extreme adversity motivated by a search for something ideal. Using this definition, most travel literature is a Grail Quest if we imagine the Grail to hold wisdom, experience, and self-knowledge.

GRAND TOUR

In the late seventeenth century, after the Reformation in England (1660), the well-heeled of Europe, especially those in Great Britain, began to make what has come to be called "The Grand Tour of the Continent." The stated purpose was to gain some experience of the wider world, although given that many Grand Tourists stuck together and ran through an identical itinerary of sights, one wonders how much learning actually took place. Rather, this pursuit seems to have been something of a status symbol and a test of tenacity, for such a journey was difficult and anything but luxurious.

Usually lasting several months (often the pleasant summer months), the Grand Tour was a way to gain a certain amount of Continental polish. Young gentlemen often went, either by desire or at their father's command, after completing their university training. In many cases, travelers were accompanied by a tutor paid to oversee the journey and to ensure that some learning took place. By the early eighteenth century, the Grand Tour was well enough established that many women, though always with a chaperone, were encouraged to make a journey to the Continent.

Typically, the route began in London, to get outfitted and to procure guidebooks and supplies, and it then proceeded to Dover to catch a ferry to Calais. From there, it was mandatory to head to Paris, Versailles, and Fontainebleau, with as many high-society engagements crammed in as possible. In addition, it was quite common to spend some weeks taking French lessons, if for no other reason than to be able to flirt with the opposite sex. After Paris, Switzerland was a common destination: the refined culture of Paris contrasted dramatically with the rugged Alps. Having walked in the mountains and taken the brisk Swiss air, the tourist was almost required to go to Florence, Venice, and Rome to look at art and architecture. More adventurous sorts might have gone as far south as Naples, especially if interested in music or the dangerous history of Mount Vesuvius. After Italy, the traveler usually headed northward again, to Germany, particularly Berlin and Potsdam, and perhaps a brief stop in one of the university towns. Finally, usually low on energy and money by now, the Grand Tourist visited Holland and Flanders to look at the paintings. Squeezing this schedule into a summer, especially given slow coach travel, made for a whirlwind tour that usually exhausted even the most energetic. Savvy travelers, however, slowed the pace down considerably; it was not uncommon for the more intrepid travelers to spend several years on a Grand Tour of Europe.

Other aspects of the Grand Tour were almost universal as well. Souvenir hunting became something of a mania. The ever-competitive wealthy sought to outdo their peers with exotic or exquisite purchases from afar. And writing was considered a daily duty. Vast quantities of letters were written to friends and family at home, both to communicate and to share the glories of the tour. Additionally, it was standard practice to keep a detailed diary or journal of events. As is to be expected, the quality of these writings varies enormously.

The Grand Tour, as a well-to-do affair, diminished with the popularization of cheap and efficient rail travel in the 1830s. By that time, the Continent was not considered especially exotic, and the wealthy sought other rites of passage. The newly mobile middle class, along with Americans, continued a sort of Grand Tour well into the twentieth century.

References: Fussell 1987

HALL, CAPTAIN BASIL

Basil Hall (Scottish, 1788–1844) showed great curiosity and exuberant energy from childhood onward. Son of a famous scientist, he finished his general education in Edinburgh by his midteens. He promptly joined the Royal Navy and spent most of the rest of his life traveling widely and writing prolifically. His *Fragments and Voyages* (1831) was published in nine volumes and represents only the "greatest hits" of his tales. Individual volumes and other travel accounts were released in multiple editions and translated into seven languages. His popularity was great among the scientific community, among lay travelers, and with the Royal Society, of which he was an honored and esteemed member.

Between his vast seafaring adventures, Hall made extensive overland trips throughout Europe and the Near East. But his true passion remained the sea. As a sailor, he was rapidly promoted to captain; over the span of his career, he traveled to the Far East, South America, the Mediterranean, and Africa. His epic journey with his family throughout the United States is chronicled in *Travels in North America in the Years 1827 and 1828* (1829).

Regardless of his destination, Hall demonstrated a keen eye for detail and a true zest for travel. As a cultural observer, he was unrivaled, particularly because he appears to have had a superior instinct for finding opportunities to see authentic or natural moments. He visited mainstream institutions, like schools, hospitals, and museums, as well as many less likely destinations, like small communities, homes of poorer families, and businesses. Thus his accounts blend the quotidian with the extraordinary. Above all, his curiosity drove him, and his enthusiasm led him to write detailed accounts of all he saw.

Because of his wide range of experiences, he very effectively compared his destination to a variety of other cultures and geographies that he knew intimately. His manner of telling tales is easy and congenial: he rarely wrote in daily diary entries, preferring instead a looser narrative form that seems to flow naturally. In fact, Hall's stories unfold much the way travel actually does: tangentially, unpredictably, at various speeds. Never shy with asides, commentary, and subjective opinions—but mostly respectful and honest—Hall's tales evoke a delightfully credible picture of what it was really like to have been there.

Hall's writing delights with its elegantly crafted phrases and engaging structure. He often introduces anecdotes in a roundabout, framed manner or by way of a flashback to a different experience. Committed to using travel as a means of learning, and writing as a means of remembering, Hall writes:

> It is amusing to look back, after a journey is over, at those objects which at the time excited the most vivid interest, but which have faded from the recollection so completely, that any description of them from memory would be feeble and unsatisfactory, while a literal transcript of the notes written on the spot would be no less inaccurate from their extravagance and high colouring. The mere proximity of some things, gives them an importance which we are apt to mistake for a permanent and intrinsic value; whereas their real consequence may not extend beyond their own small circumference. Even on the spot, it is frequently no easy job for the stranger to decide which of a variety of objects he shall devote most of his attention to. (Adams 492–493)

It is precisely this earnestness and sincere desire to capture the truth in his writing that makes Hall so satisfying to read.

As an example of a traveler driven by the need to write all of his experiences into texts that can serve to teach others, Hall has produced superior books. He devoted his life to learning of the world through engagement with far-flung people and places; the result of this quest is a set of volumes that is the next best thing to actually having been there.

References: Adams 1988

HARDY, THOMAS

Thomas Hardy (English, 1840–1928) ranks among the great nineteenth-century authors. Famous for his so-called Wessex novels, including *Far from the Madding Crowd* (1874), *The Mayor of Casterbridge* (1886), *Tess of the D'Urbervilles* (1891), and *Jude the Obscure* (1895), Hardy also wrote a considerable amount of poetry over the course of his life. Finally amassed into one edition after his death, *Collected Poems* (1931) remains a formidable poetic achievement. In terms of style and topic, his verse represents a significant literary bridge to the twentieth century.

Born into a financially struggling family, Hardy had to fend for himself from an early age. Although he did not have the luxury of foreign travel as a youth, he learned a traveler's ethos by moving from town to town looking for opportunities. By the time he made it to London (1862), he was wise to the ways of the world. After his literary success provided him with sufficient income, Hardy ventured to the Continent on several occasions. His most significant journey was a yearlong visit to the Continent with his wife in 1884–1885. Remnants of this trip appear in most of his subsequent work.

While his novels often involve moving from one town to the next, they cannot be called travel literature. Instead, they are cousins of travel literature. Being in motion,

being between places—in short, traveling—serves as an obvious symbol of the psychological or societal changes his characters experience. For example, Jude's long walk to Christminster (an Oxford stand-in) is as much about his new direction in life as it is about taking the road to a new town. Throughout the Wessex novels, Hardy's characters make numerous regional journeys: what they find is that motion may be ambivalent, but it always causes change.

Several of Hardy's works describe life as a journey. To be sure, a great deal of literature has done the same, but Hardy's is a particularly industrialized variant of that metaphor. Writes travel scholar Paul Fussell:

> That life is a "journey" is one of the oldest clichés lodged in the human imagination. That life is a railway journey became easily conceivable during the age of steam and electricity. But it took Hardy, with his flair for the portentous, the dangerous, and the uncertain, to imagine life as a risky and mysterious rail journey—despite the straight tracks and the public stations and the ticket bought for a specific destination—"towards a world unknown." (Fussell 473)

In his poetry Hardy focused more concisely and clearly on travel writing. Superior examples can be found in his *Collected Poems* as well as in a number of anthologies. All of the great themes of travel literature recur repeatedly in his delightful verses.

Travel merges with education as he wanders the classical ruins of ancient Rome in a poem called "In the Old Theatre, Fiesole." As the narrator imagines history in the ruins, a little girl approaches, selling an ancient coin. For all his imagination, the narrator needs this real moment to span the vastness of time between ancient and modern: the girl allows the scene to make sense. The narrator remarks,

> She lightly passed; nor did she once opine
> How, better than all books, she had raised
>   for me

In swift perspective Europe's history
Through the vast years of Caesar's sceptred
   line.
(Crossley-Holland 125)

Making the journey to see the ruins is part of
the lesson; engaging the culture that inhabits
the space presently is another. The experiences of travel are not limited simply to seeing the sights and reflecting internally.

Perhaps with some amount of nostalgia,
Hardy penned "Midnight on the Great Western" in 1917. It tells of a "journeying boy"
thrilled and a little afraid of his trip across a
(relatively) great distance. Such a journey
would have been impossible in Hardy's own
youth; perhaps Hardy is projecting an impossible perspective onto the boy. In this poem
we can see travel as a metaphor for potential;
the young boy stands on the threshold of becoming a man of the world, much as Hardy
had thrown himself from Dorchester to London in his youth. In the poem the character
is anxious but excited, trying to muster as
much bravery as he can. The journey stands
in for a condensed version of life: ahead lay
unexpected joys and sorrows, behind the un-
changeable past.

In "At the Inn" from 1898, we see that
travel alters the way voyagers behave: an affa-
bility and affinity shrouds those in motion.
The narrator has gone to an inn with his
lover, a vaguely illicit action in the late nineteenth century. In good, hospitable fashion,
the innkeeper welcomes the travelers:

When we as strangers sought
   Their catering care, . . .
They warmed as they opined
   Us more than friends—
That we had all resigned
   For love's dear ends.
(Ricks 465)

To travel is to escape, at least to a degree, cultural conventions and expectations. The decision to take a trip serves as an inducement to
experience; such experiences, especially when

written about, form great and lasting memories. The poem concludes with the narrator
looking back upon that time with great
fondness.

In the body of Hardy's work we can see
such travel themes repeated and praised.
Change and unpredictable interactions drive
his characters; they often seek such propulsion
literally, by moving. For Hardy, then, travel
and experience—and, we surmise, writing—
are the fundamental components of life.

References: Crossley-Holland 1986; Fussell
1987; Ricks 1987

HARRER, HEINRICH

Perhaps one of the most accomplished travelers in Tibet, Heinrich Harrer (Austrian,
1912–) blended travel and literature and
politics so gracefully that they seem one. His
journeys, his teaching, and his writing have
entertained as well as influenced. *Seven Years
in Tibet* (1953) chronicles his remarkable travels into the Tibetan culture and his amazing
relationship with the Dalai Lama.

What began as a simple adventure culmi-
nated in the makings of literature (and film;
see the 1997 movie *Seven Years in Tibet*).
Harrer was on an expedition in the Himalayas when World War II broke out; the
British imprisoned him as a refugee. He escaped by considerable guile, preferring the
wilds of the mountains to his cell. Yet he was
alone, without funds, without mountaineering equipment, and without a destination.
For two years, he wandered. He finally
ended up in Tibet, still a relatively isolated
sanctuary where the politics of the war were
distant. By a combination of good fortune
and perseverance, he met the young Dalai
Lama and eventually became his close friend
and tutor.

His book tells of how he came to know
and respect this wise young Dalai Lama and
the Tibetan people. Harrer's book is charming
in that it expresses his genuine excitement

and enthusiasm for the exchange of ideas. He knows that he is the Dalai Lama's eyes to the West, and as such, he has a grave responsibility. It is a profoundly clear example of travel that teaches of the self; in order to teach the Dalai Lama, Harrer must clearly remember himself.

Harrer describes the situation:

> I observed then, for the first time, that he liked to get to the bottom of things instead of taking them for granted. And so, later on, like many a good father who wishes to earn the respect of his son, I often spent the evening reviving my knowledge of half-forgotten things or studying new ones. I took the utmost trouble to treat every question seriously and scientifically, as it was clear to me that my answers would form the basis of his knowledge of the western world. (Rugoff 150)

Harrer's book tells of an adventure that began under the worst imaginable circumstances but that he made into something grand and significant in spite of adversity. It is this spirit of adventure and exchange that is the greatest strength of the story.

References: Rugoff 1960

HEMINGWAY, ERNEST

Nobel laureate Ernest Hemingway (American, 1899–1961) deserves mention as a figure on the fringes of travel writing. His contribution to modern literature has been noted and studied at great length; indeed, his work falls into many genres. Although travel played a great role in his life and in many of his stories, Hemingway is not usually regarded as a

Still from the movie version of The Sun Also Rises, *1957 (Photofest)*

giant of travel literature. Several of his stories, however, merit annotation in this volume because they are eminently literary and travel drives substantial portions of the plot. In this regard, aspects of Hemingway's work intersect travel literature.

As a newspaper journalist in the 1920s, Hemingway lived and worked throughout Europe and Africa. Where danger was to be found, there was Hemingway. As a supporter of the Spanish Civil War, Hemingway volunteered in both World War I and II in a variety of roles, from partisan to ambulance driver to war correspondent. When not involved with human conflict, he loved big game hunting, deep-sea fishing, and adventure sports. This obsession with danger and death is a theme that runs throughout Hemingway's life and work.

A member of the artistic and literary set of Paris dubbed the "Lost Generation," Hemingway published his first major work, *The Sun Also Rises,* in 1926. This work launched his career and marked him as the literary voice of his generation. As a modernist novelist, Hemingway's influence on literature has been enormous; as a travel writer, his influence has been more modest.

Most of his novels and short stories contain instances of travel that facilitate character development and constitute necessary elements of the plot. In *The Sun Also Rises,* the trip to Pamplona (Spain) to participate in the running of the bulls serves as the catalyst to Jake's development. In *A Farewell to Arms,* Fredric Henry's escape to Switzerland functions as a journey that allows Henry to learn of himself. In *The Old Man and the Sea,* it is a sea voyage that provides the opportunity for the protagonist to encounter the marlin that teaches him of life's grand struggle. *Green Hills of Africa* (1935) and *The Snows of Kilimanjaro* (1936) change the setting to Africa, but the role of travel remains the same. In both of these stories, the escape from familiarity and normalcy spurs the characters to introspection, conflict, and development.

The extreme situations and hardships the characters encounter bring out their best and their worst traits.

The Snows of Kilimanjaro describes a safari gone awry. As the protagonist lays dying of gangrene in his tent, his lover helpless to save him, he reminisces about his myriad of travels:

> He remembered the good times with them all, and the quarrels. They always picked the finest places to have the quarrels. And why had they always quarreled when he was feeling best? He had never written any of that because, at first, he never wanted to hurt any one and then it seemed as though there was enough to write without it. But he had always thought that he would write it finally. There was so much to write. He had seen the world change . . . and had watched the people. . . . He had been in it and he had watched it and it was his duty to write of it. (Hemingway 49)

In this passage Hemingway fuses travel, learning, and writing into a single package. An integral part of the voyage always remains the writing of the tale. As such, this story moves closer to a textbook example of modern travel literature. To ensure that his point is made, Hemingway has the adventure of the safari prompt the protagonist to muse about travel in general and then to recognize his obligation to write about it.

Perhaps the closest Hemingway ever came to pure travel writing was *A Moveable Feast* (1964). The book recalls Hemingway's early years (1921–1926) in Paris. Although written decades after the fact, the text contains remarkably precise recollections of people and events of this nearly mythical period. Hemingway's autobiographical narrator in this case details his own fascination with the strangeness of Paris. To be sure, the narrator responds to the differences between Paris and American cities with a spurt of growth and development. Indeed, the opportunities of a foreign lifestyle inspire the narrator to reflect poignantly on his former life. Nonetheless, his focus on his fellow expatriates in Paris—like

F. Scott Fitzgerald, Gertrude Stein, Ezra Pound, and his ex-wife Hadley—frustrates the conventions of travel literature. At best, this work can be labeled an experimental extension of travel literature.

Almost all of Hemingway's stories contain aspects of travel literature in one form or another. Throughout his work, travel provides an opportunity for revelation about human nature and for self-awareness. Hemingway believed that it is via exposure to the wide world, contact with the unfamiliar and extreme, and interaction with the foreign that we come to know ourselves. For his modernist recasting of travel, Hemingway may be considered a travel writer.

References: Brian 1988; Hemingway 1987

HILTON, JAMES

James Hilton (English, 1900–1954) published his best-selling novel *Lost Horizon* in 1933. It is a fine example of utopian travel literature in that the voyage to the impossibly idyllic Shangri-La exposes the faults of European society; once again, visiting the other teaches the voyager about himself. Considering that this novel was written against the backdrop of a mounting socialist threat and impending chaos in Europe, it seems clear that Hilton's utopia is meant as a corrective contrast to the world in which he lived.

The story begins with the reunion of old schoolfellows talking of a long-lost companion named Conway. Rutherford tells how he has been tracking Conway for years. Travel has becomes a sort of detective work for Rutherford: traces of Conway found here, a sighting there, a story of his presence elsewhere. Rutherford's quest to find Conway comes from having seen him and heard the story of his adventure—which he promptly wrote down as notes for a novel and has just given to the narrator. Adventure and writing about that adventure become one act; what was Conway's experience becomes Rutherford's story (which the narrator then relates to us).

Conway's story is simple: he and a random group of three others are kidnapped and flown to a remote mountain retreat. They are "rescued" by kindly monks who take them to their fabulous monastery and treat them as guests. Due to the harsh climate and extremely remote setting, contact with the outside world is infrequent and unreliable. They are to be guests for an indefinite period; in the meantime, they have access to all the delightful pleasures of the monastery: fine food, abundant nature, a library, a conservatory, conversation. Each character responds differently to the situation, but each response signals a very personal self-reflection.

The novel focuses primarily on Conway and how he comes to understand himself more fully. He is quickly accepted by the monks and is given special treatment. He comes to realize that the peace and contemplative nature of the monastic lifestyle suit him very well. In contrast, the youngest and most zealous member of the marooned group insists upon an escape at any cost. Says Conway: "If you'd had all the experiences I've had, you'd know that there are times in life when the most comfortable thing is to do nothing at all. Things happen to you and you let them happen. The War [World War I] was rather like that" (Hilton 64). We learn that this has been Conway's modus operandi in life, in travel, and in crisis. He allows whatever presents itself to occur, and then he learns from it. It is also noteworthy that he compares this adventure to war: indeed, it takes an extreme situation to teach the most profound lessons.

The radically exotic setting and culture of the monastery function as glaring contrasts to Europe and America, thus making memories of home all the more vivid for the visitors. Part of this contrast is the familiar Oriental versus Occidental comparison: the Asian is often mythologized as inscrutable, mystical, and highly spiritual, whereas the European is forthright, rational, and pragmatic. The result is often a sense of insider versus outsider, which creates a tension. But Conway bridges the gap. He is at once a European outsider and a monastic insider. In his attempts to acclimate himself, he muses: "There came a time, he realized, when the strangeness of everything made it increasingly difficult to realize the strangeness of anything; when one took things for granted merely because astonishment would have been as tedious for oneself as for others" (Hilton 165). In fact, Conway is having a genuine crisis of the self: he is sure of neither what he is nor what he wants to be.

Once informed that the four "guests" cannot leave, Conway begins a moral struggle; accepting this policy makes sense to his monastic side, while rejecting it makes sense to his European side. Remaining in Shangri-La involves taking a potion that is an elixir of youth; he is promised extreme longevity and extraordinary pleasures of the mind. The sole condition is that he can never leave the valley. This situation functions on one level as a very powerful metaphor for travel. To be away from home is to reduce home to mere memory; the longer and farther away from home the traveler is, the more fully are memories reduced to certain elemental components. Being in Shangri-La is taking that idea to the maximum degree: you can never go home, but you can spend the next two centuries remembering and making sense of those memories. In theory, the newness of Shangri-La—and the newness of the traveler's ever-changing perspective—will yield endless comparisons and revelations.

Although the offer proposed to Conway is an intriguing idea, he rejects it in order to help his young friend Mallinson escape, which requires his own departure from the valley as he accompanies him. Yet from the frame narration we learn that Conway has since sought to return to Shangri-La, which suggests that he reversed his position in the end. This apparent reversal might be read as

acknowledging that regardless of whether one is at home or abroad, there is always something desirable happening in the opposite place. Perhaps we might call this "the grass is always greener syndrome." Part of the wisdom that travel teaches us is that the world marches on without us.

As is usually the case with utopian literature, the idyllic paradise turns out to have some serious flaws. Shangri-La, while on the surface and in theory a seemingly ideal society, appears monstrously selfish at a deeper level and in practice. Preserving music, literature, philosophy, and ideas in a vacuum fails to benefit humankind and runs counter to the tradition of the Humanities. Furthermore, a society with precise and invariable rules, however benign, denies its citizens freedom. Even apparently "good" endeavors—such as art, music, and literature—can be pursued to excess. Once again given the troubled time in which Hilton wrote the novel, I feel that we must consider the book gravely skeptical of extremism of any sort.

Thus as a work of travel literature, *Lost Horizon* depicts a journey to a mythical land; but it is this journey that demands that the participants—and we as readers must be numbered among them—reflect upon their own cultures. Only by getting outside of the familiar can we see ourselves. In the best cases, this learning is then returned to the original culture, either in the individual or in the literature.

References: Hilton 1960

HOOD, THOMAS

In 1826, to depict his journey to Rotterdam, Netherlands, while his beloved remained in London, Thomas Hood (English, 1799–1845) penned his delightful poem "To ★★★★★." Hood was a minor early-Victorian figure who is noteworthy also for the array of magazines that he edited and his friendship with literary notables Charles Lamb, William

Hazlitt, and Thomas De Quincey. His own published works—among them *Faithless Nelly Gray* (1834), "The Song of the Shirt" (1843), *The Plea of the Midsummer Fairies* (1827), and *Whims and Oddities* (1826)—were courteously received but never particularly famous or lauded. Hood's influential friends promoted his works to their limits; the most common praise for them is that they are full of puns, wit, and humor.

"To ★★★★★" may strike the modern reader as a particularly odd title for a poem. The row of asterisks signifies that the poet wants to protect the identity of the real person for whom it was written. As romantic involvement was often cause for scandal, propriety dictated that anonymity was to be preserved. There is a long tradition in poetry of effacing a person's name for the sake of modesty but also as a means of teasing: readers, even the one to whom the poem was dedicated, can never be absolutely sure who the author had in mind. It causes us to wonder and to speculate on the identity of his lover.

In this poem, the narrator is torn between the excitement and adventure of a Continental visit and his remorse at being apart from his love. Perhaps the poem was written to his lover, who is stuck at home, as a token of affection and fidelity. Written in seven stanzas of eight lines each, "To ★★★★★" begins with disoriented awe at arriving. Before the stanza is finished, however, the narrator has anchored himself with a familiar memory:

> From side to side I saunter,
> And wonder where I am;—
> And can *you* be in England,
> And I at Rotterdam!
> (Crossley-Holland 168)

Each subsequent stanza ends with the same sentiment: she is at home and he is abroad. The final lines depict the narrator drinking with his newfound friends but proposing a toast to "The girl I love in England." He has imported her into the pub, if only in spirit.

Instead of embracing the strangeness of his new setting, he seeks to make it resemble his familiar haunts.

"To ★★★★★" is interesting chiefly because it describes how the difficulties of travel outweigh the joys. At every turn, what might be exciting or beautiful is tainted precisely because it is not home, the defining feature of which is the presence of his lover. Rotterdam is cast in negative light: "A sort of vulgar Venice" where "They deal in foreign gestures, / And use a foreign speech." It is the difference from what is familiar that keeps reminding him of home. Although he gripes in every stanza, the narrator tells of a luscious range of sensual pleasures he encounters while abroad, from the "silver moonbeams . . . restless in their sleep" on the canals, to the tobacco of hookahs in the coffee shop, to the variety of wines in the bar. In spite of such praiseworthy elements, the narrator remains aloof and at times snobbish. Even the rhythm of the poem suggests stiffness and constraint. Indeed, the protagonist of this poem refuses to embrace the pleasure of being in a foreign land.

References: Crossley-Holland 1986

HOUGHTON, FIRST BARON

See Milnes, Richard Monckton

HUXLEY, ALDOUS

Most famous for his utopian novel *Brave New World,* Aldous Huxley (English, 1894–1963) also wrote travel literature with considerable skill. Although raised in a prominent family and educated at Oxford University, Huxley was known for his biting criticism of pretentiousness as well as for his dry, satiric wit. He had studied medicine but never practiced due to his poor vision; nonetheless, all of his writing demonstrates his scientific background. His nearly 50 published books fall into many categories.

As an affluent and successful man of letters, Huxley traveled widely and whenever possible. His journal of a yearlong voyage through India, Burma (modern-day Myanmar), Malaysia, Japan, China, and the United States was published as *Jesting Pilate: The Diary of a Journey* (1926). A vivid and loosely kept account, *Jesting Pilate* records his observations, adventures, and encounters along this strange route. It appears that this voyage made a lasting impression on Huxley, for his beliefs and attitudes underwent a marked shift toward mysticism following this trip. It is no leap to assert that Huxley's travels changed him.

Beyond the Mexique Bay (1934) chronicles Huxley's expedition in the Caribbean, Guatemala, and Mexico. Compared to the adventures captured in *Jesting Pilate,* this journey appears to have made a less favorable impression on Huxley. He is often critical and cranky in his descriptions. By this point in his career, Huxley had adopted a spiritual mysticism as his guiding light, and perhaps the West Indies and Central America were something of a disappointment with their strong Catholic beliefs. Nonetheless, *Beyond the Mexique Bay* is significant as travel literature in that it describes a traveler reconciling his preconceived notions with what is in fact before him. The span between expectations and reality is often great; in this book Huxley focuses on what happens when a traveler bridges that gap.

Island (1962), which took its title from Lord Byron's 1823 poem of the same name, tells the story of the HMS *Bounty.* Huxley takes the tale and weaves a novel around it. While not entirely travel literature, *Island* has several elements beyond the lineage of its title that make it travel writing. Like *Brave New World, Island* creates a utopian culture, this time on an island called Pala. As readers, we become visitors to this strange and exotic place. We necessarily form cultural comparisons and experience the same sort of self-reflection that is key to any work of travel literature.

These three works in particular represent the best of Huxley's travel literature. Together they depict an enormously learned man continuing his education and honing his self-awareness by traveling and engaging foreign cultures. His voyages made a profound difference in his own life as well as in his writing. Huxley grows via cultural cross-pollination, and as readers, we can follow that development over the course of his prolific career.

See also: Byron, Lord
References: Harvey 1967; Newby 1985

J

Then yields his courage to his Enemies,
And stops their way with his hew'd flesh,
 when death
 Hath quite depriv'd him of his strength and
 breath,
 So have they spent themselves; and here they
 lye,
A famous mark of our Discovery.
(Adams 166)

As an expression of the willful sacrifices that these early explorers made—and as a dramatic tale of the human spirit—James's journal is worth a look.

References: Adams 1988; Christy 1894

JAMES, CAPTAIN THOMAS

The claim to fame of Captain Thomas James (English, 1593?–1635), a minor explorer, is the exploration of the southern reaches of Hudson Bay. He was searching for the elusive Northwest Passage. Upon returning to England, he published his account, *The Strange and Dangerous Voyage of Captain Thomas James* (1632).

His story is indeed a harrowing tale: his crew reduced to a dozen, James had his men build a shelter and sink the ship in order to save it from being crushed in the ice. They endured the frigid Canadian winter, suffering great privations and miseries, until finally the weather broke and they could raise the ship for repairs. These completed, they happily returned to England.

James's journal is at once both gripping and pitiful. It expresses the perseverance, the tenacity, and the bravery of these spirited explorers. James depicts himself as a remarkably enlightened leader: depending upon the situation, he could be incredibly compassionate, wholly democratic, or unflinchingly firm.

Upon leaving the settlement, James composed a poem to honor those who died during the winter. Its final lines express the bitter glory that marked the mission:

Their lives they spent, to the last drop of
 blood,
Seeking Gods glory and their Countries
 good.
And, as a valiant Soldier rather dyes

JAMES, HENRY (JR.)

Author of a vast number of highly acclaimed books, Henry James (American, later British, 1843–1916) penned several remarkable works of travel literature. An avid traveler and a nearly compulsive writer, wherever he went he wrote reflective, insightful, and provocative essays. His subjects ranged from history to art and architecture to profiles of individuals he encountered. His four greatest works of travel literature were published relatively early in his career: *Transatlantic Sketches* (1875), *Portraits of Places* (1883), *A Little Tour in France* (1884), and *Italian Hours* (1909). His *Collected Travel Writings* (compiled and reprinted 1993) contains a number of shorter works including *English Hours, The American Scene,* and a series of otherwise uncollected travel writings. In these books James concerned himself with invoking the history of the places he visited and then engaging that historical current in the present.

Born to a well-to-do intellectual family, James was shuttled between Europe and the United States throughout his childhood. Henry James Sr. insisted that Henry Jr. and his brother, William, be given the finest education. The family employed private tutors who traveled with the family. Perhaps this is one of the reasons that James's books conjoin travel and learning: from his earliest boyhood, his tutors used travel as a part of his education. Because of his prominent family and the considerable fame and praise he achieved on his own, James had access to the rich, powerful, and famous of both Europe and America. Lesser writers might have concentrated on profiling these glittering acquaintances and their lavish lifestyles, but James almost wholly ignores them in his travel writing in favor of more abstract and broader topics.

An astoundingly meticulous and organized fellow, James reflects his own personality in his travel writings. His narratives are extremely thorough and consistently focus on history, literature, architecture, and manners of a particular place. By way of transition, he often shares his impressions and then comments upon them, thereby framing his own seemingly objective account with his own subjectivity. Constantly fascinated with the psychology of perception, James peppers his works with many wonderfully unstable moments where he undermines his own descriptions and accounts as unreliably personal and colored by any number of extraneous factors.

James felt anxious about being an American. The rawness and lack of history in the country caused him to feel rootless; as a solution, he established ties in Europe. Effectively, like many nineteenth-century Americans, he adopted the European heritage and all its trappings. James sought social, aesthetic, and intellectual grounding in the great Continental traditions. To learn this bearing, he first read voraciously and then went to experience those places. In this regard, James used travel as an integral part of his ongoing education. In many of his novels the contrast between America and Europe plays a central role; indeed, it is by traveling between the two cultures that James was able to gain extreme insight into both.

James rightly deserves his reputation as a master stylist. His travel writing mixes cerebral meditations with emotional outbursts.

His long, complex paragraphs are often exhausting with their physical details and related cultural asides. He includes little by way of dialogue, preferring instead extended descriptions and analyses. As in his later novels, his travel literature strives for an evocative realism and psychological credibility.

As a highly educated intellectual, James spices his travel literature with an abundant array of classical literary references. From Heroditus to William Shakespeare to John Milton to Jean-Jacques Rousseau, and everyone in between, his profusion of allusions effectively enhances his accounts. James's essays roam freely off their topics, but he always seems to return to a few familiar themes.

A Little Tour in France chronicles one of his trips to France. This expedition appears to have been politically as well as sociologically motivated. James, as usual, dwells on the historical background of the places he visits. Given the weight of the French Revolution in France's history, James often anchors the places he visits in 1789 and then traces their history backward and forward from there. He also spends considerable time observing and analyzing architecturally significant places, including Chenonceaux and Fontainebleau. Lastly, James seems vexed by the general French rejection—socially, artistically, historically—of their Roman heritage. Thus when visiting, for example, Rouen, he is bothered by the apparent lack of respect for and denial of the town's ancient history.

Transatlantic Sketches and *Portraits of Places* both contain a variety of observations of Europe. Concentrating on cultural history and architecture, these books contain numerous noteworthy images of buildings, structural highlights, and common scenes. Interesting for what they include, these books provide a number of insights that only an insider could supply. As travel guides, they are interesting and useful, for they offer a particularly sophisticated series of descriptions. In addition, they afford a glimpse of what a late-nineteenth-century traveler might have found noteworthy.

The essays comprising *Italian Hours* were not collected and published until after the turn of the century. They are unrelated articles written in the 1860s and 1870s over a series of tours and travels. Said James of one such visit to Italy: "At last—for the first time—I live!" (Fussell 438). In this volume James writes often of Italy as a singular place, generalizing about behavior and national traits. There are some more specific accounts in the collection, including another loving description of Venice. As with his other works, James remains critical of modernization and change, asserting that "all this modern crudity runs riot over the relics of the great period" (Fussell 441). Yet James does not come across as insolent; rather, it is his familiarity with and obvious love for Italy that allow him to be critical without being obnoxious. *Italian Hours* reads like a loving eulogy for Italian greatness flavored with lavish examples from a variety of cities. Additionally, what James saw as lamentably modern remains extremely interesting to the contemporary reader who may be tempted to idealize nineteenth-century constructions.

His less famous and perhaps less magnificent travel writings include *The American Scene* (1907), which describes a long trip around America after two decades of absence, and *Essays on London and Elsewhere* (1893), which focuses on England.

Furthermore, travel and journeys play significant roles in many of James's novels. Very often, visiting starkly contrasting cultures causes his characters to develop in ways they had not anticipated. *The American* (1877) is a love story that contrasts French and American manners and mores. *The Europeans* (1878) depicts a fictitious European observing New England, and as such, it clearly can be labeled a travel novel. In this intricate and psychologically complex tale, travel functions not only as the backdrop for the plot, but also its very essence.

James imagined his travels as if he were observing some sort of show: the story surrounded him, and it was his job to make sense of it. He viewed himself as a detached spectator, obliged to take notes and weave a story from the great history that flowed around him. As he wrote of Venice for *Century* magazine in November 1882:

> Venice. It is a great pleasure to write the word; but I am not sure there is not certain impudence in pretending to add anything to it. Venice has been painted and described many thousands of times, and of all the cities of the world it is the easiest to visit without going there. Open the first book and you will find a rhapsody about it. . . . There is nothing more to be said about it. Every one has been there, and every one has brought back a collection of photographs. . . . It is not forbidden, however, to speak of familiar things, and I believe that, for the true Venice-lover, Venice is always in order. There is nothing new to be said about it certainly, but the old is better than any novelty. . . . I write these lines with the full consciousness of having no information whatever to offer. I do not pretend to enlighten the reader; I pretend to give a fillip to his memory. (Rugoff 607–608)

These lines epitomize James's travel writing: introspective and evocative at once, and clearly in love with the topic. For James, texts are but reminders of real places; never can an account replace an actual visit.

References: Adams 1988; Fussell 1987; Harvey 1967; Newby 1985; Rugoff 1960

JENKINSON, ANTHONY

As the Renaissance spread northward, the whole European continent found itself in a mercantile competition. Vast fortunes were to be earned from importing goods from Asia; the principal difficulty was the great distance that provided numerous opportunities for thieves, pirates, storms, wild beasts, and endless other impediments. Anthony Jenkinson (English, ?–1611) was one of many merchants of the Elizabethan era who sought his fortune by trade with Asia and his fame by writing about it.

His account of his travels, *Voyage from Moscow to the City of Bokhara* (1561), relates his attempt to find an easier—and thus more lucrative—overland route to the Silk Road. He was convinced that traversing Russia was his best bet, and toward that aim, he first journeyed to Moscow to become the captain-general of the Muscovy Company of London Merchants. He arrived in 1558 and spent the next two years trying to make it to China. After considerable difficulty—the usual storms, mutinies, thieves, illnesses—he reached the desert regions of Central Asia. Still confident, he equipped himself with a caravan of 1,000 camels and countless porters. For eight months, he plodded through the desert looking for the trading cities of Bokhara (Bukhara) and Samarkand (Samarqand).

The region at the time was firmly under Turkish command, and it had withered as a central hub of trade because Arabian merchants sought to avoid their Turkish enemies. Within weeks of finding these cities lacking in the goods he sought, Jenkinson sold his caravan and returned to Moscow with the recommendation that a Russian trade route to China was impossible.

Jenkinson's narrative is noteworthy for several reasons. First, his calm narration of harrowing and bitterly disappointing events suggests that his attitudes about travel took for granted grave danger and a strong likelihood of failure. In other words, though he sought to make his living by traveling the trade routes, he found the journey interesting and exciting in itself. Second, Jenkinson shows us the bold spirit of a newly emerging capitalist sensibility: part of the value of goods from Asia came from the difficulty of obtaining them. Travel serves as a sort of business in this case. Third, his writing style is among the best of the Elizabethan merchants. His prose is witty, dramatic, and at times quite amusing, while his opinions are bold, brave, and genuine. He does not color his description with overly excited awe, but rather with an endearing sincerity. It is this earnestness that makes him both enjoyable and interesting to read.

See also: Silk Road
References: Morgan 1886

JOHNSON, SAMUEL

An indispensable character in the history of English letters, Samuel Johnson (English, 1709–1784) remains famous in many regards. His prolific career produced many works, including the *Rambler* (a newspaper he published and edited), *A Dictionary of the English Language, Rasselas,* and *The Lives of the Poets.* Beyond these formidable contributions, he also wrote two fascinating books of travel literature: *A Journey to the Western Islands of Scotland* (1775) and *Journal of a Tour to the Hebrides* (1785).

Although he traveled periodically throughout Europe, his journey to Scotland and the Hebrides Islands (in the company of James Boswell) seemed to have most inspired his travel writing. Dr. Johnson believed progress to be propelled by observational learning. To his mind, a keen observer abroad might learn volumes that might aid Britain: "Let Observation, with its extensive view / Survey mankind from China to Peru" (Fussell 130). Significantly, he sought the nearest foreign other to study in detail.

A man of enormous energy and prominent ideas, Johnson started life with modest means and worked extremely hard to better his position. After a failed attempt at teaching, he found that he was able to eke out an existence from his writing. Slowly, the momentum of his career built, abetted significantly by his *Dictionary of the English Language* in 1755. After this point, he became moderately famous and continued his prolific textual production. His fame and fortune increased significantly, and he redoubled his

An eighteenth-century print depicting Samuel Johnson (Hulton Deutsch Collection/Corbis)

told. He that enters a town at night and surveys it in the morning, and then hastens away to another place, and guesses at the manners of the inhabitants by the entertainment which his inn afforded him, may please himself [alone]" (Fussell 241). Indeed, such superficial travelers offer readers nothing entertaining or educating. To cure this ill, Johnson took his time traveling and meeting local folk of all categories. With his tremendously broad knowledge and his easy way with conversation, he found that the best way to engage people was by talking with them. In addition, Boswell and Johnson prided themselves on utilizing a variety of methods of locomotion, from walking to barges to post carriages.

His books thus document his travels through Scotland with great detail and precision. Rather than following the traditional chronological travelogue format, Johnson's books are organized by place-names. For each town, he writes an essay describing the physical as well as the sociological specifics of the place. Although his intention was praiseworthy, Johnson's obsession with completeness tends to stifle his stories: they often plod through seemingly endless details and historical references. Nonetheless, nestled amid the facts is an extraordinarily multifaceted image of Scottish life in the late eighteenth century.

Although Dr. Johnson's modus operandi was engagement, he writes his text from a detached perspective. Rarely does he quote or recreate a conversation, preferring instead to summarize and relay what he deems to be of value in the exchange. The effect of this narrative voice is a reassuring sense of objectivity, although on some level we know that we are at his subjective mercy.

Another intriguing aspect of Johnson's text arises from the way in which he represents Scotland as almost exotic. Unable to understand the dialect in many cases, amazed at the rugged geography, and astounded at the social behavior of the villagers, Johnson depicts a land that seems as foreign as deepest Africa. Implicit in this stark contrast is a

efforts to leave his mark upon a number of disciplines. As he gained prominence, he found himself in a circle of London intellectuals, including Boswell. The two became fast friends and traveled widely together.

One of his stated goals of the trip to Scotland with Boswell (1773) was to write a different sort of travel text than was popular in his day. Generally, he found most travelogues uninspired and dull. He blamed this mostly on the mode of traveling: "The greater part of travelers tell nothing because their method of traveling supplies them with nothing to be

default comparison to his familiar life in literary London. Perhaps predictably, Johnson's book met with mixed reviews. For his conservative politics, the Scots maligned him; for his effusive praise of the beauty of Scotland, the British scorned him. Regardless, one of the enduring elements of Johnson's travel writing is that it did not shy away from controversy or offensiveness.

In the end, Johnson's travel writing values education. It is through observation and engagement that we learn of difference, and in so doing, we are often forced to adjust our own opinions. As he writes in an essay titled "Some Rather Conflicting Observations on Travel,"

All travel has its advantages. If the passenger visits better countries, he may learn to improve his own, and if the fortune carries him to worse, he may learn to enjoy it. . . . Books of travels will be good in proportion to what a man has previously in his mind; his knowing what to observe; his powers of contrasting one mode of life with another. (Newby 15)

We will let this stand as a summary of Dr. Johnson's travel projects. Irreducibly, travel and writing reside at the core of learning.

See also: Boswell, James
References: Drabble 1998; Fussell 1987; Newby 1985

KALM, PETER

Naturalist Peter Kalm (Swedish, 1716–1779) provides an interesting perspective on the United States in the decades just before the American Revolution. As a Swede, he had a rather different viewpoint than many of his contemporary French and English writers, who had significant colonial interests in America. In addition, as a scientist, Kalm attempts to maintain a stance of objectivity and distance.

Carolus Linnaeus, the botanist who codified a classification system for plants, commissioned Kalm's three-year journey. Kalm's scientific work stands as superior, but it is his personal journal that interests us. Although his travels began in 1748, his account of them was not published until some years after his return in 1751, and then another 20 years elapsed before Kalm's work was translated into English. That text, *Travels into North America* (1772), remains an interesting look mostly at colonial New England and Canada during a critical historical period.

Kalm's prose may not be as crafted as that of some of his literary peers, but it is decidedly thorough and descriptive. His focus is almost always comparative in nature; he usually categorizes people into one of three camps: Europeans, English colonists, or French colonists. Native Americans are mostly incidental and do not constitute a major portion of Kalm's study.

Yet in spite of his scientific form and rigid order, Kalm chooses to observe and comment upon a delightfully quirky selection of characteristics. Social mores and manners, fashion, regional language differences, climate, and cuisine all strike Kalm as notable. Pharmacology, linguistics, religion, and slavery interested Kalm as well. Detached from his subject, as though a fly on the wall, Kalm observes and analyzes the daily life of the figures he encounters.

He is often highly critical of the behavior of North Americans. Perhaps this is one reason it took two decades for the English edition to get published. But this is also one of the chief values of the text: his critical Swedish eye sees much that English and French travelers in North America did not. Indeed, it is Kalm's attempt at objectivity that makes him an interesting and informative source.

References: Newby 1985

KANE, ELISHA KENT

During the mid–nineteenth century, a mania for extreme expeditions captured the imaginations of European and American explorers. The magnetic poles of the earth provided particularly tempting destinations. Nations raced to be the first to field an exploration to these inhospitable extremes of the globe. A series of misadventures from 1845 to 1851 left several major excursions missing in action or thwarted. On his first major voyage, Elisha Kent Kane (American, 1820–1857) wrote the relatively dull *U.S. Grinnell Expedition in Search of Sir John Franklin* (later abridged and reprinted as *Adrift in the Arctic Ice Pack,* 1915).

In 1853, a team from the Geographical Society of New York set out for the Arctic in search of clues as to the fate of previous missions as well as in hopes of reaching the North Pole. Kane served as team doctor. With several Arctic expeditions under his belt, Kane had valuable experience and medical knowledge. This trip too was ill-fated. The crew expected a grueling and harrowing journey; what they got was vastly worse. That some members of the team survived remains remarkable. But they did succeed in setting a record—namely, they attained the distinction of traveling "Farthest North" (at the time) by reaching 80°10' north. Kane's gripping and vivid account, *Arctic Explorations* (1856), met with resounding success both because of its terrifying content and its exciting writing.

Kane's text is a great example of the desire to go where no man had gone before. He clearly demonstrates how compelling it was to go where few, if any, men had ever set foot. In one way, this sort of exploration is pure travel: the voyage is both the means and the end. In this case, Kane traveled simply to reach his destination and then to return. In the process of extreme travel, the voyager learns of himself, for adversity brings out his best and worst characteristics.

Arctic Explorations tells of the northbound route on the ship *Advance* and then subsequent forays over the ice in sleds. The treacherous ice eventually trapped the ship, and the team had to set out over the ice for northern Greenland. Already two years into the journey, the men were tired and weak. When they left the ship, they packed a month's worth of food; their trek ended up taking 83 days. Aided by friendly Etah Eskimos, what remained of the party eventually emerged in civilization.

Upon return, the team was regarded as heroic. Kane, however, was mortally weakened by the ordeal. He rushed through the writing of his book and died within a year of its release.

For its agonizing details and its understated depiction of courage and tenacity, *Arctic Explorations* ranks high on the list of adventure travel literature. As an example of travel for its own sake, the text is also noteworthy. And lastly, as a well-told story, all the more exciting for its truth, Kane's book succeeds.

References: Newby 1985

KEROUAC, JACK

Beat poet Jack Kerouac (American, 1922–1969) is often a favorite of travelers. After completing his education in New York, Kerouac embarked upon a life that would send him wandering around the globe. His extensive travels in the United States and Mexico are chronicled in his quasi-autobiographical novels and poetry. He also visited Europe, North Africa, and Asia over the course of his life.

Kerouac fits into many categories, among them travel writer. His stories embrace the excited discoveries that come from encountering a new place full of different people. *On the Road* (1957) is Kerouac's most clearly defined example of travel literature in that the plot itself is driven by the notion of motion. While there are considerable elements of travel writing in some of his other works, we will concentrate on this single text as an example.

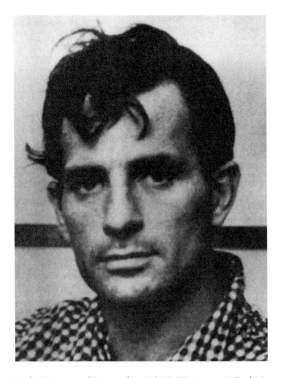

Jack Kerouac, photograph c. 1958 (Bettmann/Corbis)

On the Road remains Jack Kerouac's most famous novel. It defined beatnik attitudes about motion, travel, and inspiring places. Ultimately, the characters figure out that being on the road is better than actually being at the destination; it is the state of being in motion that inspires the imagination.

The novel is a story of a young writer named Sal Paradise (modeled on Kerouac himself) who sets out to have a few last adventures before settling down into a more mainstream and conservative lifestyle. Along the way, he encounters a host of wild and countercultural characters who help him to grow emotionally and spiritually. The most vivid and influential of his friends is Dean Moriarty (based on Neal Cassady), perhaps the ultimate Beat: "his soul was wrapped up in a fast car, a coast to reach, and a woman at the end of the road" (Kerouac 4). Dean is both ex-convict and con man, constantly stirring up trouble, yet his overwhelming charm and energy make him the likable center of attention. As such, he is descended from the traditional figure of the picaro. He inspires fierce loyalty in Sal, among others, and devotion from his string of lovers; but in the end, Dean finds himself unable to return the favor: he deserts Sal in a Mexican hospital in order to head back out on the road.

A number of colorful characters revolve around Dean. Carlo Marx (based on Allen Ginsberg), the friend with "two piercing eyes—the holy con-man with the shining mind, and the sorrowful poetic con-man with the dark mind," (7) serves as the intellectual of the bunch. Old Bull Lee (based on William S. Burroughs) is the drug-addicted elder of the group who is tied down with a wife, kids, and a house but who nonetheless manages to provide a wild time whenever anyone is passing through. Roland Major is the antithesis of Sal: he too is an aspiring writer, but instead of using travel as his muse, he stagnates, "a choleric, red-faced, pudgy hater of everything" who sits in his "silk dressing gown composing his latest Hemingwayan short story" (40–41). Remi Boncour, the Frenchman with the big heart, is down on his luck but always in a jovial mood, ready to spend what little cash he can scrape together. Terry is the Latina migrant worker who teaches Sal about trust and simple pleasure; he nonetheless deserts her. And Marylou, Camille, and Inez are the long-suffering girlfriends who try to win Dean's elusive affections. Each character has his or her own personal struggle that is deferred by the carefree times on the road.

Sal, Dean, and a combination of cohorts bounce repeatedly from New York to Denver to California with numerous detours. Each city, each region, has its own unique characteristics: "all around us was fragrant green grass and the smell of fresh manure and warm waters. 'We're in the South!'" (138). After several cross-country jaunts, they imagine the ultimate road trip: from New York down to South America. Once they immerse themselves in the foreignness of Mexico, they begin to realize how closed-minded they have been. Encountering a radically different culture forces them to become even more aware of the constraints under which they had lived. Once removed from familiar expectations, they experience the most magical and mystical—but unsustainable—time of their lives.

The state of being on the road is characterized by a nearly limitless openness to any chance happening; unexpected turns in the road are what thrill. As a response to the staid American 1950s, Kerouac's novel provides a means of protest against conservative expectations. Where the mainstream culture sought order and predictability, the Beat generation embraced disorder and happenstance. The road provided a seemingly unending source of new people and places. Both literally and symbolically, *On the Road* is filled with confrontations between the establishment and the counterculture: for mainstream culture, the road is a means to an end; for the Beats, the road is an end in itself.

Perhaps the novel depicts travel as an ambivalent metaphor for life: to live, to travel, is to have great potential but also to leave some things behind: "What is that feeling when you're driving away from people and they recede on the plain till you see their specks dispersing?—it's the too-huge world vaulting us, and it's good-by. But we lean forward to the next crazy venture beneath the skies" (156). Ultimately, *On the Road* presents travel as rebellion and freedom.

See also: Picaro
References: Kerouac 1976

KINGLAKE, ALEXANDER WILLIAM

Historian Alexander Kinglake (English, 1809–1891) wrote one of the classics of travel literature. His *Eothen* (1844) remains a singular masterpiece of storytelling and adventure. The text is at once thrilling, emblematic of the Victorian age, and a benchmark example of engaging travel writing.

As a student of the classics at Cambridge University and then a law student in London, Kinglake was known for his skeptical views and cheerful disposition. After taking his degrees, he opted for an extended tour of the Near East in 1834. With his loyal translator and friend Mysseri, Kinglake sought exotic adventures throughout the Islamic Ottoman Empire.

Abundant adventures and crucial life lessons greeted Kinglake over the next 15 months. Though he made copious notes and sent some interesting letters home, his text was not published for 10 years. During this time, he crafted the stories for maximum effect and polished his prose to its gleaming present state. When *Eothen*—Greek for "out of the East"—was released, it met with immediate praise and affection. For more than a century, Kinglake's text reigned as one of the finest and most popular examples of travel literature. Contemporaneous travel writer Jan Morris described *Eothen* as "one of the most original, graceful, and creative of all travel books, which has cast a sort of spell over the genre from that day to this" (Fussell 328).

Written as a series of letters to his schoolmate Eliot Warburton, *Eothen* feels congenial and intimate. Yet we rapidly discover that the epistolary form is but a device: the letters grow far too lengthy to be actual. Over the course of the text, Kinglake proffers advice on travel and routes, remarks on architecture, engages a bewildering selection of people, and reflects on the nature of travel. Always cheerful, positive, and good-humored, he sets the standard for happily allowing his adventures to occur. In this regard, we might imagine his book more novelistic in that the central focus of the story is as much on Kinglake's own character as it is on his destinations.

One of the factors that makes this text pure travel literature is Kinglake's own insistence that his book is simply a story of his own experience. He presumes no grand or lofty motives save entertainment and the occasional intuitive lesson. In his preface Kinglake describes his book as

quite superficial in its character. I have endeavoured to discard from it all valuable matter derived from the works of others, and it appears to me that my efforts in this direction have been attended with great success; I believe I may truly acknowledge that from all the details of geographical discovery or antiquarian research—from all displays of 'sound learning and religious knowledge'—from all historical and scientific illustrations—from all moral reflections, this volume is thoroughly free. (Kinglake 1)

Indeed, Kinglake's realm is not science or history or theology, but rather life experience and the human spirit.

Charming and unflappable, Kinglake plunges into his adventures with zest and glee. Though Cairo reeled under the plague, he delights in his time there; though lost in the forests of Servia (Serbia), he marvels as the vast unspoiled nature of the place; though delayed in the scorching desert, he finds great beauty and peace. Regardless of his adventures, Kinglake casts them in a positive light, learning from every single experience.

Often hilariously funny, *Eothen* reads like a journey, rambling and amiable. Never shy to launch into obtuse tangential asides, Kinglake evokes the free-associative thinking that is a feature of travel. Constantly comparing foreign manners and behavior to English standards, Kinglake gently learns of and recognizes the arbitrary construct of such codes. Graceful and inoffensive expression of these lessons may be one of the primary merits of the text: it teaches of life and happiness with humor, humility, and patience.

Without a doubt, Kinglake's text has had a great influence on modern travel writers. His imprecise itinerary would become the traveler's norm. His jocund and merry tone embodies the ideal gentleman traveler of the nineteenth century. And his nonjudgmental perspective would serve as an example to many of the great travelers of the next century. Kinglake subtitled his story *Traces Brought Home from the East,* and undoubtedly the fragments of experience and wisdom that he collected are still precious today.

References: D'Oyley 1932; Fussell 1987; Kinglake 1908; Newby 1985

KNIGHT, SARAH KEMBLE

As a bold young woman, Sarah Kemble Knight (American, 1666–1727) wrote a much-praised account of her journeys in the colonial Northeast. Her diary, *The Journal of Mme. Knight,* remains a valuable historical document for its precise geographic detail and for its commentary about gender roles in early eighteenth-century New England. Meticulously accurate about street names, descriptions of buildings, geography, and other physical details, she provides a clear picture of the region. In addition, she narrates the actions and words of nearly all whom she encounters, thus demonstrating social interactions.

Her account details a trip from Boston to New York to New Haven in 1724–1725 (along what is now known as the Boston Post Road). Employing a sophisticated narrative voice, Madame Knight depicts herself as a fearless—and tireless—judge of character and social critic. Each day's account is thorough and often ends with an original poem. Her work is filled with lively accounts of adventures: unpalatable food, wretched weather, bizarre characters, and unexpected occurrences. As a woman from a well-established family, she would have been expected to stay with well-to-do acquaintances along the way. Shunning cultural expectations, she stayed at several roadhouses with people she met on her journey. The result is that she travels through social classes as well as from town to town. At every turn, however, she maintains a joyous sense of humor and a keen wit. Always quick to step back and to make the best of a situation, Madame Knight stands out as an embodiment of the spirit of travel.

LA SALLE, RENÉ-ROBERT CAVELIER, SIEUR DE

René-Robert Cavelier, Sieur de La Salle (French, 1643–1687), was one of the most intrepid explorers of the New World. As a writer of travel literature, La Salle poses something of a problem: unfortunately, he neither kept a journal or a diary, nor was he a faithful correspondent. Yet his stories and deeds are astounding. We know of them via loyal comrades who wrote exhaustively about him and his explorations. Because his travels were so vast and grand, La Salle deserves to be included in this volume despite the fact that he did not personally write the accounts.

Compounding the matter is the fact that he did not have a single and constant biographer. Rather, a sequence of followers wrote and published their accounts of La Salle's adventures. Father Membré chronicled La Salle's voyage down the Mississippi River in 1682; La Salle's brother Jean wrote of his explorations of Canada; Louis Hennepin compiled and embellished a set of stories allegedly told by La Salle; Father Chrestien Le Clercq described La Salle on his ships; Father Anastasius Douay focused on La Salle's late travels in the southwestern portion of America; and Henri Joutel attempted a life story of La Salle. Undoubtedly, to merit this quantity of interest, his actions must have been extraordinary. Excerpts from all of these writers have been collected by I. J. Cox into a two-volume set called *The Journeys of René-Robert Cavelier Sieur de La Salle* (1922).

Well educated and from a prosperous family, La Salle made his first excursion to the New World with his older brother Jean in 1666. The two La Salles bought land and prospered, but both brothers had the urge to explore. After learning a number of Native American languages and making numerous small sorties, the two decided to seek a passage to the Pacific. Other North American explorers, including Samuel de Champlain, Alvar Núñez Cabeza de Vaca, and Hernando de Soto, had sought a Northwest Passage or a river route to the West Coast; apparently, these voyagers had little sense of the vast width of the North American continent.

La Salle had heard the Native Americans talk of a vast body of water to the west; he surmised that this might be the Pacific Ocean. At the time, Pennsylvania and Ohio were fairly well mapped, so La Salle took the Ohio River west and eventually reached the Great Lakes. He explored and mapped the region now known as the Midwest with great precision. Building small forts, trading with the natives, and living mostly off the land, La Salle's tales are fascinating for their complex representations of Native American cultures, for their accounts of the vastness of the heartland wilderness, and for their descriptions of the ingenuity of this tiny party of travelers.

The years 1673–1685 La Salle spent making extended trips to the frontier, then back to the East Cost, and several times returning to France. After the Midwest, he turned his sights on the South and followed the Mississippi down to the Gulf of Mexico. Following a less elaborate visit to the Gulf, La Salle focused his attention on Texas and Mexico. His travels in the Southwest were also filled with considerable adventure and excitement. Father Douay's account of this portion of La Salle's career is quite good and renders a detailed picture of the man and his ideas. It also provides an account of La Salle's death: allegedly, he was betrayed and killed by some of his followers.

As La Salle was a major explorer with such a collection of secondhand contemporary sources telling his tales, we can bend the rules a little and include him in this volume. For, indeed, all accounts suggest that he was a man who loved to travel and who loved to learn. On his many journeys, he engaged an array of cultures with equal openness and honesty; throughout, he set an example for all with his forthright manner and deep sense of piety.

See also: Cabeza de Vaca, Alvar Núñez; Champlain, Samuel de; Northwest Passage
References: Adams 1988; Cox 1922

LAHONTAN, LOUIS-ARMAND DE LOM D'ARCE, BARON DE

One of travel literature's many enigmatic characters, Louis-Armand, Baron de Lahontan (French, 1666–1715), undoubtedly felt the need to be in motion. His life was filled with explorations, adventures, and travels near and far. He published a wildly successful volume titled *New Voyages to North America* that was revised and expanded several times as well as translated into numerous languages. In addition, contemporaries have told many of his tales in other works. In this regard, he is perhaps more famous as a traveler than as a writer. The combination of his legendary adventures and his single best-seller, however, earns him a place in this volume.

Born to wealth and privilege, Lahontan exerted his formidable leadership skills as a teenager. By age 17 he was a bold French officer stationed in Canada serving under La Salle. A soldier and a philosopher, Lahontan was concerned with the conquest of the North American wilderness and the spread of Christianity to the native populations. It should be noted that he was often critical of the missionary zeal exhibited by many of his fellow officers and explorers. He nonetheless led forces in numerous battles with a variety of Native American tribes. Legends of vast deposits of gold in the Southwest and in Mexico lured him away from Canada and the French military into expeditions of his own. These prospecting ventures succeeded in finding nothing but more stories—wild tales that are almost certainly exaggerated in Lahontan's writings.

His disappointment at not finding great mineral wealth and his dismay at not discovering (by chance) what is now known as the Northwest Passage evidently bothered Lahontan considerably. His letters suggest a mounting sense of failure as an explorer; this led him to ever more desperate schemes. He returned to Europe and wandered there, selling his services as a spy, explorer, and general adventurer. He never published his writings from this period.

While he might have thought himself a failure, Lahontan's writings made a considerable impression on eighteenth-century Europe. Perhaps his greatest contribution was the form he chose to employ for his writings. His book contains numerous "letters"—some actually sent, most contrived diary entries—and intellectual "dialogues." In the latter, he recounts his alleged discourses with a Canadian Native American named Adario. Like Plato, Lahontan uses the dialogue format as a rhetorical device rather than as an attempt at reportage. This form of polemical discourse is said to have influenced such major figures as Denis Diderot and Jean-Jacques Rousseau (Adams 174).

In the dialogues Lahontan and Adario discuss a range of topics, although the recurrent theme is Christianity. The dialogues represent a pedantic approach to constructing a "noble savage"—the conception of an innately simplistic and virtuous non-European who has not been corrupted by Western civilization—who shames the proselytizing Christian conquerors. Says Adario:

> If your Religion differs from ours, it do's not follow that we have none at all. Thou knowest that I have been in France, New-York, and

Quebec; where I Study'd the Customs and Doctrines of the English and French. The Jesuits allege, that out of five or six hundred sorts of Religions, there's only one that is the good and true Religion, and that's their own; out of which no Man shall 'scape the Flames of a fire that will burn his Soul to all Eternity. This is their allegation: But when they have said all, they cannot offer any Proof for it. (Adams 182)

Throughout the dialogues, Lahontan challenges the status quo European ideology and justification for conquest of the New World.

Lahontan's letters, on the other hand, are more factual and touch on cultural differences, geography, myths, family structure, diets, daily life, and much in between. They remain interesting as material history and for their details, but they lack the literary flair and ideological punch of the dialogues.

In the end, Lahontan's is a difficult case to categorize. His writings amount to a hybrid: part fact, part fabrication, they defy neat boundaries. To confound matters, his position seemed to change over the course of his career. In his early works he exhibits a brutal cruelty toward Native Americans, whereas in his later writing he seems wholly sympathetic to them. Perhaps he learned from his travels to question his beliefs. Regardless, for his daring deeds and for his formal innovations, he deserves a position as a noteworthy figure in the history of travel literature.

See also: La Salle, René-Robert Cavelier, Sieur de; Northwest Passage
References: Adams 1988

LAWRENCE, D. H.

Another major literary figure whose artistic production includes several works of travel literature is David Herbert Lawrence (English, 1885–1930). Author of numerous novels, poems, essays, and short stories, Lawrence belongs in many categories at once. In his life and in several of his books, however, Lawrence may be considered a traveler. *Twi-light in Italy* (1916), *Sea and Sardinia* (1921), *Mornings in Mexico* (1927), and *Etruscan Places* (1927, posthumously published in 1932) are each delightful and provocative in their own respect. Besides these purer forms of travel literature, Lawrence's novels often contain exotic locales and challenging journeys; they often rely upon travel and exploration to propel their plots. His collected letters, variously published, also contain many examples of fine travel writing.

Although English by birth, D. H. Lawrence spent most of his life living abroad. Remarkably, over the course of his life, he lived in Italy, Germany, Ceylon, Australia, New Zealand, Tahiti, France, Mexico, and the United States. His novels and poems received both praise and sanction; some of his earlier work was banned as scandalously sexual. Such prudery enraged Lawrence and led him abroad. In addition, he is often noted for his naturalism and his mysticism. All three of these fascinations—for sensuality, nature, and mysticism—figure prominently in his travel writing. As his body of work grew, he came to be recognized as one of the finest and most innovative writers of the twentieth century.

Lawrence needed to be in motion. He sought to invigorate himself by changing cultures radically. Learning a new set of customs, manners, geography, and habits thrilled him and kept his astounding powers of observation occupied. A man of gigantic passions, he loved discovery and newness perhaps most of all. With his wife, Frieda, he wandered the globe, trying to discover the minuscule differences between cultures while all the time confirming some universal human characteristics. For Lawrence, nature was a kind of god, and the more he traveled, the more he learned of a singular natural world.

Delighted by the residue of classical history, Lawrence visited repeatedly and later lived in Italy. Both *Twilight in Italy* and *Etruscan Places* sprout from an attempt to reconcile the past with the present. Although both texts roam widely through Italy, they are interesting to contrast: the earlier text reads more like a standard modern travelogue, whereas the latter is a more general eulogy to travel and motion. Both texts propose the existence of a sort of spirit that colors a place and that represents history. To be sure, Lawrence idealizes Italy and its romanticized classical history. Nonetheless, his queer and seemingly random set of observations lends realism to each of the texts and makes them highly evocative. Included in *Twilight in Italy* are several sections devoted to Switzerland and Germany, while *Etruscan Places* remains only in Italy, tracing Etruscan tomb paintings.

Following a brief visit to Sardinia in 1921, Lawrence allegedly wrote *Sea and Sardinia* in a mere six weeks (Fussell 475). Always fond of islands—he thought they increased the intensity of every emotion—Lawrence creates with this text a vivid sketch of his impressions. Nearly obsessed with color, light, the contrast between water and land, he writes often breathlessly of his sensations. Gently blending geographic specifics with historical references and subjective opinions, Lawrence's book reads more like a novel than a travelogue. Full of richly textured descriptions of encounters, activities, and reflections, *Sea and Sardinia* must be one of the most genial and enthusiastic examples of travel literature in the canon—that collection of works deemed the authoritative list of literary classics.

Entranced by legends of the Aztec civilization and deeply intrigued by mysticism, Lawrence also authored *Mornings in Mexico,* which reads like a collage of images pasted roughly together. The tropic flora and fauna of Mexico seem to fascinate him. Ever capricious, this story too wanders gently and discovers a strange assortment of people, places, and ideas. Perhaps Lawrence sought to mimic the pleasure of exploration in his writing, for, indeed, the book feels like the first evening in a foreign place. His paragraphs meander like winding streets; his sentences have the texture of cobbles protruding.

Travel and writing are the stuff of Lawrence's life; he seems to have found equivalent joy in getting there, being there, and writing about there. As he commented to his wife in *Sea and Sardinia,* "To tell the truth there is something in the long, slow lift of the ship, and her long, slow slide forward which makes my heart beat with joy. It is the motion of freedom" (Fussell 1987). Such freedom Lawrence certainly enjoyed and shared with his readers.

References: Fussell 1987; Rugoff 1960

LAWRENCE, T. E.

Thomas Edward Lawrence (English, 1888–1935)—also known as Lawrence of Arabia—regarded adventure as a duty. Rigorously educated as a classicist and archeologist at Oxford University, Lawrence set out for Syria, where he traveled and excavated. As the turmoil of World War I approached, he was commissioned by British Intelligence to serve as a spy and a soldier. For more than a decade, he traveled the Middle East, blending his duties as an intelligence officer with his interest in archeological history and his fascination with Arab cultures.

His lone book is a classic of travel literature: *The Pillars of Wisdom* (1926). Its creation is a legendary story in itself: the original manuscript was lost in 1919, so he rewrote it without notes. But he deemed the result unsatisfactory and destroyed this version too. Finally, he produced a third version that he tentatively sent to press. Originally printed in very limited numbers and then released again in a much larger run in 1935, at the end of Lawrence's life, the text continues to be popular and to remain in print.

The scarcity of the original, first edition only fueled the fire for the text: copies were coveted, and the text was discussed as something rare and precious. An abridged version was first released in 1927 and is titled *Revolt*

Photograph of T. E. Lawrence riding a camel (Bettmann/Corbis)

in the Desert; it sold very well. Surprised and rather bothered by the sensational success of his book and the fame it brought him, Lawrence changed his surname to Shaw in 1927 and became a pilot in the Royal Air Force. He refused a knighthood and the Victoria Cross (a military award granted for valor) for reasons that are unclear.

The Pillars of Wisdom chronicles Lawrence's quest for a contribution to archeology and his political influence with Arab leaders. His extensive travels in the region led the British government to recall Lawrence to Egypt in 1916. At the briefing in Cairo, he learned that he was to aid the sharif of Mecca in his uprising against the Turkish forces. His success in leading the rebel forces was phenomenal. Through craft, guile, and bravery, he led his troops in a series of legendary exploits. Part of his genius was his unpredictability: at times he favored traditional military engagement, while at other times he devised smashingly effective guerilla campaigns.

Lawrence's writing is curious as well. Sometimes his prose swaggers with bravado, and sometimes it is gently inflected with tender sympathy. Much more than a tale of insurrection, Lawrence's campaigns are treated like strange holidays: his observations are more cultural, historical, linguistic, and geographic than militaristic. His experiences, however, are often harrowing and terrifying, yet he rarely acknowledges difficulty in favor of a detached, matter-of-fact tone. In addition, his education manifests itself, for his account brims with classical, Elizabethan, and romantic allusions and references.

Lawrence's quirky behavior provides a fascinating subject for extended study. Presuming that he was in earnest in his modesty, we can consider him one of the true travelers of his day. For Lawrence, travel and adventure were not extreme moments to be captured and brought home as ornamental sources of fame; rather, they were moments in life, chances to learn, and part of ordinary behavior. His arduous strife for literary perfection seems to have been driven by a sense of obligation, which implies that, for Lawrence, travel and writing were inseparable.

References: Harvey 1967; Newby 1985

LEONOWENS, ANNA

Recently rediscovered as a figure well worth serious study, Anna Leonowens (Welsh, 1834–1914) is a fascinating subject. Her four books, *The Romance of the Harem* (1873; sometimes listed as *The Romance of Siamese Harem Life*), *The City of Veiled Women* (1872), *The English Governess at the Siamese Court* (1870), and *Life and Travel in India* (1884) are splendid examples of the most sophisticated sort of travel literature: part autobiographical travelogue, part adventure fiction, and part philosophical treatise. It is hard to decide whether to treat each book as a separate subject or her life as a single work; I have chosen the latter option, particularly having been persuaded by Susan Morgan's introduction to the University of Virginia Press edition of *The Romance of the Harem.*

As a young girl, Leonowens (born Crawford) was left with a governess while her parents went to India. Her father was killed and her mother remarried, and only as a teenager was Anna allowed to join her mother. Evidently fascinated by these exotic lands and ill-treated by her family, Anna made several solo journeys throughout India and the Middle East. She met Major Thomas Louis Leonowens in Bombay and married him a year later. After seven years, Major Leonowens died and left Anna with two children. She attempted various ways of making a living—among them serving as governess and running a school—and eventually set out for Bangkok. Why she chose Bangkok remains a mystery.

At least this is the traditional story. New scholarship has cast some significant doubt on this history (for a fuller account, see Morgan 1991). Nonetheless, it is certainly the case that she arrived in Siam (now Thailand) to work as a royal governess. From these experiences, she wrote her novels.

They must be considered novels, regardless of the historical and "factual" data they employ, because they contain numerous contradictions and historical inaccuracies. No one doubts that Leonowens had an incredibly privileged perspective on the court of Siam; indeed, it is perhaps the only Western account of this subject ever written. As a woman, she had access to the City of Veiled Women and King Mongkut's harem—two things no European male had ever seen. Such secrets made her books extremely desirable. She had traveled where all the male adventurers could never manage to go; the resulting allure was irresistible. Her stories have been retold variously in other forms, perhaps the most famous being the Rodgers and Hammerstein musical *The King and I.*

Her novels revolve around her own story of earning the respect of King Mongkut, who apparently took an especial liking to Leonowens. The stories tell of their relationship: both parties teach each other of their hugely differing cultures. She crosses not only class but cultural boundaries; in so doing, she is an intrepid voyager. The relationship between Leonowens and the king is troubling. While it appears to have been an intellectual fascination, little in her writing suggests that Leonowens had a particularly keen intellect. Perhaps we shall never know the full details, but this much is certain: she had some clear influence on the king and a level of freedom unheard of in a restrictive, absolutist society.

Leonowens's storytelling is a vivid first-person narrative that slips occasionally into a rather believable free indirect discourse. Her tales are often haunting and graphic: torture, enslavement, and brutality pepper the text. But if her tales reflect the darker side of Siamese culture, they also describe Buddhism in a very favorable light and the City of Veiled Women as something of a sanctuary.

Her descriptions of these almost mythical places are some of her best work. In terms of the City of Veiled Women, she tells of an almost utopian society of females and eunuchs. While many were wives and concubines of the king and his court, many were also female teachers and merchants. In all, she boasts that this thriving city had a population of around 9,000 residents! In *The Romance of the Harem,* she presents us with the converse: the sugar-coated slavery of concubinage. Instead of wallowing in the anguish of the situation, however, Leonowens gives us the story of how these women overcome their terrible lot.

The issues addressed in Leonowens's work are many, including gender roles, absolutist politics, imperialism, slavery, and the relationship of literature to history. In looking at a radically different culture, Leonowens urged her Victorian readers to evaluate their own culture. By concentrating on the other, she makes her analysis of her own culture more palatable. As literature, her books are progressive and exceptional; as history, her life appears to have been equally so.

References: Morgan 1991; Rugoff 1960

LEVANT

Levant refers to the countries of the eastern Mediterranean. The word is derived from the ancient French *levant,* the present participle of *lever* (to rise). It was adopted into English to mean the point where the sun rises. Thus the countries of the East, particularly the eastern Mediterranean, are said to be "the Levant." For example, "Many years spent in the Levant had darkened his skin."

The name obviously is Eurocentric; the Levant to a Turk would be India, the Levant to an Indian would be Oceania. Using the word in its fullest sense anchors one's perspective in Europe.

It is also possible to argue that we tend to figure a day as progressively developing like a human; it begins like a child and ends as an old man. As such, the East, the Levant, is the infant undeveloped. Only in the West, that is to say Europe, does the brightest point of the day emerge. To extend the metaphor, west of Europe is the decline, the move into darkness. Clearly, this sense of the word makes *Levant* a problematic term. Perhaps this is why the term is rarely used any longer.

References: OED

LEWIS, NORMAN

Norman Lewis (English, 1914–) has visited an astounding number of places. His novels, travel essays, and magazine articles are numerous and diverse. He penned significant texts that describe Italy, Spain, the Balkans, the Middle East, and Southeast Asia. While his novels are set in a variety of international and exotic locales, the are not usually considered travel literature. His nonfiction, however, is among some of the best travel writing of the late twentieth century.

A Dragon Apparent (1951) describes the turmoil and anguish in Vietnam, Cambodia, and Laos caused by a succession of ruthless colonial governments. It can easily be read as prophetic of the horrors that loomed on the horizon for the U.S. intervention in the region at the end of the decade. In addition, it addresses the always-thorny question of what happens to folk wisdom and ancient customs when "modernization" and "progress" are ushered in.

An Empire of the East (1994) finds Lewis fascinated on his journey through Indonesia. With some 15,000 islands, a complete tour of Indonesia is obviously impossible. More interested in politics and ethnic differences within Indonesia, Lewis restricts this book to three islands: Sumatra, East Timor, and Irian Jaya. Like many of Lewis's travel books, this one is endearing in its seemingly random set of observations. Lewis becomes like a fly on the wall watching and describing what he sees. In this manner, the book bounces lightly from strange and wonderful characters to climate to quirky anomalies of a culture that has modernized very rapidly. Just as the contrast between the familiar West and the exotic islands of Indonesia causes interesting tension, so does the contrast between old tribal ways and modern global standardization. In these tense intersections, we find Lewis telling his story and dubiously wondering at the nature of so-called progress.

A Goddess in the Stones (1992) chronicles his expedition to India. Lewis's perspective is rare: although he sees with the eyes of a European accustomed to certain material conveniences, he appears quite willing to live in the grueling poverty of the locals and is little bothered by such conditions. Instead of complaining about the wretched conditions, he earns the locals' respect—and consequently their trust—by sharing their plight. He enthusiastically narrates his experiences in feudal states like Bihar, in the slums of Calcutta, and among some of the small, rather hostile tribes. The massive beauty of Indian history and culture is blended with the very real human squalor; the result is a tale of human spirit and courage that cannot help but cause readers to reflect upon their own will to survive.

Voices of the Old Sea (1985) is a charming tale of Spain and Catalonia. It focuses on the old traditions of fishing villages and the hearty attitudes that come with relying on nature for employment. When not fishing, the people are tending to cork trees. Tender and amusing, it is filled with folk wisdom and an appealing look at a culture that seems impossible in the modern era. Once again, the clash between contemporary city life and the remnants of the Old World is a deeply moving and provocative subject that encourages us to wonder at the sense of modern society.

An odd mix of autobiography that reads like fiction, *The World, the World* (1988) might be called a metatravel tale. In disjointed essays of various excursions and encounters throughout the wide world, decades apart, the narrator tells of his initiation into and subsequent infatuation with the world of travel and travelers. In constant motion himself, and recounting the letters and tales of other travelers whom he meets, this is a rich and interesting treatise on the compelling nature of travel. With episodes on four continents, this book may be one of the best samples of Lewis's travel writing available. As he revisits places after decades of absence, we begin to see that travel is always about growth and change, both on the part of the place and on the part of the traveler.

Lewis blends descriptions with analytical commentary seamlessly and gracefully. Exotic places and situations serve as more than drama: they make a difference in his ideas and in his understanding of himself. From his hilarious scenes at the traditional Vietnamese banquet to his delight at the colors of jungle foliage, Lewis has a keen eye for detail and an amiable way of telling a tale. His tone is familiar and delighted with the endless distinctions between the foreign cultures and his more familiar English ways.

References: Newby 1985

LITHGOW, WILLIAM

The history of William Lithgow (Scottish, 1582–1645) strains the imagination. Part traveler, part sideshow, Lithgow claimed to have walked nearly 40,000 miles through Europe, Asia, and Africa over the course of a two-decades-long tour! He was jocosely known as "Cut-lugged Willie" as a result of having lost his ears—they were cut off by four brothers who happened to discover William amorously entangled with their sister (Newby 112). More than a curious anecdote, this early misadventure prefigured a raft of difficulties and unfortunate accidents that were to befall Lithgow throughout his life. Metaphorically, life is often described as like a journey; in Lithgow's case, most of his life literally was one extended journey.

Lithgow meticulously chronicled his epic voyage and published his book shortly after his return to Scotland in 1629. The title is rich indeed: *The Totall Discourse, of Rare Adventures, and Painful Peregrinations of a Long Nineteene Yeares Travayles* (1632). In fact, in the 1682 Wright and Passinger London edition, the full title provides a great summary of the book:

> Lithgow's nineteen years travels through the most eminent places in the habitable world: containing an exact description of the customs, laws, religion, policies and government of emperors, kings, and princes: also of the countries and cities, trades, rivers, and commerce in all the places through which he travell'd: also an account of the tortures he suffered under the Spanish Inquisition by racking and other inhumane usages, for his owning the Protestant religion: together with his miraculous deliverance from the cruelties of the papists, which far exceeded any of the heathen countries herein described

Quite a mouthful for a title!

Like his contemporary Thomas Coryate, Lithgow provides a wealth of fascinating stories of incredible adversity. Unlike Coryate, however, Lithgow seems to have had consistently bad luck. Discerning how much of his story to believe is a tricky matter; generally, Lithgow's tale is thought to be reasonably accurate. Nonetheless, for centuries readers have gone wide-eyed with wonder at his tales. There is some evidence to suggest that Voltaire's character Candide owes some debt to Lithgow.

In fact, *Rare Adventures and Painful Peregrinations* (an alternative shortening of the title in some editions after 1770) often feels more like a farce than a travelogue. Lithgow found himself tortured by the Inquisition, beaten and robbed by bandits, chased by wild animals, buffeted by the elements, jailed, and beset by illness over the course of his travels. To be fair, we must remember that all this took place over a span of 19 years. Conversely, he also found himself dining with princes, exploring the holy lands of Jerusalem, experiencing natural and man-made wonders, and encountering things beyond the limits of imagination.

Lithgow's writing style is astoundingly straightforward. He recounts nonchalantly the most harrowing experiences—which occur in nearly every episode. For example, in Transylvania he finds trouble with bandits:

> I was beset with six murders, Hungarians and Moldavians: where having with many prayers saved my life, they robbed mee of threescore Hungar Duccats of gold, and all my Turkish clothes, leaving me stark naked. . . . For their better security, they caryed mee a little out of the way, and bound my naked body fast about the middle to an Oaken tree . . . swearing to me that if I cryed for helpe, or marred them of their designes before the Sun set, they would turne back and kill me. . . . But night come, and I forgotten, was left here in a trembling feare, for Wolves and wild Boares till the morrow. (Newby 112–113)

Always, he persevered and continued on to additional adventures, all described with detail and detachment.

Beyond being simply exciting to read, Lithgow's book provides an invaluable insight into daily life in the early seventeenth century. His attention to detail, aided considerably by his apparent knack for languages, allows his readers a substantive look into many foreign lands and cultures. Although some travelers sought goods to bring home to trade, Lithgow sought only stories. Ideas, descriptions, tales were what he brought home and shared with Britain, thus teaching of foreign cultures, of geography, and of difference. Such literary production remains one of the fundamental motives of all subsequent travel literature. Within the history of travel literature, Lithgow, Coryate, and others represent a distinct stage. While seafaring voyages and explorations had a sense of glory and grace, overland peregrinations before roughly 1650 were rare and agonizing endeavors. Unlike later travel writing, which often served to promote or glorify the foreign, overland travel of the sixteenth and early seventeenth centuries was dangerous, painful, and generally unpleasant. It served as a reminder of why one would not want to stray too far from home. Those who did dare were obliged to write of the adventure; such writings served as a replacement for travel.

See also: Coryate, Thomas; Voltaire
References: D'Oyley 1932; Newby 1985

LIVINGSTONE, DAVID

Another of the famous African adventurers of the nineteenth century, David Livingstone (Scottish, 1813–1873) must be noted as a fascinating character whose deeds were more impressive than his writing. But his journeys were so overwhelmingly dramatic that even the often-ponderous journals are interesting to read.

Portrait of Rev. David Livingstone, c. 1850–1900 (Library of Congress)

As a medical missionary, Livingstone first went to Africa with extraordinary compassion for the native peoples. He soon found, however, that geography and exploration were even greater passions. Spurred on by the common Victorian urge to go where no white man had gone before, Livingstone spent 30 years seeking new peoples and places in Africa. "And always," writes Milton Rugoff, "underlying all other motives, was the daemon of the explorer, an irresistible desire to go on and on" (Rugoff 320).

Livingstone's collected journals run many hefty volumes. For decades, he made faithful daily entries; this exercise alone is fascinating. To be able to trace the daily activities of anyone for nearly 30 years is remarkable. His observations cover an amazing range of topics as well. Both the natural world and the various cultures he encountered figure prominently in his journals, but he also dives into philosophical discourses, theological debates, medical research, and political theory. His journals are an astounding testament to a man who devoted his life to learning. Over the years he seems to have retained a love of learning and an open mind; within his journals are numerous examples of changing his mind or learning something new that forces him to admit to having made a mistake.

Apparently very hardy, Livingstone rarely found himself ill. As a white man in the interior, he was already intriguing; combine that with a shrewd mind and medical learning, and it is no wonder that the natives respected him deeply. Due to the permanence of his travels, Livingstone was able to retain a select core of companions whose devotion was unflinching. When he died, his native friends preserved his body and carried it 1,500 miles through the jungle to the coast (Rugoff 321).

Livingstone's motivation for travel and writing was clearly mixed: on the one hand were the thrills of adventure and discovery, and on the other was his ardent desire to stop the slave trade and to improve the living conditions for Africans. In his introduction to the account of his 1866 voyage to explore the Nile's source, he writes: "Now that I am on the point of starting on another trip into Africa, I feel quite exhilarated: when one travels with the specific object in view of ameliorating the condition of the natives, every act becomes ennobled" (Livingstone ii).

He believed that his travels and his writing, though hard work, were a credit to himself and to his culture. His glory comes from his seemingly sincere desire to help the African peoples; along the way, he gained fame as a brave and bold explorer. It is also interesting to note that while the ostensible purpose of the journey is to explore, he implies that by so doing he can improve the situation of the natives.

One of the more remarkable aspects of Livingstone's character was that hardships never seemed to discourage him. By his logic, the harder the struggle, the greater the glory; by extension, the greater the glory, the greater the pleasure. Therefore, to Livingstone, adversity equated with pleasure. This is demonstrated most clearly in the story of his final days. Without a doubt one of the most dramatic passages in all of travel literature, we as readers get to watch as his journal entries diminish to nothing.

Various editors have compiled and arranged the journals and stories of those who were with Livingstone in order to recreate a description of his brave demise. In spite of pain, delirium, and utter disability, Livingstone insisted upon going forward, even if it meant being carried in a sort of litter. Virtually paralyzed with various maladies, Livingstone pressed his company to continue. Finally he expired, praying, after an agonizing few days. The narrative itself demonstrates the tenacity of this man; that it is completed by his friends demonstrates how truly beloved he was.

As one of the great travel tales of our culture, Livingstone's journeys embody the spirit of adventure as a means to learning. Travel in Livingstone's journals is hard and dangerous work; the product of that labor is glory and progress. His impact upon various native peoples was great; his contribution to geographic knowledge was significant. But more important to this project, Livingstone is a legend whose deeds function almost as myth. While his writing may not constitute great literature in itself, Livingstone himself functions as a literary character. In this regard, the story of Livingstone's adventures can teach us quite a lot.

See also: Stanley, Sir Henry Morton
References: Livingstone 1874; Rugoff 1960

LORD, W. B., AND THOMAS BAINES

W. B. Lord (English, fl. 1870s) and Thomas Baines (English, 1822–1875) were both travelers and writers. Lord was a military man, and having served in the Victorian era when British colonial ventures were booming, he saw his share of military excursions. Baines was an artist and a minor explorer who had completed excursions to Africa and Australia. While neither has the distinction of writing exquisite travel literature, they did combine to write a singularly valuable resource for travelers: *Shifts and Expedients of Camp Life, Travel, and Exploration* (1876).

The book is a massive work, filled with detailed illustrations and vast in scope. Because of its physical size—no tiny paperback volume was printed—it must have been intended as something of an encyclopedia of travel and exploration skills. Indeed, it can still serve as a course in creative problem solving in the bush. As prerequisite reading for adventure travel, Lord and Baines's text set the standard. Although it is impossible to tell just how many travelers saved themselves by practicing what they had learned in *Shifts and Expedients,* it is safe to assume that the history of travel literature would be less rich had they not written this book.

In this astounding compendium, Lord and Baines cover a huge assortment of topics, from treating snakebite to constructing

rudimentary shelter to navigation via stars, and a bewildering number of issues in between. More than a simple survival handbook, however, *Shifts and Expedients* is fascinating because of its at times bizarre solutions (which I can only presume would be effective). For example, "In cases of extreme necessity, and when the preservation of human life depends on the obtainment of water, the supply to be found in the stomach of the camel should not be overlooked or forgotten" (Newby 17). Indeed not!

Utilizing sources as diverse as tribal customs, folk wisdom, British military survival manuals, and the science of the day, Lord and Baines compiled solutions to thousands of potential problems. By reading this manual as a list of what adversity might occur while on an expedition, we can see clearly that tourism and adventure travel are very distant cousins.

References: Newby 1985

LOTI, PIERRE

Pierre Loti is the pen name for Louis–Marie–Julien Viaud (French, 1850–1923). He began his career at age 17 as a naval officer, the result of which was a fascination with foreign places and peoples. Indulging in his creative urges, he selected a nom de plume and began writing sentimental adventures set in exotic locales while progressing through the military ranks. Naval service provided him endless opportunities for travel and ample time to capture the stories on paper.

Loti's books combine evocative, impressionistic descriptions with melodramatic encounters between European and local characters. The result is a series of romanticized tales of travel, exploration, and (often-amorous) cultural engagement. Later in his career, his novels focused on France, and while they have elements of travel in them, they are certainly not travel literature. This mature work is often more heavily praised, but his earlier work is why he appears in this volume.

Loti's literary output amounts to a great number of books. His travel literature alone includes at least 10 volumes; his letters and correspondences increase the number. Often thinly disguised, the narrators of his fictional tales resemble the author himself. His novels, conveniently, are set in places he had visited. Says Percy Adams, a scholar of travel literature, of Loti's novels: "They are in fact travel books disguised as novels" (Adams 595). Although the plots of these novels are exaggerated—if not fabricated—their wealth of detail makes them fascinating as well as entertaining.

Loti's travel novels are many. I will briefly summarize the best that have been translated into English. *Aziyadé* (1879), set in Constantinople and on the Turkish Aegean coast, may be the most cliché and manic of Loti's novels, but it contains extraordinary details of the sultan's opulence—replete with a famous harem scene. *The Iceland Fisherman* (1886) describes a North Sea romance. Set in Brittany, it is the story of a woman waiting for her seafaring lover. *Madame Chrysanthème* (1887) is the story of a Japanese geisha and her French "husband." It also served as one of several sources for Puccini's opera *Madame Butterfly*. *The Exile* (1891) recounts the romance between a sailor and a Romanian princess. They meet in various European ports and delight in the variety of architectural, cultural, and historical differences.

In all cases, there is an overwhelming sentimentality to Loti's novels: love is at the center of them all. They are filled with vivid and scintillating descriptions of their settings. They often end sadly, even tragically, as the male sets out for new adventures. We might read this trend in several different ways. Perhaps it suggests that travel is a greater lure than romance: once hooked on the life of adventure, a man cannot be held down. Or perhaps more subtly we may interpret this pattern as a way of recognizing substantive cultural differences: the male "heroes" believe that they can understand their lovers, but in fact they are always wrong. We might infer that Loti's novels sought to warn nonchalant men of the potential pain they could cause by being irresponsible and culturally ignorant.

In addition to his novels, Loti wrote a number of travelogues. Oddly, he used his pseudonym but told the stories in a travelogue form. Nonetheless, his accounts are often as breathless and exuberant as his novels. *Le Mariage de Loti* (1880) takes place in Tahiti and is a dreamy, idealized account of an island paradise that had the reputation of uninhibited sexuality. *Jérusalem* (1885) and *Galilée* (1885) both describe Loti's visit to the Holy Land. His reflections on religious history and the usual ancient sights are especially rich with detail. *Impressions* (1898) is particularly interesting: its subject is travel in general. This text should be among the classics of travel literature, but because Loti is often maligned as monothematic and overly sentimental, it is usually overlooked. His impressionistic vignettes of various travels and his discussions on memory, learning, and pleasure (to say nothing of romance) make this text a first-rate collection of travel musings. *India without the English* (1903) represents a slight political barb: the colonial competition between France and England manifests itself in Loti's repeated critique of the Raj. Politics aside, it is a wondrous foray into a richly historical culture. *Toward Isfahan* (1904) describes Loti's excursion to the Middle East. As always, he is enchanted with the difficulties: the harsh desert, the nasty camels, Bedouin bandits, and so forth.

Throughout, Loti's style of writing is dramatic and his adventures are described with novelistic flair. Like a child wide-eyed with wonder, Loti narrates his voyages in great torrents of adjectives and modifiers. With his superior eye for detail, he gushes descriptions in his travelogues—the result of which is that his texts hover on the edge of unbelievability.

While exotic places feature prominently in almost all of Loti's writing, such locales function primarily as a backdrop for his romantic novels. In most of his stories his narrator is blasé about places but passionate about what happens to occur there. One example, from *The Exile,* will suffice: "Still, on the present occasion, I scarcely look at this marvelous Venice; the only value it has to me now is that of being a charming accessory, a somewhat ideal background or frame to the sweetly sad figure of the queen, the fairy I have come to visit" (Adams 596). We may also read into this passage a hint that it is the process of the visit—or any travel—that matters. Simply achieving the goal, be it a visit or a journey, may be the ostensible aim of the exercise, but the entire process is where the lessons lurk.

Another theme that runs throughout Loti's writing is the necessity of engaging local peoples whenever possible. Such interactions and exchanges help the traveler to better know foreign places. In *Madame Chrysanthème,* for example, the French naval officers are having an afternoon's holiday in the Japanese countryside. One Frenchman exclaims delightedly how far away from home they are. The narrator muses, "There can be no doubt that in this spot we are a great deal farther away from France than we were this morning on board the *Triomphante.* Whilst one is on his own ship, that travelling house he has brought with him, he is surrounded by the faces of his own countrymen, by all the customs and habits of his land, and this deludes him" (Adams 603). The distance—both physical and psychological—between Japan and France is more clearly manifest when they have escaped the familiar space of their ship. Upon encountering the unfamiliar, the sailors must quicken the pace of their learning: they come to see their own and the foreign cultures more clearly.

All in all, Loti's contribution to travel literature has been considerable. The sheer magnitude of his travels and the quantity of his published work mark him as a major figure. The quality of his writing and its universal interest in travel make him a joy to read as well as a valuable source of historical, cultural, and geographical data.

References: Adams 1988; D'Oyley 1932

M

MACLEAN, SIR FITZROY

Sir Fitzroy MacLean (Scottish, 1911–1996) is one of the adventure travelers who carried the traditions of nineteenth-century travel literature into the modern era. Much like Robert Byron in terms of route as well as literary style, MacLean describes an arduous series of destinations in his decidedly modern work of travel literature, *Eastern Approaches* (1949). While author of a number of travel books, including *Escape to Adventure* (1950), *A Person from England, and Other Travellers* (1958), *Back to Bokhara* (1959), *Yugoslavia* (1969), *To the Back of Beyond: An Illustrated Companion to Central Asia and Mongolia* (1974), and *To Caucasus, the End of All the Earth: An Illustrated Companion to the Caucasus and Transcaucasia* (1976), MacLean's best work of travel literature remains *Eastern Approaches*.

Over the course of his career, MacLean wore several hats: diplomat, traveler, member of Parliament, writer, and spy. His courage, tenacity, and quick wit are all readily apparent to any reader of his texts.

Eastern Approaches tells of MacLean's defiant journey into the Soviet Union beginning in 1937. Naturally, the political climate was tense, but with the brashness of his youth and the pluck of his character, MacLean succeeded in traveling throughout Central Asia. He used his employment as an official of the British government to facilitate some parts of his journey, but mostly his travels were driven by his own curiosity. Indeed, the fact that there was so much political resistance to foreign travelers in the Soviet Central Asian states seems to have made them all the more desirable as destinations. Part of the joy of visiting a forbidden or foreboding place is the difficulty one must encounter. In this regard, MacLean carries the heritage of the true travelers: adversity makes the journey sweeter and piques the traveler's desire to go.

The story begins with MacLean departing Paris for Moscow. As with every departure, there is a momentary sadness at leaving. Quickly, he recovers his zeal and asserts, "But now it was time for a change. I have always relished contrasts, and what more complete contrast could there be after Paris than Moscow? I had seen something of the West. Now I wanted to see the East" (MacLean 11). His journey begins with a desire to contrast the familiar to the foreign, and throughout his epic journey he notes differences and learns from the other.

From his post in Moscow he plans his trip, first making a sort of reconnaissance voyage to Baku. This miniature voyage turns out to be a success and fires MacLean to renew his planning. Ostensibly, he embarks on a journey to Siberia, a less restricted region, but surreptitiously switches trains in a provincial city. With Soviet agents tailing him at a safe distance, MacLean heads toward Central Asia.

His difficulties range from the simply inconvenient to the life threatening. He describes endless bureaucracy, treachery, and bad food as well as incredible monuments, amazing history, and a warm welcome from apolitical locals. Playing cat and mouse with various agents assigned to monitor his activities, MacLean bluffs, bribes, and chances his way safely across vast distances, from Alma-Ata to Tashkent and finally to Samarqand. Rather than satisfying him, this trip only increases his desires.

Over the course of the next two years, while based in Moscow, MacLean makes a number of different, and ever more daring, journeys to Central Asia. The triangular contrast is interesting: a Scotsman living in Moscow and visiting Central Asia compares all three. Subsequent forays include travels to Mongolia, Chinese Turkestan, Kazakhstan, Uzbekistan, and Afghanistan.

By 1940 the war was on, and MacLean was recruited by British Intelligence. He writes of the interview: "For [the last] six years, they said, I had been learning my job" (MacLean 148). He responded in characteristic fashion: this was another sort of journey, sweet because of its risks.

The second half of *Eastern Approaches* finds him based in Cairo. MacLean's intelligence-gathering trips send him across North Africa and the Middle East. With the same traveler's eye, he describes his wartime adventures. After a time, MacLean is rotated to the Balkans, where his shrewd travel skills are again employed for Allied intelligence gathering.

Part traveler's tale, part war story, part history, *Eastern Approaches* is a fascinating work of modern travel writing. Laced with heavy-handed literary allusions and tinted with vivid descriptions, MacLean's work captures the essence of travel with his excitement and his willingness to take risks. In this regard, he is one of the last of the great travelers, for most who follow are more tourists than adventurers.

See also: Byron, Robert
References: MacLean 1951

MACNEICE, LOUIS

Much has been written about Louis Mac-Neice (Irish-born, English, 1907–1963), a major twentieth-century poet. He is not usually noted as a travel writer, but his many volumes, including *Blind Fireworks* (1929), *Collected Poems* (1949), *Autumn Sequel* (1954), *Eighty-five Poems* (1961), and *Solstices* (1961), contain several notable examples of travel verse. His own peregrinations were mostly touristic in nature, but these safe vacations inspired and influenced him considerably.

Closely associated with W. H. Auden, MacNeice counted among his friends some of the era's finest minds. He was a scholar of classics, a mild social activist, and a writer, and his poems are still well respected and often anthologized. *The Oxford Book of Travel Verse,* for example, contains six of his poems. Later in life, he became famous as a lecturer and presenter on BBC radio. For the sake of brevity, two examples can demonstrate Mac-Neice's skill as a poet and his interests as a traveler. As a lauded speaker and poet, he was afforded the opportunity—or perhaps sometimes coerced—to travel widely.

"Solitary Travel" is a curious, 24-line poem that seems to lament the antiseptic nature of modern travel and the deep loneliness that traveling alone can inspire. MacNeice begins with a list of cities on several continents: "Breakfasting alone in Karachi, Deli, Calcutta, / Dacca, Singapore, Kuala Lumpur, Colombo, Cape Town" (Crossley-Holland 26). What is striking is how different these words sound, how exotic, how exciting. With their foreign textures, the words perform an abbreviated version of the distinction between such diverse places. But he goes on to comment not about the places themselves, but rather about the alienating accommodations, which adhere to a sort of world standard: "The hotels are all the same." Though some specifics may change, though the waiters are of different races—"coffee-coloured or yellow or black"—the experience is the same.

From bland hotels, he moves to "indistinguishable airports" and the identical game of customs, regardless of the country. It is only in the final stanza that MacNeice offers a solution: " . . . If I could only / Escape into icebox or oven, escape among the people." This is the traveler's dream: to escape the rote—to shun the familiar routine of the global tourist and to encounter difference in a foreign place. With his somber words and flat tone, MacNeice evokes drudgery; it is travel, that bright and bold exposure to the new and different, gone horribly awry.

In contrast, MacNeice's poem "Mahabali-puram" describes his visit to India and the spiritual as well as physical excitement he found there. With its long and highly embellished lines, the poem describes an ornate and beautiful holy site. In the dark, slightly threatening space, he describes the fantastic and provocative sculpted reliefs of the Hindu gods Vishnu and Siva and exclaims, "Behold what a joy of life—" (Crossley-Holland 317). The experience of the foreign in this case has helped MacNeice's narrator to see value and joy in his own life. His awe at the aesthetic and spiritual beauty of the scene affirms his own vitality. Indeed, is this not one of the principal and ideal values of travel?

He continues for several elaborate stanzas to describe the experience of these works of art. At the end he concludes,

> But the visitor must move on and the waves
>   assault the temple,
> Living granite against dead water, and time
>   with its weathering action
>   Make phrase and feature blurred;
> Still from today we know what an avatar is,
>   we have seen
> God take shape and dwell among shapes, we
>   have felt
> Our ageing limbs respond to those ageless
>   limbs in the rock
>   Reliefs. Relief is the word.
> (Crossley-Holland 319)

The traveler has been touched by what he has seen and has learned from this wholly foreign icon. His encounter with the strange has shed light upon the familiar, and he feels a sense of satisfaction and fulfillment. In this exposure to both a distant culture and a different time (the reliefs are thousands of years old), the narrator feels part of something larger, perhaps a human history that transcends individuals or even single cultures.

Thus in some of his poems MacNeice demonstrates several of the core themes of travel literature. Sprinkled throughout his poems and letters are many such nuggets that mark MacNeice, among other things, as an interesting travel writer. Perhaps MacNeice can best be considered a travel writer in that he laments the antiseptic replacement of travel with tourism.

References: Crossley-Holland 1986; Harvey 1967

MAGELLAN, FERDINAND

A mere three decades after Christopher Columbus had made it across the Atlantic Ocean, Magellan (Portuguese, 1480–1521) set out to circumnavigate the globe. Attempting the journey would have been bold enough; Magellan actually completed it, thereby proving that the earth was undoubtedly round. Like Columbus, Magellan was driven by the desire to find a trade route to the East. His story is told in *Voyage round the World* (1522).

While both Columbus and Magellan sailed under a Spanish flag, neither one was a Spaniard. Because of Spain's great wealth, power, and ardent desire for a better trade route, explorers from surrounding countries found ready support there for their voyages. Magellan was Portuguese by birth, but he seemed to have little allegiance to his homeland.

In 1519, Magellan set off on his mission to locate the Moluccas (the Spice Islands). Finding sailors for his small fleet had been a great problem, for the bold nature of the voyage, its formidable duration, and lingering fears of the flatness of the earth dissuaded many a man. Only the deep pockets of King Charles V of Spain saved the expedition. With roughly 50 men on each of his five ships, Magellan embarked.

In spite of encountering all imaginable difficulties en route, Magellan reached the coast of South America. But his voyage had only just begun. Working his way down to the southern tip of the continent proved to be slow and treacherous. A full year after leaving Spain he finally reached the howling strait that is now named after him: the Strait of Magellan. One of the more dramatic moments in travel literature, Magellan's account of the terrifying wind and waves still strikes fear in the hearts of sailors. Although he had succeeded in reaching the Pacific, his fleet was in shambles, his crew was starving and mutinous, and his confidence was shaken. Reduced to barbaric conditions, Magellan's ships sailed onward, claiming the Philippines for Spain. Soon after doing so, Magellan was killed by one of the natives.

A small crew of survivors continued on to the Moluccas, loaded their single remaining ship with cloves, and sailed home to Spain. Eighteen survived the three-year journey. Of course, if Magellan died halfway through the trip, how is it that we have an account of Magellan's circumnavigation of the globe? His secretary, an Italian nobleman named Antonio Pigafetti, faithfully transcribed the first year of Magellan's dictation; when Magellan was killed, Pigafetti continued the journals for his captain.

The joint work is remarkable because it represents so many first impressions. Many of the sights and peoples had never before been observed by Europeans; as such, the journals are often fantastic and exaggerated. After the point where Magellan died, the narrative gets less literal and more imaginative; perhaps Pigafetti was rather more gullible than his late master. Nonetheless, as a testament of bravery, determination, and spirit, the record stands as a great travel story.

The journals are also interesting in that they provide a wonderful lesson in economics. As mentioned, the ostensible purpose of the journey was to find a trade route to the Spice Islands. Spices in Europe were very rare and thus quite valuable; in the East they were common and relatively cheap. Yet along the way, the small trading that Magellan and his crew engaged in seems to me very telling. In an economy with no universal currency, *anything* can be valuable. Thus we see Magellan

trading seemingly worthless items for food and supplies: "We made excellent bargains here: for a hook or a knife we purchased five or six fowls; a comb brought us two geese; a small looking glass, or a pair of scissors, as much fish as would serve ten people. . . . Our playing cards were an equally advantageous object of barter; for a king of spades I obtained half a dozen fowls, and the hawker deemed his bargain an excellent one" (Rugoff 396–397). Magellan goes on to talk about how this sort of barter has made him think of the value of everyday items. Indeed, when put in a radically different context, the most worthless of commodities can become a rare treasure.

In the words of his secretary Pigafetti, Magellan "was adorned with every virtue; in midst of the greatest adversity he constantly possessed an immovable firmness. At sea he subjected himself to the same privations as his men. Better skilled than anyone in the knowledge of nautical charts, he was a perfect master of navigation, as he proved in making the tour of the world, an attempt on which none before him had ventured" (Rugoff 406). As a great adventurer and a subtle observer of differences, Magellan must be praised. The spirit of his memory propelled his men to complete the journey even after his death; it is that same spirit that makes his journals great.

References: Rugoff 1960

MARVELL, ANDREW

A well-educated and somewhat privileged fellow, Andrew Marvell (English, 1621–1678) had both opportunities and desires to engage in the turbulent politics of his era. He is most famous for his association with John Milton and with Oliver Cromwell, as well as for his scathing satires attacking the monarchy, but in earlier days he penned a number of significant poems that can nominally be called travel literature.

Marvell spent four well-documented years traveling on the Continent and exchanging ideas with whomsoever he could engage. He was a gifted linguist who was passionate about his ideas, and his travels are the stuff of legends. Less concerned with geography, climate, and customs, Marvell remained focused on the realm of ideas, particularly politics and religion. Although his poems circulated widely in pamphlet form or in private editions, it was not until 1681 that they were officially, and posthumously, published. Thus within his collected works there are poems on many themes and topics; scattered among the early works are several examples of travel literature, including "Bermuda" (1652?) and "The Character of Holland" (1651?). In addition, much of his early work, though devoted to more general themes, contains striking instances where he uses travel as a metaphor for understanding and knowing.

"Bermuda" served as a gift to a number of English exiles setting out for the West Indies to escape religious persecution and political turmoil. Although Marvell had never been there, the myth of the New World was vivid for him. Employing the images of the pastoral, he constructs a Bermuda that resembles a paradise found. A deeply religious man, Marvell attributes all the beauty and goodness of the New World to a kind and generous God. Thus the garden of Bermuda is bathed in "eternal spring" and is formed by a "grassy stage, / Safe from the storms" (Crossley-Holland 364–365). A land of heavenly abundance, "[God] makes the figs our mouths to meet, / And throws the melons at our feet" (365). The poem is interesting for its imaginative rendering of a foreign place and its idealized sense of elsewhere: paradise is always somewhere else, usually just over the horizon.

Marvell's long poem "The Character of Holland" is peculiar and challenging to read. While it ostensibly functions as travel literature—it contrasts the familiar to the foreign and learns as a result of the encounter—it also addresses political and religious issues.

Complex in its balance of oppositional ideas, yet engaging with its lyrical beauty and subtlety, the poem merits sustained and detailed study, which is beyond the scope of this volume. As for its being a travel tale, suffice it to say that in it Marvell takes great pains to describe the reclaimed nature of the Dutch land, its laws and politics, and its economy all within the frame of his comparison between Holland and England.

As a major metaphysical poet, Marvell has many claims to literary fame. In a small way, he may also be named a poet of travel literature for his unusual blending of travel with politics and religion. Perhaps one way to read Marvell is to imagine life itself as a journey to salvation.

References: Crossley-Holland 1986; Fussell 1987; Harvey 1967

MASEFIELD, JOHN

As a very young man, John Masefield (English, 1878–1967) set out to sea to find his fortune in the world. Meeting with grand experiences but little fortune that could sustain him, Masefield moved to the United States and bounced around the country doing odd jobs. Finding this wandering lifestyle unsuitable, he returned to England in 1901 to try his hand at writing for a living.

Drawing on his early adventures as a seaman, Masefield found he had substantial literary talent. Publishing poems, essays, articles, and fiction wherever he could, he amassed quite a record of success. Much of his early work relies on the theme of travel and adventure for its motivation, whereas his later work moves in many other directions. Although published in a variety of forms, his two early books of travel poems are usually called *Salt Water Ballads* (1902) and *Ballads and Poems* (1910). Echoes of his travels are prominent in *Dauber* (1913) and in many of his short stories, including "A Mainsail Haul" (1905) and "A Tarpaulin Muster" (1907).

Photograph of John Masefield by Pirie MacDonald, 1933 (Library of Congress)

Masefield went on to publish dozens of books on a wide range of themes. His success was great enough for him to have been named British poet laureate in 1930.

For the sake of brevity, one example from *Salt Water Ballads* can demonstrate Masefield's style and thematic focus. Often printed as an excerpt titled "Sea Fever," the passage reads:

> I must down to the seas again, to the lonely
>   sea and the sky,
> And all I ask is a tall ship and a star to steer
>   her by,
> And the wheel's kick and the wind's song and
>   the white sails shaking,
> And a grey mist on the sea's face and a grey
>   dawn breaking.
>
> I must go down to the seas again, for the call
>   of the running tide

Is a wild call and a clear call that may not be
    denied;
And all I ask is a windy day with the white
    clouds flying,
And the flung spray and the blown spume,
    and the sea-gulls crying.

I must go down to the seas again, to the
    vagrant gypsy life,
To the gull's way and the whale's way where
    the wind's like a whetted knife
And all I ask is a merry yarn from a laughing
    fellow-rover,
And quiet sleep and a sweet dream when the
    long trick's over.
(Crossley-Holland 21)

We can see quite obviously a number of major themes of travel literature in this section. The narrator values the journey more than the destination; being at sea, being in motion, is an end unto itself. He feels drawn to motion: note the repeated imperative, "I *must* go down to the seas again" (my italics). For Masefield, travel functions as an antidote to London society: it is a "vagrant gypsy life." To be on the seas is to be immersed in the natural world of the stars, wind, mist, tides, spume, gulls, and whales. Finally, his last request, perhaps most important, is to hear "a merry yarn from a laughing fellow-rover." Masefield recognizes the crucial role of stories in travel. To live stories and to share narratives are fundamental elements of travel; to capture those stories in writing is what makes travel literature.

References: Crossley-Holland 1986; Harvey 1967

MAYLE, PETER

In 1989, Peter Mayle (English, 1939–), an advertising executive turned writer, moved with his wife and two dogs to Provence, France. The resulting books, *A Year in Provence* (1989), *Toujours Provence* (1991), and *Hotel Pastis* (1993), chronicle some of their more memorable moments while trying to assimilate into rural French society. The tales are charming, funny, and deliciously Epicurean; they flow like an easy dinner conversation, one idea leading genially, if haphazardly, to the next. In each of the books, Mayle seems to have one underlying theme: How different is France from Britain? Fortunately, difference in this case is not negative but rather exciting; it inspires Mayle to reflect upon both his former and present homelands.

A Year in Provence follows a linear structure: it is a month-by-month account of the Mayles' first year of residence. From practical issues like actually buying the house, to linguistic peculiarities of Provençal French, to understanding rural rituals, Mayle tells even banal tales with wit and modesty. Often the butt of his own jokes, Mayle is able to laugh at his own assumptions and preconceived notions about France and the French.

Gradually, the Mayles become comfortable as expatriates; their incessant stream of British and American guests, however, serve as reminders of non-Provençal normalcy. Fools serving as comic foils to the hero, the vacationers cause us to laugh at ourselves. A businessman with a neurotic need to phone the office, weak-stomached acquaintances, sunburned idiots who refuse to wear sunscreen, and friends of friends who insist upon hospitality all remind the Mayles of the culture that they have abandoned. It is by observing and by asking often-embarrassing questions that they learn to love, and to be accepted, in their foreign home.

The second book, *Toujours Provence,* is more loosely organized around stories. They seem to flow like a forest path, one leading to another and to another, with no particular destination in mind. Our protagonists have "gone native" (in a positive sense) and seem to make far fewer mistakes. Adventures continue, guests return again and again, and the delightful characters that live in the Lubéron district continue their marvelous antics.

By the end of these two books, Mayle declares that he uses the natural world as his calendar and the sun and the moon as his clock. The rhythm of country life has forever changed the way he views the passage of time. Of course, this is a contrast to the way most of us exist, utterly dependent upon our watches and planners. Perhaps this is part of the point of the books: what we take for granted as the way everyone lives is in fact highly culture specific, not to mention class specific. Mayle has journeyed to a foreign country but also to a foreign class. Shifting from yuppie culture to farming culture is a voyage in its own right.

Hotel Pastis, though published last, actually narrates the Mayles' decision to move to France; we might consider it a "prequel" to the other two books. Without having read the subsequent history, however, the story falls flat. Most of the sterling moments of the text remind me too much of more carefully crafted experiences in the other two stories. For these reasons, *Hotel Pastis* feels like an afterthought. Regardless, when read as a trilogy, in the order of publication, this set of tales satisfies and amuses greatly.

All along the way, Mayle learns with joy. And as a result, he recites his lessons joyously. It is difference that stimulates and drives Mayle; it is also difference that teaches him lessons. By being elsewhere, by knowing and even becoming the other, Mayle learns of himself and helps us to see our own cultural quirks and foolishness. Make no mistake: Mayle is also critical, as only an outsider can be, of the French and their peculiarities. The clear vantage point provided by being away from home does not discriminate; both home and home-away-from-home receive scrutiny.

He concludes at the end of the first book, "It had been a self-absorbed year, confined mostly to the house and the valley, fascinating to us in its daily detail, sometimes frustrating, often uncomfortable, but never dull or disappointing. And above all, we felt at home" (Mayle 207). It seems to me that this is a fine description of the best sort of travel. In this self-absorption are lessons, and from fascination, frustration, and discomfort, self-reflection can follow. In the grand tradition of travel literature, Mayle both learns from his journey and then writes his lessons in order to teach with his tales.

References: Mayle 1989

MELVILLE, HERMAN

Herman Melville (American, 1819–1891) is universally known for his masterpieces *Billy Budd* and *Moby Dick,* but he also wrote a large quantity of outstanding travel literature. His travel books include *Typee* (1846), *Omoo* (1847), *Mardi* (1849), *Redburn* (1849), *Journal up the Straits* (posthumously 1935*), Journal of a Visit to London and the Continent* (posthumously 1948), and *Journal of a Visit to Europe and the Levant* (posthumously 1955). It was in fact his travel literature that nineteenth-century audiences appreciated far above his later novels.

Born into a well-to-do family that saw a sharp reversal of fortune when he was 12, Melville had to make his own way in the world after having grown up in relative ease. He most assuredly rose to the occasion. After working at various odd jobs in New York, and despising the drudgery and structure of his workaday life, Melville shipped off as a cabin boy on a transatlantic ship in 1839. So began a lifetime of travels, adventures, and literary accounts thereof.

Although the work was hard, unfamiliar, and among salty sailors, Melville found the sea to possess irresistible allure. After returning, he attempted to teach school but found the enticement of motion too strong: in 1841, he shipped out to the South Seas for an 18-month cruise on a whaling boat. Most of the factual details for *Moby Dick* were gained during this time. Bouncing about the South Sea Islands, he found adventures aplenty. He jumped ship with a friend on several occasions, was held captive by natives in the Marquesas islands, stowed away on a trading ship, worked in Tahiti, and eventually made it back to Hawaii as a whaler. This epic adventure satisfied Melville for a time. He returned to the East Coast confident that he had sufficient literary material from which to draw.

Melville was fond of claiming that the seafaring life was his education; he once remarked that, as a poor young man, the sea was the only university open to him. Travel as an invaluable form of learning is a theme that appears in almost all of his books. His early work, all travel romances, met with considerable success, and this freedom allowed him to pursue the more highly literary and abstract novels of his most famous middle period.

As a renowned man of American letters, new opportunities opened up for Melville. He went to London and Paris in 1849 but found he preferred the quiet life on his Massachusetts farm to the glittering international life of the literati. For more than a decade in the 1850s and 1860s, he remained mostly in the States, writing his masterpieces and making only brief journeys abroad. But even these small adventures had a great effect on Melville.

After this period of relative stability and prolific literary production, Melville again felt the need to travel. Some scholars attribute this restlessness to the fact that his literary reputation, surprisingly, had faltered. He found his great works did not sell nearly as well as his earlier travel writing. His solution was to make a series of lecture tours in the United States and abroad. His later years were peppered with travels across North America, Europe, the Levant, and the Mediterranean. On these trips he kept fabulously detailed notes and made typically brilliant observations. These journals were essentially lost until Melville's reputation was resuscitated in the 1920s, and they were finally published in their unpolished but nonetheless remarkable form in the 1940s.

Generally, Melville is noted as both a shrewd stylist and a gifted wordsmith. His works consistently blend realism with philosophic abstraction, and his tales are filled with allegorical or symbolic characters that have astounding complexity and depth. Behind his abstract devices, however, rests a sizable quantity of firsthand factual data. All of his travel novels are set in places he visited in his travels. Frequently, his travel writing posits natural phenomena as spiritually significant; in a sense, travel serves as a form of worship in Melville's texts.

Typee was Melville's first novel and is based largely on his own voyage to the South Seas. That said, many of the accounts are significantly exaggerated or embellished for dramatic purposes. After more than a year at sea on a whaling ship, the narrator (Tom) and his friend (Toby) jump ship in the Marquesas Islands. Tired of lousy food, backbreaking work, and a tyrannical captain, they abscond to paradise. A perfect antidote to their hellish ship, Typee delights them. They are revered by the natives, treated as honored guests, feted, fed, and allowed access to beautiful girls. Amid tropical splendor and perpetually abundant leisure, they live among carefree natives on an enchanted island. It is a sort of paradise found, an island populated by noble savages—those deemed virtuous and pure on the basis of never having been influenced by Western civilization. Indeed, throughout the text, the narrator rails against the corrupting influence of white men upon the idyllic natives.

Tom falls sick, and Toby sets out to get help. He meets with misadventure and cannot return, leaving Tom alone. Rather quickly thereafter, Tom tires of the paradise, dubious of the cannibalistic practices and the warring ways of the islanders. He enlists the help of a friendly turncoat islander to make his way to an Australian vessel. There is some suggestion at the end of the novel that one of his reasons for leaving was to be able to tell his fantastic tales to white men (and to find his friend Toby).

Typee contains long, languid descriptions of the natural beauty of the island, the quaint—and simple—customs of the inhabitants, and, of course, a native love interest, the beautiful and innocent Faraway. More romance than travelogue, the novel chronicles various prosaic and poetic moments. Frequently, Melville overtly compares the island to Europe, mostly to the praise of the island. Such cultural comparisons anchor the text in a Western perspective and target the Western reader's desire for an Eden that bears some resemblance to the familiar. For example, the narrator frequently visits the sex-segregated bachelor chiefs at a lodge called Ti. Writes Melville, "The Ti was a right jovial place. It did my heart, as well as my body, good to visit it. Secure from female inclusion, there was no restraint upon the hilarity of the warriors, who, like the gentlemen of Europe after the cloth is drawn, and the ladies retire, freely indulged their mirth" (Rugoff 458–459). Such comparisons, although casual asides, serve to make Melville's account more inviting and less alien to his readership.

Omoo acts as the sequel to *Typee*. The novel picks up with Tom, injured and weak, signing on as a seaman. This ship too turns out to be poorly equipped and a hotbed of strife and deceit. The crew revolts but fails to gain control of the ship. They are incarcerated and then deserted on Tahiti. Island life suits them, though they quickly press the hospitality of the generous natives. Tom and his new friend, Dr. Long Ghost, smell trouble brewing and set off for nearby Imeeo. They find work as field hands but feel such labor is too taxing.

Amid the tropical abundance, poverty is not an issue. The doctor and Tom set out to study the natives and relax in the second half of the novel. In this section Melville incorporates his own studies of Polynesian peoples. Manners, customs, clothing, food, religion, and language receive elaborate descriptions. In the midst of the novel, then, a travelogue resides. Valuable for its factual data but somewhat long-winded after the quick pace of the first half of the novel, the section is a curious inclusion. After a time, cultural anthropology loses its fascination for Tom, and he leaves his friend to press onward. He signs on as a whaler on the provocatively named ship *Leviathan.*

Perhaps the intellectual sequel to *Omoo* is *Mardi,* although the narrator and the tone shift significantly. Taji is the hero of this novel; he and his friend Jarl desert their whaling ship in the South Pacific. Through several misadventures, they find themselves adrift in a lifeboat with a third character, Samoa. Incredibly, they encounter a native priest taking a beautiful white woman, Yillah, to be sacrificed. They rescue her, Taji falls in love, and they land on the island of Mardi, another paradise. Alas, Yillah soon vanishes mysteriously, and the despondent Taji seeks her far and wide. For many chapters, he scours the Marquesas Islands.

Though implausibly motivated, this voyage is one of the best examples of Melville's travel writing. Not only are his descriptions superb, Taji and his companions have a continuous discussion about the nature of travel and exploration. In addition, they make extended—and often sarcastic—comparisons of the various colonial powers that "own" the islands. The tale ends enigmatically: Taji leaves his companions to continue his search "over an endless sea," but we are no longer sure if he is seeking Yillah or himself. Either way, Melville depicts travel as the only means to satisfaction and self-knowledge.

Having nearly exhausted his experiences in the South Seas, Melville turned back to his first transatlantic voyage in 1839 for his material in *Redburn*. Although he is much more capable as an author here, the story describes a much less able traveler. Writing himself as Wellingborough Redburn, Melville describes his gaffes as a novice seaman. The sailors loathe him, the passengers condescend to him, and he is hopelessly lonely. His salvation is his excitement with being in motion and knowing that he will soon be able to explore, however briefly, England.

Once ashore, the narrative follows Redburn's wanderings in Liverpool. His wide-eyed wonder and innocence make him a first-rate cultural critic. Skeptical of England's mythical status as superior to America, Redburn finds numerous ways in which it compares unfavorably to his home. As often happens, when at home, the protagonist criticizes America, but when abroad, he becomes remarkably patriotic. Redburn and his new friend, Harry, make a boisterous trip to London and then sign on to return to the United States.

The novel ends rather tragically and bitterly. The homeward passage is a nightmare of disease, privation, and deceit. When they arrive, the captain refuses to pay their wages. Redburn returns to where he started, poor and aimless, and Harry signs on to a whaling ship, where he is killed. Such an abruptly tragic ending represents a rarely mentioned aspect of travel: it can be dangerous and destructive.

Melville's posthumously published travel journals are also quite interesting. Much less dramatic than his novels, they nonetheless contain engaging exploits and adventures. With his ever-critical eye, Melville cuts to the quick of cultural difference and laments the usual tourist practice. *Journal up the Straits* describes his journey to the Holy Land and his desire to find some sort of spiritual reassurance from the ancient relics. *Journal of a Visit to London and the Continent* and *Journal of a Visit to Europe and the Levant* both cover the mainstays of European travel but, once again, from Melville's skeptical perspective. More often than not, he finds himself nonplussed by that which awes others. Rich in details and punctuated with comical snap judgments, these texts lend an insight into Melville the traveler.

Over his long and fruitful career, Melville used travel as inspiration for his writing. A source for engaging stories and excitement as well as a tool for learning and self-reflection, travel lies at the heart of his work. His enthusiastic embrace of the unfamiliar and his idealization of his own experiences into romances make his work a sort of literary hybrid. His books fuse fact and fiction into a strange composite that epitomizes travel literature.

References: Hart 1965; Rugoff, 1960

MILLER, HENRY

Henry Miller (American, 1891–1980) may be an embodiment of a restless century. Constantly in search of new excitement and trends, he spent large portions of his life in transition. As a major American writer, Miller fits into many categories. While his literary production was vast, several of his most famous works are notable as travel literature.

To understand Miller's books, which are mostly autobiographical, we need to realize that he rejected the United States as his home and moved to Europe from 1930 to 1940. It is during this decade that he focused on cultural comparison, first writing of Europe from an American perspective in *Tropic of Cancer* (1934) and then adopting a European perspective to write of his own childhood in New York in *Tropic of Capricorn* (1939). Although these two texts are only nominally travel literature, they may be included in this encyclopedia in that the fundamental theme of each is getting to know oneself through experiencing different cultures. In a particularly modern manner, Miller describes his own adolescence in his home country as a voyage of learning and self-understanding. In addition, it is by going to different places—both at home and abroad—that Miller's characters develop and grow. Lastly, these two texts read like travel literature: there is a vivid descriptive energy in these books that suggests a traveler's wide-eyed wonder at discovering people, places, and things.

Although less daring and innovative as novels, several other of Miller's books are more clearly travel literature. *The Colossus of Maroussi* (1941) grew out of Miller's own trip to Greece and describes the people, the ruins, and the geography with breathtaking detail. The novel begins as a standard chronicle of a holiday but grows into a remarkably impressionistic set of sketches and scenes of Greece. World War II had just begun, and Miller seemed to be reaching for a greater sense of civilization than the twentieth century could provide him, thus *The Colossus of Maroussi* evokes classical Greek history. Although delighted with the ruins, myths, and antique heritage, Miller's narrator finds the spirit of the contemporary people to be the greatest genius of Greece. In this regard, Miller's travel novel can be compared to the travel writing of his contemporary D. H. Lawrence. Rejecting the idealized history of Greece in favor of a real present represents a shift away from so many eighteenth- and nineteenth-century works of travel literature, and thus this shift marks Miller as an innovator and a progressive within the history of the genre.

After many years living in numerous countries, Miller returned to his native United States and made an extensive tour. His reflections, reactions, and insights were published in the very successful novel *The Air-Conditioned Nightmare* (1945) and its sequel, *Remember to Remember* (1947). Both books reside in the intersection between novel and travelogue; they clearly represent an autobiographical account, but they read as fiction with the emphasis more on perception than on objective facts and details. Deeply critical of American values and attitudes, these texts met with hugely polarized receptions. Both texts show Miller, who was both wealthy and famous as a result of his earlier work, jesting, provoking, and scandalizing any number of people. The result is an amusing and enlightening story that uses Miller's sharp wit and audacious cynicism to make the entire society seem to be riddled with dotards, idiots, and fanatics.

Throughout his life, Miller both lived and wrote of his own wide travels. Each trip represented a journey of self-discovery and an opportunity to teach others of their own myopia. Miller's employment of travel literature as social criticism has deep roots, but his style and form were uniquely his own and can be said to have had a significant influence on much of the travel writing of the late twentieth century.

See also: Lawrence, D. H.
References: Benét 1965; Harvey 1967; Newby 1985

MILNES, RICHARD MONCKTON

Richard Monckton Milnes, First Baron Houghton (English, 1809–1885), was a minor Victorian figure with a passion for travel poems. Educated at Cambridge University and friendly with some of the literary greats of his day, including Alfred, Lord Tennyson and William Makepeace Thackeray, Milnes went on to write scholarly studies of John Keats and to serve in a number of political capacities. For our purposes, his *Poetical Works* (1876) is his claim to fame: it contains numerous substantial and interesting travel poems.

Milnes's social standing afforded him great opportunities. His sense of loyalty and duty to Great Britain, however, prevented him from living abroad. Yet he did travel extensively throughout continental Europe, Greece, and Turkey. His travels anchored his somewhat arrogant impression of Britain and served to augment his already strong patriotism. Whereas some travelers use their exposure to cultural difference as a means of critiquing their homeland, Milnes responded to his journeys with a renewed certainty that his familiar culture was superior.

A product of the Victorian era, Milnes's verse is highly dramatic and excited. History, particularly British or classical, provides a richly textured backdrop for every monument, building, or city. In one long cycle called "The Ionian Islands," Milnes dwells upon the past glories of Greece, specifically as

seen from the eyes of a nineteenth-century English traveler. The poem begins,

> Thou pleasant island, whose rich garden-
> shores
> Have a long-lived fame of loveliness;
> Recorded in the historic song, that framed
> The unknown poet of an unknown time,
> Illustrating his native Ithaca,
> And all her bright society of isles,—
> Most pleasant land! To us, who journeying
> come
> From the far west, and fall upon thy charms.
> (Crossley-Holland 146–147)

The travelers experience bliss in the present by basking in the long-gone glories of the mythical ancient Greece of literature. In good colonial fashion, the narrator shifts focus after some 30 gushing lines: he claims to see a similarity between ancient Greece and his own Britain. Indeed, to be immersed in a foreign time and place can only bring the narrator to reflect upon his own home. This response was certainly not unique to Milnes; many other writers and tourists had used voyages to Greece to affirm their belief that Britain was a modern embodiment of ancient Greek ideals.

In the same poem Milnes closes with the notion that travel is a great teacher. Urging the traveler ever forward, he notes that his own memory of the voyage (and the poetic lines that describe the experience) "Will bear the fruit of many an after-thought, / Bright in the dubious track of after-years" (Crossley-Holland 148). The journey, and its written account, will fix life lessons in his mind.

To Milnes, as to many travelers, the past is indeed a foreign country. Thus to visit foreign lands, particularly those locales with famous ancient histories, is to encounter the wisdom of that long-lost era. In the conclusion of "The Burden of Egypt," Milnes notes:

> Where is for them the tale of history told?
> How is their world advancing on its way?
> How are they wiser, better, or more bold,
> That they were not created yesterday?

Undated engraving of Matteo Ricci, sixteenth-century Italian missionary, with Li Paul (Bettmann/Corbis)

Why are we life-taught men, why poor
    ephemerals they?
(Crossley-Holland 265)

A complicated passage, to be sure, but it suggests on one level that the voyage teaches of
history and relative progress, that it provides
wisdom and strength of character. For this
sort of blending of travel, learning, and writing, Milnes rates a position as a noteworthy
travel writer.

References: Crossley-Holland 1986; Harvey
1967

MISSIONARY

The general definition of *missionary* as a noun
is anyone who is sent on a mission by a religious organization to preach, teach, work, or
proselytize in a foreign country. In the context of European and American history, missionary work is generally Christian and suggests that the land to which the missionary is
sent is heathen.

Many travelers, particularly in the sixteenth and seventeenth centuries, were considered missionaries. The Jesuit order was
particularly vigorous in its missionary efforts,
although numerous other Catholic orders in
France, Spain, and Portugal funded substantial numbers of missionaries.

The history of missionary travel is inextricably tangled with the history of colonialism;
because the early modern states were not entirely distinct from the church, political and
religious histories were often united. The
major European powers justified their colonial conquest of the New World as saving the
pagan natives from eternal damnation by
converting them, via missionaries, to Catholicism. Under the same rationale, missionary
efforts were sent to the South Pacific, China,
Africa, and just about everywhere else
human life could be found.

It is decidedly a tricky designation to call
the writings of missionaries travel literature.
In this encyclopedia I have included only

those writings that have substantial literary
merit and those accounts that represent a
major cultural, geographic, or historic discovery. In many cases, missionaries were simply travelers with deep religious convictions
who combined a love of travel, learning, and
adventure with the opportunities provided
by their respective churches.

MOLUCCAS

See Spice Islands

MONTAGU, LADY MARY WORTLEY

As the daughter of a marquis and a lady of
fashion, Lady Mary Wortley Montagu (English, 1689–1762) might have lived an entirely
unremarkable upper-class life. But Montagu
had a passion for learning. Adept in the Latin
and Greek languages at an early age, she
quickly became an accomplished student of
the classics. Her voracious appetite for art,
music, and literature impelled her toward the
loftiest artistic circle of the day; she was a
friend, correspondent, and sometime satirist
of the likes of Alexander Pope, Joseph Addison, and William Congreve. In addition,
Montagu was noted as beautiful, witty, and
vivacious.

Her husband was appointed ambassador to
Turkey, so the couple moved to Istanbul.
How their marriage survived remains a mystery: she was lively, by all accounts, and he
was dull and stolid. Perhaps by writing she
was able to escape from what is thought to
have been a grave mismatch. It is from Istanbul that her finest work of travel literature
was written: *Letters and Works of Lady Mary
Wortley Montagu* (1718). A collection of letters, small essays, anecdotes, and tales mostly
of her life in the upper reaches of Turkish
society, this work demonstrates Montagu's
hearty travel spirit. She recounts her experiences at coffeehouses, Turkish baths, social
engagements, and state functions; in every

Engraving of Lady Mary Wortley Montagu in Turkish garb (Michael Nicholson/Corbis)

case, she is a keen observer of difference. Her stories invariably contrast social behavior of the "European" and the Turk.

Furthermore, Montagu offers us a rare picture of the daily life of Islamic women in the eighteenth century. Once again, from her English perspective, we must wonder how much bias is built into her accounts, but in many instances her descriptions appear to be among the most objective available.

Montagu's fascination with difference suggests a slight uneasiness with the splendor of Turkey. Implicitly, to her, Turkey cannot rival Britain, yet much that she sees—be it architectural, historical, cultural, or artistic—is magnificent. Repeatedly, she notes that her class standing outranks those around her, as though to reassure herself of her personal superiority. As a diplomatic wife with a free spirit and an educated mind, she had the freedom to access almost any aspect of Turkish culture with little actual risk. In this regard, her accounts are valuable. But more interesting are the moments where Montagu learns of herself and finds that the world as she knew it in England is heavily colored by perspective. These rare and precious moments of growth make this text genuine travel literature, and fun to boot.

After Turkey, she returned to England and seems to have separated from her husband. She moved to Italy for a time and then to France. Letters from this later period of her life are also contained in her collected writing, and many of these are fine examples of travel writing. Ever witty, scandalous, and shrewd, Montagu offers us numerous cultural insights and descriptions of a rich selection of destinations.

References: Pick 1988; Rugoff 1960

MONTESQUIEU, CHARLES

Charles-Louis de Secondat, Baron de La Brède et de Montesquieu (French, 1689–1755), who wrote under the name Charles Montesquieu,

was a man of letters, a lawyer, a philosopher, and a nobleman. He wrote a number of very different books, including his seminal piece of travel literature, *Persian Letters* (1721), which remains a magnificently complex and subtle work that is part travel fiction, part social commentary, and part historical document. To gather material for this work, Montesquieu made a brief voyage to the Levant and then supplemented his experience with vigorous textual research. From 1728 to 1731, he traveled throughout continental Europe and Great Britain, but by this time he unfortunately had turned his attention away from travel writing in favor of other genres and topics.

A wealthy, powerful, and well-educated Frenchman, Montesquieu seems to have been a born politician. His family was actively political, and he was sent to Paris to study law as a young man. To his surprise, he found Paris both fascinating and somewhat ridiculous. Full of youthful vigor and a scathing wit, he wrote the marvelously incisive *Persian Letters* as a satire of the Parisian high society that shocked him so. To preserve his good family name, he published the book anonymously in Holland; it ran through 10 editions in its first year and sold briskly for the next several decades.

Persian Letters is a remarkable novel and an early example of a wildly innovative adaptation of the tradition of travel literature. Playing off of the popular eighteenth-century epistolary form, Montesquieu penned 161 fictitious letters (mostly) among a Persian sheik named Usbek, his servants, and the wives and eunuchs in his harem. Usbek is on an extended visit to Paris and has left his possessions in the capable hands of a trusted eunuch; the letters detail daily life in the harem and Usbek's adventures and observations in France.

The principal delight of the tale is a clever and subtle inversion of the Orientalist tradition: instead of a European noble commenting upon strange foreign lands, Montesquieu reverses the roles so that a foreign gentleman critiques Paris. As the tale progresses, the mockery of Parisian social and sexual politics becomes more and more apparent.

One of the strongest appeals of the book is the suggestive eroticism of the harem. Although the myth of the harem is always present, Usbek's harem is uncomfortably reminiscent of Parisian high society. Within the harem, sexual desire and deception destabilize the community; by extension, the same drives are implied to be weakening Paris.

The complex issue of cultural critique in this novel needs a few words of explication. Montesquieu is behind the scenes pulling all the strings, to be sure, but he writes essentially two travel books at once: the first is a somewhat fantastic account of life in a harem, and the second is a fake foreign perspective on France. In both directions, the foreigner learns of himself by being outside of his element: the fictitious Usbek learns many great lessons from Paris, while real Parisian readers learn many lessons from the Persians.

Like his contemporary Jonathan Swift in *Gulliver's Travels,* Montesquieu deftly blends fiction with enough verisimilitude to create powerful social satire. Masked in the form of travel literature, *Persian Letters* indeed teaches great lessons and mandates sustained self-reflection by frustrating the relationship between the foreign and the familiar. The implied message is the stuff of pure and proper travel literature: by voyaging to see the other, we learn of ourselves.

See also: Swift, Jonathan
References: Benét 1965

MOODIE, SUSANNA

Novelist Susanna Moodie (English-born, Canadian, 1803–1885) wrote several novels and books of poetry over the course of her career. None, however, is as vivid and passionate as her first novel *Roughing It in the Bush, or Life in Canada* (1852). Born Susanna Strickland in Suffolk, she grew up in a middle-class family. A durable and ambitious young woman, she was greatly frustrated by the delicacy with which English women of the era were treated. She eventually married J. W. D. Moodie, a military officer, and the couple moved to Canada in 1832.

Rather than stopping in one of the larger cities, they settled far into the provinces. *Roughing It in the Bush* is the story of her hardships as a pioneer and her discovery of a radically different way of life. Her novel is interesting in that it follows her transition into, and acceptance of, a new culture. Moodie found all the certainties of English life missing; in response, she was forced to relearn just about everything. One of the consequences, quite logically, was that her journey caused her to reflect upon her own character at great length. In this sense, *Roughing It in the Bush* is a fine work of travel literature.

Full of folk wisdom and quirky but often charming characters, Moodie's novel surpasses most frontier tales of homesteading by its elegant prose and sophisticated narrator. She is objective in her voice but likable as well. Moodie's choice of details moves the novel along at a swift pace while remaining highly evocative.

Constantly under duress, Moodie tells of her struggles to maintain a decent household for her family. The weather is a constant threat, from the icy temperatures in the winter to the great storms in the spring. During one particular cold snap, Moodie finds her house on fire from overstoking the stove. After sending her kitchen girl to fetch help, the indefatigable Moodie writes, "I was left quite alone, with the house burning over my head, I paused one moment to reflect what had best be done" (Robinson 388). Coolly, she begins evacuating the cabin of its most precious contents—the children and the most essential possessions. She worries that "to expose the young, tender things to the direful cold was almost as bad as leaving them to the mercy of the fire. At last I hit upon a plan to keep them from freezing. I emptied all the clothes out of a large, deep chest of drawers, and dragged the empty drawers up the hill; these I lined with blankets, and placed a child in each drawer, covering it well over with the bedding" . . . (Robinson 388). The fire causes severe damage, but not enough to deter the Moodies.

Throughout, Moodie narrates the joys and sorrows of the pioneer family with good humor, insight, and patience. Her humility and tenacity make her endearing, her keen eye for details and distinctions makes her a valuable source of information. In sum, *Roughing It in the Bush* is a travelogue that reads like a novel. The heart of the story, however, remains a tale of character development caused by encountering—and besting—the unfamiliar.

References: Benét 1965; Robinson 1994

MOORE, THOMAS

One of the most praised and popular poets of the romantic era, Thomas Moore (Irish, 1779–1852) penned great verse on a myriad of topics. In his collected works are several superior examples of travel verse. Across the board, his poetry is notable for its astounding musicality and gentle texture.

The son of a Dublin grocer, Moore used his skills in music and language to work his way through Trinity College. Restless, he wandered about Great Britain in search of himself. As a young man, he published his first book, *Poetical Works* (1801), under the assumed name of Thomas Little. From 1819 to 1822, he lived in Italy, and he had a property in Bermuda that he presumably visited at some point. After a variety of alternating successes and setbacks, he was finally given a literary pension in 1835. Over the years he wrote songs, essays, satires, a novel, and several plays. Only in his verse does he pick up the themes that allow him to be called a travel writer.

One of the best examples of Moore's travel literature is a multipart set of poems called *Rhymes on the Road*. Written after touring the British Isles, the poems have several unusual components that make them fascinating and engaging. Throughout, there is an animosity between the narrator—an Irishman—and the various Englishmen he encounters. Playing with the idea that encountering the foreign can teach us of the familiar, this narrator finds that meeting the English other reminds him of how well he likes the Irish. Moore begins one section with this exclamation:

And is there then no earthly place
    Where we can rest, in dream Elysian,
Without some cursed, round English face,
    Popping up near, to break the vision?
(Crossley-Holland 12)

The influx of English visiting Ireland may have started the complaint, but the narrator goes on to imagine the silliest sort of English travelers at some of the world's great monuments. Indeed,

. . . [no] fear of Mameluks [Egyptian military
    caste] forbids
Young ladies, with pink parasols,
To glide among the Pyramids
(13)

Or for that matter, the narrator expects

. . . flying to the Eastward, [to] see
Some Mrs Hopkins, taking tea
And toast upon the Wall of China!
(13)

Rhymes on the Road covers many topics usually not blended into travel literature. Intensely political, Moore uses travel both as a literal action and a metaphoric description of life in general. Thus in his wanderings the narrator encounters carefully fabricated elements chosen by Moore to provoke and to anchor a political stance. In this series travel is the backdrop for the exchange of ideas and for criticism.

Using travel as a figurative replacement for the journey of life, Moore is able to merge didactic lessons with credible narratives. In "Song of the Evil Spirit of the Woods," a traveler finds himself lost and imperiled by a host of real and symbolic dangers. The message seems to be one of caution and prudence, for evil lurks along the roadside of life. With energized and magnificently powerful lines, Moore writes of his stricken wanderer:

> Hither bend you, turn you hither
> Eyes that blast and wings that wither!
> Cross the wandering Christian's way,
> Lead him, ere the glimpse of day,
> Many a mile of mad'ning error
> Through the maze of night and terror,
> Till the morn behold him lying
> O'er the damp earth, pale and dying!
> (Crossley-Holland 368)

Such powerful tales of doom and danger spin the meaning of travel literature quite differently than usual.

For the quality of his verse and the innovative application of common themes, Moore's travel poems are spectacular indeed. They mark themselves as travel literature that then wraps itself around political or pedantic ends such that the association of travel with life cannot be denied. For Moore, adventurous journeys—and scintillating tales thereof—need not be to the far-flung and exotic; they can easily be found in one's own backyard.

References: Crossley-Holland 1986; Harvey 1967

MORITZ, KARL PHILIPP

An embodiment of German romanticism, Karl Philipp Moritz (German, 1757–1793) tried his hand at many professions. Over his brief but full life, he dabbled in acting, teaching, writing, psychology, and even clerical pursuits. When he met Johann Wolfgang von Goethe in Rome, the two became fast friends, and Moritz was subsequently introduced to the great figures of the day: Friedrich von Schiller, Johann Gottfried von Herder, and Gotthold Ephraim Lessing, among others. It is a testament to Moritz's abilities that he was able to charm and fascinate the likes of this crowd.

Extremely well read, Moritz was an avid observer of cultural difference. He spoke English almost as well as his native German—not to mention Latin and Greek—and had a particular fascination with English literary history. This led him to repeated visits to Great Britain, the accounts of which appear in *Karl Philipp Moritz in England* (1782).

His stories are remarkable in that they are full of wry irony. As a foreigner, he found himself treated as a guest, but often the hospitality offered seems absurd or ridiculous. As an example of the cultural outsider coming to England and observing the oddities of that culture, Moritz's text is superior. Because of his knowledge of the language and the history of Britain, he is able to toy with numerous references; in several cases, it becomes clear that Moritz knows more about English history than the Englishman with whom he speaks.

Moritz's writing concentrates on the natural and the social rather than the artistic. He insisted upon walking wherever possible—a 40-mile trek from one town to another would not have been unusual—and staying at small inns. As a result, Moritz is exposed to the more common folk instead of the upper class. Partly with fascination, partly with horror, he relates his encounters with innkeepers, maids, drivers, farmers, and bartenders.

For example, in Windsor, Moritz finds an inn that looks nice and has a pleasant innkeeper but that has the surliest of servants. The episode proceeds genially up until the climax, when Moritz is forced to share his room with a drunken soldier because of an overbooking. He leaves the inn in the morning followed by the curses of the servants whom he has refused to tip. Throughout, Moritz never loses his sense of humor and his detached, traveler's perspective. In Oxford he meets a drunken crew of clergymen who immediately befriend him. His competency in Latin and his rhetorical skills so impress his new friends that they insist upon toast after toast. A drunken party ensues and a story results.

In these and many other episodes Moritz cultivates casual encounters into stories. His focus seems to be on human interaction rather than famous landmarks or geographic sights. As an outsider to the British culture who nonetheless speaks English, Moritz is able to observe what might go unnoticed by a Briton. In this regard, to English audiences, Moritz's book is a very telling set of observations that often pokes gentle fun at Britain.

See also: Goethe, Johann Wolfgang von
References: Adams 1988; Fussell 1987; Newby 1985

MORRIS, JAN

Jan Morris (born James Humphry Morris; English, 1926–) has a passion for all sorts of adventure. As a university student, Morris developed a reputation for crackling energy and unpredictability; in subsequent years he would live up to that early reputation in every way.

As a soldier and war correspondent in World War II, Morris first discovered his abilities for travel under duress and reportage. After the war, he was employed by the London *Times*. Morris gained significant fame in 1953 when he joined Sir Edmund Hillary's successful assault on Mount Everest as the expedition's reporter. With a sufficient level of name recognition, Morris found he could travel and write for a living.

His books of travel writing are many and varied. The short list includes *As I Saw the U.S.A.* (1956), *Islam Inflamed: The Middle East Picture* (1957), *Coronation Everest* (1958), *South African Winter* (1958), *The World of Venice* (1960), *South America* (1961), *The Road to Huddersfield: A Journey to Five Continents* (1963), *Places* (1972), *Travels* (1974), *Journeys* (1984), *Hong Kong* (1988), and *Sydney* (1992). Indeed, Morris has visited and written about all five continents.

In 1972, after a long and agonizing struggle, Morris underwent surgery to complete his gender transformation: James had become Jan. The "journey" of becoming a transsexual is chronicled in her memoir *Conundrum* (1972). Morris's case remains an interesting study in "gendered language": Is there a structural, stylistic, or thematic change in her writing over the course of this transition? The jury is still out.

Regardless, Morris's writing is exceptionally engaging and her adventures are variously thrilling. One of the most descriptive and exhaustively thorough writers in the modern era, Morris's prose often behaves like a photograph: she tries to capture a "snapshot" of the place and the moment. Though fabulously rich in details, her writing is sophisticated also because she always reminds us that she, the author, is there behind the scenes. So, for example, after a vivid description of Hong Kong, she writes:

> There are flashes of sun on distant windows. I leave my typewriter for a moment, open the sliding glass doors and walk out to the balcony; and away from the hotel's insulated stillness, instantly like the blast of history itself, the frantic noise of Hong Kong hits me, the roar of that traffic, the thumping of that jack-hammer, the chatter of a million voices across the city below; and once again the smell of greasy duck and gasoline reaches me headily out of China. (Robinson 306)

While relying on the details to evoke the place and add ironclad credibility to her tales, Morris repeatedly anchors the experience of travel in the process of writing. She implies that the reason she is traveling is to write for us, to see what we cannot, and to capture it for us. The act of writing is always part of travel for Morris; as such, she distinguishes herself as a noteworthy and influential writer of travel literature.

References: Fussell 1987; Robinson 1994

MORRIS, WILLIAM

For his writing, for his images, for his design, for his politics, and for his architecture, William Morris (English, 1834–1896) is deservedly famous. His prominence as a poet and artist began in his student days at Oxford University; over the course of his life, Morris demonstrated a dazzling array of talents. For a time linked with the Pre-Raphaelite Brotherhood, Morris was intimately associated with some of the finest creators of the Victorian era. Among his accomplishments are a number of poems that function beautifully as travel literature.

One of Morris's intellectual fascinations was with Norse mythology. To study these ancient sagas—and their relationship to British literature—Morris made two extended visits to Iceland, first in 1871 and then in 1873. Not only were these trips fruitful in terms of his scholarly work, but they made a remarkable impression on him personally. His *Poems by the Way* (1891) describes aspects of this voyage as well as an array of reflections on Iceland, myths, and the nature of travel.

Within this collection is a wide variety of different poetic styles and literary themes. From lighthearted and rousing songs like "Ode to the Last Pot of Marmalade" to the more stern and patterned "Gunnar's Howe above the House at Lithend," Morris displays multiple talents. In almost all cases, however, he seems fascinated with the Icelandic language and how its texture marks it as different from Morris's soft and polished English. Constantly, he includes names of people and places, Icelandic expressions and exclamations. For example, the chorus of "Ode to the Last Pot of Marmalade" is: "Come! Up with the Smör! Come! Out with the Brod, / We'll have one more Spise that's fit for a god" (Crossley-Holland 227). The result of this linguistic contrast is perhaps akin to the social experience of the foreign: feeling the distinction between languages begins the cultural, historic, and geographic recognition of difference.

At once decisive and inquisitive, Morris has a special talent for gracefully balancing the factual with the speculative. As a traveler, he easily notes what he sees, but as a poet, he distances himself and wonders at the nature of perception. In other words, he questions his motivation and the reasons for his emotional responses to his adventures, as though asking himself "Why do I see it thus?" In "Iceland First Seen," the traveler has just landed at his destination; already he is exuberant but quizzical as well. The first stanza of this 84-line poem describes the physical landscape with dramatic excitement: the traveler remains in the realm of the physical with his "toothed rocks," with the "desolate green," with the "mountains / all cloud-wreathed and snow-flecked and grey." But immediately in the second stanza, the intellect pipes in:

> Ah! what came we forth to see
> that our hearts are so hot with desire? . . .
> Why do we long to wend forth?
> (Crossley-Holland 224)

It is such ambivalence that makes Morris's travel verse so interesting and provocative.

For Morris, a journey to a foreign land is about learning stories—and then writing about those stories. Thus when he exclaims to the island, "O land, as some cave by the sea / where the treasures of old have been laid," the treasures are ancient stories. His insistence that travel and tales are inextricably linked argues well for Morris's status as a writer of travel literature.

References: Crossley-Holland 1986; Harvey 1967

NAIPAUL, SIR V. S.

N

Sir V. S. Naipaul (Trinidad-born, Indian, 1932–) writes both novels and criticism. Born into a family of Indian immigrants to Trinidad, and later educated at Oxford University, Naipaul embodies travel writing in the second half of the twentieth century: his prose is profoundly decentered. If one of the defining characteristics of travel literature is the encounter of the foreign that causes a reassessment of the familiar, what happens when the traveler is genuinely multicultural and transnational? While this is problematic for the analysis of travel writing, it is also a great strength for writers like Naipaul. He has the ability to see with a fascinatingly composite perspective; his observations and interpretations are all the more insightful as a result.

Travel scholar Paul Fussell writes of Naipaul: "It is as a displaced person that he views the world, exploring Africa, India, Iran, and South America only to recoil from their various perversions or simplifications of the Western ideal" (Fussell 784). In this regard, Naipaul can address the lingering ramifications of colonialism in his travel writing. But it is not all gloom and doom in Naipaul: his novels are peppered with hilarious frustrations and ironic, dark moments of humor. More than inserted simply for amusement value, these lighter interludes can be very effective at teaching us of difference—and at encouraging tolerance, patience, and a sense of humor.

We might call Naipaul a "post-touristic" writer in that his characters travel not for the escape of a vacation, but for some deeper lesson. His books often include a character that writes about his journey, thus fusing travel and literature together. Scornful and almost always disappointed with tourist sights and attractions, Naipaul is one of the few modern writers who makes an absolute distinction between travel and tourism. The former is a chance to learn—often of oneself—whereas the latter is a chance to escape into empty denial.

Naipaul's literary production has been significant both in its quantity and its quality. Almost all of his novels can be called travel literature in that encountering a foreign culture is at the center of the plot, and travel serves as more than a convenient excuse for an exotic background. However, his most lauded novel, *A House for Mr. Biswas* (1961), is generally not considered a work of travel literature. A brief listing of some of his better examples of travel literature follows. Naipaul writes in a highly autobiographical style for his fiction and a rather novelistic style for his nonfiction. It is thus difficult, and perhaps pointless, to distinguish between the forms.

Photograph of V. S. Naipaul, November 1968 (Hulton-Deutsch Collection/Corbis)

An Area of Darkness (1965) features India and highlights the difficulties and joys of a character that discovers his heritage only to find that it is simultaneously familiar and foreign. As in many of the classic novels of self-discovery, the protagonist of this tale comes to realize the power of racial/cultural history.

A Bend in the River (1979) roams Africa with an exiled Indian. The narrator, Salim, finds a small town that is caught between the modern and tribal worlds. Salim's journey—both physical and spiritual—becomes one with the fate of this town: both are in transition and struggling to find an identity. Slowly things unravel, and instead of stability and peace, chaos and violence erupt. The implication is that the motion of change—sometimes called progress—proceeds continuously; in other words, there can be no rest or peace in this world. Often considered overly cynical and dark, this is a travel tale that does not promote Africa in the least.

Among the Believers (1982) chronicles a journey through the Islamic world and addresses the power and problems of Islamic fundamentalism. *Beyond Belief* (1998) is the sequel (of sorts) that broadens the scope of Islamic cultures to include Indonesia and Malaysia and that fills in some of the holes from his earlier work. His concentration focuses again on the power of stories: modern politics reconciled with the ancient narratives and traditions. Naipaul introduces his readers to an array of very believable characters who illustrate the ambivalence that often accompanies fundamentalism. The story tries to approximate an objective study of faith while wearing the robes of a novel.

In a Free State (1971) is an odd compilation of short stories, a novella, and extracts from Naipaul's travel journals. The thematic glue is the idea of freedom, in all its forms: personal, political, spiritual, and intellectual. Travel is the teacher, as in most of Naipaul's work. It also deals at length with issues of exile, a kind of forced travel, and intolerance.

The Enigma of Arrival (1987) is even more autobiographical than his other novels. It tells the story of a journey from Trinidad to England, with all the culture shock and comparative lessons one would expect. Although written relatively late in his career, this novel returns to Naipaul's early formative years. For this reason, it is a good starting point for a study of his collected works.

A Turn in the South (1990) is set in the United States and directs Naipaul's critical eye to American culture. Concentrating on the volatile mix of the endearing and the maddening aspects of Southern provincialism, Southern history, and Southern autonomous identity, this book is political and provocative. In its characterization the South looks as odd and threatening as any of the exotic locales of Naipaul's other works. With its racial economy, its cultural traditions, and its extraordinary regionalism, the South appears as a world apart from the rest of the United States.

One of Naipaul's most sophisticated examples of cultural comparison, *The Middle Passages* (1962) provides his impressions and reflections on the colonial powers—Great Britain, France, and Holland—and their influence on West Indies and South American cultures. A hugely complex and wonderfully insightful study, this book epitomizes Naipaul's position as outside of any one culture. He is indeed a "postnational" citizen of the world.

As an example of his elegant prose and his meditative themes, we might look at a passage from *An Area of Darkness*. En route to India, and anxious, Naipaul writes,

It had been a slow journey, its impressions varied and superficial. But it had been a preparation for the East. After the bazaar of Cairo the bazaar of Karachi was no surprise; and *bakshish* was the same in both languages. The change from the Mediterranean winter to the sticky high summer of the Red Sea had been swift.

The Last Voyage of Henry Hudson, *John Collier, 1881, a quest for the Northwest Passage (Tate Gallery, London / Art Resource, NY)*

But other changes had been slower. From Athens to Bombay another idea of man had defined itself by degrees, a new type of authority and subservience. The physique of Europe had melted away first into that of Africa and then, through Semitic Arabia, into Aryan Asia. Men had been diminished and deformed; they begged and whined. Hysteria had been my reaction, and a brutality dictated by a new awareness of myself as a whole human being and a determination, touched with fear, to remain what I was. It mattered little through whose eyes I was seeing the East; there had as yet been no time for this type of self-assessment. (Fussell 788)

In this passage we can see a wealth of important themes and a richness of description. The journey is critical as a frame or a prelude to the arrival; it establishes the parameters in no uncertain terms. The levels of cultural, social, linguistic, and even psychological comparison are many and varied. And finally, the exposure to the foreign leads to self-knowledge and introspective reflection: to see the other is to be forced to look closely at the self.

Naipaul's popularity and critical acclaim has been wide and mighty. In 1971, he won the Booker Prize and in 1989 he was knighted. He continues to travel and to write; his travel literature is undeniably among the most influential and experimental in modern times.

References: Fussell 1987

NORTHWEST PASSAGE

The water route from the Atlantic to the Pacific Ocean through the Arctic islands of Canada. Sixteenth-century explorers imagined a short trade route from Europe to the Pacific basin; they found it possible but extremely hazardous. Various travel accounts from the sixteenth to the nineteenth centuries document exploration of the Northwest Passage.

See also: Champlain, Samuel de; Dampier, William; James, Captain Thomas; La Salle, René-Robert Cavelier, Sieur de

NÚÑEZ CABEZA DE VACA, ALVAR

See Cabeza de Vaca, Alvar Núñez

OLEARIUS, ADAM

We might imagine Adam Olearius (German, 1603–1671) as a professional traveler. His voyages were state missions, for the most part, but his stories are travel literature. A well-respected man of letters, Olearius was sent by Duke Frederick of Holstein first to Russia and then to Persia. The first of his nine volumes of journals and accounts was published in 1656. They very rapidly became seminally popular and were translated into all the major European languages. The first English edition is titled *The Voyages and Travels of the Ambassadors from the Duke of Holstein, to the Great Duke of Muscovy, and the King of Persia* (1662).

Olearius's first journey was to Moscow in 1633, with the sole purpose of gaining permission for a longer stay and then passage to Persia. This precursor took two years but served to teach Olearius the Russian language. His subsequent voyage back to Moscow and then down to Persia (1635–1639) had a more practical purpose: he was sent to open a trade route to Isfahan. A third trip to Moscow in 1647 seems to have been made simply to thank the duke of Muscovy, who encouraged Olearius to stay and to settle in Russia. He refused, preferring to return to Holstein to write his books.

A compulsive diarist, Olearius sought to capture as much of the culture, art, politics, and manners of a place as possible. His writings are interesting, however, because he took great care to edit, correct, and compile them into a narrative; as a result, it was not until many years later that he published the account. His sense of literary craftsmanship helped to produce fascinating documents that are highly accessible and enjoyable. To this day, his accounts of seventeenth-century Russia are considered some of the finest and most detailed.

Woven into Olearius's observations are his retrospective comments. He often corrects himself or checks his facts elsewhere. In so doing, he presents his reader with a narrative that seems to be writing itself. The effect is a persuasive trustworthiness: we read the accounts and imagine that he has meticulously researched and confirmed his observations and assessments. As a scholar, he utilized whatever outside sources he could find. His book contains references to German, Latin, Russian, and Persian texts. His obsession with writing and telling the tale accurately suggests how important he felt his words to be. Indeed, while the simple ostensible objective of his journeys was to foster trade, a secondary, if unspoken, mission was to teach the court of Holstein of the Russians and the Persians.

His topics range from religious rituals to architectural history, from court manners to public behavior. Each volume differs somewhat in subject matter, although there is a chronology that flows through the entire series. While his texts are structured as travelogues—that is to say, written in the form of daily entries—he buries tangential essays, reflections, and asides between his observations of the process of travel. Open-minded, tolerant, and inquisitive, Olearius remains one of the more enduring and endearing writers of classical travel literature.

References: Adams 1988

OSSOLI, MARCHIONESS

See Fuller, Margaret

PARDOE, JULIA

A phenomenally energetic author of the romantic period, Julia Pardoe (English, 1806–1862) was already writing publishable poems as a teenager. Somewhat reclusive, she led a quiet but prolific life with her father, Major Thomas Pardoe. They seem to have had an unusually strong relationship; at age 29, she moved with him to Constantinople (now Istanbul). Her verse is perhaps her more famous contribution to history, but her two books of travel literature are noteworthy for our purposes. *The City of the Sultan and Domestic Manners of the Turks* (1837) and *The Beauties of the Bosphorus* (1839) both resulted from her extended residence in Turkey.

The City of the Sultan is a formal attempt to compare daily life in Constantinople, for a privileged European woman at least, to that in London. With a very subtle eye for details both physical and cultural, Pardoe provides a vivid picture of the beauty and exotic nature of life in Constantinople. With a relatively open mind, she seeks to describe the decidedly foreign way of life she adopted as her own.

In her second look at Turkey, Pardoe indulges in a little more romantic excitement and titillation. Evoking the myth of the harem and the (mostly male) fantasy of this idea with her title, *The Beauties of the Bosphorus,* Pardoe produced a book that celebrates Constantinople. Whereas the title suggests, and the content confirms, an interest in the harem, Pardoe has played a joke upon her

readers: instead of being about harem girls, the book is about the building in which the harem resides and other architectural "beauties" of the city. The book contains Pardoe's own drawings and descriptions of art and architecture. To be sure, she plays with the exclusive nature of the harem: she draws the structure that houses it, along with much of Topkapi (the sultan's palace complex in Istanbul), painstakingly, even longingly. She can see and capture only the outside of these places, but her imagination wants to suggest what goes on inside. By reading Pardoe through her images and descriptions, we can see a delicious ambivalence toward the life of the Turkish court.

Both books remain interesting and vivid representations of an incredibly opulent and politically significant moment in history. In addition, if her works are read in the context of colonial subjugation, Pardoe becomes culpable as a cultural imperialist. Finally, for her lyrical and carefully crafted prose, Pardoe can be read as a sort of loving connoisseur of the exotic other.

References: Newby 1985

PARK, MUNGO

Mungo Park (Scottish, 1771–1806) is said to have feared nothing. After completing his medical training at Edinburgh University, he volunteered as a ship's doctor on an East India Company vessel bound for Sumatra. After this voyage, Park never stopped traveling, adventuring, exploring, and risking his neck. His most famous journey was in search of the source of the Niger River, published as *Travels in the Interior of Africa* (1799). He returned to Africa in 1805 to continue his exploration of the Niger headwaters, but his luck did not hold out: he died in a roaring river after a bloody skirmish with natives.

While some of Park's journals, notes, and letters survive, his only major publication remains *Travels in the Interior of Africa*. Nonetheless, this single book is a major work of travel literature that influenced many of the romantic and Victorian accounts of adventure. With his deadpan tone and nonchalant bravado, Park is much admired and loved as a storyteller.

The tale is complex and full of adventures. Arriving in Gambia, he spent several months readying his excursion. Unlike the overstaffed and elaborate exploration parties of some of his contemporaries, Park's was highly limited: a single servant named Johnson, a boy porter, and three pack animals. Park's own gear was amazingly sparse. He claims he carried, "a few changes of linen, an umbrella, a pocket sextant, a magnetic compass and a thermometer; two fowling pieces and two pairs of pistols" (*Oxford Atlas of Exploration* 60). In addition, he wore a large hat, under which he hid his papers and documents. With this light load, Park and his party spent two years exploring more than 500 miles of West Africa.

Part anthropology, part naturalism, and part geographic exploration, Park's account is fascinatingly diverse. His encounters with a variety of sub-Saharan peoples remain a valuable anthropological record, while his descriptions of various flora and fauna excite naturalists. Geographically, Park was the first European to determine that the Niger did in fact flow eastward. His explications brim with precise and discriminating details, and his engaging narrative moves at a fast pace. Clever and inquisitive, Park treats his expedition as a sort of grand puzzle to be solved for great glory. His text reflects his progress toward the solution, and it goes a long way toward exposing the process by which he resolved problems.

Dauntless of spirit and remarkably tough, Park refused to quit. He had been commissioned by the British Africa Association to explore the commercial and navigational possibilities of the river, and his indomitable 23-year-old spirit spurred him ever onward.

Held prisoner for months by the king of Ludamar, stymied by a torrential rainy season, often near starvation, suffering from fever, and ill equipped, Park endured and pressed forward. Although he had not achieved his objective, eventually Park had to turn back: "worn down by sickness, exhausted with hunger and fatigue, half-naked, and without any article of value by which I might procure provisions, clothes, or lodging, I began to reflect seriously on my situation" (Newby 42). Expedition organizers in Britain had thought him dead, thus his return was met with great surprise and excitement. A hero's welcome ensured eventual brisk sales of his book.

Travels in the Interior of Africa fascinates for its earnestness and its courage. Despite the horrendous difficulties Park faces throughout, he refuses to complain. His description of native peoples—though they often tried to kill him—is sensitive, open-minded, and refreshingly unpretentious. His adventures are magnificent and thrilling, but most exquisite in this text is Park's own character. Crafty and shrewd, his wit saves his skin on various occasions. For example, when held captive by a Muslim tribe, Park finds his belongings impounded. The chief of the tribe, curious about Park's compass, asks how it is that the needle always points to the great desert. Aware that the tool is invaluable to his survival, Park must find a way to make it repugnant to the chief. Cleverly, Park tells the chief,

> that my mother resided far beyond the sands of Zaharra [the Sahara], and that whilst she was alive the piece of iron would always point that way and serve as a guide to conduct me to her, and that if she was dead it would point to her grave. Ali now looked at the compass with redoubled amazement; turned it round and round repeatedly; but observing that it always pointed the same way, he took it up with great caution and returned it to me, manifesting that he thought there were something magic in it and was afraid of keeping so dangerous an instrument in his possession. (Rugoff 266–267)

Such adventures fill this text with excitement and suggest the sterling character of Park himself.

The second voyage was ill-fated from the beginning. Well funded and equipped with a guard of 30 soldiers, Park set out in 1805. The soldiers did not last long: hostile tribes, a brutal climate, and disease took a heavy toll. Before they even reached the Niger, Park had lost most of his party. In spite of such great losses—including his brother-in-law—Park and his men continued. With his reduced crew, Park sailed nearly 1,000 miles down the Niger River. Finally, with only 4 Europeans (of an original 45) and a few porters, Park decided to head back. Precisely what happened is something of a mystery; the lone survivor tells of an ambush of natives in roaring rapids. Park and the rest of his party were never seen again.

As one of the legends of travel literature, Mungo Park's adventures continue to interest and entertain readers. For Park, grand and terrible adventures were the stuff of life; to explore was the finest glory. It seems that Park respected adversity as a test of character and that by enduring extreme hardship he could learn of his own limits.

References: Newby 1985; *Oxford Atlas of Exploration* 1997; Rugoff 1960

PECK, ANNIE

Annie Smith Peck (American, 1850–1935) had an extraordinary passion for adventure. Her feats as a female mountaineer are legendary, her love for Latin American culture seems boundless, and her zeal for women's rights is inspiring. We can learn much about this remarkable figure by her four books that blend many of her interests under the single banner of travel writing: *A Search for the Apex of America* (1911), *The South American Tour* (1913), *Industrial and Commercial South America* (1922), and *Flying over South America: Twenty Thousand Miles by Air* (1932). Her travels and

Studio photograph of Annie S. Peck in her mountain-climbing outfit, 1934 (Bettmann/Corbis)

her writings mark Peck as a brave traveler with a social conscience—a woman who undertook adventures few men in her day dared dream of.

After completing her education with high honors, Peck bounced around various universities in the United States and in Europe. She taught at several places and showed great promise as a classics scholar. But her real passions lay elsewhere. On a tour of Europe she found the Alps to be enchanting and vowed to return to scale the Matterhorn; many of her professors and male friends insisted that such a climb was too rigorous for a woman.

Thus Peck latched onto the notion of mountaineering as a means to proving that men and women are equal. In the late nineteenth century, scaling mountains was an activity mostly reserved for the heartiest and bravest of men. After a rigorous apprenticeship and training regimen in the United States, Peck felt ready to attempt more dangerous peaks. She quickly proved that she could be just as tough as the boys. Her early adventures in the Alps led to high peaks in Mexico (1897) and the Andes (1908). Not only was she a woman but in many of her later climbs she was in her late forties and early fifties! With her indomitable will and boundless energy, she amassed a stunning record of ascents.

Not content to be simply a mountaineer, she devoted herself to the suffrage movement with equivalent zeal. Between expeditions and while training she continued to write articles—both scholarly and for a mass audience—and was much sought after as a lecturer. Her focus was upon the abilities of women and the sexism that held them down. Upon reaching the summit of Mt. Coropunain (1911) in Peru, she unfurled a banner that read "Votes for Women" and left it atop the mountain as a statement. In this small example we can see how Peck blended her love for physical adventure with her sociopolitical interests. Such a fusion of physical and intellectual passions would remain constant throughout her life.

Very early in her career Peck realized that mountaineering was an expensive business that needed sponsorship. She proceeded deftly to use her writing skills and her feminist agenda to gain the funding and support of various newspapers and magazines; hence her accounts were widely read in the popular press. In 1897, with support from Joseph Pulitzer's *Sunday New York World,* Peck traveled to Mexico and climbed Mt. Popocatapetl (17,883 ft.), and after that Mt. Orizaba (18,660 ft.). The latter peak gave Peck the honor of having climbed higher than any other woman.

These early expeditions led to seven other trips to Central and South America to scale mountains. *A Search for the Apex of America* chronicles these early mountaineering adventures in Mexico and the Peruvian Andes. Peck's early writing bristles with annoyance

at the sexism she encountered in Mexico. However, this obstacle, like all others, proves no match for Peck: she overcomes it as easily as she traverses glaciers. More than a simple account of adventure, Peck's tale describes the planning of her trips and the human interaction with her fellow climbers, with porters, and with villagers they meet along the way. With obvious fascination and interest, Peck writes a travelogue that contains richly drawn characters as well as political essays. It is a curious and original text in which we begin to see the dry wit that becomes so prominent in her later writing.

The South American Tour picks up with the later of Peck's climbing adventures. Since the peaks she is attempting are becoming more difficult, the amount of organization and planning has increased as well; thus this text is set in a variety of towns and villages where Peck is preparing her Andean mountain assaults. Knowing that she was supposed to be writing lectures to be delivered upon her return—both about mountaineering and about women's rights—Peck included in this book an assortment of essays about labor rights and gender relations that she wrote while organizing her expeditions.

Over the course of these first two books we come to know Peck as indefatigable. Despite injury, hardship, and brutal conditions, she refuses to quit. Five times she fails to summit a particular peak; finally on the sixth exasperated attempt she succeeds. With her funds dwindling, she always finds the dogged determination to write an article or present a lecture in order to replenish her purse. One cannot help but admire her tenacity and spirit.

As she grew older, Peck found that she was less able to spend months in the mountains living in a tent. Instead of retiring to the sedate life of a writer, she wrote an interesting book called *Industrial and Commercial South America.* While this is not strictly a work of travel literature, it is a loving look at the business climate of South America. Over a two-year lecture tour of much of South America,

Peck wrote this collection of essays on the culture and the commercial climate. The book greatly encouraged American and European firms to invest in Latin America.

After a stint in politics in the United States, Peck returned again to Latin America. In her eighties, she was no longer able to climb mountains, so she sought another form of adventure travel: by air. Commercial air travel was still quite exotic and even slightly suspect. Intrepid as always, Peck followed the coastline of South America on an assortment of airlines. She stopped to observe and to lecture in the major cities and then pressed onward. *Flying over South America: Twenty Thousand Miles by Air* can be greatly amusing to modern readers because the hardships of air travel seem at times to be of the same magnitude as high alpine mountaineering! In other places, she waxes poetic at the tremendous views of the peaks that she had loved so dearly all of her life. Ever political, Peck chronicles her meetings with ambassadors and local politicians, with women's groups and laborers, and with fellow travelers. It is a lively account of travel in the 1930s from a woman who spent her life in motion. In many ways, this final book is her best example of travel writing in that it celebrates the myriad of different people and places that it is possible to know in a lifetime of travel.

Peck's final travels—a cruise to the West Indies followed by a return to her beloved Greece—were never captured as a text. She collapsed at the Acropolis and had to be sent back to the United States, where she died a few months later. Her life had been used up traveling and writing about those adventures.

References: Robinson 1994; Stefoff 1992

PERIPLUS

Rarely used any longer, the word *periplus* means a circumnavigation or account of such a voyage. Coming from the Greek, it literally means "sailing around." Employed frequently in eighteenth-century translations of classical travel literature and subsequently in English travel accounts, many travelers refer to an around-the-world voyages as a periplus. Thus we might read, "Drake's periplus remains significant centuries later." In addition, any motion around something—for example, sailing around the coast of Madagascar—can also be called a periplus. To take another example, in 1853, English author Thomas De Quincey used the word to refer to a walking circuit: "My mother now entered upon a *periplus,* or systematic circumnavigation of all England" (OED). For our purposes, the word is noteworthy because it conflates the journey and the account—the travel and the literature—in a single word.

References: OED

PICARESQUE

The name of a genre of novels that depicts the adventures and exploits of a likable rogue, a picaro (from the original Spanish *pícaro*). Usually in the form of a novel, the picaresque story chronicles the ups and downs of a scoundrel who tricks his way through adversity. Often the structure of the story is based on episodes in a series of different places casually connected. Examples of picaresque elements appear in Miguel de Cervantes' *Don Quixote,* Daniel Defoe's *Moll Flanders,* Henry Fielding's *Tom Jones,* and Mark Twain's *Adventures of Huckleberry Finn.*

PICARO

Technically speaking, the picaro is the character featured in a picaresque story. The term has been borrowed from the Spanish *pícaro* (rogue or rascal), which is derived from the verb *picar* (variously used as to sting, bite [insects] or nip; as well as to itch or to burn). More generally, we describe any character who is a likable rogue as a picaro. Looking at the etymology of the word, we see that it suggests various minor discomforts—a sting, a (mosquito) bite, a (squirrel's) nip—instead of more serious bodily harm. By extension, the picaro is guilty of lesser transgressions rather than egregious crimes; he is a trickster who dupes someone out of money, or steals a lover, or cons a friend into doing his work for him.

The picaro must be likable and forgivable; often he is funny and his tricks are aimed at characters who deserve what they get. He uses his wits to move the story forward and employs pranks to get ahead in the world. Usually the picaro mends his ways once he has accomplished his principle objective in the story. In scholarly usage, characters from any form or genre of literature can be referred to as a picaro.

PRINCE, NANCY

As a free woman of color, Nancy Prince (née Gardener; American, 1799–1860?) penned an autobiography, *A Narrative of the Life and Travels of Mrs. Nancy Prince* (1850, revised 1853 and 1856), that deserves mention. After marrying Nero Prince, an officer attached to the court of the czar of Russia, Nancy moved to Russia and wrote an account of her life. Later, the couple moved to Jamaica and then back to the United States; both places are included in her book.

Her narrative is mostly a chronological account, orderly but lacking structural innovation. At her best, Prince nonchalantly narrates some extraordinarily harrowing situations including floods, revolutions, kidnappings, attempts at enslaving her, and a shipwreck. Between these interludes, however, she often rambles excessively. In addition, modern readers may balk at Prince's religious motivation for her journeys: she was deeply committed to missionary work and raising funds to support her mission. Nonetheless, her perspective remains unique, and as such, she can provide valuable insight into the cultures she observes. For Prince, life and travel are the same thing; she writes of her life as a marvelous journey, here perilous, there rewarding, elsewhere surprising.

References: Schriber 1995

PRIVATEER

See Buccaneer

these three aspects of his character, we can see how Sir Walter Raleigh can be considered a travel writer.

His first major journey in the colony called "Virginia" (now North Carolina) was to help secure the lost colony of Roanoke Island in 1584–1586. The expedition accomplished little except to cost Raleigh and his backers a considerable sum of money. Nonetheless, Raleigh was a prominent enough figure to publish a mediocre book about his rather dull journey. In England, as political proponent of colonization of the New World, he used his book as evidence of the potential for extracting riches from America. Ironically, his actual journey had done nothing of the sort: rather than producing great profit, it had incurred great loss.

It was not until 1595 that Raleigh returned to the life of adventure and travel. His

RAJ

The name given to the British rule over the Indian subcontinent up until 1947. Literally, it means sovereignty, rule, or kingdom. It comes from the Hindi *raj,* which means to reign or to rule. Loose uses of the word abound; one could be "in India with the Raj," or the word can be used metonymically, as in "the Raj administered brutal discipline." Ironically, in more modern Hindi *raja* has come to mean any petty chief, official, or dignitary.

An overwhelmingly colonialist term, *Raj* rarely sees nonironic contemporary usage; however, from the mid–nineteenth century to the mid–twentieth century, the word was commonly accepted.

RALEIGH, SIR WALTER

Sir Walter Raleigh (English, 1554?–1618) appears to have lived many lives in his 64 years. As a favorite of Queen Elizabeth, he must be noted as a courtier and politician who spent time both in Parliament and in jail (when he found himself on the wrong side of political debates). As a close friend of the likes of Edmund Spenser, Christopher Marlowe, Sir Philip Sidney, and George Chapman, and as the author of a number of very fine poems, Raleigh can also claim the title of artist. Finally, as an adventurer to the New World and the British colonies in North America, Raleigh can be called a traveler. Combining

Portrait of Sir Walter Raleigh (Library of Congress)

expedition set out to explore the Orinoco River in what are now Venezuela and Brazil. He sought the legendary city of Manoa (also known as Eldorado) and pursued various tales of golden statues; neither did he find. He returned to England with a pitiful quantity of loot and little by way of geographic accomplishment. To save face, however, he published *The Discoverie of the Large, Rich, and Beautiful Empyre of Guiana, with a Relation of the Great and Golden City of Manoa (Which the Spanyards call El Dorado)*. The title alone suggests Raleigh's insecurity with the project. And while *Discoverie* lacks the drama and narrative of some of the great travelers' tales, it has a number of remarkably vivid naturalistic passages. Perhaps for this reason, the book sold well.

In addition to the value of its descriptive details, Raleigh's *Discoverie* is often read as a defense of colonialism. Much as with his earlier work on Roanoke, Raleigh urges Europeans to civilize native peoples—to his mind, that meant to convert them to Christianity. In this regard, his book had its most lasting effect. As a part of the legacy of exploitation of the New World, Raleigh may find his reputation now slightly tarnished.

See also: Eldorado
References: Adams 1988; Harlow 1928; Newby 1985

RICCI, MATTEO

Father Matteo Ricci (Italian, 1552–1610) is often noted as the first successful Jesuit missionary in China, where he went by the name Li Matou. *China in the Sixteenth Century: The Journals of Matteo Ricci, 1583–1610* (1612?), originally written in Latin, is an impressive legacy to a man of great learning and seemingly boundless energy. It includes detailed journal entries that span decades of his life in China, elaborate maps, illustrations, anecdotes, philosophical/theological essays, and transcripts of many Chinese tales. His missionary work, his love of books, and his travels seem fused in one neat and substantial package.

Perhaps the driving force behind Ricci was his endless love for learning. He quickly learned the Mandarin language and customs and then proceeded to encourage intellectual exchange with the local scholars. In Peking he established a small library of European texts, maps, and artifacts: these objects fascinated the Chinese, and Ricci spent vast amounts of time explaining the political, social, and spiritual differences between Europe and China. Adept in astronomy, cosmography, and the fine arts, as well as theology, Ricci spent the first decade of his missionary work simply exchanging ideas in an open and nonproselytizing manner. As Arnold H. Rowbotham notes, "From the first the Jesuits realized the value and influence of the printed page; the picture, the engraving, the map, and the textbook were throughout the history of the missionary a powerful aid to propaganda" (Rowbotham 56). Ricci thus promoted himself under the banner of learning and exchange. He might easily have used this as a sly means toward conversion, but it appears that he chose a less aggressive sort of missionary behavior.

His accounts detail some of the technological marvels of China. He describes in vivid detail exquisite fireworks, massive wooden temples, and 200-year-old telescopes that were superior to anything Europe had yet produced. Clearly, the Chinese man of learning was equal, if not superior, to the European. This notion fascinated and perhaps troubled Ricci throughout his life in China.

In addition, Ricci tells of local as well as imperial politics, of manners, of government structures, and of ideologies. In nearly every case, he preaches tolerance of difference; often he admits having learned mighty spiritual lessons from his Chinese hosts. Perhaps this is what makes him great as a travel writer: he can see where his own prejudices interfere with his pursuit of wisdom.

One of his tales serves as a perfect example. Ricci, an avid cartographer, produced a map of the world using Chinese characters for the emperor. As would have been normal for a European, Ricci drew Europe along the central axis and China in the lower right corner. The emperor, after complimenting him on his work, noted this peculiar marginalization of his great empire; Ricci tells us that he had to quickly promise to draw a new map. The point is that Ricci was made to see his own perspectival bias. It is a classic moment of travel literature: the traveler comes to realize that how he has heretofore seen the world is limited by his own personal viewpoint.

In sum, Ricci was generally liked and tolerated by the Chinese precisely because he was not overly zealous as a missionary. Rather, he was zealous as a traveler and as a transcriber of the marvels of China and its rich history. He began by learning of the other in an effort to convert him; in the end, it appears that the other had more of an impact on Ricci. His later writings suggest an acceptance of Confucian beliefs and ancestry "worship" as perhaps compatible with Christian notions. He realized that a hybrid harmony was possible so long as open exchange and compromise took place.

References: Rowbotham 1942

ROGERS, SAMUEL

Samuel Rogers (English, 1763–1855) wrote popular and well-crafted poetry. His verse is less extreme in its passions than that of his friends William Wordsworth and Lord Byron; nevertheless, Rogers, a man of wealth, fame, and power, was noted for his prominent wit and sophisticated formulation of ideas. His personal travels appear to have been limited to continental Europe and the Mediterranean, for as with many well-to-do gentlemen of his era, he undertook a Grand Tour after finishing his education. His verse often combines his three fascinations: travel, recollection, and poetic language. Repeatedly, he mixes these notions in different proportions, but the result is usually consistent: memory, like poetry, is not fixed, but rather an evocative representation.

His best examples of travel verse are also some of his most famous works: "The Pleasures of Memory" (1792), "Columbus" (1814), and *Italy* (1828), a collection of poetic tales of his travels. His ability to project his narrator into a wide range of situations is one of his finest skills. Stylistically, Rogers's verse suggests stability and order framing a tempered enthusiasm. His images are sensual and powerfully visual.

As travel literature, Rogers's poems strive to demonstrate the subjective nature of perception, particularly perception of the foreign. In *Italy,* for example, his narrator struggles to keep his preconceived notions, formed by his classical education, from overwhelming his observations. The competition between fact and fiction resides at the heart of Rogers's poetry. Thus he writes:

> Fable and Truth have shed, in rivalry,
> Each her peculiar influence. Fable came
> And laughed and sung, arraying Truth in
>   flowers,
> . . .
>   Yet here, methinks,
> Truth wants no ornament, in her own shape
> Filling the mind by turns with awe and love.
> (Crossley-Holland 99)

In short, Rogers provides a different sort of romantic travel verse. His quest to represent the emotions and sensations of his travels, rather than attempting simply to capture the details, anchors him in his era, but his precise technique is unique. As a precursor to the rise of realism, the style of most modern travel literature, the romantic movement must be regarded as an important influence.

See also: Byron, Lord; Grand Tour; Wordsworth, William
References: Crossley-Holland 1986; Harvey 1967

SAND, GEORGE

When talking of George Sand (French, 1804–1876), one is always tempted to emphasize her fascinating and rebellious life over her fine writing. To succumb would be a shame. However, a few words about her history are in order.

George Sand is the pseudonym for Amandine-Aurore-Lucile (or Lucie) Dudevant (née Dupin), an aristocratic French lady who refused to behave like one. After a failed marriage, she decided to live life on her own terms. Her cigar smoking and her masculine attire combined with her quick tongue made her an instant spectacle in Paris. Public, passionate relationships with Alfred de Musset and later Frédéric Chopin served to enhance her reputation as a freethinking and radical woman. Her many novels and books of social criticism were hailed as progressive and unique. As a brash but persuasive voice for women, workers, and the poor in general, Sand was highly effective at inciting debate.

In addition, she wrote a singularly interesting book of travel literature: *Lettres d'un Voyageur* (1837). Comprised of a dozen lengthy "letters" from her travels in Europe, the book is both amusing and influential. These letters were not sent to friends; rather, they were published in a variety of periodicals. Parisians found them fascinating. Here was a flamboyant woman dressing as a man and engaging in various forms of masculine freedom all over the Continent. It should be noted that throughout Europe it was strictly illegal for women simply to wear trousers, let alone to don a fake mustache and impersonate a male for extended periods. Nonetheless, Sand's skill at disguises and her outspoken character allowed her to complete the ruse without running afoul of the law.

Her tales are remarkably forthright and emotionally honest. Behind her narrative often lurks the anguish of her recent difficulties with her lover, de Musset; thus Sand swings from passionate joy to dark despair over only a few pages. Invariably, the excitement of seeing something new or meeting someone interesting lifted her from despond. It is the joy of the traveler to have fresh and unexpected experiences waiting around every corner.

Through Italy, the Alps, and parts of France, Sand continued her masquerade. Just as the voyage is always about learning of the self, being disguised can be a powerful tool for self-reflection. Combining travel with the anonymity of a disguise makes this journey one of revelation and development for Sand. Happily for readers, she took the time to transcribe her experiences into an engaging and intimate story. As travel literature, *Lettres d'un Voyageur* is rare and precious for its range of topics, its provocative perspective, and its insistence that travel, writing, and life are irreducibly one.

SCOTT, ROBERT F.

The great Antarctic explorer Robert Falcon Scott (English, 1868–1912) wrote one of the most interesting accounts of polar expedition. Compiled as *Scott's Last Voyage* (1913), it tells a harrowing tale of adventure and disappointment. The work comprises two volumes; the first contains his journals from young adulthood onward, while the second is devoted to his final journey. In both cases, Scott's writing richly develops his character. For its vivid descriptions and for its spirit, Scott's tale merits consideration.

Caricature of French novelist George Sand (Leonard de Selva/Corbis)

Scott returned to England in 1904 from three long years exploring the Antarctic. Lauded as a hero, he enjoyed his success, but he also yearned to be the first man to the South Pole. That goal had proved elusive to Scott and a number of other adventurers all seeking to be the first to set foot on an abstract and otherwise undistinguished spot. Using his newfound popularity, he began to organize a team to try again. Overcoming significant resistance and a dearth of funds, he finally pieced together an ill-equipped and poorly trained team. What they lacked in finances and experience they made up for in spirit—they had the hottest sort of adventurer's fire in their blood.

In 1910, he set out for the Ross Sea in his ragtag vessel *Terra Nova*. After a year of trying to sail as far south as possible, navigating the tricky ice floes and ever-changing inlets, he and his three companions continued on foot, pulling their sleds. Nearly three months later they succeeded in reaching the Pole, exhausted but thrilled, only to find the Norwegian flag of Roald Amundsen already flying. He had reached the Pole first, by a matter of weeks.

Demoralized, the team began the long trek back to the ship. They never made it. A search party nearly a year later found the men frozen in their tents. Among their effects were Scott's journals, which provide a daily log of the horror story. For 60 days, they had toiled heroically against extreme fatigue, illness, and a shocking lack of supplies. Aware that he had made several major miscalculations and bad decisions, Scott completes a narrative that spirals into tragic despair as the end nears.

With he and his men frostbitten, gangrenous, and out of supplies, and with temperatures at −40 degrees Fahrenheit, Scott's final entries are riveting. Aware that they were within two days' journey from a resupply depot, he realizes that they cannot make it. One ailing member has wandered off to die in order to avoid being a burden. Scott's last entry reads:

Thursday, March 29—Since the 21st we have had a continuous gale from the W.S.W. and S.W. We had fuel to make two cups of tea apiece and bare food [emergency rations] for two days. . . . Every day we have been ready to start for our depot *11 miles away,* but outside the door of the tent it remains a scene of whirling drift. I do not think we can hope for any better things now. We shall stick it out to the end, but we are getting weaker, of course, and the end cannot be far.

It seems a pity, but I do not think I can write more.

R. Scott.

For God's sake look after our people [families]. (Scott 278)

This moving tale of a brilliantly charismatic man remains one of the great examples of travel as obsession. As in the best sort of literature, Scott's recognition of his hubris, or excessive pride, after it is too late makes for a fascinating character study. In addition, his descriptions of the desolate and howling Antarctic are some of the best available. Even with his incredible fortitude and burning desires, Scott could not avoid his mortality and his humanity. With his remarkable honor, courage, and humility in the face of failure, Scott learns the ultimate lesson from travel.

References: Newby 1985; Scott 1913

SEDGWICK, CATHARINE MARIA

The writing of Catharine Maria Sedgwick (American, 1789–1867) is most noteworthy for its constant comparisons of Europe to America. As a successful American novelist—she published 12 novels—Sedgwick was shocked to find how differently Europeans viewed the United States. Accordingly, her work *Letters from Abroad to Kindred at Home* (1841) serves as a great example of learning about oneself, either individually or culturally, by traveling to meet the other.

Sedgwick writes:

With my strong American feelings, and my love of home so excited that my nerves were all on the outside, I was a good deal shocked to find how very little interest was felt about America in the circles I chanced to be in. The truth is, we are so far off, we have so little apparent influence on the political machinery of Europe, such slight relations with the literary world, and none with that of art and fashion, that except to the philosopher, the man of science, and the manufacturing and labouring classes, America is yet an undiscovered country as distant and as dim [as] Heaven. (Schriber 77–78)

Indeed, it never occurs to Sedgwick that America in 1841 was not an equal of the great European nations. We can also see from the text how American isolation, geographic as well as cultural, leads Sedgwick toward a sort of countercolonialism: the former possession, the United States, desperately seeks influence with the former master.

Amusing and engaging, Sedgwick's text describes a journey of self-understanding. As in Homer's *Odyssey,* the child has to know the parent before she can know herself. Sedgwick, as a stand-in for all Americans, needs to travel to the Old World in order to more fully understand who she is.

References: Schriber 1995

SÉVIGNÉ, MARQUISE DE

The Marquise de Sévigné (French, 1626–1696)—born Marie de Rabutin-Chantal—found herself widowed, with two young children, at age 25. Already established as a prominent woman of fashion, she chose not to throw herself back into the marriage market, but rather to live a life of privilege and taste as a widow. One of her obsessions was art, in all of its forms. Amid the baroque splendor of Louis XIV's court, Sévigné indulged in her passion for beauty.

Her literary legacy is a collection of over 1,500 letters, mostly to her daughter and some to her intimate circle of aristocratic friends. These letters are published variously; Roger Duchêne edited a three-volume edition titled *Correspondance* (1972). As a person of wealth and noble heritage, Sévigné made a number of trips throughout Europe. Her letters from these places are rich with detail, wit, and wisdom. Not only are they a wonderful sketch of the luxury of the era, but they represent a rare portrait of how a single, if aristocratic, woman was treated.

Sévigné's travel letters are also interesting in that she does not restrict herself to discussing high-society functions and luxury. Instead, she takes great care to describe, with goodwill and sometimes humor, her encounters with coachmen, housekeepers, and other ordinary folks. This is in keeping with her consistently upbeat and generally optimistic tone. While she does note the quotidian, her primary focus is on the foppery of the upper classes.

Throughout her letters, she provides charming and comical moments. Her gentle mockery most often falls upon the ridiculous men and women of the higher classes. In one particularly funny letter, Sévigné is at Vichy to take a water cure. Slightly skeptical but a sport nonetheless, she has great fun laughing at some of the other persnickety matrons who imagine the waters a panacea. She relates: "We are advised Madam de Pecquigny has also arrived or is expected. She is the Cumaean Sibyl, and wishes to be cured of her sixty-six years which she resents; this place is becoming a mad-house" (Newby 116). The reference to Cumaean Sibyl is particularly acerbic: she was a prophet who was granted 1,000 years of life. Unfortunately, she forgot to bargain for youth and thus lived out the majority of her days as a wretched hag in her cave (Zimmerman 75–76). Sévigné therefore jests with this old woman who wishes to be cured of her age.

The example above is but a brief taste of her writing. Even when she is at home in Paris, she writes as if she were observing something very foreign. Perhaps this is her gift: to see and question all as if it were exotic. When she is indeed traveling, her acute vision is magnified further still. Sévigné constantly uses the context of travel as a way to question, doubt, and provoke her own class, culture, and milieu.

References: Benét 1965; Newby 1985; Zimmerman 1964

SHAW, T. E.

See Lawrence, T. E.

SHELLEY, MARY WOLLSTONECRAFT

There is some risk in calling Mary Wollstonecraft Shelley (English, 1797–1851) a travel writer. Usually Shelley is considered a Gothic novelist or a romantic writer; with these designations, I will not quibble. Yet for her life and for two of her books, I believe she can be productively included in the category of travel writers.

Her mother, Mary Wollstonecraft, died several days after giving birth to Mary. She grew up rebellious and bold. In 1814, at age 17, she left England with Percy Bysshe Shelley and settled on the Continent. When his wife died two years later, Percy and Mary were married. Their life was a continuous sequence of travels and textual production. Anchored in Switzerland for many years, they made extended and frequent trips to Italy, Greece, Germany, and France.

Shelley's travel books are two: *Rambles in Germany and Italy in 1840, 1842, and 1843* (1844) and her classic novel *Frankenstein.* Given the popularity of her fiction and the middling quality of her travelogue, I will focus more attention on *Frankenstein.* In both cases, Shelley seems to crackle with electric excitement at the notion of travel: the energy of a voyage inspires as well as delights her.

Portrait of Mary Shelley, by R. Rothwell (Bettmann/ Corbis)

The novel *Frankenstein; or, The Modern Prometheus* was first released in 1818 and then underwent substantial revisions for a third edition in 1831. Most scholars generally recognize the revisions as enhancing the text, thus I refer to the 1831 edition in this summary.

Through a sophisticated suspended narrative, Shelley has blended three distinct stories—from three different perspectives—into one novel. The first level is the story of explorer and adventurer Robert Walton writing letters to his sister (Mrs. Saville) about his voyage to the North Pole. Within these letters, we read the story of Walton's encounter with Victor Frankenstein, the scientist who created an artificial humanoid. Nested within this story is Victor's recounting of the monster's own story. While decidedly different stories, each of the three tales elegantly engages the others; hence the formal construction of the novel beautifully accents its thematic content.

The outermost layer, sometimes called a frame narrative, is what makes this story a superb example of travel literature. The story begins as an epistolary novel (i.e., the novel consists of a series of letters), although we are privy only to Walton's missives. These letters serve to set the stage and to establish some of the major themes: Walton is making his way to the Arctic; clearly he is a sensitive and at least moderately educated gentleman; he delights in telling of his exotic setting, especially of the climate; and he seems to want to share with his sister a sense of peril that only bravery and tenacity can overcome.

In the first letter we learn of Walton's motivation for the journey: a spirit of adventure and an intrepid desire to observe on the behalf of all humankind what has never been seen before. He asks himself, "What may not be expected in a country of eternal light? I may there discover the wondrous power which attracts the needle; and may regulate a thousand celestial observations. . . . I shall satiate my ardent curiosity with the sight of a part of the world never before visited, and may tread a land never before imprinted by the foot of man" (Shelley 16). This quest for glory erases all fear and all pain in Walton, yet he is still nagged by an intense loneliness. He feels friendless and alone in the frigid north. Perhaps the isolation, often the result of travel, is the inspiration for the whole text.

Other bedrock elements of travel literature appear in the epistolary frame: nature—in this case, weather and icebergs—is figured as a force that would thwart the adventurer; the exotic land is supposed to hide great and marvelous mysteries; and travel is a form of labor. Says Walton of his letters/journals, "I am practically industrious—pains-taking;—a workman to execute with perseverance and labour" (21).

When Walton meets the stranded and ill Victor Frankenstein, the letters become an impossibly extensive retelling of Victor's history. The epistolary frame dissolves into a more conventional narrative. We learn that Victor attempts to forget his sorrows by going on a journey, which distracts him from the guilt he cannot escape. Like Walton, Victor seeks rugged and dangerous nature as a solace.

In chapter 11, Victor tells the story that the monster told him. Fundamentally, the monster has been an unwilling traveler in a foreign culture: he has had to find a way to communicate; he has had to endure harsh elements; and his life has been governed by travelers' needs—food, shelter, and clothing. His encounters are a lesson in misunderstanding the other, for every person he meets assumes that because he looks different—he is often described as "hideous"—he is evil. In this section of the novel we learn that he can be kind, generous, and just.

Throughout the novel, the images of motion and travel link the tales together. In a perfect three-way example of observing the other, Victor, Walton, and the monster all learn of themselves by looking at one another. That this intensely productive learning occurs while under the extreme conditions of a voyage is no simple coincidence.

Much later in her career Shelley penned a travelogue that also deserves note. *Rambles in Germany and Italy* resulted from a long series of trips and voyages over the years 1840–1843. Just as Shelley rambled between places, so too does the narrative ramble along with little formal structure. Instead, the book is a compilation of stories, anecdotes, observations, and musings inspired by her travels. In this text Shelley repeatedly balances the grandeur of nature with the pettiness of society. To her conception, art is the force that mediates between the two. Carefully crafted, vivid, and at times quite emotional, this text provided an interesting picture of travel and adventure in the romantic era.

Although Shelley is not traditionally listed as one of the great travel writers, I contend that with these two texts to her credit, one could persuasively argue for her inclusion. In her life and in her writing, she employed travel as inspiration, motivation, and pedagogy. What more could we ask?

References: Shelley 1969

SILK ROAD

The series of trade routes running from southeast China to Europe is called the Silk Road (also known as the Silk Route). As shown by the accompanying map, this is not one fixed route but a series of possibilities and options. The Silk Road is no longer used for trade, although numerous groups of hearty adventure travelers have attempted to follow parts of this ancient route.

Initially the general path of trade caravans—often transporting precious silk—from China in the second century B.C.E., this route continues to be the principal "road" across Eurasia. For many centuries before Europe congealed into trading states, the Central Asian cities along the route flourished as money and ideas flowed in as a result of this commerce. Such cities provided a nexus of exchange and understanding: they were travelers' cities where all things unfamiliar and exotic could be found.

In the late Middle Ages, Europeans began to take an interest in these trade routes. By the Renaissance, European travelers had documented much of the Silk Road. It was only after sailing vessels and navigation became sufficiently advanced in the seventeenth century that overland trading cities began their demise. Nonetheless, well into the twentieth century, the architecture, history, and continued small-scale trade of goods from Asia along the Silk Road kept travelers interested.

With its mystique, its harsh geography, and its exotic products, the Silk Road has figured prominently in many travel accounts and examples of travel literature. The collapse of the Soviet Union in 1991 made travel along much of the route easier, hence many of the once-grand cities along this trade route have reopened and emerged as exotic markets for carpets, silks, spices, and textiles.

References: Muqi 1989

Contemporary photograph of the Silk Road, Pakistan, 1993 (David Samuel Robbins/Corbis)

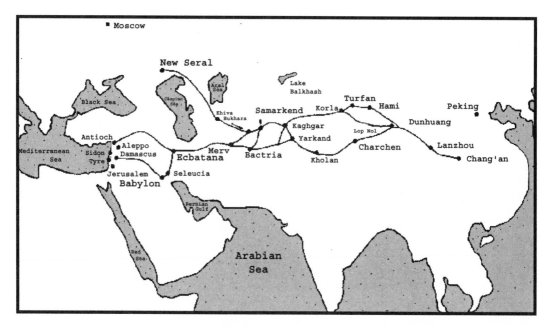

Map showing the route of the Silk Road (Magellan)

SLOCUM, JOSHUA

Little remembered by history but nearly legendary among sailors, Joshua Slocum (Canadian, later American, 1844–1909?) was the first man to sail alone around the globe. He recounts his epic solo circumnavigation in his book *Sailing Alone around the World* (1898). His two earlier books, *The Voyage of the Liberdade* (1894) and *The Voyage of the Destroyer* (1896), are rare and relatively uninteresting. *Sailing Alone,* however, is a genuinely great work of travel literature.

As a young man, he joined the merchant marine and saw his share of success, attaining the rank of captain at age 25. For many years, he journeyed near and far. As steamships increased in number, sailing captains found work scarce. Slocum had to accept ever-riskier commissions for meager pay. With his wife, herself an avid traveler, and family, Slocum sailed the South Seas, the Atlantic, and the Indian Ocean. Tragically, his wife died on a voyage to South America, and Slocum found himself deeply grieved.

Several turns of bad luck further degraded his reputation and, more significantly, his fortune. A cholera epidemic forced his ship into quarantine, where the cargo rotted. Slocum prevented an attempted mutiny off Uruguay by shooting the two leaders, but the resulting lengthy court case diminished his finances even more. Finally, he inexplicably ran his ship into a sandbar. Broke, alone, and depressed in South America, Slocum had to reinvent himself.

Never one to quit, he found a new wife—who happened to have two adventurous, seafaring sons—and began to build a ship from scratch. From his imagination and experience on many sorts of boats, Slocum built an astonishing 35-foot vessel that is said to have cost about $100 to build. She proved to be unshakably seaworthy, transporting the family back to the United States without a fuss.

Middle-aged and full of fire again, Slocum began the serious work of restoring abandoned vessels. This was not the hobby of an idly rich man; rather, it was his ticket out of poverty. His ingenuity and dedication to his boats astound; while his friends mocked him, he patiently refurbished, and in many cases greatly improved, his ships.

The modest success of his two first books and his reputation as a crack renovator led to an offer he could not refuse: in 1892, a distant acquaintance offered him an old fishing boat to restore and use as he saw fit. Christened *Spray,* this unorthodox sailing vessel became the dream project of Joshua Slocum.

The voyage and its telling are vintage maritime travel literature. Salty, humorous, and personable, Slocum's book tells the tale of a mature and experienced sailor seeking nothing so much as a good voyage. This is not an account written by a young and shrill captain imagining he is the first to see the wonders of the world. Instead, it is a sober, often-philosophical account of introspection and interaction with all parts of the globe.

Upon setting out, Slocum stated his intention was simply to travel. In an age of steamships and mechanized devices, here was one man sailing a ship he effectively built by hand. Wrote Slocum: "If the *Spray* discovered no continents on her voyage, it may be that there were no more continents to be discovered; she did not seek new worlds, or sail to powwow about the dangers of the seas. The sea has been much maligned. To find one's way to lands already discovered is a good thing" (Kanellos 77).

Beyond simply venturing, Slocum had his share of adventures: pirates repeatedly gave chase, storms buffeted the ship, and supplies ran low. Wry and experienced, his account is a joy to read. Like a vaudeville hero, Slocum thwarted intruders by leaving tacks on deck or using stuffed dummies. Exhaustion played a part as well, leading to hallucinations and bleary confusion.

Never did Slocum complain, however. Quite to the contrary, the various adversities seem to have made his voyage all the sweeter. At every port, Slocum found interesting people to populate his text. Some were famous, some infamous, and some were just local folks curious to see an old man in a strange craft, but all are brilliantly described in Slocum's book.

Repeatedly, Slocum found that he could learn much of himself and of human nature by visiting far-flung places. His life may be read entirely as one grand study of foreign and familiar cultures from the vantage point of a sailing ship. In a rapidly modernizing world, Slocum is a clear voice for slowing down the pace and seeing all the majesty of the world and its inhabitants.

References: Kanellos 1999

SMITH, CAPTAIN JOHN

John Smith (English, 1580?–1631) spent his life having adventures and then writing them down. He has nine books to his credit, including *A True Relation of Virginia* (1608), *A Description of New England* (1616), *The Generall Historie of Virginia* (1624), and *The True Travels, Adventures, and Observations of Captaine John Smith* (1630). At 16 years of age, he left England to sell his services as a soldier of fortune in the war against the Turks in central Europe. He was captured and imprisoned in Constantinople for a time, but eventually he escaped and fled to Russia. While working his way back to England, he vowed his next journey would be to the New World.

From 1606 onward, he labored in the service of the English monarchy as a colonial sea captain. His various books tell of different voyages and adventures. Smith is credited with exploring and mapping the Atlantic coast south of Jamestown; it was during these topographical missions that he befriended several native tribes. Throughout his career, Smith sought to convert the Native Americans to Christianity, but he did so with a considerable quantity of compassion and openness. He rose through various civil and military ranks until he was governor of Virginia and later admiral of New England.

How They Took Him Prisoner in the Oaze, 1607; *illustration from* The True Travels, Adventures, and Observations of Captaine John Smith *(Library of Congress)*

Much of Smith's writing is dry and purely descriptive. As a historical record, the material is valuable, but as travel literature, it often lacks an engaging style or a sense of drama. Curiously, Smith often writes in the third person, perhaps trying to suggest that the tale is more objective than an obviously subjective first-person narrative. Thus when we read "Smith, little dreaming of that accident . . . ," it appears a history rather than a personal narrative; the fact remains, however, that Smith is both the author and the protagonist of his tales. Nonetheless, scattered throughout his works are moments of fabulous excitement; for such accounts, Smith is worth reading.

One of Smith's most famous passages—from *The Generall Historie of Virginia*—describes his first encounter with the child Pocahontas in 1607. According to Smith's account, Pocahontas risked her life to save him. Having been taken to Chief Powhatan, Smith finds himself ready to be slaughtered: "the conclusion was, two great stones were brought before Powhatan: then as many as could layd hands on him [Smith], dragged

him to them and thereon laid his head, and being ready with their clubs, to beate out his braines, Pocahontas the King's dearest daughter, when no intreaty could prevaile, got his head in her armes, and laid her owne [head] upon his to save him from death" (Adams 151). So began a relationship that has been the subject of considerable speculation and embellishment. In Smith's book we see his friendship with the girl lead to a friendship with the tribe; he becomes their trading partner and adviser. Eventually, Powhatan came to consider Captain Smith one of his sons, although this does not imply a marriage between Smith and Pocahontas. In fact, in his later work *The True Travels,* Smith writes to the queen of England, telling of Pocahontas and her marriage to an Englishman. Rather quickly, it seems, Smith tired of Powhatan and his daughter and moved on to newer adventures.

Time and time again, Smith demonstrated his insatiable desire to see, to learn, and to write about new people and places. His struggle to record objectively the world around him has earned him a place in the annals of history. As a brave and determined traveler, he seemed to live to be in motion: upon arriving somewhere, he began to look to the next journey.

References: Adams 1988; D'Oyley 1932; Newby 1985

SMOLLETT, TOBIAS

A gifted novelist with many different literary skills, Tobias Smollett (Scottish, 1721–1771) penned several extremely popular and interesting tales of travel. While *Travels through France and Italy* (1766) remains his most famous work of travel literature, he has a number of books to his credit, including *Roderick Random* (1748), *Peregrine Pickle* (1751), *The Expedition of Humphry Clinker* (1771), and *A Compendium of Authentic and Entertaining Voyages* (1756).

Many scholars and historians have commented upon the exchange between Smollett and Laurence Sterne, whose novel *A Sentimental Journey through France and Italy* (1768) contains a character comically named "Smelfungus" who is clearly a parody of Smollett. Indeed, upon the publication of Sterne's book, Smollett's *Travels through France and Italy* saw a marked decrease in sales and remained out of print for more than a century (Adams 345).

Sterne not withstanding, Smollett's tale has regained its rightful place in the literary canon (the authoritative body of works accepted by scholars) because it is indeed a very fine tale that demonstrates the pedagogical potential of travel. To boot, it is a fun and often-funny tale.

The ostensible purpose of Smollett's voyage was to improve his failing health. He was not a wealthy man, and he had just lost his daughter; as tonic, he and his wife decided upon a journey. Curiously, he felt he could not live without a sizable quantity of books, so he shipped a library of some 150 volumes along with him. Imagine a sickly, underfunded, cantankerous Scottish intellectual grumbling and griping through the French and Italian countryside, and you will have a fairly accurate picture of Smollett. He chronicles with great, even absurd, detail the disputes he has with a variety of innkeepers, coachmen, waiters, travelers. His pages are rife with complaints to the point that the modern reader is usually inclined to read Smollett through the lens of irony or misanthropy.

The 40-odd letters that make up the book were never actually posted; they are addressed, in fact, to a fictional friend. His stories are ripe with brash criticism and erudite verbalizations of very common traveler's woes: a slightly seedy inn leads to the proclamation that "All the inns of France are execrable"; and upon finding some French plumbing inadequate, he proclaims the French "beastly." He is also given to critical, if humorous, generalizations: "If a Frenchman is admitted into your family . . . the first return he makes for your civilities is to make love to your wife, if she is handsome; if not, to your sister, or daughter, or niece" (Fussell 200). Such cultural criticism delighted British readers—one can imagine how the book was received in France—and, on a more sophisticated level, forced readers into looking at their habits and familiar surroundings in a slightly different light. Smollett's book is at its best when it asks the reader to note—and to appreciate—what s/he might easily take for granted.

By comparing culture, the "us" and the "them" of Britain and France, Smollett is indeed demonstrating that he has learned from his journey. As an intellectual, he is not content to possess his knowledge idly; rather, he seeks to share it in his writing. Throughout his book, he gently transforms his wry observations into lessons:

The French, however, with all their absurdities, preserve a certain ascendancy over us, which is very disgraceful to our nation; and this appears in nothing more than in the article of dress. We are contented to be thought their apes in fashion; but, in fact, we are slaves to their tailors, mantua-makers, barbers, and other trades-men. . . . When the natives of France come to London, they appear in all public places, with cloaths made according to the fashion of their own country. . . . Why, therefore, don't we follow it implicitly? No, we pique ourselves upon a most ridiculous deviation from the very modes we admire, and please ourselves with thinking this deviation is a mark of our spirit and liberty. But, we have not spirit enough to persist in this deviation, when we visit their country. . . . [Indeed,] the fashions of both countries are equally absurd. (Adams 347)

France is not the only subject attacked in this journey, to be sure. Smollett's response to Italy ranges from racist tirades to classist laments to simple kvetching. If the people do not elicit a complaint, then the climate does; if the ruins are exciting, then the landscape is almost invariably terrible. That which pertains to or dates from the classical era is sure to meet with Smollett's favor; that which is contemporary and Italian is sure to be a subject of scorn. Such nationalism is amusing in retrospect; perhaps it can help us avoid being similarly overimpressed with ourselves.

One of the advantages of toting a huge collection of books is that Smollett is able to quote at length from Ovid, Horace, Virgil, and the like, in an attempt to see the same sights about which they wrote. Thus the book is deeply literary, with Smollett quoting the classics and then commenting upon how badly the same vista, structure, or characteristic has changed.

His other works are worth a brief note as well. *A Compendium of Authentic and Entertaining Voyages* is a collection of traveler's tales that Smollett compiled and then entirely rewrote. For the sake of this book, I am more interested in hearing travelers tell of their own tales in their own words, but as a source of amusing narratives and clearly told stories, Smollett's book is superb.

Humphry Clinker, Roderick Random, and *Peregrine Pickle* are picaresque novels that defy categorization. As fictional epistolary tales, they are pure novelistic; in that their letters tell credible travel tales of real places, they may approach being considered travel writing. The stories contain a single, central hero, who develops and grows in a realistic but also sarcastic manner. Whatever else they may be, these texts offer fine stories that reside on the edge of travel literature.

See also: Grand Tour; Picaresque; Sterne, Laurence

References: Adams 1988; Fussell 1987; Newby 1985

SOUTHEY, ROBERT

Although Robert Southey (English, 1774–1843) was a prominent poet in his day, his reputation has suffered of late. One of the so-called Lake Poets, Southey wrote vast amounts of prose and verse that are usually categorized simply as romantic. He served as poet laureate from 1813 to 1843. Many contemporary readers find him less thrilling and melodramatic than Lord Byron and Percy Bysshe Shelley and less technically gifted than his friend Samuel Taylor Coleridge. Such judgments do injustice to a fascinating writer who composed an astounding quantity of poetry, prose, and essays.

As with any prolific oeuvre (body of work), Southey's varies enormously. Tucked within his poems and letters are a fair number of very fine works of travel literature. Southey's own travels to Spain, Portugal, and Italy were very fruitful; his literary production from abroad is dominated by the theme of travel. A very short list of some of his best travel writing includes *History of Brazil* (1810–1819), "Thalaba" (1801), "A Tale of Paraguay" (1825), "My Days among the Dead Are Past" (1822), and "Recollections of a Day's Journey in Spain" (1797).

Generally speaking, Southey's travel writing exposes the tension between feeling excitement for the foreign and feeling nostalgia for the familiar. Whereas the unfamiliar and the exotic provide beauty and inspiration, the traveler must realize the fleeting nature of the experience. The philosophical difficulty for Southey lurks in the impossibility of memory (or poetry) to capture the real experience. Thus the traveler must wrangle with his own knowledge that his recollection provides but a paltry and flat representation of that vanished moment.

We find a singularly fine example of this idea in his poem "Recollections of a Day's Journey in Spain." The title locates the narrator already removed from the actual experience and the readers doubly removed in that we receive a poetic, textual representation of a memory of an event. Delightedly, the narrator calls to mind "wild and lovely scenes" of Spain and "retraces" and "reviews" the vistas with a pleasure "not less delighted" than that with which he "beheld them first" (Crossley-Holland 78). All seems well for the traveler remembering his excursion.

In the second stanza, emotional trouble begins. We learn that his voyage was a year ago, and he is recollecting the sunny happiness of Spain from rainy, gloomy, cold England. But even the memory is tainted, for the narrator admits that when he was in Spain he longingly thought "of England, and all my heart held dear / And wished this day [the return home] were come" (78). While traveling, he projected himself to the safe and comfortable future space of recollecting his adventures. Indeed, wheresoever the narrator is, he longs to be elsewhere. When in Spain, he thought of his familiar, dear home; when at home, he longs for his foreign adventures again. Such is the nature of travel: it confounds our desires.

The third and fourth stanzas expand upon the glorious recollections of Spain. Vividly, enticingly, Southey describes the scene with minute and enchanting details that evoke sensuous memories of various sorts. This is an idealized recollection, the stuff of retouched memory, rather than a transcription of the reality of the moment with its aching feet, burning thirst, and disorientation.

In the last few lines of the poem, Southey yanks us back to the present. He writes in conclusion,

> . . . O lovely scenes!
> I gazed upon you with intense delight,
> And yet with thoughts that weight the spirit down.
> I was a stranger in a foreign land;
> And, knowing that these eyes should nevermore
> Behold that glorious prospect, Earth itself
> Appeared the place of pilgrimage it is.
> (80)

Both originally and in retrospect, the narrator realizes that the experience of travel is comprised of singular and unrepeatable moments. As soon as a sight is seen, it vanishes into the flat representation of memory. In addition, perspective matters. Foreign eyes see and note a scene very differently from local eyes. What passes unnoticed in daily life may be extraordinary to the outsider. Finally, Southey concludes that all of life is this sort of journey. Human life is nothing more than a pilgrimage, a travel that is more about the journey than the destination.

Southey's vision is a deep and at times troubling one. His sense of travel as both the stuff of life and the deferral of death, along with his conflation of memory and textual representation, makes him a sophisticated travel writer. Throughout his works, one can find incidents and examples of superior and provocative travel literature.

References: Crossley-Holland 1986; Harvey 1967

SPEKE, JOHN HANNING

Serving in India with the British army gave John Hanning Speke (English, 1827–1864) his first taste of travel and adventure. It also conditioned him to think only in imperialist terms. After multiple treks into the Himalayas, Speke became rather well known as an explorer. But in his early years, his journals lack any special gift for storytelling. By 1850, however, Speke had befriended travel legend Richard Burton, and it seems to have had a remarkable effect on his travels, his writing, and his life.

Burton taught him much about travel and travel writing; after all, Burton was already widely idolized as the ultimate adventurer. Together, Burton and Speke ventured into East Africa, but Speke was seriously wounded in a skirmish with natives and had to abandon the journey. Burton continued on, a fact that enraged the jealous Speke.

Both Burton and Speke had a single goal: to discover and document the vast lakes that serve as the source of the Nile River. What began as a friendship quickly deteriorated into a bitter rivalry. Eventually, Speke did "beat" Burton by discovering Lake Victoria and publishing the story in his *Journal of the Discovery of the Source of the Nile* (1863). The story tells of his three years, 1860–1863, tracing backward from the Nile to Lake Victoria as substantial proof.

The journal itself is only mildly interesting. He includes the usual wealth of geological, botanical, and cultural observations, but scattered among these facts are a handful of more dramatic—even melodramatic—accounts that seem to mock Burton's heroic narratives. In one memorable scene, Speke and his cohorts battle a family of rhinos with their swords! Even in these moments of fancy, however, Speke is unable to escape his Victorian sensibilities. To his mind, Africa is a diversion, a game, and travel is a competition. Little in his journal suggests anything more significant than factual learning; on the whole, Speke is a good example of a travel writer who can tell us about the imperialistic attitudes of the nineteenth-century British explorer.

See also: Burton, Sir Richard Francis
References: Rugoff 1960

SPICE ISLANDS

The grouping of islands now known as the Moluccas, a scattered range of islands and atolls in eastern Indonesia. Numbering over a thousand and spread over a million square miles of sea, these islands have always been remote. During the European Middle Ages, Arab and Chinese traders explored and mapped these precious sources of cloves and nutmeg. Only after the Age of Discovery (roughly the fifteenth and sixteenth centuries) did the Europeans begin to explore and exploit these islands.

Such an ardent desire for spices may seem odd to the modern reader, but we must remember that spices were used to preserve and to cure perishable foods—and to mask the smell of slightly spoiled ingredients. Thus, along with salt and smoke, spices became essential to prolonged stays away from sources of fresh food. In other words, lengthy seafaring voyages, travels to inhospitable climates, and scores of other ventures that required self-sufficiency were made easier by access to spices. In addition, as with any highly sought commodity, spices also provided a source of enormous wealth; he who succeeded in returning to Europe safely with a cargo of cloves and nutmeg had an instant fortune.

These tiny tropical islands were the cause of intense competition, colonial squabbles, naval skirmishes, and even wars. Empires were built on the wealth of goods acquired from far-flung colonies; the Spice Islands figured prominently in early Dutch, Portuguese, and English colonial pursuits.

STANLEY, SIR HENRY MORTON

One of the major names in the exploration of Africa, Sir Henry Morton Stanley (born

Welsh, American 1841–1904) is to this day a legend. Inextricably bundled with the explorer David Livingstone, Stanley's famous words, "Dr. Livingstone, I presume?" do not do justice to the merits of his own exploration and writing. He devoted his life to African expeditions and, as a result, penned several valuable and interesting books, including *How I Found Livingstone: Travels, Adventures, and Discoveries in Central Africa* (1872), *Through the Dark Continent* (1878), *The Congo and the Founding of Its Free State* (1885), and *In Darkest Africa* (1890).

From Stanley's history we may be able to more fully understand his fearless tenacity and dogged perseverance. As a poor orphan, Stanley had to learn to fend for himself quite early in life. By age 17, he had already sailed from England to find his fortune in America. Taken in by a merchant, Stanley found instant success. He and his adoptive father made numerous voyages through Missouri and Arkansas, as well as all along the frontier. It was during this period that Stanley decided to travel and to write for a living. After serving in the Civil War, Stanley landed a job as a newspaper correspondent. Following a string of successful reports, Stanley was sent to seek the long-lost African explorer David Livingstone. Never one to waste a journey, Stanley filed reports from the Suez Canal, Crimea, Palestine, Persia, and India on his way to Africa. One wonders at his sense of geography!

His chronicle of finding Livingstone provides an example of Stanley's immense spirit and extreme fortitude. Slogging through Africa was both dangerous and difficult, and Stanley had to search blindly, mostly on rumors, for many months before he even found tangible evidence that Livingstone was still alive. Starting with a party of nearly 200 porters and trackers, Stanley finds attrition shockingly rapidly. To disease, skirmishes, desertion, natural disasters, and even a disciplinary execution, he loses members of his ever-dwindling team. Through a never-ending series of difficulties, while surmounting various human and natural adversaries, Stanley finally succeeds in achieving his objective. But as with any travel, reaching the destination is somewhat anticlimactic; it is the process of getting there that makes this a great story.

For four months, Livingston and Stanley explored together, and under such great tutelage, Stanley became quite an explorer himself. His subsequent trips to Africa—and their corresponding accounts—are also significant to geographic history and travel literature.

The first trip, described in *Through the Dark Continent,* tells of Stanley's 1,000-day journey down the Congo River. His next trip sent him to central Africa again, this time with the idea of founding a state there. Stanley's final journey, perhaps his most brash, was an attempt to bring support on behalf of Great Britain to Emin Pasha, the governor of the Egyptian Sudan. Insurrection had pinned down the governor near Lake Albert, and his situation looked grim. *In Darkest Africa* tells the tale of this journey.

On all of his journeys, a similar ending arises: what Stanley expects to find bears little resemblance to the actual situation. Whether he is discovering Livingstone or Emin Pasha, Stanley finds that these hearty explorers neither need to be saved nor wish to be returned to civilization. Though his journeys often had tangible objectives, in his writing Stanley focus on the voyage itself: indeed, the true value of travel is the process, not the result.

Over the course of these journeys, Stanley casts himself as heroic. Through the most horrific of experiences, he keeps his head—both literally and figuratively—and leads his party ever onward. Perhaps Stanley is one of the eminent examples of grace under pressure: he never cracks. One of the greatest values of his writing remains that his stories describe a sort of rugged travel that pushes men to their limits. Under such circumstances, core characteristics come to the fore; it may be that encountering extreme adversity is the ultimate way of learning of oneself.

Studio photograph of Sir Henry Morton Stanley, 1871 (Hulton-Deutsch Collection/Corbis)

Although the horror of his adventures often overshadows his texts, Stanley's travel writing is vastly superior to that of most explorers. While his prose stumbles at times and his structure wavers, he does a good job of preserving a sense of drama and excitement. Contemporary readers often find his dead-pan nonchalance astounding; he relates life-threatening encounters in precisely the same tone as his discovery of a new botanical subspecies. Although his format of daily entries often feels stilted and constraining, Stanley ably makes pure description interesting.

See also: Livingstone, David
References: Newby 1985; Rugoff 1960

STEINBECK, JOHN

One of the great novelists of the twentieth century, John Steinbeck (American, 1902–1968) has been studied in many capacities. His contribution to modern literature has been great in numerous regards. His collected works contain many aspects of travel literature and several books that figure prominently as pure travel writing. Perhaps significantly, his earliest and his latest books are most truly travel literature: they may be said to frame all of his other work.

Awarded both the Pulitzer Prize (1940) and the Nobel Prize (1962), Steinbeck's writing is a staple of the American canon—those works of literature comprising the authoritative collection approved by the literary establishment. His characters are credible, complex, and memorable; his themes are broad reaching, poignant, and decidedly modern. His stories tell of migrant farmworkers, country folk, cannery laborers, pearl divers, and alienated city dwellers. They are vivid and sensitive tales of the human spirit struggling tirelessly to overcome adversity. In nearly all of his books, physical movement marks the beginning of change and development. Generally speaking, travel in his novels operates on both literal and metaphoric levels: the specific journey is but a distillation of the larger journey of life with unexpected joys and sorrows just down the road or around the bend.

Cup of Gold: A Life of Sir Henry Morgan, Buccaneer, with Occasional References to History (1929) reflects Steinbeck's lifelong interest in seafaring, adventure, and conflict. An idealized romance, the novel imagines the life of Privateer Henry Morgan, who left no literary account himself. The story tells of high seas adventures in the Panama, Jamaica, and the Caribbean. Although Steinbeck did considerable research on the topic, many of the incidents are wholly fabricated or extrapolated from the tiny bit of historic data that exists. As travel and adventure, the story is interesting, but it is perhaps more unusual as a hybrid of travel fact and travel fiction.

The Sea of Cortez (1941, later reissued and expanded as The Log of the Sea of Cortez in 1951) is a pure travelogue. This text provides an account of Steinbeck's travels with marine biologist Edward F. Ricketts throughout the Gulf of California. Part travelogue, part essay on the journey of life and the evocative power of the sea, the book is an interesting counterpart to Cup of Gold in that it is nonfiction that often reads like a novel. Using his formidable literary talent, Steinbeck writes a highly readable record of an actual journey.

The Wayward Bus (1947) is a novel about the social interaction and sexual misadventures of travelers stuck at a rest station. The scenario transmutes common travel into a microcosm of modern American society. The frustrated travelers have to interact in spite of animosity and distrust—some of it quite justified. The story provides an example of travel gone awry and made challenging, but it also notes the precious affinity that travelers often feel with one another. In daily life, these characters would have no affinity or interest in one another, but in the context of travel—and mild adversity—they form friendships and bonds. Perhaps we might read The Wayward Bus as an elegy to the power of travel to influence behavior and human interaction.

Russian Journal (1948) represents Steinbeck's travels in Russia during World War II. As a war correspondent, his reportage is more political and sociological than personal, but once again Steinbeck blends forms and describes a complex and very human response to war. His focus on individual anecdotes and small details makes this a rare example of war reporting that is also travel literature.

Even his tales of Europe—The Moon Is Down (1942), The Short Reign of Pippin IV

John Steinbeck enjoying a stroll with his French poodle Charley, the star of Travels with Charley, *November 1962 (Bettmann/Corbis)*

(1957), and *Bombs Away* (1942) among them—can be read as observations of different cultures that cause the reader to reflect on being American. Though set elsewhere, the dominant themes of a struggle, strife, and transcendence build a bridge between the Old World and America; regardless of when and where, there are similarities in all human existence.

Travels with Charley (1962) is a journalistic account of Steinbeck's road trip across the United States with his old poodle. Late in his life, he declared, "I did not know my own country" and thus bought a pickup truck and drove through 30-odd states in search of knowledge, understanding, and experience. Steinbeck described his companion, Charley, as "an old French gentleman poodle" (Newby 439). With his magnificent ear for regional dialects and his carefree itinerary, Steinbeck makes of this journey a celebration of the subtle diversity of America—from its geography to its dazzling array of people. Enhanced by characteristic realism and readability, *Travels with Charley* reads like an exceptionally well-crafted novel. The protagonist, however, is Steinbeck himself. Every encounter spurs him to reflect on his country and himself. It is one of the finest accounts of travel produced in the twentieth century.

Throughout his works, Steinbeck demonstrates a remarkable respect for—sometimes even awe of—travel. All of his travel writing evokes both the physical setting and the narrator's psychological response to the journey. For this two-pronged focus, Steinbeck's travel literature must be regarded as highly sophisticated. His enormous talent as an author allows him to compose believable, moving, and uncommonly accessible travel literature that blends different genres. Steinbeck's literary hybrids paved the way for modern, posttouristic travel writing.

References: Benét 1965; Hart 1965; Newby 1985

STEPHENS, JOHN LLOYD

John Lloyd Stephens (American, 1805–1852) had a particular knack for inspiring people to trust him. Although trained as a lawyer, Stephens found the lure of travel irresistible. What began as recreational visits to Greek and Roman historic sites throughout Europe and the Near East turned into three substantial journeys, the accounts of which were published as *Incidents of Travel in Egypt, Arabia, Petraea and the Holy Land* (1837); *Incidents of Travel in Greece, Turkey, Russia and Poland* (1838); and *Incidents of Travel in Central America, Chiapas and Yucatan* (1843). His easy manner and candid interaction with people make his travel writing both endearing and informative.

Well-educated and moderately prosperous, Stephens was torn between his comfortable life as a New York lawyer and his thrilling adventures as an amateur archaeologist and ardent traveler. His compromise was to throw himself fully into lengthy trips, but between trips he returned to New York to practice law. It was an admirable scheme that he kept up the whole of his life.

One of Stephens's primary interests was in ancient cultures. His travels were always partly devoted to archaeology and art research; he earned considerable fame in scholarly circles with his book *Incidents of Travel in Egypt, Arabia, Petraea and the Holy Land*. Yet the story he tells is much more than a scientific journal—it has warmth and charm that comes from Stephens's unpretentious interest in the people who live among the relics and ruins of the ancient world. His route was a whirlwind tour of a North Africa and much of the Middle East; his desire seems to have been to see as much as possible. Along the way he encountered a colorful cast of characters, from tradesmen to sheiks. His stories are dramatic in that they tell of wild places, exotic animals, magnificent ruins, and strange cultural practices.

Stephens's first work follows in a long line of travelogues that chronicle the famous classical sites of the region. Yet his writing stands out for its lucid energy and exuberant style: he writes with genuine excitement and the apparent desire to construct a narrative out of history. Stephens seems to have had keen instincts that led him to sniff out trouble—without recklessly endangering himself—and thus he was privy to scenes of torture, unrest, rare rituals, and improbably coincidental meetings. After the book's publication, many viewed it with skepticism: they thought it must have been considerably exaggerated. Stephens staunchly maintained that he had simply captured what he had been lucky enough to see. We shall never know for sure if his tales are strictly accurate, but we can certainly find them amusing and thrilling as stories.

Having found success with his first book, Stephens immediately began planning his next trip, a logical extension of his first voyage. He recalled the classical ruins of Greece and Turkey from an earlier visit, but this time he sought to describe and investigate them systematically. On the way back to Europe he made strategic stops in Poland and Russia, hence the title of his book: *Incidents of Travel in Greece, Turkey, Russia and Poland*. Stephens captures a remarkable series of adventures with his customary ease and detachment. Though situations often deteriorate to threatening, his narrative voice remains objective and unafraid. This is not to say unemotional, however: throughout all of his books, Stephens describes his journeys with passion and feeling.

His return to the States led Stephens to engage in legal work for the U.S. State Department on a treaty with Central America (1839). In this capacity he was sent to negotiate with Central American governments, but he found that political power was scattered widely and difficult to trace. This scuttled the project, at least politically. Instead, Stephens devoted his vast energy to a study of the cultural and archaeological history of the region.

This book, published as *Incidents of Travel in Central America, Chiapas and Yucatan,* further increased his fame. As with his earlier books, this study meticulously chronicles his quest for noted ancient ruins. For this third project, Stephens enlisted an artist named Frederick Catherwood, who illustrated the project lavishly. These drawings were some of the most comprehensive and detailed of the era, and as such they had great archaeological and scholarly value. The pair traversed most of Central America, covering more than two thousand miles and documenting many of the finest Mayan ruins (Rugoff 746).

If anything, this Latin American trip proved to be the most arduous. Many of the ruins they sought were hidden deep in the jungles; access to these sites proved dangerous as well as difficult. While Stephens retains his interest in local people, much of the trip was spent slogging through uninhabited wilds, hence natural elements—both flora and fauna—play a larger role than in his previous books. As if to compensate for the long passages in the bush, Stephens seems to have redoubled his efforts to capture the spirited times he had in the towns and cities. We are privy to several splendid fiestas, replete with exotic cocktails and alluring native women; gory bullfights; dramatic Catholic masses; and gargantuan feasts featuring strange local delicacies. To my mind this third text is Stephens's finest work in that it gracefully combines the social and the archaeological in equal measure.

A small example of his prose should suffice to convey Stephens's pleasant and readable style. He had just discovered the lost Mayan city of Copán when he wrote:

It is impossible to describe the interest with which I explored these ruins. The ground was entirely new; there were no guidebooks or guides; the whole was a virgin soil. We could not see ten yards before us, and never knew what we should stumble upon next. At one time we stopped to cut away branches and vines, which concealed the face of a monument, and dug around to bring to light a fragment, a sculptured corner of which protruded from the earth. I leaned over with breathless anxiety while the Indians worked, and an eye, an ear, a foot, or a hand was disentombed. . . . The beauty of the sculpture, the solemn stillness of the woods disturbed only by the scrambling of monkeys and the chattering of parrots, the desolation of the city, and the mystery that hung over it, all created an interest higher, if possible, than I had ever felt among the ruins of the Old World. (Newby 472–473)

Fittingly, Stephens returned to the States to considerable acclaim, in spite of the fact that he had failed at his diplomatic mission.

Overall, we can read Stephens as an early American voice in travel literature, perhaps prone at times to hyperbole and childlike outbursts of excitement. He takes the tradition of travel writing and applies his own style to the rendering of his stories; in this regard he can be considered an important pioneer in the field. In addition, his balance of scholarly focus with literary craftsmanship is an encouraging example to subsequent travel writers.

References: Newby 1985; Rugoff 1960

STERNE, LAURENCE

Novelist Laurence Sterne (Irish, 1713–1768) followed his more celebrated masterpiece, *The Life and Opinions of Tristram Shandy* (1760), with a travelogue. Although both have elements of the picaresque, *A Sentimental Journey* (1768) remains the better example of his travel writing. The text was inspired by Sterne's own seven-month journey through France and Italy. He was terminally ill at the time, and he seemed to imagine his journey abroad as a sort of warm-up for his own journey into death.

A Sentimental Journey is a great piece of travel literature for several reasons. First, Sterne compresses the act of traveling and the act of writing into one action; journeying and writing become the fundamental elements of existence. Second, Yorick, Sterne's quasi-autobiographical protagonist, expressly employs travel as a means of gaining experience and wisdom. And third, Yorick positions travel as an activity above the political fray; in the end, it matters very little whether he is French or British.

To briefly summarize, the novel tells the tale of Parson Yorick and his wanderings in France with his servant La Fleur. Their principal activity—at least as recounted in the text—is getting from one place to the other

and, in the process, encountering an array of lovely women. From shopgirls to a merchant's wife to a rich widow, chance meetings provide delightful diversions for Yorick. One interlude flows until another intersects it; it is this course that Yorick—and thus the narrative—follows until another chance meeting takes him in yet another new direction. Just as his journey bounces from one place to another, so too does the story progress from tale to tale, a series of only loosely connected stories and asides. It is precisely this unexpected set of twists and turns that makes the journey—and the novel—so interesting; nothing follows in a linear manner, and so nothing is easily foreseen.

In this manner, writing and travel are conflated. The text demonstrates its own plot and, as such, can be called a manifesto. As every page is turned, a new help or hindrance appears, just as each day presents new opportunities. Spontaneous actions and responses to whatever chance events occur drive Yorick and, in turn, the story. Travel becomes not a means to an end, but rather an end in and of itself; likewise, the adventures that Yorick lives lead to no overwhelming truth or unified climax. Instead, the object of the exercise remains very simply to continue traveling and writing haphazardly: in short, the object of the exercise is to live.

As with many picaresque novels, Sterne includes generous doses of satire and sarcasm. Yorick is as much a buffoon as a hero, as much the butt of the joke as the joker. He elaborates a sort of taxonomy of travelers very early in the first volume:

Idle Travellers
Inquisitive Travellers
Lying Travellers
Proud Travellers
Vain Travellers
Splenetic Travellers

Then follow the Travellers of Necessity
The delinquent and felonious Traveller
The unfortunate and innocent Traveller

The simple Traveller,
And last of all (if you please)
The Sentimental Traveller. (Sterne 34–35)

The list itself is facetious, yet Sterne rescues Yorick by having him add wisely, "It is sufficient for my reader, if he has been a traveler himself, that with study and reflection hereupon he may be able to determine his own place and rank in the catalogue—it will be one step towards knowing himself" (35). Such good sense tends to balance the satiric oversentimentality of Yorick; the result is a satire that is both moralizing and playful. Over the course of his own journey, Yorick comes to find that he is indeed a joke of sorts—indeed, his name is borrowed from one of Shakespeare's finest fools, a reference mentioned repeatedly in the novel. The final product is a novel regarded at once as great travel literature and as a great spoof of travel literature.

Throughout classical literature—as in Dante, Homer, and Virgil—life has been figured as a journey, with the ultimate destination being death. On several levels, Sterne has incorporated this idea into his novel. Although the original title page indicates that this is an account of *A Sentimental Journey through France and Italy,* Yorick dies before reaching Italy. In part, this hasty denouement is due to Sterne's own failing health; some scholars contend that he died before he could finish the text. Regardless, the association is made: death and destination are in one camp, and life and travel are in another. In the plot of the story, this notion is demonstrated by Yorick's stubborn desire to continue at all costs. Upon realizing that he had forgotten to secure a passport to France, and realizing that France and England were at war, Yorick finds himself in a dangerous position. Viewed as a spy, he has the police on his tail, yet he refuses to return home—"Go but to the end of the street, I have a moral aversion for returning back now wiser than I set out" (92)—even if that means grave danger to himself.

The goal of Yorick's adventure ostensibly remains the pursuit of wisdom. Whether roaming through foreign lands or marching through a series of years, both aging and traveling are supposed to supply wisdom. Says Yorick, "so it fares with the poor Traveller, sailing and posting through the politer kingdoms of the globe in pursuit of knowledge and improvements" (36). Yorick seems to understand that it is through observing difference that he will best be able to understand himself and his own culture. Instead of seeking to catalog the art treasures available for viewing at the sites he visits, Yorick desires to see the people and the landscapes (which are also popular subjects in contemporaneous painting); he seeks to know the original rather than the reproduction. He is quite certain that to *really* know the other is valuable: "I could wish . . . to spy the *nakedness* of their hearts, and through the different disguises of customs, climates, and religion, find out what is good in them to fashion my own by—and therefore am I come" (108). To learn from the other is one of the irreducible motives of true travel literature.

If the acquisition of wisdom is Yorick's goal, then certainly he is successful. Through a series of encounters with men and women of several classes, Yorick realizes that there is a human community that transcends nationalism. Though his and his servant's nations are at war, Yorick can employ and love the French La Fleur. In spite of national grievances, Yorick and Mons. le Count de B★★★★ can become friends and allies on the strength of honor, decency, and individual personality. Travel, in Sterne's novel, serves as an antidote to politics; it functions as a means by which free citizens can interact outside of the realm of governments and blind policy. It seems clear that Sterne is suggesting that travel leads to knowledge of the other, which in turn leads to understanding, which ends in peace.

In fine form, the novel both begins and ends in the middle of things; the first line is in midconversation, the last in midsentence.

This suggests that perhaps the text is to be imagined as an encounter whilst on a journey. As a brief series of jolly tales, the novel reads much like an evening of talk at a pub; stories and characters come and go, perhaps exaggerated, perhaps wholly fabricated, but genial nonetheless. To make a modern analogy, this novel is like a holiday snapshot: there may be one story at the center, but there are many others that are cut off or left out of the frame.

See also: Picaresque
References: Fussell 1987; Sterne 1987

STEVENS, THOMAS

A most curious traveler, Thomas Stevens (American, 1855–?) has a single, if monumental, claim in the history of travel. In the spring of 1884, he set off to ride around the globe on his bicycle. His diary is published as *Around the World on a Bicycle* (1887). His trip is astounding for its daft energy; his journal is amusing simply for his account of the reactions he received.

His route crossed the middle of the United States without a hitch. He then sailed to Germany and pedaled through south-central Europe into the Balkans. Next, he followed a route based on the Silk Road through Central Asia and into China. Then he looped down for good measure to the Malay Peninsula before heading north to Japan. After nearly three years and 15,000 miles, Stevens sailed back to America. He was lauded as a hero and celebrated on both coasts.

Arriving in various cities where bicycles were strange beasts provided both excitement and challenges. His account tells of excited throngs enthusiastically encouraging him but at the same time causing him peril and difficulty. Predictably, the roads through Asia were often abysmal. For his hearty endurance of great distances and extreme duress, Stevens deserves praise.

His narrative is a straightforward compilation of observations organized into vignettes.

Stevens's eye for detail is good, but his sense of humor is better. Rarely, in the text at any rate, does he lose his cheerful optimism. For example, after having reached an impassable stretch of road in China, he writes, "Hours are consumed scrambling for three or four miles up and down steps, and over the most abominable course a bicycle was ever dragged, carried, up-ended and lugged over" (Newby 362). No fuss, just the will to press ever onward. This tenacity and dauntless spirit make Stevens worthy of reading.

See also: Silk Road
References: Newby 1985

STEVENSON, ROBERT LOUIS

One of the most famous and most beloved of all travel writers, Robert Louis Stevenson (Scottish, 1850–1894) has had an enormous influence on travel literature. With his actual adventures, his novels, his travelogues, his essays, his poetry, and his letters, he demonstrates a love for adventure and experience. As a pillar of the genre, Stevenson provides a diverse and fascinating body of work that remains exciting, charming, and beautiful more than a century after it was penned.

As a teenager, Stevenson already had burning urges to roam, observe, and write. Due to a chronic pulmonary infection, which later developed into tuberculosis and became a lifelong ailment, he was sent on many small trips to take the fresh air. Stevenson cast these therapeutic journeys in a positive light: they were excuses to explore new places and to write about them. By the time he entered college, he was already an avid, and published, writer. Although he studied law and engineering at Edinburgh University, there can be no mistaking his true love: travel.

We can divide Stevenson's travel literature into three categories according to where the action takes place: in Europe, in North America, and in the South Seas. While there

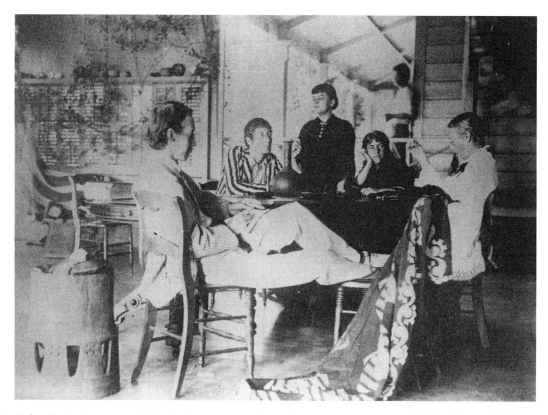

Robert Louis Stevenson with his family sitting around a table at his home in the Hawaiian Islands, c. 1921 (Library of Congress)

are many thematic and stylistic strands that remain constant, his work matured considerably over the course of his life. His earlier phases are anchored in de facto descriptions and accounts, whereas his later periods are wildly imaginative and more evocative than realistic. Also note that it often took Stevenson a decade or more to publish his accounts. This suggests a highly crafted, revisionary writing process: while he obviously made copious notes and sketches, his published work is edited, polished, and arranged for maximum entertainment and emotional effect. His oeuvre is indeed vast and not limited to travel literature—*The Strange Case of Dr. Jekyll and Mr. Hyde* (1886) being the most famous example. For the sake of space, only some of his finer works of travel writing are listed here.

Inland Voyage (1878) narrates a tour of the waterways of Belgium, France, and Germany. In his canoe, always in good spirits in spite of

constant difficulties, Stevenson has ample time to observe and to muse. As a result, the tale is as much about his reveries and impressions as it is about specific people and places. Although a travelogue, it reads more like a novel: our protagonist undergoes a development of character as the book proceeds. Instead of strictly chronicling his days, Stevenson writes in vignettes that mostly amuse and delight. A master at telling tales with drama, timing, and exactly enough detail to ensure credibility without weighing the story down, Stevenson captures the sensations of lightness, freedom, and expectation that are the principal allures of travel.

Travels with a Donkey in the Cévennes (1879) finds Stevenson again opting for alternative travel through rural France. Ostensibly, the trip represented another cure for his TB. Stevenson sought to camp for months amid the crisp mountain air of the Alps and in other parts of southern France. A highly subjective, often very funny account of a rather slow and awkward journey, *Travels with a Donkey* displays Stevenson at his jovial, good-humored best. Fascinated by people and their customs, manners, and quirks, Stevenson delights in staying weeks in backwater hamlets, baffling the locals. Of a village called Monastier, where he spent a month, Stevenson writes: "in this little mountain-town . . . they all hate, loathe, decry, and calumniate each other. Except for business purposes, or to give each other the lie in a tavern brawl, they have laid aside even the civility of speech. . . . In the midst of this Babylon I found myself a rallying-point; every one was anxious to be kind and helpful to the stranger" (Fussell 417). Page after page, Stevenson's account is an endearing blend of observations and amusing reactions to all he saw. In this regard, the story is as much about the narrator as it is about the French.

In this tale Stevenson also employs a wonderful conceit—an extended metaphor that likens two seemingly dissimilar things, usually one concrete and one more abstract: namely, while it is true that the narrator does indeed purchase a donkey as his companion and aid, we come to see that our narrator himself may be donkeylike in his stubbornness and obstinacy. As he learns to cajole, command, and load his beast, we can chuckle as we see him learning to control himself as well. He must learn a decidedly different way of life in the hills, and just as for his donkey, it occasionally takes a crop to teach the lesson.

In 1879, Stevenson set off for the United States, first sailing to New York and then taking the train across the country to California. The story of his journey is told in *The Amateur Emigrant* (1895). From the cramped ship's cabins to the rattling, smoky, noisy train carriage, the journey is decidedly unromantic and downright painful. Mingled with personal narrative are numerous details about the history of the railroads, customs, and travel protocol. Perhaps one of Stevenson's less

interesting stories, it remains fascinating for its historical details. As this journey occurred before Stevenson met with fame and fortune, he identifies with the poor immigrants he meets, many of whom are on journeys of hope and expectation. Amid optimistic squalor, Stevenson observes America through the window. Upon arrival, he finds a land of rambunctious and unpredictable behavior. As his somewhat refined European manners scrape against the ways of the Old West, a variety of embarrassing and comical situations occur. *Across the Plains* (1892), also published years after this experience, is another of Stevenson's books that draws deeply on the material gathered in America.

Stevenson had followed his fiancée to America; they married and settled for several years. In addition to his books, Stevenson concentrated during this period on shorter stories, essays, and poems, many of which were published and received with great praise. In fact, his works began earning enough money to support him. A number of smaller texts, mostly autobiographical, were published in a volume called *Virginibus Puerisque* (1881). This period also saw the publication of *The Silverado Squatters* (1883), a story about Calistoga and the strange congregation of fortune seekers, travelers, and wanderers he encountered there. Hoping to strike silver in the local mine and finding a harsh natural environment instead, the early pioneers of the West who inhabit this story provide a picture of relentless determination. *The New Arabian Nights* (1882) similarly highlights the behavior and adventure mentality of the American Wild West. Compared to the Old World, America was exotic, magical, and full of excitement; such a stark difference propelled Stevenson's imagination to great heights.

By the time Stevenson returned to Great Britain in the early 1880s, he had been working on what is perhaps his fictional masterpiece for years; finally, in 1883, *Treasure Island* was published in book form. Part romance, part adventure tale, this novel is often labeled travel literature. In many ways, it is. Jim Hawkins narrates the story of his association with an old pirate who has a map describing the whereabouts of Captain Flint's buried treasure. Jim inadvertently outwits the evil pirate Pew and his gang to secure the map, which he promptly gives to Squire Trelawney and Dr. Livesey. The three set off in search of treasure. Through various adventures, battles, and obstacles, not the least of which is archnemesis Long John Silver, they find the booty.

The elements of travel literature in this novel are several. First, the stark contrast between the pirate's life and a British boy's life causes Jim to reflect on both states. Second, the treasure, or destination, is not all that important; instead, it is the excuse for a good adventure. As such, the journey itself contains the value—not to mention the bulk—of the excursion. Third, travel and adventure teach great lessons. Along the way, Jim learns about honor, trust, fidelity, and compassion: these are the (ideal) lessons of experience. The status of *Treasure Island* as a classic of travel literature thus seems well deserved.

By 1888, Stevenson had moved again, this time to the South Pacific. After an extensive tour, he settled in Samoa, where he died suddenly in 1894. He was buried atop a mountain, and to this day his grave remains something of a cult tourist attraction. During his later years, he continued to write novels, essays, and poetry as well as his constant travelogues.

Island Nights' Entertainments (1893) and *In the South Seas* (1896) tell tales of Stevenson's adventures from 1888 to 1892. These collections of tales represent a rather arbitrary assortment of unconnected stories about Hawaii, Tahiti, the Marshall Islands, the Gilbert Islands, and Australia. I suspect he selected and compiled these particular stories for their dramatic appeal and jolly tone. As a trader, traveler, and seeker of stories, Stevenson wandered far and wide over the islands. Sometimes engaging natives, other times colonialists, these works paint the South Pacific as a wonderfully exciting and hospitable region. Perhaps the most significant value of

these texts is the elegant way in which they balance human personalities with geographic places: there always seems to be a relationship between the characters and the island upon which they live. Also significant is the way the islanders—both natives and expatriates—regard Europe. Frequently, Stevenson is confronted with amusing and challenging impressions of his homeland. To see an island king, for example, display his "fine manners" is to see a parody of European behavior. These marvelously pedantic moments are some of the finest in Stevenson's writing simply because he is intellectually nimble enough to laugh at his own distorted cultural reflection.

In his glorious travel verse, Stevenson describes magnificent adventures but often with a substantive nod to the ambivalence of leaving home (again). In "Christmas at Sea," for example, the narrator is in a fierce squall, ice in the riggings, and the ship in peril. And though it be Christmas, a holiday ostensibly of spiritual significance, the excitement of the moment drives all other thoughts away. Then, just as the vessel breaks into calmer seas, the peril gone, the passengers "all heaved a mighty breath, every soul on board but me": "But all that I could think of, in the darkness and the cold, / Was just that I was leaving home and my folks were growing old" (Crossley-Holland 19). Even for a hearty, lifelong traveler, there is ambivalence in travel: while the rewards are great, so too are the costs.

As Stevenson himself observed, "We are all travellers in what John Bunyan calls the wilderness of this world" (Fussell 417). Indeed, all of his life was a journey. Few travelers have maintained the pace and constant enthusiasm for newness that Stevenson made appear effortless. With his buoyant spirit, in spite of perennial poor health, he provides us with an example of passion and drive. And with his numerous works of wonderfully vivid, carefully wrought, and lovingly rendered travel literature, Stevenson offers us a world of texts that teach us of our humanity and of our foolishness.

References: Adams 1988; Cox 1949; Crossley-Holland 1986; Fussell 1987; Harvey 1967; Rugoff 1960

STRAIT OF MAGELLAN

The narrow passage between the southern tip of South America and Tierra del Fuego is called the Strait of Magellan. Exploring this intricate and dangerously complex series of channels, Ferdinand Magellan finally found a navigable sequence in 1520 and thus bestowed upon it his name. Upon reaching the open sea and finding it calm, Magellan proclaimed it "Pacific" (peaceful, tranquil).

One of the great challenges of navigating around the tip of South America is the difficult choice of routes: both possibilities have elements of extreme danger. Even with Magellan's map, risking the shallow, narrow, and confusing strait proved fatal to many captains. Alternatively, rounding the ferocious Cape Horn south of Tierra del Fuego meant enduring monumental seas, frequent storms, and vicious winds.

In subsequent centuries navigation charts improved considerably, and the Strait of Magellan became the preferred route. However, a new peril arose in the seventeenth century: buccaneers. The maze of channels and calm water was the perfect setting for marauding pirates to ambush trading ships and then escape. Heavy cargo ships and even the large galleons (warships) could not maneuver as well as the smaller, more nimble pirate vessels. Hence the Strait of Magellan became treacherous once again as the site of many great battles.

See also: Cape Horn; Magellan, Ferdinand
References: Oxford Atlas of Exploration 1997

SWIFT, JONATHAN

One of the greatest talents of Jonathan Swift (born Irish, English, 1667–1745) was to be many things at once. So it is with his writing: his great works can be read from various vantage points with equally satisfying results. Thus, although he is known as a satirist, a political pundit, and a clergyman, we might also read him as one of the finest of travel writers. His most famous work, *Gulliver's Travels* (1726), is also arguably one of the finest pieces of travel literature of the eighteenth century.

Throughout his life, Swift was torn between Dublin, his home, and London, the center of his literary, political, and ecclesiastical careers. His personal travels were few and not particularly adventurous, but between these cities he journeyed many times. Just as any of the great travelers, Swift keenly observed these two sites, often alternating between being the insider and the outsider. Indeed, his strange status as neither (or both) Irish and English, at a time of intense rivalry and antagonism between the two, is a fascinating story in and of itself. For a variety of reasons, Swift was able to critique both places and politics with equal ease.

Swift's numerous publications delve into a wide range of subjects, but among the majority of them there is a commonality: social satire. Repeatedly, Swift attacked social behavior, political dealings, foreign policy, and education with his cutting wit and incisive satiric tales; in short, society was his target.

His singular work of travel fiction, and to a degree travel satire, is *Gulliver's Travels.* On a purely formal level, he took the travel narrative—an ambiguous form that could be either fact or fiction—and toyed with it. To European audiences of the eighteenth century, exotic travel accounts of the South Pacific, Africa, and the Americas provided an increasingly shocking and astounding source of wild tales. Cannibalism, strange hybrid creatures, bizarre rituals, and sexual immodesty were the stock and trade of popular travel stories of the day. Swift plays off this tradition by anchoring Gulliver in the almost plausible and then pushing him off into the realm of the satirically impossible.

With his characteristic good humor and energetic wit, Swift fabricated a text that could not be categorized. Much of it was

Gulliver in Brobdingnag; *illustration from Jonathan Swift's* Gulliver's Travels *(Bettmann / Corbis)*

thought to have been partly or wholly true. Debates raged around the text, as they often did around Swift's writing. His deft parody of form and theme left Swift's contemporary readers off balance: to right themselves, they had either to accept the tale as true or to reject it as enchanting fantasy. Either way, to this day, the utopian tale has been swallowed on some level: the rationality of the cultures that Gulliver visits makes too much sense to be denied entirely.

The story is fairly complex. Lemuel Gulliver, doctor on a sailing ship, narrates his tale of adventure. His voyages are presented as travelogues that read, by and large, very much like so many other "real" accounts. These journeys take him to four separate places—Lilliput, Brobdingnag, Laputa, and Houyhnhnm-

land—each of which teaches Gulliver a new lesson. Perhaps unrealistically, each adventure is written as a individual excursion framed by a return to the ship.

The first part of the book introduces the character of Gulliver and sets him quickly off to sea. Promptly, he is shipwrecked and finds himself a survivor in Lilliput, the inhabitants of which are a mere six inches tall. Everything physical is scaled down in size; but as though to compensate for their physical stature, the Lilliputians are hugely pompous and self-important. These irritable and querulous folk are constantly bickering, squabbling, and fighting over the most trivial of matters. As a result, Gulliver deems them a ridiculous people. Throughout, there are multiple veiled references to English and Irish issues that mark

Lilliput as a satire. Indeed, by making his readers look at a foolish foreign "race," Swift has made them also look in the mirror.

In contrast, giants populate Brobdingnag. Accidentally left on the shore of this land, Gulliver finds here the inverse of Lilliput. He assumes that because the natives are gigantic, they must be brutes; instead, they prove to be precisely the opposite. In this section Gulliver is made to tell the king all about the manners, customs, and political structure of Europe. When described and critiqued by the king, the familiar ways of Europe seem laughably petty and unthinkably stupid. Proclaims His Majesty at the end of Gulliver's account, "I cannot but conclude the bulk of your natives to be the most pernicious race of little odious vermin that nature ever suffered to crawl upon the surface of the earth" (Swift 2095). Once again, observing the foreign causes Gulliver, and Swift's readers, to reflect inwardly.

Gulliver's next destination is Laputa, a floating island filled with "wise men." These wise men—scientists, philosophers, historians, and the like—prove, of course, to be fools. Their theories and ideas provide a hilarious mockery of many of Swift's contemporaries. The wise men are so enthralled by their studies that they have no conception of the practical details of daily life. Their absurd experiments, irrational conclusions, and universal misery make Laputa decidedly distasteful to Gulliver.

Finally, our protagonist sails to Houyhnhnmland, where the eponymous Houyhnhnms and Yahoos dwell. The former are horses with human intellect; the latter are human bodies with the intellect of beasts. Gulliver assumes physical form to be an indication of intellectual capacity, thus he is shocked to find his expectations frustrated by the reverse. What appear to be horses are deeply logical, compassionate, and inquisitive creatures. In a word, the Houyhnhnms are exemplary in their humanistic rationality. In contrast, what appears to be human turns out to be base, vile, cruel, and brutish. Ugly and selfish desires and passions drive the Yahoos. This confusion sends Gulliver into a great depression of self-doubt, for he has to wonder what he is. When he is expelled by the Houyhnhnms, he finds that a deep and intractable misanthropy dominates him.

After all is said and done, both Gulliver and Swift's readers have learned from the foreign. Gulliver is a ruined man who cannot return to his home because it is too grim and horrible after what he has seen. His exposure to the wildly exotic has changed his perception of the familiar. Similarly, readers have been made to reflect on their social, intellectual, and individual structure.

Through these adventures, Swift's details disguise the text as travel literature. Notation of flora and fauna, precise observations and descriptions of his hosts, and the frame story of Gulliver being a ship surgeon on a journey with these tales his letters home all suggest a true tale of travel. And while the various races he meets are odd indeed, they are not so exaggerated as to be entirely unbelievable. We therefore read the tale as a travelogue, accepting the fantasy of strange and wondrous races in far-flung places. Swift has caught us with his craft, and we believe the illusion.

The result is a bitter and wry critique of the folly of humanity. Foolish, brutish, irrational, and endlessly corruptible, mankind appears a bungled mistake. If these are the lessons that *Gulliver's Travels* presents its readers, we have assuredly been taken on a wild journey into self-reflection and analysis of what it is to be "enlightened" and "civilized."

References: Fussell 1987; Harvey 1967; Swift 1987

TATCHELL, FRANK

A mostly unknown English vicar, Frank Tatchell (fl. 1920) composed a single rather interesting travel book. His book of travel advice, titled *The Happy Traveler: A Book for Poor Men* (1923), is a delight. Although he lived in Sussex, judging from his text, he must have wandered far and wide. Above all, Tatchell describes travel as a form of learning: from the experience of travel, one can learn volumes.

As his title suggests, Tatchell was an advocate of traveling on the cheap. For him, travel, motion, and experience were simply different facets of the same experience. Full of somewhat dubious tips for the nearly destitute traveler, this text amuses for its enthusiasm. Whether proffering advice as to how to thwart stray dogs or explaining the fineries of ditch camping, Tatchell provides a rare voice for the impoverished wanderer. For him, tourism—with its hotels, servants, and private cars—is not travel at all; it is only under duress that a traveler can engage a foreign culture.

References: Newby 1985

TAYLOR, JOHN

Known in his day as "the water poet" because he worked as a waterman on the Thames River, John Taylor (English, 1580–1653) supplemented his wages by writing verse. Eventually, the verse caught the ear of Ben Jonson, who sponsored Taylor's literary efforts.

Beloved for his bawdy and energetic rhymes, he began to publish pamphlets. Thus encouraged, Taylor made a series of journeys in order to write about them: indeed, the stated objective of the adventures was to produce texts about the journeys. Over the years he published a fair number of works, which he collected and published as *All the Workes of John Taylor, the Water Poet* (1630). This volume contains a variety of voyaging tales. Among the best are *The Penniless Pilgrimage* (1618), which tells of Taylor's trek from London to Edinburgh on foot, and *Taylor's Travels from London to Prague,* which chronicles his lengthy voyage to pay tribute to the queen of Bohemia. In all of his work, Taylor demonstrates an acute eye for detail and difference.

Quirky, daft, and bold, Taylor's adventures are indeed remarkable. Combined with his considerable talent as a poet, Taylor's tales make for interesting travel literature. It remains a considerable achievement to have survived such adventures and to have retold them in clear, clean verse. In addition, Taylor can be noted as an uncommon voice of a less educated traveler who attempted, to the best of his ability, to capture objectively what he observed.

References: Crossley-Holland 1986; Harvey 1967

THACKERAY, WILLIAM MAKEPEACE

William Makepeace Thackeray (English, 1811–1863) may be well known as a Victorian novelist, but much of his early career was devoted to travel writing. Even his greatest novels—*Vanity Fair, Henry Esmond,* and *Barry Lyndon*—contain significant remnants of his early wandering and echoes of his conviction that restlessness encourages change. For Thackeray, motion signaled transition, for better or for worse. In his life as in his writing, moving from one culture to another

Portrait of William Makepeace Thackeray (Library of Congress)

provided an outward manifestation of psychological and emotional changes.

Born in Calcutta into the family of an English civil servant, Thackeray began his life from a foreign perspective. Perhaps his foreign early years caused England always to seem odd to him: often he found much of his life in Britain maddening. When his father died, the family returned to England, and Thackeray, age six, was sent to the best schools. He refused to apply himself at Cambridge University and left without a degree in order to travel in Europe with some friends. This trip seems to have inspired him to write.

An accomplished draftsman as well as writer, Thackeray submitted some of his sketches and essays for publication. In 1836, he had some drawings accepted, and a number of small successes followed. He moved to Paris to become a correspondent but found himself uncomfortable there too. Nonetheless, he wrote *The Paris Sketchbook* (1840)

during this uneasy time. It contains drawings and commentary about the lifestyle, sights, manners, and fashions of the French capital.

His next journey was to Ireland. The results of this expedition were disappointingly similar to his Paris experiment: he found Ireland less than he expected, but he wrote a book, again containing drawings and commentary, called, unimaginatively, *The Irish Sketchbook* (1843). Nevertheless, in conjunction with his fiction, these sketchbooks sold and were received courteously by critics. They remain interesting as an insight into Thackeray's own unstable period: the things he notices and comments upon are quite telling.

With his rising success, Thackeray gained greater confidence and thus took more literary chances. His great works unfolded rather quickly thereafter. Still restless, he sailed to Athens, Constantinople, Jerusalem, and Cairo in 1844. On this trip he wrote the extremely interesting *Notes of a Journey from Cornhill to Grand Cairo* (1846). It is in this text that he finally uses his significant literary talents to write travel literature. Although this work was composed as a sequence of notes and vignettes, Thackeray finally escapes the rigid confines of simple observation to delve into interpretation and a more evocative style. He begins to play with major issues like cynicism, difference, and the disappointment resulting from frustrated expectations (often what he found when he traveled). Continuing with his pattern of sketchbooks, this one is illustrated with his original drawings as well.

In addition to his novels and travel tales, Thackeray is also noted for his poetry. A number of fine examples have been anthologized and reprinted, perhaps the best among them being "The Ballad of Bouillabaisse." The poem tells of a traveling narrator who revisits his favorite haunt in Paris, a small hotel that serves sublime bouillabaisse. The return to a familiar, yet still foreign, place is often cause for conflicted emotions; indeed, in memory pleasant things have a way of becoming impossibly nice. Finding that the proprietor has died, the narrator laments the swift passage of years and the impossibility of reliving fond memories. Dispirited at the news, he sinks into his recollections. To his happy surprise, the new cook's soup proves to be different but remarkably pleasant nonetheless. What could have been a somber poem about loss turns out to be a celebration of the new. To be sure, it is travel that provides the setting and the frame for this lesson.

The themes of travel literature are most apparent in Thackeray's travel sketches, but in his novels, as well as in his life, travel plays a crucial role. Most often, travel opens his eyes not so much to the nature of the foreigner, but to his own state of mind. It is this self-reflective learning that marks Thackeray's work as travel writing.

References: Crossley-Holland 1986; Harvey 1967; Newby 1985

THEROUX, PAUL

Paul Theroux (American, 1941–) has been one of the dominant voices in travel literature since the publication of his first travel book in 1975. Often deemed post-touristic because of his emphasis on the travail of travel, he is among the most entertaining and sophisticated of the contemporary travel writers. Keenly aware of the history of travel literature, Theroux often plays with many of the canonical travel authors by borrowing some of their mannerisms, writing styles, textual structures, or destinations. His output has been vast but of consistently superior quality.

A fairly ordinary, middle-class upbringing led to the usual soul-searching in college. After graduation, still unsure of what he wanted to do, Theroux made a journey to Africa. This journey inspired him to write, and he published several interesting pieces of reportage in various magazines and newspapers. The travel bug had bitten him, but freelancing as a young journalist proved to be the fast track to poverty. He joined the Peace

Corps and seemed to like it well enough, but he refused to stifle his political opinions. Particularly, he vociferously protested the U.S. involvement in Vietnam; after several warnings, the Peace Corps expelled him.

Teaching English seemed a natural option. From 1968 to 1971, he taught in Singapore and devoted his spare time to travel and writing. This proved to be the recipe for success. He continued to explore Asia far and wide, gathering ideas for his first best-selling travelogue, *The Great Railway Bazaar.* He moved to England in 1972 to write full time and to live with his family.

For Theroux, it is unthinkable to write simply from imagination. Instead, he writes of what he knows; his novels are autobiographical in that they record real experiences but novelistic in that they are composed, edited, and polished for maximum literary punch. After his first handful of successful travel books, Theroux branched out into a variety of different novelistic genres, although in almost all of them there are substantial elements of travel and a lively array of exotic settings.

The Great Railway Bazaar (1975) launched Theroux's career. Although written as a first-person travelogue, the story reads more like a novel. It tells the story of one man's encounter with the largest continent on earth. Along this epic railway odyssey, Theroux vividly evokes a picture of travel as decidedly distinct from tourism. Rather than making the usual codified observations of tourist attractions and describing the superficial traits of the locals, Theroux develops his characters with considerable care. From a sequence of famous rail routes—the Orient Express, the Khyber Mail, and the Trans-Siberian Express—he observes the vast quantity of difference to be found. Through Turkey, Iran, India, Southeast Asia, Japan, and the Soviet Union, Theroux experiences the faded glory of once-opulent rail travel. In a nod to the great nineteenth-century travelers, he feels nostalgia for the elegant train cars and stations of old. Indeed, the slowness of rail travel delights Theroux: only in slow transitions can one note many of the subtle changes that occur culturally, geographically, and emotionally.

Throughout the story, Theroux's focus is on people. Never one to sugarcoat his experiences, he seems just as comfortable critiquing as praising. Perhaps this is one aspect of his insistence that he is a traveler, not a tourist: whereas the tourist is inclined to gush effusively, the traveler would rather tell a story that balances the good with the bad. Often indulgently wild, as though looking for a great story, Theroux takes a number of moderate risks. Drugs, contraband, prostitutes, and dealings with petty criminals recur repeatedly. At its heart, as with all pure travel literature, *The Great Railway Bazaar* is mostly about its narrator. The variety of things that annoy or even outrage him, the numerous fabricated identities he assumes, and the development that he undergoes make the story a novel about a traveler rather than observations of a sequence of places. In the end, the novel itself reflects Theroux's flagging energy: in its tone, language, and scope, the novel loses steam as the journey winds down.

The Old Patagonian Express (1979) describes Theroux's next great railway excursion. Instead of Asia, he tackles the Americas. From Boston to southern Argentina, Theroux rides the rails again. Predictably, he encounters a myriad of fascinating characters and plenty of difficulties. His incisive observations regarding the considerable effort of travel are at once humorous and alarming. The vast quantity of time this journey takes allows the narrative to flow at a gentle and easy pace; some find it a bit too slow. As in his earlier work, Theroux tells his story as he sees it: nothing in this book is whitewashed in order to make it pleasant. Travel for Theroux is hard work, an integral part of which is prolonged observation and keeping a written account.

Riding the Iron Rooster (1988) describes Theroux's railway voyage through China.

With his adventurous spirit and rich prose, he has produced a fascinating study of the ordinary people's China. His commentary ranges from the cultural revolution to Mao Tsetung, from the stoic perseverance of Chinese farmers to the curious tokens of Western capitalism visible in the cities. Much of this study is overtly directed at wondering not what China can learn from the West, but what the West can learn from China. This theme of cultural cross-pollination is rarely expressed so openly; perhaps it reflects Theroux's own openness to foreign ideas and ways. In stark contrast to this overarching theme, much of Theroux's individual descriptions are highly negative and critical of the Chinese. While many find him offensively cantankerous, Theroux always attacks genuine problems that are, in most cases, quite possible to fix. In this travel book, as in his first two, he clearly marks himself not as a tourist seeking simply to be amused, but as a traveler there to learn and to write a story.

The Happy Isles of Oceania: Paddling the Pacific (1992) tells of Theroux's journey through dozens of Pacific islands in a kayak. He starts in New Zealand and then proceeds to New Guinea; from there, he ranges far and wide. Wandering, or rather paddling, to many of the famous South Seas destinations, Theroux follows in the wake of Herman Melville, Robert Louis Stevenson, W. Somerset Maugham, Louis-Antoine de Bougainville, and many other famous travel writers. Instead of idealizing these places and finding them paradise regained, Theroux is often critical. This island is pest-ridden, the food on that one is bad, everything is dirty, the natives are absurdly superstitious—these are only a few of his complaints. But rather than simply whining, Theroux is playing against the tradition: where his predecessors romanticized these places, Theroux is demystifying them. They are just real, human places with beauty and flaws. Such honesty and realism met with considerable public criticism: most people want to keep these places mythically pure.

Theroux's objective seems to be travel for the sake of travel. Tautological as that sounds, it in fact recalls the aesthetic movement's "art for art's sake" doctrine. The comparison works: travel for Theroux is a worthy end in itself. One result is that the focus shifts away from the place and its people to the author and his struggles to make sense of what he sees. Always, Theroux's adventures are admirably bold, and in spite of his complaining, he displays extraordinary tenacity. His work blends precise and vivid observation of the region with a more complex narrative of the nature of travel. At his best, he offers fascinating insights into the power of isolation and the grueling self-reflection that occurs on such a journey.

In addition to a number of very fine works of short travel stories, Theroux has published many book-length works that intersect the genre of travel literature in some fashion. *The Mosquito Coast* (1981) fictionally depicts the adventures of an expatriate father and son in South America. *Kingdom by the Sea: A Journey around the Coast of Great Britain* (1983) is a comic, teasing look at the British—their manners and their sense of identity. *The Pillars of Hercules* (1995) represents Theroux's Grand Tour of the Mediterranean, where he revisits many of the cities of classic travel literature. *My Other Life* (1996) revisits Theroux's early days in Africa, Singapore, and London as a struggling travel writer. *On the Edge of the Great Rift* (1996) contains three separate, wholly fictive novels of Africa. *Kowloon* (1997) addresses identity issues in the politically challenged city of Hong Kong. *Sir Vidia's Shadow* (1998) chronicles Theroux's journey as a writer, from his earliest days of reading travel literature to his huge success.

Throughout his oeuvre (body of work), Theroux plays the foreigner, always remaining detached and irascible but perfectly observant. There is always a gap between him and the locals whom he encounters. This distance is what the travel writer seeks to bridge, however artificially. In this regard, Theroux is successful, for he allows his readers to have various experiences without actually sitting on a train for 12 weeks. Additionally, his constant awareness of the process of writing represents a sophisticated literary device. Repeatedly, the narrator is asked what he is doing in a given place; his answer, writing a book. The labor of travel produces literature. Theroux recognizes that the work of a journey results in insight and wisdom that he can share with his readers.

See also: Grand Tour
References: Fussell 1987; Newby 1985

THOMPSON, HUNTER S.

Hunter S. Thompson (American, 1935–) writes a strange type of parodic travel literature. His stories often tangle travel, drugs, and lawlessness into a happy, illicit bundle. As a result, his novels are wildly popular with some readers and infamous among others. One thing is sure: his stories tell of wanton, capricious trips whereon the journey is the object of the exercise.

In the early 1960s, Thompson recognized his wanderlust. He had found middling success as a journalist in the States and apparently figured that he could find equal success in a more interesting locale. Thus he moved to Rio de Janeiro to serve as a foreign correspondent. After two years, he had published journalistic and creative pieces and had discovered a wild style of living. Many of his travel vignettes are told in his best-seller *The Great Shark Hunt* (1962). He returned to San Francisco and promptly went undercover to write a book-length exposé of the Hell's Angels motorcycle gang. His other major travel piece is *Fear and Loathing in Las Vegas* (1971).

The Great Shark Hunt is a rather whimsical title for a book that has little to do with fishing. Instead, the "sharks" are stories, some of which are dangerous and might consume a person. As a reporter, Thompson's reason for traveling is to gather tales, write them up in a dramatically entertaining fashion, and publish them for cash. Travel functions as his labor, and writing is what his stories are about. Thus we see Thompson arriving in a poor Latin American village: "As I came over the brink of the cliff, a few children laughed, an old hag began screeching, and the men just stared. Here was a white man with twelve Yankee dollars in his pocket and more than $500 worth of camera gear slung over his shoulders, hauling a typewriter, grinning, sweating, no hope of speaking the language, no place to stay—and somehow they were going to have to deal with me" (Newby 494). To be sure, Thompson is no escape-oriented tourist, but rather a traveler ready to coax stories out of his travel experiences.

Similarly, in *Fear and Loathing in Las Vegas,* the purpose of the journey is to write. The narrator is on assignment from his magazine to cover a convention: "I was, after all, a professional journalist; so I had an obligation to *cover the story,* for good or ill" (Thompson 4). Thompson takes a relatively tame scenario and blows it into a surreal vision of travel made monstrous. Through an outrageously heavy drug and alcohol haze, the narrator experiences every possible traveler's nightmare, from botched reservations to legal trouble. In lieu of a tourist's sedate and rational response to such adversities, Thompson's narrator responds in the worst possible way (but never gets caught): with violence, hysteria, and deception. In the end, he has taken the mother of all road trips, and therein resides the story.

Thompson's travel literature also implicitly recognizes travel as the best means for self-reflection. Through their difficulties, the characters grow and learn of themselves. Whether in South America or the Nevada desert, the experience of a different geography and a strange culture jostles the traveler's perspective sufficiently to allow him to see differently. As a postmodern example of travel literature,

Thompson's work bends traditions in odd and interesting directions without discarding them entirely.

References: Newby 1985; Thompson 1971

THOREAU, HENRY DAVID

Noted essayist and philosopher Henry David Thoreau (American, 1817–1862) can be considered a travel writer as well. While his writing addressees many issues—naturalism, self-reliance, politics, and spiritualism—simultaneously, his works fundamentally are travelogues that describe his impressions of and response to various locales. Indeed, for Thoreau, life is a sort of journey in which the

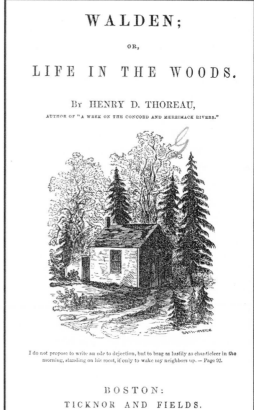

Title page of Walden; or Life in the Woods, *1854, showing Thoreau's hut at Walden Pond, Massachusetts (Library of Congress)*

experience of various people and places encourages self-discovery. As a transcendentalist philosopher, perhaps Thoreau would also have agreed that spiritual growth is an idealized journey that behaves very much like physical travel.

Several of Thoreau's works can well be seen as travel literature. *A Week on the Concord and Merrimack Rivers* (1849), *The Maine Woods* (1864), *Cape Cod* (1865), and *A Yankee in Canada* (1866) all contain considerable elements of travel and exposure to cultural difference. Thoreau's journeys were occasions to learn and to reflect upon the nature of humanity. But it his most famous work, *Walden* (1854), that is perhaps best read as travel writing.

In 1845, Thoreau began his famous experiment with self-reliance: he moved into an isolated cabin and vowed to "live deliberately." For two years, he more or less sustained himself independently. His elaborate daily journals were then crafted and shaped into the collection of reflections that we know as *Walden*. It is key to note that one of the objectives of his self-exile was to force himself to write. The journey thus functioned as an impetus toward literary production.

The book tells of Thoreau coming to know himself in the strange and silent forest. By escaping conventions of society, like shopping or wearing ornamental clothes, he was able to reflect upon the nature of that society. By stepping outside of the familiar, Thoreau gained a new perspective. This shift in viewpoint is the traveler's principal trick. To be sure, Thoreau gives us numerous beautiful details of his "foreign land," yet the primary emphasis of his story is on how the experience caused him to see himself and his former lifestyle very differently.

Thoreau's exuberant style of writing and his obvious enthusiasm for his project lead to some breathlessly beautiful passages. His deep affection for nature, labor, idealism, and simplicity manifests itself in most of the 18 essays of the book. As a travelogue, his book thrills, for we are given an account of an incredible journey inward toward what Thoreau imagined is best in humanity.

References: Hart 1965

TOCQUEVILLE, ALEXIS DE

Historian and political theorist Alexis de Tocqueville (French, 1805–1859) may be best known for his studies of democracy, political upheaval, and social structures, but he also penned two significant works of travel literature. While his famous histories, *L'Ancien régime et la révolution* (1856) and *De la démocratie en Amérique* (1835), were published in his lifetime, Tocqueville's vast quantity of personal travel notes—carefully organized and revised—was not edited or translated until well into the twentieth century. J. P. Mayer and Yale University Press issued several volumes of Tocqueville's travel writing in 1959;

Portrait of Alexis de Tocqueville (Library of Congress)

they are published in English as *Journeys to England and Ireland* and *Journey to America.*

Deeply concerned with encouraging political freedom and civil rights, Tocqueville made extensive visits to England and Ireland in the 1830s and 1840s. His purpose was to compare and to contrast the relatively stable politics of England with the turbulent politics of France. In a scholarly manner, Tocqueville did what all great travelers do: he went abroad to help learn of his homeland. What he found was a system of government that was arcane and tangled up in an immense history. The common people whom he met had little sense of their practical role in government; the parliamentarians and minor politicians, in contrast, had an inflated sense of duty. As an exercise in precise observation, *Journeys to England and Ireland* is invaluable. Not only does it provide one of the enduring pictures of British society of the era, but also it asks numerous provocative and insightful questions about the ideal role of government. Tocqueville possesses a rare intellectual methodology that balances a highly sophisticated theoretical apparatus with sociological data and real interviews.

Still seeking other perspectives on the same subjects, Tocqueville set off for America in 1831. He wanted to observe a fledgling democracy firsthand. For nearly a year, he toured New York, Boston, New Orleans, and many parts in between. His observations appear in *Journey to America,* although it contains but a selection of the 14 volumes he originally composed (Adams 516). His experiences in the United States were deeply moving: many of the ideas from this journey appear in more highly developed, theoretical form in his later political writings.

Ever thorough, Tocqueville sought a large sample of important personages. University presidents, Supreme Court judges, prominent businessmen, and local politicians all appear in his account. His method was to engage people in animated and intricate discourse; essentially, Tocqueville interviewed dozens of people. Not content to visit only the powerful, he also sought out former slaves, Native Americans, and farmers. For his breadth of subjects, Tocqueville is rare and valuable. The topics he discussed were often thorny: the justice system, taxation, civics, North versus South animosity, and the breach with England. Charming and witty, Tocqueville had a great gift for inspiring people to talk about their ideas. Faithfully, he recorded them.

In addition to Tocqueville's social and political observations, *Journey to America* contains several substantive essays on the natural splendor and vastness of the United States. Greatly impressed by the scale of the country and by the myth of the frontier, Tocqueville made trips into the wilderness with American Indian guides. He believed that abundant wilderness had a decided influence upon the collective character of Americans.

In his travels in America, Tocqueville found what he was seeking: something to inspire hope for the future of democracy. Armed with this evidence, he returned to his homeland with a clarified vision of French history. His subsequent political writing owes much to his observations—some of them clearly idealized or romanticized—of America. His voyages taught him to see his familiar France in a slightly different light.

Certainly, Tocqueville is not the most exciting of travel writers, but what he lacks in physical adventure he more than makes up for in intellectual brilliance. This brand of literary and theoretical travel literature reminds us of the significant impact travel can have on both individuals and politics.

References: Adams 1988; Benét 1965

TRENCH, RICHARD CHENEVIX

As the Anglican archbishop of Dublin, Richard Chenevix Trench (English, 1807–1886) had both great privileges and great power. After completing his education, he embarked upon the first of numerous visits throughout

Europe and to North Africa; these trips would impel a portion of his writing toward travel. Beyond his political and religious abilities, he was a poet and an intellectual as well. His work with the Philological Society supported the project to move ahead with the *Oxford New English Dictionary*. In addition, he has several volumes to his name, including *Poems from Eastern Sources* (1842), *The Study of Words* (1851), *English Past and Present* (1855), and *Alma and Other Poems* (1865). While not a major travel poet, some of his poems are interesting illustrations.

"Gibraltar," for example, figures travel as a tool of self-awareness and patriotism.

> England, we love thee better than we
>   know.—
>   And this I learned when, after wand'rings
>   long
> 'Mid people of another stock and tongue,
> I heard again thy martial music blow,
> And saw thy gallant children to and fro
>   Pace, keeping ward at one of those huge
>   gates,
>   Twin giants watching the Herculean
>   Straits.
> When first I came in sight of that brave show,
>   It made the very heart within me dance,
>   To think that thou thy proud foot shouldst
>   advance
>   Forward so far into the mighty sea.
> Joy was it and exultation to behold
>   Thine ancient standard's rich
>   emblazonry,
>   A glorious picture by the wind unrolled.
> (Crossley-Holland 84)

As all readers are sure to note, this poem gushes with patriotism and nationalism. In good Victorian fashion, England is figured as the mighty mother. She is stable, strong, and forgiving as she watches her "gallant children to and fro." The state and the queen—the body politic and the monarch's body—conflate into a single entity. Remember that Trench is writing during the height of the British Empire, thus British influence is truly global.

Yet the narrator is not sailing home to Great Britain at all. He is, as the title of the poem indicates, passing through the Straits of Gibraltar. We must recall that Gibraltar was under British control at the time and was therefore guarded by towers, flags, armed men, and gates, all under Her Majesty's control. The narrator feels both pride and a sense of security. We might read between the lines a bit to infer that he has felt rather alienated in those lands not under British dominion.

The key to the poem as a work of travel literature is in the first three lines. The narrator suggests that only by long wanderings in foreign lands does he recognize how much he loves his motherland (and mother tongue). Said otherwise, by extensively visiting foreign places, the narrator comes to know his home—and, by extension, he comes to know himself. Perhaps we can see in "Gibraltar" a moment of clear self-recognition, where the narrator realizes what he has learned from his travels. It is just such an epiphany—that travel teaches us of ourselves—that marks this poem, to my mind, as great travel writing.

References: Crossley-Holland 1986

TROLLOPE, ANTHONY

Like his mother, Frances Milton Trollope, Anthony Trollope (English, 1815–1882) wrote an enormous quantity of books. Famous for his novels of Victorian life, particularly the Barsetshire series and the parliamentary cycle known as the Palliser novels, he also wrote several interesting and praiseworthy travel books. Describing his intention, Trollope said, "A novel should give a picture of common life enlivened by humor and sweetened by pathos" (Benét 1027). He could equally have been describing his travel literature.

Born into a poor family, he started his career as a low-grade post office official. After observing his mother's literary success, he started moonlighting as a writer. His first novel was published in 1847, although he kept his day job for many years, even after his literary success and popularity were considerable. Evidently a man of extraordinary energy, he found time between his office work, his writing, and his fairly active social schedule to make a number of major voyages and journeys.

Trollope's travel books are dully titled but quite interesting to read. They are *The West Indies and Spanish Main* (1859), *North America* (1862), *Travelling Sketches* (1866), *Australia* (1873), and *South Africa* (1878). All five books are voluminous, meticulous, and very tidily organized, yet they all have moments of novelistic excitement and imaginative evocations. He insisted upon reworking, editing, and polishing his work considerably; the result is a superior literary quality. A single example will serve to illustrate. In describing miners in *South Africa,* he writes, "Perhaps the most interesting sight at the mine is the escaping of the men from their labour at six o'clock. Then, at the sound of some welcomed gong, they begin to swarm up the sides close to each other's heels apparently altogether indifferent as to whether there be a path or no. They come as flies come up a wall, only capering as flies never caper—and shouting as they come. In endless strings, as ants follow each other, they move on" (Rugoff 359).

His first major journey was ostensibly in an official capacity: he was charged with observing and restructuring the postal system in the West Indies. From this journey grew his first travel book, *The West Indies and Spanish Main.* The most factual and businesslike of his travel books, it contains lengthy descriptions of commerce, politics, geography, and culture. Modern readers may balk at Trollope's unquestioning sense of British superiority and native incompetence. In spite of some unsavory elements, the account offers a wealth of data and insight into the British commercial, colonial, and intellectual interests in the West Indies.

With his mother and some of his siblings in America, Trollope made four journeys to the United States. His first journey corresponded to the beginning of the Civil War, thus much of the book *North America* is a lucid and objective discussion of both the Northern and Southern positions. Like his mother, although not quite so vitriolic, he roundly criticized American manners and social graces. Nonetheless, he expresses a wide-eyed fascination with the cities and the people whom he encountered. His description of Washington, D.C., mostly under construction, is a great reminder to modern Americans of the brevity of our history. In his travels to the frontier, mainly the Midwest, he finds the excitement and rawness that he had hoped to experience.

His son had immigrated to Australia, causing Trollope twice to sail the Pacific Ocean to visit. *Australia* describes the journeys and his impressions. If Trollope was critical of the United States, he was disparaging of Australia. With its penal atmosphere and extreme isolation, yet its relative lack of exotic natives, Australia, for Trollope, had little to recommend it. The possible exception was the honesty and forthrightness he found there: unlike America, Australia had no pretense of being "civilized," innovative, or independent. Scarcely redeeming qualities!

Late in his life, Trollope felt the need to visit the only major British colony he had not seen: South Africa. His two-volume account, *South Africa,* ranges broadly over the culture and the natural beauty of the colony. On horseback he crisscrossed the substantial distances of colony. His interaction with Boer farmers provides a rare glimpse at the unrest that would lead to the Boer War (1899–1902). With great excitement, he describes the diamond mines, the wildlife, and the positive influence of British rule on the "natives." In some ways, his last effort is his best: he takes more literary chances and bounces more wildly than ever before among his images and his themes.

In addition to his actual travel accounts, Trollope wrote a magnificent book called *Travelling Sketches* that can best be described as a series of essays on aspects of travel. In this book he addresses the benefits and difficulties of traveling alone, obstacles to female travelers, reasons for travel, tips for emigrating families, travel as entertainment, as adventure, and as education, and finally, in an essay so titled, "Tourists Who Don't Like Their Travels." A wonderful primer that sold quite well, it provides us with a glimpse of Trollope's theories on travel.

Throughout his travel writing, Trollope maintained a comparative stance: in all five books his scrutiny of his destination is in comparison to Britain. In this regard, travel taught Trollope to know his homeland. In the colonies he was confronted often with unpleasant interpretations of familiar ideas, manners, and customs. Trollope had an open enough mind to see his own society reflected in the colonies, not always in the best light. Furthermore, for his orderly structures and well-crafted style, Trollope remains one of the great literary reporters of foreign travels.

See also: Trollope, Frances
References: Benét 1965; Harvey 1967; Rugoff 1960

TROLLOPE, FRANCES

Frances (née Milton) Trollope (English, 1780–1863) has many claims to fame. Author of 40-odd books, family breadwinner, and mother to equally prolific Victorian author Anthony Trollope, Frances Trollope inspires with her energy and strength. She also wrote several famous works of travel literature.

Frances Trollope refused to conform to the gender roles advocated by her era. Finding her family reduced to poverty, she began her monumental literary career, eventually supporting them comfortably with her writing. Her early novels tend toward sentimentality and sensationalism, and they had

correspondingly weak sales. It was only after she set out to observe and reflect upon the world that her writing became popular and more literary.

After a three-year stint in the United States, she published her masterpiece of travel literature, *Domestic Manners of the Americans* (1832). The book met with wildly mixed reviews: the Americans took great offense at her representation, whereas the English found it wonderfully sound. Such raging debate about her work assured her a level of fame that made her subsequent dozen books best-sellers.

Never one to soft-pedal her ideas, Trollope spoke forcefully and earnestly on a wide range of subjects. A great critic of puritanical prudery, an advocate of women's rights, a vehement antislavery activist, and a sophisticated theorist of democracy, she courted controversy with her writing. Said Mark Twain of her *Domestic Manners,* "She knew her subject well, and she set it forth fairly and squarely without any ifs and ands and buts. She deserved gratitude but it is an error to suppose she got it" (Fussell 295).

While in the United States, she lived for almost two years in Cincinnati, then in a small frontier town. The rest of the time she traveled widely and compiled a wonderful selection of tales and reflections. Her descriptions of Niagara Falls, New Orleans, and Washington, D.C., are particularly strong.

Her Cincinnati writings are deeply critical of American behavior. She begins the section of *Domestic Manners* on this city by proclaiming, "I never saw any people who appeared to live so much without amusement. . . . I am tempted to believe that a stranger from the continent of Europe would be inclined, on first reconnoitering the city, to suppose that the places of worship were the theatres and cafés of the place" (Fussell 296). Astonished at the puritanical obsession with appearing modest, pious, and chaste, Trollope rails against the lack of discourse, culture, and intellectual freedom. To her mind, such oppressive religious obsessions were exactly what the early Americans had fled from in Europe; to recreate them in the New World seems to her abominable.

America was supposed to be a land of social innovation and fresh ideas, yet Trollope finds it to be as stagnant and exclusionary as Europe. Instead of finding townspeople building a social network around a variety of institutions—school, town hall, neighborhood, etc.—she was disappointed to discover that the church still dominated American social affinities, as it did in Europe. Furthermore, while girls could be educated and granted diplomas, unlike in Europe, they were not allowed to do anything with their education. While the rhetoric of America insisted upon social equality and a degree of class mobility, Trollope finds little to demonstrate these ideas in practice.

Other notable observations in the book include her scathing attack against the treatment of slaves, her lament at the lack of refined manners and taste, and her enthusiasm at the magnificent diversity of the country's geography. Although the title suggests a singular concern with domestic space, much of her book in fact addresses the public and artistic spheres. Commercial habits were of special interest to Trollope, who attempted to start a sort of "bazaar" of European goods in Cincinnati. It failed miserably, much to her chagrin.

In spite of Trollope's enthusiastic lambasting of America, one gets the sense that her criticism is constructive and corrective. She implies that she wants to like the United States and wants to see the immense and obvious promise of this new democracy come to fruition. Indeed, she strives to be fair-minded and equitable in her perceptions. When something merits praise, she eagerly grants it; but when an occasion deserves critique, she is equally eager.

As a traveler, Trollope understood that she was an outsider. She made a considerable effort toward recognizing her potential bias. For example, while on a riverboat from New

Orleans, shortly after arriving, she writes: "I know it is equally easy and invidious to ridicule the peculiarities of appearance and manner in people of a different nation from ourselves; we may, too, at the same moment, be undergoing the same ordeal in their estimation; and moreover, I am by no means disposed to consider whatever is new to me as therefore objectionable; but, nevertheless, it was impossible not to feel repugnance to many of the novelties that now surrounded me" (Adams 511). Much of her book overtly compares America to Europe, presumably with the hope of exchanging some of their respective strengths.

Energetic, insightful, and at times very witty, Trollope's vision of early-nineteenth-century America is a valuable description of both the larger cities—Boston, New York, Washington—and small-town life in a frontier town. She captures a huge quantity of material details and provides a very credible picture of the era. Especially when combined with a smattering of contemporary responses, her book represents a significant contribution to the literature of travel.

See also: Trollope, Anthony
References: Adams 1988; Fussell 1987; Harvey 1967; Robinson 1994

TWAIN, MARK

Mark Twain (American, 1835–1910), the pen name of Samuel Langhorne Clemens, stands as one of the masters of literature; his oeuvre (or collective body of work) includes a number of examples of innovative and exciting travel writing. His travelogues, social commentary, and travel tales are universally praised and appreciated. Witty, incisive, and often irreverent, Twain provides a particularly American voice for literature—travel or otherwise. His impact upon later writers both in the United States and abroad has been monumental.

Photograph of Samuel Langhorne Clemens, c. 1900–1910 (Library of Congress)

Following early days as a Missouri scamp, then riverman, then apprentice printer, Twain set out for the somewhat Wild West of Nevada. Upon arrival, he quickly found work simultaneously as a miner and as a journalist. So began his career of writing accounts of various places, first for newspapers and later for his books. In 1865, his first major story appeared in print: "The Celebrated Jumping Frog of Calaveras County." After this success, Twain made a lecture tour that only inspired him to travel farther and wider.

In 1867, he made his first journey to the Old World, sailing the Mediterranean and visiting historic sites. The chronicle of this voyage he published as *The Innocents Abroad; or, The Pilgrim's Progress* (1869). The book met with wild approval, selling well over 100,000 copies in its first years of publication. Success with this story led him to write a travel account of his early days as a journalist; this he

titled *Roughing It* (1872). A second trip to Europe, this time an extended stay on the Continent, inspired *A Tramp Abroad* (1880). His last travel book, *Following the Equator* (1897), describes a global lecture tour that Twain made in 1895. Between these travel books, Twain wrote numerous novels, short stories, and essays. While not his most famous works, Twain's travel literature has an especial charm and energy that makes it among the most beloved travel writing of all time.

In general, Twain's travel literature is highly readable. He employs a hearty quantity of slang, idiom, and coinages to describe his destinations. The stories are dramatic, exaggerated, and populated with impossibly rich characters, often composites of several people whom he actually met. Twain's travelogues relate the history of a journey, not event by event, but rather in an impressionistic and scattered manner. The result is a sort of realism and believability of setting and events, but with the inclusion of characters that are pure caricature. Nonetheless, his travel tales are primarily autobiographical and written from the narrative perspective of Twain himself. In sum, his tales are easily accessible on the informative or descriptive level, but then they bounce into sarcastic or outrageous exaggeration. As for focus, Twain is more interested in people than places, and he seems as likely to concentrate on his fellow travelers as on the locals.

Innocents Abroad, Twain's first book-length travel piece, is in fact a compilation and reworking of letters written for a variety of newspapers. Steaming on a luxury ship through Italy, Greece, Turkey, Egypt, and the Holy Land, Twain finds more than enough to amuse him. The text somewhat cynically laughs at both his destinations and his fellow travelers. Twain exhibits his trademark irreverence, this time toward the great relics of antiquity.

Throughout the text, he berates tourism and the herd mentality of his fellows. He jests incessantly with the hucksters in the tourist trade and laughs at the poor tourists who are innocent enough to get duped by guides, innkeepers, shop owners, and even corrupt officials. Twain's account delights in that he pokes fun at nearly everything but particularly at cultural behaviors that he does not understand. For good measure, he also ridicules European manners and customs. With their severe awe and overblown sincerity as they encounter the most famous ruins and residue of ancient history, Twain's companions provide ample laughs.

Roughing It continues the same raucous style with a different focus: the western United States. Twain begins his journey in St. Louis and heads west with stops in Nevada, Utah, and California. The text ends with Twain's journey to the Sandwich Islands (now the Hawaiian Islands), where, in real-life chronology, his previous book began. Once

again, the central focus of the story is not on places themselves, but on how the narrator—fairly closely modeled on Twain himself—responds to his variety of experiences.

In this tale we see Twain attempt to live as a miner, journalist, humorist, and writer. Set on the free-spirited frontier, the adventures are exaggerated for effect, as though to prop up the myth of the American West. Facts melt under Twain's obvious desire to be entertaining, thus the story is more bawdy and comical than historically or geographically accurate. Nonetheless, he lauds the frontier spirit that encourages a man to wander. In the end, we can read the story as a tale of growth and development, for the narrator indeed shifts his position from tentative resistance to wandering to a strong acceptance of travel as a grand teacher.

A Tramp Abroad marks Twain's return to Europe. It describes a walking tour through the Black Forest, the Alps, and northern Italy. The pun in the title suggests the story's contents: in its verb form, *tramp* is to trek or wander on foot, but in its noun form, *tramp* is a beggar or homeless wanderer. Playing off both senses of the word, Twain found while on his tour that he was often treated not as a guest, but as an inconvenience. He attributes his tepid welcome to the fact that he is an American, providing one more reason to continue his comic attack on Europe.

A Tramp Abroad represents Twain's most ambitious attempt to address an extensive selection of topics. It is also perhaps the most traditional of all of his travel writing in its style and form. Less vernacular and more romantic in his language, Twain writes at length about the natural beauty he finds, folktales he hears, manners he notes, history he remembers, and art he observes. Although this trip seems to have been the most pleasant of all his travels, he slyly includes his praise for the comparable facets of the United States alongside of his praise for Europe. There remains a subtle hint of satire flowing just beneath the surface; occasionally, this gentle subversion erupts into blatantly satiric tangential accounts of, for example, "the awful German Language" or "The Great French Duel." With its sophisticated structure and themes, this may be Twain's most accomplished travelogue.

Following the Equator reverses many of the trends in Twain's first three travel books. Struggling with debt from failed speculation, Twain was forced to make a world lecture tour. Reluctantly, he set out for Asia, Australia, and India (with stops along the way). The text tells of this forced travel, and as such, none of the joy of free wandering is present. Instead, Twain is bitter and sardonic with his highly complex and analytical cultural comparisons. He focuses a large portion of the text on Australia, evidently fascinated by the profound differences between it and his homeland. As both are former British colonies geographically isolated from England, one might suppose great similarities, yet Twain finds that they bear no resemblance whatsoever.

Interestingly, in his last text Twain dwells on the pain of transportation as never before. But ironically, these unpleasant moments facilitate his writing and make up his story. Whereas in his earlier works his carping is amusing because of its crafted dramatic impact and impeccable timing, in *Following the Equator* Twain comes across simply as whining. For example, his section on India depicts him exhausted and overwhelmed by the population density; the radically unfamiliar culture, myths, and manners; and the plagues, famines, and natural disasters that seem to be everywhere. Rather than the insightful outsider seeing from a different perspective, he instead resembles a misanthrope. In spite of its negative emphasis, the text is still amusing, especially when read in conjunction with his earlier works.

For Twain, travel is about encountering stories. Throughout his works, we meet a variety of characters that tell some of the most magnificent—if unbelievable—stories of all.

Twain recognized the value of the tales he could pick up along the way. In *Innocents Abroad* he writes,

> The Old Travelers—those delightful parrots who have "been here before," and know more about the country than [the king]. . . . We love to hear them prate and drivel and lie. We can tell them the moment we see them. They always throw out a few feelers: they never cast themselves adrift till they have sounded every individual and know that he has not traveled. Then they open their throttle-valves, and how they do brag, and sneer, and swell, and soar, and blaspheme the sacred name of Truth! . . . But I still love the Old Travelers. I love them for their witless platitudes; for their supernatural ability to bore; for their delightful asinine vanity; for their luxuriant fertility of imagination; for their startling, their brilliant, their overwhelming mendacity! (Fussell 394)

Indeed, these storytellers often make Twain's stories come to life.

Even Twain's famous novels, *The Adventures of Tom Sawyer* (1876), *Life on the Mississippi* (1883), and *The Adventures of Huckleberry Finn* (1884), poignantly demonstrate the deep lessons that travel can facilitate. *Huck Finn* serves well as an example, although any of these three could easily be called travel fiction.

Elements of travel literature abound in these novels. Huck and Tom are figured as American picaros who do whatever is necessary to survive, including relying on their boyish charm, which is often affected. Through an array of adventures, Huck and Tom learn of the wide world by participating in it; from the family feud between the Grangerfords and the Shepherdsons, to the trickster Duke and the con man King, to the unpredictable nature of the river, they receive quite an education on their adventures. Travel—life on the river—offers them liberty; it is being in motion that gives them freedom, for every day delivers a new set of events ripe for their response.

The desire to travel initiates the primary narrative of the story: when Huck's abusive alcoholic father reemerges to kidnap his estranged son, Huck responds by flight: "All I wanted was to go somewheres; all I wanted was a change, I warn't particular" (Twain 12). It is this desire to see and to participate in difference that inspires the journey. In the end, travel facilitates a deep and meaningful friendship wherein Tom and Huck will take significant risks for the others whom they encounter. Only by being in unpredictable situations— namely, by being in motion—can the events of this story and the growth of Huck occur.

Over his entire career, Twain seemed to assert that it is travel that teaches and travel literature that relates that learning, perhaps teaching the lessons again. Twain himself learned these lessons over a lifetime of travels and shared his experience with the world in his many books. In his life and in his writing—in his travels and in his literature— Twain recognized the value of stepping outside of the familiar.

See also: Picaresque, Picaro
References: Fussell 1987; Hart 1965; Harvey 1967; Rugoff 1960; Twain 1959

TYRRELL, ALBERT E.

A curious and reclusive writer about whom very little is known, Albert E. Tyrrell (Canadian American, fl. 1990) published a single highly provocative work of travel literature titled *Misadventures of an American Abroad* (1990). This self-proclaimed jack-of-all-trades turned to travel and writing rather late in life after working in a variety of engineering jobs. Feeling a need to shift the focus of his life again, Tyrrell established himself as a publisher and then set out to write a book. In order to do so, he needed material, thus he organized a voyage.

Tyrell embarked upon a whirlwind tour of the globe in three months—a nod to Jules Verne's *Around the World in Eighty Days*— with the express purpose of using that voyage as the material for his book. Written as a disjointed travelogue of seemingly random encounters with individuals and institutions, the text carries us from Los Angeles to New Zealand, to Australia, to Southeast Asia, to Europe, and then back to North America. Although Tyrrell's book assumes the form of a travelogue, with chronological entries describing each city, its form also swerves toward novelistic: above the structure of the journey, he has overlaid a consistent and recurrent adversary and a narrator who undergoes a significant degree of growth.

The book is subtitled *Big Brother Exposed,* a reference to George Orwell's *Nineteen Eighty Four* (published in 1949), which describes a nightmare society in which the government constantly scrutinizes citizens in order to control them. Orwell's futurist vision becomes Tyrell's present reality, and the theme of surveillance recurs throughout the text. Constantly scrutinized and tracked by various passport agencies, government information groups, and comical mystery characters that appear repeatedly, Tyrrell blends reportage with postmodern novelistic paranoia. This playful pastiche serves a particular purpose: to note the ubiquitous power of bureaucracy as it curtails the freedom of travel. Subject to constant official monitoring, the narrator mocks and jeers at the waste of energy spent gathering useless information about a harmless traveler.

In some regards, like Paul Theroux, Tyrrell can be called post-touristic: travel in the postmodern world serves not as an escape, but as confirmation that Euro-American domination has run amok. Instead of finding a genuinely different world in the far-flung corners of the globe, the narrator finds a garish and horrible reflection of North America. Of course, these echoes of the familiar serve powerfully to accentuate the absurdity of global capitalism and cultural hegemony.

As an example of a hybrid form of travel literature, the novel is a provocative experiment. Witty and humorous moments pepper the text, although there are many failed attempts as well. In spite of its strange structure, the novel anchors itself in the classic tropes—or figurative representations—of travel literature: travel as labor, travel as pedagogy, and travel as self-reflection. In a world where tourism and tourist writing dominate, Tyrrell's effort is refreshing.

wherein the sultan's wife takes quite a fancy to him. To dissuade her advances, he plays still another role:

> V Finally, the lot fell upon me to be mad. Having then taken this enterprise upon myself, it behoved me to do such things as were natural to madmen. Truly, I never found myself so wearied or so exhausted as during the first three days that I feigned madness. The reason was that I had constantly behind me fifty or sixty little children, who threw stones at me, and I threw stones at them [!]. . . . I had my shirt constantly full of stones, and acted like a madman. The queen was always at her window with her damsels, and remained there from morning till evening to see me and talk with me; and I, being mocked by many men and merchants, taking off my shirt, went, quite naked as I was, before the queen, who took the greatest delight in seeing me, and would not let me leave her, and gave me sound food to eat. (Newby 257)

VARTHEMA, LODOVICO DE

Remarkably, Lodovico de Varthema's (Italian, fl. 1505) *Travels* has been in print almost continuously since its original edition in 1510. It has been translated into at least eight languages, and it is almost always excerpted in anthologies of travel literature. Varthema's popularity is deserved: his gifts as a storyteller are exceptional.

His tales are unabashedly in the first person and lively; we can get a good sense of the man by reading his stories. In a line, Varthema was one of the original great adventurers whose wit and cleverness carried him into—and more importantly, out of—truly extraordinary situations. In some ways, Varthema can be considered a picaro—that is, a likable rogue who gets into potentially dangerous situations but narrowly escapes.

The most famous tales from his book occur in the Middle East. Fascinated by the bustling trade of the caravans, Varthema decides to pass himself off as an Arab. He quickly learns Arabic, "converts" to Islam, and disguises himself convincingly as a *Mameluke,* a mercenary of the sultan. Employed as a guard of the caravan, he finds that he has great freedom to engage in adventures and exploits. He is noted as only the second non-Muslim to have visited the holy city of Mecca. Disguised, he finds friendship and romance, riches and high times, and excitement and drama in the extreme. He gets himself into considerable trouble, including one sequence

The image is a hilarious one: Varthema pelting children and then strutting nude before the queen. Yet the result is perfect in that he is rewarded with food and friendship (and who knows what else). For Varthema, life is but a series of adventures and conquests; being in motion and in a foreign land simply facilitates them.

Driven by his intense curiosity and an insatiable desire for excitement, Varthema's exploits are irreverent, astoundingly bold, and often haphazard. Perhaps this is part of their charm, for the way they are recounted in his text makes it seem as though he really is making it all up as he goes along. Indeed, such a fancy-free attitude embodies the spirit of travel: we go simply to go, not necessarily to get anywhere. Varthema takes it a step further in that he often risks his life for a bit of fun or for a joke; in him, we see the traveler who will do anything for an adventure.

See also: Picaro
References: Adams 1988; Hammond 1963; Newby 1985

VERNE, JULES

Novelist Jules Verne (French, 1828–1905) wrote some of the most beloved adventure fiction of his era. His fabulously famous tales include *Journey to the Center of the Earth* (1864), *Twenty Thousand Leagues under the Sea* (1870), *Around the World in Eighty Days* (1873), and *The Mysterious Island* (1874). Fantastically imaginative, his adventure romances are cousins to travel literature in that they describe travels into the imaginary realm.

Verne's tales tell of wondrous expeditions to impossible places; because of the popularity of his books, these destinations have become mythical. While his novels do not address actual journeys, they do demonstrate the nature of travel. In these four books particularly, Verne's narrators note cultural difference, propose travel as a means to self-reflection, and utilize adventures en route to growth. In order to be considered travel literature, travel must work as the engine of a book's plot; in all four of Verne's stories, it surely does.

Photograph of Jules Verne, 1888 (Library of Congress)

Unbelievably prophetic, Verne's stories pressed the science of the day well into the hypothetical. It is difficult for modern readers—for whom submarines, global balloon flights, and excursions beneath the earth's crust are hardly newsworthy—to understand how wildly outrageous these devices seemed to Verne's audience. For nineteenth-century readers, Verne's tales were science fiction, yet it is significant to note that these novels propose travel, exploration, and adventure as worthy extensions of science. As with space travel in the modern era, Verne's fanciful journeys represent the vast potential for science when combined with boundless human curiosity.

Journey to the Center of the Earth recounts the adventures of Otto Lidenbrock, an impetuous German professor of geology. He stumbles upon a Renaissance manuscript that describes a route to reach the center of the earth. He hurriedly readies an expedition to explore this new world, enlisting his nephew and several other vivid characters along the way. They travel to an extinct volcano in Iceland and descend into the literal underworld—which, tellingly, bears some interesting resemblance to mythical, especially Dantean, hell. For several months, they explore this land of natural wonders, vast forests, fantastic creatures, and barbaric cavemen. They escape from the core by riding a volcanic eruption and land, conveniently, off the coast of Italy.

In some ways, the novel describes a voyage back in time. Verne's center of the earth is similar to prehistoric surface civilizations, and thus the story may be read as a contrast between civilized and precivilized life. Of course, the explorers are cast as the good guys, whereas the uncivilized natives are threatening and mostly devoid of the loftier of human sentiments. Nonetheless, there is a magnificent element of cultural comparison in this tale: the underworld represents the antithesis of (idealized) Western civilization.

Twenty Thousand Leagues under the Sea tells of a group of traveling scientists trying to understand a series of undersea anomalies. Something has been sinking ships, and many suspect a sea monster. An explosion kills most of the team, but Aronnax, the narrator, and two companions survive. They are captured by Captain Nemo, an enigmatic villain who takes them aboard his submarine. From Ceylon to the South Pole, they voyage with Nemo, breathlessly describing the strange and unknown undersea world. Their adventure then becomes a struggle with ethics, as Nemo, megalomaniacal but charismatic, holds them captive. Both fascinated and horrified at the way Nemo uses his magnificent ship, the prisoners must thwart his evil intentions. Life on board the closed society of the submarine functions as a microcosm of the larger world, and as such, the novel addresses numerous social issues, including freedom, power, and selflessness.

Around the World in Eighty Days is one of Verne's later novels. His maturity as a novelist allows him to address some subtle issues, and his ideas of travel are quite sophisticated in this tale. The plot is a simple one: sedentary gentleman Phileas Fogg makes a bet at his London club that he can circumnavigate the globe in fewer than 90 days. This ambitious bet sends Fogg and his faithful servant Passepartout through a series of grand adventures in the most exotic—and highly embellished—places on earth. Through cleverness, determination, and loyalty, they succeed handily, managing the task in a mere 80 days. Once again, good intentions and boundless curiosity defeat adversity.

Employing every means of transportation available—train, ship, coach, sled, elephants, and so forth—Fogg defies death and trickery in accomplishing his journey. As the story is simply about travel—indeed, the object of the exercise is not to get somewhere, but simply to pass through—there are many moments where Fogg reflects upon the restorative and invigorating nature of being in motion. Upon his return, Fogg finds that he is a new man with renewed hope and energy.

A Walk at the Bottom of the Sea; *illustration from* Twenty Thousand Leagues under the Sea *by Jules Verne, 1870 (Bettmann/Corbis)*

Such is the power of travel and, to a lesser degree, travel literature.

The Mysterious Island traces the adventures of a party of travelers who find themselves marooned on a remote island. Five passengers, fleeing the American Civil War in a balloon, blow hopelessly off course and crash-land into total isolation. Their task is to rebuild a society using whatever survivalist savvy and skills they have. Pirates, natives, weather, beasts, and their own desires provide ample adversity for the story. Eventually, they are rescued by a passing ship and return to the familiar world whence they came.

This novel is often read as a sort of utopian tale, wherein a small group is given the opportunity to build society anew, if on a vastly diminished scale. Their successes and failures teach great lessons about their original culture. In this regard, we might read *The Mysterious Island* as mildly critical of Euro-American society: when stranded in a radically foreign environment, inherent prejudices, misconceptions, and foolishness become painfully obvious. Yet cooler heads ultimately prevail, and the perceived strengths of Western civilization win out in the end.

In all cases, Verne's stories propose a marriage between science and exploration. When combined, the two can afford mankind access to the sublime wonders of the world. Invariably, the heroes are those characters who can balance their love for adventure and travel with "good" intentions and proper applications. Travel therefore has enormous power for Verne, including the power to change minds and to better the lot of humanity.

References: Benét 1965

VIAUD, LOUIS-MARIE-JULIEN

See Loti, Pierre

VOLTAIRE

Voltaire (French, 1694–1778)—the pseudonym of François-Marie Arouet—ranks among the finest authors of his time. He wrote in many different genres: tragedy, epic, history, philosophical treatise, fiction, and a combination thereof. *Candide; or, Optimism* (1759) may be considered many different ways, but for our purposes, it has some significant elements of superior travel literature.

Restless in France, Voltaire resided in several cities but found each one to be unsatisfactory for some reason. In 1726, he moved to England for a period of roughly two years, having been exiled from France for his political beliefs. He returned to Paris to remain only briefly and then moved again to Berlin, later to Geneva. Various journeys punctuated

his residences: he visited much of Prussia, Russia, large portions of Europe, and the Mediterranean basin. His travels contributed to his encyclopedic knowledge of cultures, politics, and history.

Many of his ideas and experiences were distilled into *Candide*. The story is simple enough: young and naive Candide falls in love with Cunégonde but finds that an unimaginable series of obstacles intercedes their union. Faithful until the end, he remains devoted to his love in spite of extreme difficulties and diversions. He never ceases to progress toward rescuing Cunégonde from her own string of misfortunes. This pursuit takes Candide throughout Europe, to the New World, and then back to Turkey. Although the story is not actually a travel narrative, the incidental journeys that Candide must make are treated in a particularly fine way. In addition, *Candide* contains a number of picaresque elements.

Throughout the tale, coincidence plays a significant role in Candide's life. While in motion, while traveling, he by chance meets a series of tricksters and rogues who play upon his trusting nature. Most often in the guise of fellow travelers, these cheats, swindlers, and villains mightily abuse Candide. Early in the story, our penniless protagonist thinks it is his good fortune to meet some friendly travelers on the road. They begin by offering to buy him dinner and end by abducting him into the Bulgarian army. The moral seems to be that while circulating in the wide world may offer opportunities, it also poses risks: those who seem friendly may not be so. This is Candide's first travel lesson, one that is repeated a number of times in the story.

Another lesson Candide learns is that in other cultures, things are not always what they appear to be. This has the effect of making Candide aware of his own European culture as different from other cultures, particularly those in the New World. First he sees "two girls, completely naked, who were running swiftly along the edge of the meadow, pursued by two monkeys who snapped at their buttocks" (Voltaire 31). Behaving chivalrously, Candide shoots the monkeys, thereby saving the girls. Or so he thinks. In fact, he has killed their lovers! Candide's companion Cacambo explains the situation and chides Candide that he is "always astonished by everything. Why do you think it so strange that in some countries monkeys succeed in obtaining the good graces of women? They are one quarter human, just as I am one quarter Spanish" (32). This cultural relativism, although here presented in a humorous light, underscores the value of travel.

Again by extraordinary chance and incredible luck, Candide manages to "discover" the mythical city of Eldorado, which proves to be the complete opposite of Europe. Cultural differences provide great humor in these chapters as Candide learns of this strange society; in so doing, Voltaire is mocking European ways. It is by spending time deep within another culture that Candide learns of his home. Likewise, it is by this device that Voltaire satirizes European culture. The utopia that is Eldorado directly contrasts and opposes the reality of France in the eighteenth century: where Eldorado is peaceful, egalitarian, humble, and charitable, France is warring, aristocratic, vain, and greedy.

Finally, Candide obtains his beloved Cunégonde, the process of which takes them to Turkey. Once again, this culture provides a contrast to, but also a critique of, France. Greed and lust again oppose Candide, but he prevails. Finally he has all his heart desires: his love, though now she is old and ugly; his mentor, though he has changed his tune considerably; and stability from the wanderings. Yet such motionlessness is dull. In a searing passage, the character of a wise old woman states: "I should like to know which is worse, being raped a hundred times by negro pirates, having a buttock cut off, running the gauntlet in the Bulgar army, being flogged and hanged in an auto-da-fé, being dissected and rowing in the galleys—experiencing, in a word, all the miseries through which we have passed—or else just sitting here and doing nothing?" (75). Candide has to admit that the question is a tough one.

Indeed, it is the freedom of motion, the unpredictable nature of travel, that has value. Travel exists as one form of action. Such action is the opposite of complacent inaction. Voltaire, through Candide, seems to be challenging the closed-minded security of staying home, where everything is safe and predictable. Action, activity, motion, all animate life—it is better to move and suffer than to stay still and feel nothing. In this regard, *Candide* works to promote adventure and to proclaim itself travel literature.

See also: Eldorado; Picaresque
References: Voltaire 1966

WAUGH, EVELYN

Evelyn Waugh (English, 1903–1966) wrote a great number of novels, short stories, and essays, most of them characterized as witty, wry, and ironic. As a successful and prominent man of letters, Waugh could afford to satirize the ridiculous behavior of the British upper classes. Among his dozens of novels are several travel tales that deserve mention for their influence on the genre.

Waugh's public persona radiated British fastidiousness. Although a veteran traveler, he never got used to the disruption and unpredictability of travel—or perhaps it is better said that he never tired of complaining about it. From 1928 to 1937, he traveled almost constantly, producing novels and travel books simultaneously.

Generally speaking, his travel literature mocks the traditionally lauded aspects of travel. Instead of finding truth and transcendence, Waugh's narrators find an interminable stream of kitsch, filth, unpleasantness, and inane fellow travelers. Commenting on the nature of tourism, Waugh is quoted as saying that the tourist "debauches the great monuments of antiquity . . . [and is] a comic figure, always inapt in his comments, incongruous in his appearance. . . . Avarice and deceit attack him at every step; the shops that he patronizes are full of forgeries . . . [but] we need feel no scruple or twinge of uncertainty; *we* are travellers and cosmopolitans; the tourist is the other fellow" (Fussell 653). Indeed, the tourist is pathetic, but who admits to being a tourist?

Waugh has poked a sharp jab at all who assuage their guilt by blaming their fellows for ugly touristic behavior.

One of Waugh's most significant contributions is theoretic: he argues for a fundamental distinction between travelers and tourists. Travelers ply a trade; voyaging is both their job and identity. Tourists are interlopers who dart near and far seeking quick thrills and momentary glimpses of what they feel they ought to see. In vernacular terms, the tourist is the "been there, done that, it's Tuesday so this must be Paris" visitor. In contrast, the true traveler deeply feels the places he visits and often values the process of the journey as much as the arrival. Travelers seek to encounter the foreign, while tourists seek to discover the familiar abroad. Wealthy Brits, particularly, were notorious for

Portrait of Evelyn Waugh, 1940 (Library of Congress)

their insistence upon finding where all the British tourists were. Waugh's parodies address this issue repeatedly. Yet we must note that to make these distinctions and to parody such behavior, Waugh needed to have plenty of firsthand experience.

His first travel book, *Labels* (1930), chronicles his Mediterranean cruise. The title refers to all the stickers on his luggage from various ports of call, as though rather than stories, the tourist travels simply to amass an impressive collection of appliqués on her portmanteau. Written as a travelogue, the book describes unspeakably ugly touristic behavior. Drunken debauches, revels with streetwalkers, deceit, and generally rambunctious behavior make up the meat of this tale. While amusing, and occasionally very funny, the book puts the reader in the uncomfortable position of feeling embarrassed for the narrator. Given Waugh's skill as a novelist, one can only presume that this was entirely intentional. His description of Mount Etna will serve nicely as an example: "I do not think I shall ever forget the sight of Etna at sunset; the mountain almost invisible in a blur of pastel grey, glowing on the top and then repeating its shape, as though reflected, in a whisp of grey smoke, with the whole horizon behind radiant with pink light fading gently into a pastel grey sky. Nothing I have ever seen in Art or Nature was quite so revolting" (Newby 178).

In later tales he breaks away from the posh travel depicted in *Labels*. *Ninety-two Days* (1934) describes a rough and arduous excursion through British Guiana and Brazil. On foot and on horseback, the traveling party slogs through the merciless jungle hoping to reach Manos. They fail because their boat never arrives. Even when off the beaten path, Waugh chooses to dwell on negative reactions. Repeatedly, his grand expectations are left unfulfilled: "All that extravagant and highly improbable expectation had been obliterated like a sand castle beneath the encroaching tide" (Fussell 519). Squalor, inconvenience, and unfamiliarity grate on Waugh;

in short, it is difference that he cannot accommodate. In this regard, his travel writing reverses a long-standing trend of openness and eagerness to encounter the cultural other.

Even his short travel story "Cruise" approaches being sardonic. An innovative tale, it simply reprints one side of a postal correspondence between a lady of leisure on a cruise and her beloved at home. Though cheerful, the postcards and letters describe a myriad of petty disasters and intrigues. The lady's buoyant and bubbly reportage is in direct contrast to the fact that she is having dull time as a tourist but a grand time socializing with her fellows. In fact, she informs her beau in one note, "Darling, I can't wait to tell you I'm engaged to Arthur. Arthur is the one I thought was a pansy" (Craig 116). Deadpan and ironic "Cruise" presents an amusing—if fabricated—perspective in a very effective form.

Contemporary readers may find Waugh politically incorrect and hopelessly snobbish, but if we remember that his body of work leans almost fully toward mockery and satire, we might resuscitate his position. In addition, Waugh's disenchanted tone and his distinction between travelers and tourists cannot be denied as major influences on post-touristic travel writing. Authors like Robert Byron, Paul Theroux, and Eric Newby clearly owe a debt to Waugh's innovations.

References: Craig 1996; Fussell 1987; Harvey 1967; Newby 1985

WELLSLEY, DOROTHY, DUCHESS OF

Much admired by the esteemed writer William Butler Yeats for her extremely rich verse, Dorothy, Duchess of Wellsley (English, 1889–1956) was an avid traveler as well as a poet. Her collected verse was published after her death as *Early Light* (1956). Among her many exquisite poems are several great examples of travel verse.

A wealthy and privileged woman with a keen desire to see the world, she made voyages to the Mediterranean and to the Middle East. Much of her work blends luscious images of nature overlaid with history. Her verse has a dreamy quality that idealizes her subjects without crossing into absurd abstraction. Two of her best travel poems are "First Flight" and "Camels in Persia."

"First Flight" describes her impressions of Persia. The poem begins,

> Here is the perfect vision: in the dawn,
> In smudgy dusk I rise above the plain
> Of the Persian desert
> (Crossley-Holland 21–22)

It then proceeds to describe the aching beauty of the vista upon which she gazes. Her experience of an exotic location evokes a sense of history and vast understanding: the place contains all of its past, its legends, and its lore. As a poet, she feels bygone times lingering in the geography as she continues:

> The desert skims below.
> Like caterpillar trails the camels go
> Marked broadly by their stacks of camel
>   thorn.
> (22)

The ancient history of the Silk Road remains tangible and alive.

Under the canopy of endless sky and desert, she feels unified by geography in that the same sky hangs over her English home:

> Beside my hand the stars hang close, go out,
> Spent candles. Now the moon most surely
>   dies,
> So haggard hands she on the Persian peaks,
> Who whitens misty on an English lawn.
> (22)

For Wellsley, travel and experience of foreign lands serve to demonstrate a human commonality under a universal earthly geography; in a similar way, travel also serves to condense the past and the present into a state of timelessness.

In "Camels in Persia," Wellsley writes what begins as a reflection of camels but ends by using the beast and his burden as a metaphor for life. As the animals plod reluctantly along their desolate path, they march toward an inevitable end. Strewn along the caravan path are the "arched white ribs of his kind," the bones of fallen beasts and emblems of mortality. Personifying the pachyderm, she continues,

> The camel is sullen and proud, he is not
>   my friend,
> Will have none of my fellowship.
> Soon he knows he will fail, he will fall by
>   the way
> And his caravan pass, and leave him to
>   vultures, but now
> He knows he will drink his fill at the
>   journey's end,
> And be at peace by the palms in the heat
>   of day.
> (Crossley-Holland 270)

He bears his brutish burden aware but shows no resistance.

Abruptly she switches tone and focus, and her metaphor becomes clear: "Past the tall stone tomb where once King Cyrus lay, / Who carved a maxim for all he would subjugate: 'Traveller, pause! For you will pass this way . . . '" (270–271). Human and camel both are part of the mortal, natural order and cannot escape their inevitable fate. If we return then to the descriptions of the camel in the first five stanzas and read them as shared human traits, we must be like these beasts, stubborn and groaning until our time is up.

In both poems, as well as in many of Wellsley's works, experience in the world helps her to reflect upon the human condition and the futile arrogance of Western civilization. It becomes an easy leap to suggest that Wellsley would agree that life itself is a form of journey whereupon the voyage supersedes the destination in terms of joy, excitement, and importance.

See also: Silk Road

References: Crossley-Holland 1986; Harvey 1967

WHARTON, EDITH

The literary contribution of Edith Wharton (American, 1862–1937) cannot be denied. Author of dozens of highly acclaimed and beloved novels, Wharton must be noted as one of the great writers of her era. While it is true that travel and exotic locations feature prominently in many of her novels, most of them are not, strictly speaking, travel literature. But travel was a lifelong passion for Wharton, thus she penned several significant travel books that are largely ignored, including *Italian Backgrounds* (1905), *A Motor-Flight through France* (1908), *In Morocco* (1920), and her recently discovered *The Cruise of the Vanadis* (written 1888, published 1992). Like her novels, Wharton's travel books are lyrical, vivid, and delightfully entertaining.

Born into a prominent family, Wharton learned to travel when she was very young. At age four, she and her family moved from New York to Europe, residing in Paris and Rome and traveling extensively over the next six years. In her autobiography Wharton claimed that this "wild early pilgrimage . . . [gave her] an incurable passion for the road" (Wharton xvii). Indeed, over the course of her prolific life, she would make more than 60 transatlantic crossings, voyage into foreign and threatening landscapes most often forbidden to women, and indulge in literally hundreds of smaller, but no less interesting, trips.

Privately and meticulously educated, Wharton initially encountered Europe as a grand field trip. Desirous of showing her the treasures of art, architecture, culture, and history, her family used their wealth and leisure to school Wharton in the best the Continent had to offer. This sense of travel as pedagogy

Photograph of Edith Wharton, 1905 (Bettmann/ Corbis)

never left Wharton; even in her later years, she insisted upon carefully researching her destination before embarking. Explains Wharton scholar Sarah Bird Wright, "Her 'passion' for travel and the 'obsession' to tell stories joined together to form the primary springboard of Edith Wharton's creativity. These activities often proceeded apace— travel providing the occasion (and the necessary leisure) to write" (Wharton xviii). This commingling of travel and literature marks Wharton as a pure travel writer.

Rather than simply jotting down the usual clichés and breathless babble, Wharton sought to evoke the places she visited and to suggest her psychological or emotional response to the scene. The resulting prose delights as both highly visual and deeply, charmingly subjective. Yet it would be gravely misleading simply to relegate Wharton's writing to the realm of pleasing: beneath its lustrous surface rests extraordinary insight, knowledge, and incisiveness. As a cultural critic and a theorist of the nature of travel, Wharton has few peers. As if this were not enough, Wharton adds to this already potent mix a profound sense of literary craft that infuses her stories with drama, character development, and tension. All told, her travel writing is among the best.

Italian Backgrounds is the result of nearly two decades of various trips to Italy. Written in conjunction with her architectural study *Italian Villas and Their Gardens* (1904), *Italian Backgrounds* represents something of a "greatest hits" of her Italian adventures. The tale is peppered with costumes and characters that recall commedia dell'arte, a form of Italian comedy prominent in the sixteenth to the eighteenth century that features stock situations and characters. Thus we find Wharton mountaineering on a rope team in the Alps. Then she visits an ascetic monastery in San Vivaldo to research a particular artist. Another passage reflects upon the merits of architectural renovation in Milan and how poor restoration might have a terribly detrimental effect upon the local culture. From place to place, from idea to idea, Wharton bounces effortlessly.

Written as a series of smaller essays, each on a particular place and topic, *Italian Backgrounds* has an intellectual, theoretical tone behind its sparkling descriptions of people and places. In conclusion, Wharton writes: "[Famous art and architecture] are among the catalogued riches of the city. The guidebooks point to them, they lie in the beaten track of sight-seeing, and it is rather in the intervals between such systematized study of the past, in the parentheses of travel, that one obtains those more intimate glimpses which

can help compose the image of each city, to preserve its personality in the traveller's mind" (Wharton 111). It is the process of travel, the unexpected encounters, the daily minutiae that make the voyage resonate.

In *A Motor-Flight through France,* Wharton likens her journey to a medieval pilgrimage, with its joyful camaraderie and hopeful glee. Anchoring herself in the history of travel literature, Wharton and Henry James packed the works of George Sand along for reading. Demonstrating her independence, Wharton insisted on traveling wheresoever she desired to do whatever it was that struck her fancy (much as George Sand had done). Rouen, Fontainebleau, Paris, and Poitiers made up the poles of her voyage, with assorted side trips and diversions in between. Enthusiastic throughout, some of Wharton's most provocatively poetic images can be found in this text.

Due to the fast pace and freedom of car travel—as opposed to coach or even train— Wharton altered her structure and style of writing in this work. Rather than musing leisurely over towns and vistas, *A Motor-Flight* leaps from place to place in torrents of description, almost as if France were a blur outside the window. Perhaps as a function of her own aging, Wharton seems constantly pressed for time. The resulting chapters are thus somewhat jittery and disjointed but no less literary and evocative.

In Morocco represents Wharton's attempt to write a guidebook for Morocco. She described the work as a "slight sketch of the history and art of the country [for] happy wanderers." Traveling in 1917, at the height of World War I, Wharton also seems to have wanted a slight escape to a culture not embroiled in war. To achieve this goal, Wharton procured an invitation by the French minister of war, General Lyautey, to come to Morocco. As the country was a French colony, much of Wharton's text rings with a colonialist tone. This ideological bias aside, her writing remains interesting and enjoyable.

An absolute outsider, she immediately recognized her alien perspective: she was a woman in an Islamic country, and a famous novelist to boot. Her three-week journey gave her ample material on the exotic and exciting Islamic culture. The bazaars provide her especial fodder, the customs strike her as noteworthy and meaningful, and Muslim autocracy impresses her as antithetical to Christian democracy. Mimicking, perhaps mocking, the male obsession with harems, Wharton made a visit to one herself: not surprisingly, she wonders what all the fuss is about. Throughout the book, she evokes the specter of *1001 Arabian Nights* and its ingenious, if fanciful, storyteller, Scheherazade. In the end, her guide was no Baedeker's, but it remains a quirky and useful study of Morocco.

The Cruise of the Vanadis was only discovered in 1991. It appears to have been Wharton's personal diary of a cruise she took with her husband in 1888. Her journal includes remarkable accounts by a young and unpolished ingenue: wandering classical ruins, delighting in the exoticism of North Africa, and informally interviewing anyone whom she encountered.

She is often credited with being the first American to have written an account of Mount Athos. Located on a peninsula in the Greek Aegean, Athos is home to more than a dozen monasteries. No females are allowed on the mountain—not even female livestock. Monks prevented Wharton's landing, but she was able to observe and explore from a small launch.

Written as a series of daily entries, *The Cruise of the Vanadis* is filled with factual information that Wharton usually omitted from her finished works. Even in this early work, Wharton's range of interests is vast; from food to architecture, from history to languages, from culture to nature, she seems to want to capture everything. We might characterize Wharton as a ravenous consumer of experiences, intellectually hungry for the new, exciting, and unpredictable.

Wharton's travel books distinguish her as both scholar and poet; her accounts are meticulously researched and reasoned, but they are represented with the utmost skill and accessibility. Feisty and witty, she had the background and the experience to make broad and meaningful comparisons among geographies, cultures, and perspectives. With her sophisticated theory of travel as entertainment, as a source of wisdom, and as the root of a story, Wharton exemplifies the great travel writer.

See also: James, Henry; Sand, George
References: Newby 1985; Wharton 1995

WILLARD, EMMA HART

Emma Hart Willard (American, 1787–1870) is a rather understudied American woman of great and diverse accomplishment. As a scholar and educator of women, she worked in many disciplines, including science, geography, philosophy, and history. Her travels were broad and her journals elaborately detailed. Her major work, *Journal and Letters, from France and Great-Britain* (1833), provides a very fine account of how much freedom and respect a learned woman could have in both Europe and America in the nineteenth century.

In her elaborate preface to the book, Willard claims to have set out to make "observations not only for myself, but for my country women" (Schriber 4). An early advocate of women's rights—both in the Western world and elsewhere—Willard insisted that the road to equality begins with education. Essential to the pursuit of knowledge and wisdom, argued Willard, are experiences and exposures to different cultures and different ideas. Thus to travel—or in lieu of actually going, to read a detailed account like the one she wrote—is to begin to question traditional, and inflexible, gender roles.

While much of her work is pure detail, Willard frequently interjects her own passionate opinions. For example, while in Paris she notes the social acceptance of women working for a living, a practice much stigmatized in America at the time:

> Much evil among us, originates in a prejudice from which the French seem, in great measure, free—that there is something degrading in a woman's doing anything to earn money. In families with us, where the father employs his hands from morning till night in cutting off yards of calico, as tying up pounds of tea, not for charity—but for profit—his daughters would consider it a shocking degradation to employ theirs, to earn money, by making caps, or hats, or dresses for others. (Schriber 26)

Essential to Emma Hart Willard's vision is an exchange of ideas from different cultures and even subcultures. Travel encourages this sort of social cross-pollination.

References: Schriber 1995

WILLIAMS, WILLIAM CARLOS

Modernist poet William Carlos Williams (American, 1883–1963) is most famous for his imagist poetry. Vivid, transient, economic, and realistic, his verse is widely known and appreciated. Less well known are his prose works, which share many characteristics with his poetry. Among his fiction resides one very fine work of travel literature titled *A Voyage to Pagany* (1928).

At the insistence of his friend Ezra Pound, Williams made a single six-month tour of Europe. He had always been unabashedly American and expressed great dismay at seeing many of the great American writers—Pound, T. S. Eliot, F. Scott Fitzgerald, Ernest Hemingway, and many others—flee to Europe. The Old World was thought to be the place where great ideas could come to fruition; Williams had always rejected this notion categorically. Nonetheless, he did go to see what all the fuss was about, and his response was an unapologetic rejection.

Although technically a novel, *A Voyage to Pagany* borrows liberally from his actual experiences. The title itself sets the tone: *Pagany* is a coinage that is supposed to mean "the place where Pagans live." The story charts the misadventures of middle-aged Dr. Evans, who is a facsimile of Williams himself. A first-time traveler to Europe, he attempts to see the standard tourist sites but finds the herd mentality of this venture stifling. A romantic and astute voyager, Dr. Evans finds all of his expectations mightily frustrated. In spite of his displeasure—or perhaps because of it—Evans keeps a travelogue that details his experience.

Playfully, Williams has turned the tables of travel literature. Endless accounts of Europeans visiting and deriding America have achieved fame in the established literary canon (Alexis de Tocqueville, both Frances and Anthony Trollope, and Charles Dickens are but a few examples), but Williams writes of an American in Europe who is every bit as skeptical and dissatisfied as these famous voyagers in the United States. Even as a carping traveler, however, Evans (and Williams) recognizes the need to capture the experience in textual form.

Dripping with sarcasm, *A Voyage to Pagany* is clearly a parody. Williams seems to have set out to critique the Europe that his generation almost universally lauded. Rather than idealizing Europe by tinting it with romanticized shades, Williams dwells on the banal observations of a tourist. Time drags interminably as Evans scurries from town to town, from train station to hotel, and from misunderstanding to mistreatment.

In spite of its cynicism, or maybe because of it, the novel is damned entertaining and stylistically innovative. Williams writes with a voice unique in literature; for example, in Genoa an unexpected delay gives rise to the following reflection:

> Genoa. The name sounded hollow, depressing as the coldly sulphurous gallery through which he was passing, baggage in hand. . . . He knew

no Italian. The porter shrugged and walked away. Evans wandered around aimlessly until he found the check room. 12:05 to Florence. Thank God. Only two hours to kill. . . . Steps, hill upon hill, street lights at the bottoms of funnels. *Giovanezza*—arm in arm, drunk. *Giovanezza*—a mob shouting drunk—towers going up into night without top. No direction. No north, no south. Only the street to the railroad station; home. Lonely stairs, up. Up— nowhere. Where is the sea Columbus sailed on? (Fussell 662–663)

Indeed, the tone of this book marks a shift in American travel writing that made posttouristic authors like Paul Theroux possible.

As a travel book that breaks with tradition and stands expectation on its head, Williams's book is remarkable. Good fun as well as provocative, *A Voyage to Pagany* merits close attention. To be sure, it demonstrates that travel is not for everyone.

References: Fussell 1987

WOLFF, JOSEPH

Trouble seemed to follow Joseph Wolff (German, 1795–1862) no matter where he went. His single literary claim to fame, *Narrative of a Mission to Bokhara* (1845), is a harrowing account of his ill-advised adventures. Perhaps overly dramatic and exaggerated, his story was an instant success.

Although his father was a prominent rabbi, Wolff converted to Catholicism at age 11, an act that precipitated his expulsion from his home. He bounced around various monasteries and schools, eventually landing in Rome and procuring an audience with the pope. In 1819, however, he moved to England and converted to the Church of England and signed on as a missionary. The next five years he spent in Eastern Europe, the Middle East, and Central Asia converting Jews to Anglicanism. Evidently, this was not exciting enough for Wolff: from 1843 to 1845, he sought to discover the fate of two

British officers being held by the emir of Bokhara (Bukhara).

His book tells of his incredible journey and the endless string of difficulties he encountered. As a Christian in the Islamic world, Wolff was considered an infidel and thus persecuted variously. When he arrived, he found that the officers whom he sought, Colonel Stoddart and Captain Conolly, had suffered heinous torture and were already dead. This did not bode well for Wolff. In spite of his precarious situation, he obstinately refused to convert to Islam—a strange position given his series of previous conversions. Sentenced to death, he stoically prepared by taking opium to dull the pain of decapitation. A reprieve was granted him at the last minute, and he scurried out of Bokhara but continued to run into difficulties all the way home.

A lively tale that alternates between bravery and foolishness, Wolff's book served to confirm European fear of Muslim peoples. Vastly less suave, clever, and romantic than many of the great Islamic voyagers—Sir Richard Burton at the top of the list—Wolff comes across as a bungling wanderer. Perhaps because he was not larger than life, although his adventures were hair-raising, his book sold extremely well and is referred to by many later travelers to the same region.

References: Newby 1985

WORDSWORTH, DOROTHY

Dorothy Wordsworth (English, 1771–1855) lived much of her life with her poetic brother, William. Herself an accomplished writer, she produced several volumes of interesting work, including one book of travel literature. Her memoirs, published posthumously, also contain some extremely fine travel writing.

In 1803, Dorothy Wordsworth accompanied her brother and Samuel Taylor Coleridge on a lengthy trek through Scotland. The record of this journey she published as

Recollections of a Tour Made in Scotland (1803). Her book interests on several levels. First, when read in conjunction with William Wordsworth's and Coleridge's writings from the same trip, an interesting triangulation appears. Each author wrote a very different account of the same experience; each noticed and noted very different aspects of the tour. Second, Dorothy Wordsworth's writing merits study for its gentle, dreamy qualities. Finally, her book offers a travelogue that fills in many of the contextual details that can help us to make sense of her brother's somewhat obtuse poetry.

Although Coleridge bailed out of the excursion quite early, the Wordsworth siblings carried on. Much has been made of their mounting dependence on opium during this period, but from reading Dorothy's account, one would never suspect a problem. In addition, *Recollections* paints a valuable picture of the relationship between Dorothy and William: she alternates between mothering him and toiling as a stern critic of his work.

The travelogue is written in diary form. It provides great and wonderfully literary descriptions of Scotland: rustic, weather-beaten, and hospitable. Her choice of language and imagery evokes nature in its many moods, from angrily lashing to softly warming to coldly forbidding. With her plethora of precise details, Dorothy Wordsworth offers us a vivid picture of a strange holiday indeed.

Much of the time the Wordsworths stayed in rustic and desolate accommodations, but Dorothy found this thrilling. In one passage describing their stay in a ferryman's "hut" in Perthshire, Wordsworth writes:

We caroused over cups of coffee, laughing like children at the strange atmosphere in which we were: the smoke came in gusts, and spread along the walls and above our heads in the chimney, where the hens were roosting like light clouds in the sky. We laughed and laughed again, in spite of the smarting of our eyes, yet had a quieter pleasure in observing the beauty of the beams and rafters gleaming between the clouds of smoke. . . . When we had eaten our supper we sat about half an hour, and I think I had never felt so deeply the blessing of a hospitable welcome and a warm fire. (Newby 222)

Such things that are normally taken for granted are noteworthy on a voyage, and often these little details provide the greatest pleasure. Wordsworth had arrived in a strange and unfamiliar world; her response was to reflect with excitement on its difference and her appreciation thereof.

See also: Coleridge, Samuel Taylor; Wordsworth, William
References: Harvey 1967; Newby 1985

WORDSWORTH, WILLIAM

William Wordsworth (English, 1770–1850) is celebrated as one of the finest poets of the romantic era. His vast body of work demonstrates many different abilities; one facet of Wordsworth's oeuvre is his travel writing. Over his career, he published many outstanding examples of travel verse that were beloved then as now.

After something of a slow start, including an undistinguishing performance at St. John's College in Cambridge, Wordsworth discovered his muse: nature. In 1790, on a walking tour of France, Italy, and the Alps, he found inspiration. The drama of the mountains, the ferocity of the winds, the might of glaciers, the copious quantities of Italian sunlight, and the colors—man-made as well as natural—of foreign places were revelations to Wordsworth. To these vivid images, first observed and noted on that initial voyage, he would return for the rest of his life. It was travel that caused Wordsworth to see the beauty of the world around him.

During his lifetime, he made dozens of journeys and travels, mostly in Europe. In 1801, he first toured Scotland, then in 1802, he set off for France again (he had lived there for a year in 1791–1792). In 1814, he returned to Scotland to complete *The Excursion*. After his 1820 tour of the Continent, he published *Memorials of a Tour on the Continent* (1822). His 1829 trip to Ireland and Scotland inspired "Yarrow Revisited." A return to Italy in 1837 provided much of the material for *Poems Chiefly of Early and Late Years* (1842). Indeed, there are scattered travel poems in every one of his books. In addition, he wrote a single book of travel prose: *A Description of the Scenery of the Lakes in the North of England* (1810, revised 1822). Clearly, travel mattered greatly to Wordsworth's poetic process.

It is challenging to write a brief account of such a vast body of work that varies so greatly. Suffice to say generally that Wordsworth's travel verse evokes majestically vivid images of nature, seeks to compare cultural characteristics, and often addresses political difference. Overall, Wordsworth's travel literature suggests that by voyaging to the unfamiliar one can be jolted into introspection. It is precisely this soul-searching that causes the traveler to know himself and therefore to know his place in the natural world.

Images of nature abound in Wordsworth's poetry. The physical world often serves as ingress into the sublime, that ambivalently awesome and terrifying realm so popular with thinkers of this era. When not provoking extraordinary emotions, nature is simply beautiful, thus inspiring in a more modest manner as well. For Wordsworth, new experiences, as on a journey, cause the traveler to oscillate between the sublime and the beautiful.

In many of his poems (and in his *Description of the Scenery*) Wordsworth insists upon making detailed cultural comparisons. In *The Prelude,* for instance, he concentrates at length upon the differences between the Continent and England. Each can learn from the other, thus Wordsworth proposes himself as a sort of cultural ambassador who transfers ideas in both directions. The benefits of such a cross-pollination of cultures appear throughout Wordsworth's work.

It would be a mistake to ignore Wordsworth's political interests. He lived, after all, in France during the French Revolution and in England during significant political strife, debates, wars, and reforms. Blending his interest in foreign places with his interest in government, Wordsworth wrote several interesting travel poems that frame cultural and geographic difference with politics. Traveling to see foreign governments in action represents an unusual motive and an even more unusual subject for travel literature.

Another interesting characteristic of Wordsworth's poetry is ambivalence. Travel is not pure good, for it has a cost. Recognizing the consequences of travel, or accommodating both the foreign and the familiar, Wordsworth can stabilize what are often unstable binary opposites. For example, the following poem simultaneously celebrates an exotic foreign land and home. Very clearly, Wordsworth spells out his message: to know home well, one needs to know elsewhere also:

> I travelled among unknown Men
> In Lands beyond the Sea;
> Nor, England! did I know till then
> What love I bore to thee.
> (Crossley-Holland 385)

Yet the narrator goes on to vow never to leave England again, in this case because of a particularly beloved woman. The poem is part of a long series of so-called Lucy poems because it identifies Lucy as the object of desire and the motivation for the narrator's actions. Wordsworth sets love and travel in opposition; in this poem travel is paid for by separation from the beloved.

Given that women were generally discouraged from even the most local travel until the mid–nineteenth century, going on a journey abroad meant a significant time away from one's wife or lover. While traveling afforded access to new and exciting things, its consequence is absence. When abroad, one misses all that happens in the familiar world.

Wordsworth's nine-book poem *The Excursion* (1814) represents travel verse at its most complex and sophisticated. Wordsworth's own subtitle, *On Man, on Nature, and on Human Life,* suggests the wide range of ideas contained in the story. The plot is simple: a poet and a wanderer encounter various sorts of characters in their travels. Their discussions with each other and with those they meet lead to growth, development, and familiarity with nature, God, and society. A worthy result of travel indeed!

For his gushing enthusiasm and his astounding talent as a poet, Wordsworth as a travel writer is significant. A highly sophisticated and experienced traveler, he understood and reflected upon the idea that travel inspires. Although his poetry resists easy access, perseverance and tenacity will lead the reader on a wonderfully satisfying journey.

References: Crossley-Holland 1985; Harvey 1967

WORKMAN, FANNY BULLOCK

One of the great woman travelers, Fanny Bullock Workman (American, 1859–1925) astounded the world with her accounts of mountaineering and exploration. Her two most famous works of travel literature are *Through Town and Jungle* (1904) and *In the Ice World of the Himálaya* (1900). Both books share with readers the excitement of travel and demonstrate that women can be every bit as adventurous as men.

Fanny Bullock married a well-to-do Massachusetts doctor in 1881. They seemed a match made in heaven: both were adventurous, intelligent, and full of life. They moved to Europe in order to more easily travel the Old World (1889–1898). And travel they certainly did! Mountaineering expeditions, a bicycle trip along much of the Mediterranean coast, a photographic safari to Central Asia, and the usual stops in major European capitals were only a few of their many excursions.

They spent nearly 25 years traveling together in every direction.

Among Fanny Bullock Workman's accomplishments is the altitude record for a female mountaineer. At age 46 she bested Annie Peck's record by scaling Silver Throne Plateau in Pakistan. She went on to beat her own record twice, retaining her title until 1934. More than simply a tourist, Workman vociferously promoted women's rights. Like Peck, Workman planted a sign that proclaimed "Votes for Women" atop several high peaks (Stefoff 59).

With her husband, Fanny Bullock Workman set off to explore India and to document the art and architecture of the region. For added thrills, they planned to cross the country on bicycles! The journey began in 1897, and it took them nearly three years to pedal the roughly 14,000 miles across the subcontinent. One of the results of the trip is the very fine book *Through Town and Jungle.* It tells of their spirited adventures and hardships, their astounding reception by curious locals, and their joyous engagement with an ever-changing geography. Writing with pluck and humor, Workman narrates the tale as if she were writing an account of Sunday afternoon in the park. At the time, India was still a British colony, and Workman makes no attempt to hide her annoyance with the fragile British women who are constantly afraid of the heat, the cold, or the damp. The intrepid Americans endured these all and found themselves no worse for the wear.

Upon their return the book was published, to considerable acclaim. Perhaps this inspired the couple to take on an even more ambitious voyage for an encore. So began the planning stage of a trip that would cover the highest peaks in the world: an extensive tour of the Himalayan and Karakoram mountain ranges. Much of the region was as yet unexplored by Westerners; parts were even closed to all travel by despotic princes and isolationist rulers. Such resistance seems only to have spurred Workman and her husband onward. The story of this vast adventure is told in *In the Ice World of the Himálaya*.

An earlier visit to Kashmir had enchanted the Workmans. European and American climbers were racing to map and conquer the great peaks of the region, and the Workmans wanted to be part of the excitement. As mountaineering was a new sport, they had to design much of their own equipment. Improvisation and quick thinking were essential. The text describes their numerous assaults and the daft cast of characters that happened to find the great peaks irresistible. All told, their expedition lasted an astounding 13 years (1899–1912)! During this period they made six major expeditions to remote mountains and dozens of lesser forays to the tops of smaller peaks.

In Workman's narrative we see the husband-and-wife team functioning as complete equals; this was one of her objectives. In addition, both appear to have been astoundingly hardy and able to endure life-threatening cold and long periods of extreme exertion. With courage and boundless enthusiasm they climbed; in the evenings, while many of the other mountaineers slept, Fanny wrote her journal.

In addition to Fanny's travelogues, the couple wrote or contributed to a number of geographical studies. Their mapping, measuring, and climatic data represent a serious contribution to the early study of the Himalayan Mountains. The most famous of their geographic writing details an arduous expedition to the Siachen Glacier in the eastern Karakoram called *Two Summers in the Ice Wilds of the Eastern Karakoram: The Exploration of Nineteen Hundred Square Miles of Mountains and Glaciers* (1917). Upon their return, they were honored by an invitation to speak at the prestigious British Royal Geographical Society. In addition, Fanny Workman was asked to lecture at the Sorbonne in Paris, making her the first woman lecturer at the university (Stefoff 66).

After their long stay in the mountains, the couple retired comfortably to the south of France. Fanny went on numerous lecture tours and wrote essays now and again. Upon her death, true to her beliefs, she left a considerable amount of money to several women's colleges in the United States.

References: Robinson 1994; Stefoff 1992

his observations by contrasting his whereabouts to his English home; in this way, he must be considered exemplary as a writer of travel literature. For him, travel, writing, and learning were one exercise.

We can see his zeal for travel—and his cultivated desire to further his geographic and geologic inquiries—in almost every entry. Mildly vexed by the French custom of eating a formal meal at midday, the genial but energized Young observes:

YOUNG, ARTHUR

An odd and rarely studied fellow, Arthur Young (English, 1741–1820) earned his reputation not as a travel writer, but as an agricultural writer. His massive history of world agriculture remained a benchmark until the twentieth century. However successful his "professional" writing might have been, it is his travel writing that earned him an entry in this volume.

Although a dull farming authority in one situation, Young became a seemingly different person when on the road. Lavishly praised by novelist Fanny Burney as a scintillating and erudite gentleman, Young appears to have come to life as something of a socialite charmer whilst on his visits throughout the British Isles and to France. He published five travel books, but only one of them, *A Year's Travels in France* (1892), was still in print in the twentieth century. He writes a sort of autobiographical diary that is both thoughtful and detailed and that chronicles his various adventures and observations in lands only slightly removed, though wholly different, from his homeland of Suffolk.

Because of his charm and social graces, Young was welcomed everywhere, and he counted among his friends many influential intellectuals and politicians. One of his great tricks was to spend sufficient time in a given locale to ensure that he met and came to know the inhabitants as friends rather than as cursory travel acquaintances. As with many writers of his day, Young almost always frames

> As the ceremony of dressing is kept up, you must be at home from any morning's excursion by twelve o'clock. This single circumstance, if adhered to, would be sufficient to destroy any pursuits, except the most frivolous. Dividing the day exactly in halves, destroys it for any expedition, enquiry, or business that demands seven or eight hours' attention, uninterrupted by any calls to the table or the toilette. . . . We dress for dinner in England with propriety, as the rest of the day is dedicated to ease, to converse, and relaxation; but by doing it at noon, too much time is lost. What is a man good for after his silk breeches and stockings are on, his hat under his arm, and his head *bien poudrè*—Can he botanize in a watered meadow?—Can he clamber the rocks to mineralize? (Adams 446)

We should also note several other elements of the above passage. Young's explanation about differing dining customs in England employs "we," suggesting that he may have envisioned a foreign reader. Indeed, his travelogue was published in France, as were at least two of his other travel books. Unlike many of his contemporaries, Young's gentle critiques do not bemoan the differences; rather they simply observe, with as much neutrality as possible. Perhaps this is the sort of tact that allowed him to make friends wherever he went.

By comparison to some of the more bombastic of the eighteenth century's travel writers, Young is tame; but in his sober observations there is much to be learned about both the cultures he visits and the culture that created him. We might imagine him as one of the ideal gentleman travelers of the era, well bred and content to note the daily experiences of travel as though they were extraordinary. In so doing, Young has written a body of work that most assuredly values the process of travel as a singular endeavor directed toward understanding himself as well as coming to know those from elsewhere.

References: Adams 1988

REFERENCES

Abrams, M. H., ed. 1987. *The Norton Anthology of English Literature,* 5th ed., 2 vols. New York and London: W. W. Norton.

Adams, Douglas. 1996. *The Ultimate Hitchhiker's Guide.* Avenel, NJ: Wings Books.

Adams, Percy G. 1962. *Travelers and Travel Liars, 1660–1800.* Berkeley and Los Angeles: University of California Press.

————, ed. 1988. *Travel Literature through the Ages.* London and New York: Garland Publishing.

Addison, Joseph. 1726. *Remarks on Several Parts of Italy . . . .* London: J. Tonson.

Baudrillard, Jean. 1988. *America.* Trans. Chris Turner. New York: Verso.

Benét, William Rose. 1965. *The Reader's Encyclopedia,* 2nd ed. New York: Thomas Y. Crowell Co.

Brent, J. Theodore. 1893. *Early Voyages and Travels in the Levant.* London: Hakluyt Society.

Brian, Denis. 1988. *The True Gen.* New York: Grove Press.

Byron, Robert. [1937] 1966. *The Road to Oxiana.* New York: Oxford University Press.

Carre, Abbé. 1947. *The Travels of Abbé Carre in India and the Near East, 1672–1674,* 3 vols. London: Hakluyt Society.

Céline, Louis-Ferdinand. [1932] 1960. *Journey to the End of the Night.* Trans. John H. P. Marks. New York: New Directions.

Champlain, Samuel de. 1927. *Writings of Samuel de Champlain,* 6 vols. Toronto: Champlain Society.

Christy, Miller, ed. 1894. *The Strange and Dangerous Voyage of Captain Thomas James.* London: Hakluyt Society.

Cooper, James Fenimore. 1983. *Gleanings in Europe, France.* Introduction and notes by Thomas Philbrick. Albany: State University of New York Press.

Cox, Edward Godfrey. 1965. *A Reference Guide to the Literature of Travel,* 3 vols. Westport, CT: Greenwood Press.

Cox, I. J., ed. 1922. *The Journeys of René Robert Cavelier Sieur de La Salle,* 2 vols. New York: Allerton.

Craig, Patricia, ed. 1996. *The Oxford Book of Travel Stories.* New York and Oxford: Oxford University Press.

Crossley-Holland, Kevin, ed. 1986. *The Oxford Book of Travel Verse.* New York: Oxford University Press.

Darwin, Charles [1839] 1906. *The Voyage of the Beagle.* London: J. M. Dent.

Davidson, Robyn. 1995. *Tracks.* New York: Vintage.

D'Oyley, Elizabeth, ed. 1932. *Great Travel Stories of All Nations.* London: George Harrap and Co.

Drabble, Margaret, ed. 1998. *The Oxford Companion to English Literature,* revised edition. New York and Oxford: Oxford University Press.

France, Peter, ed. 1995. *The New Oxford Companion to Literature in French.* Oxford: Clarendon Press.

Fussell, Paul, ed. 1987. *The Norton Book of Travel.* New York: W. W. Norton.

Hammond, Lincoln Davis. 1963. *Travelers in Disguise: Narratives of Eastern Travel by Poggio Bracciolini and Ludovico de Varthema.* Cambridge, MA: Harvard University Press.

Harlow, V. T., ed. 1928. *Sir Walter Ralegh's Discoverie of the Large, Rich, and Beautiful Empyre of Guiana . . . (1596).* London: Argonaut Press.

Hart, James D. 1965. *The Oxford Companion to American Literature,* 4th ed. New York: Oxford University Press.

Harvey, Sir Paul. 1967. *The Oxford Companion to English Literature,* 4th ed. Oxford: Clarendon Press.

Hemingway, Ernest. 1987. *The Complete Short Stories of Ernest Hemingway.* Ed. Finca Vigía. New York: Charles Scribner's Sons.

Hilton, James. 1960. *Lost Horizon.* New York: Pocket Books.

Kanellos, Michael. 1999. "First around Alone." *Escape,* vol. 6, no. 1 (January).

Kerouac, Jack. 1976. *On the Road.* London: Penguin.

Kinglake, Alexander William. 1908. *Eothen.* London: J. M. Dent and Co.

Livingstone, David. 1874. *The Last Journals of David Livingstone.* London: J. Murray.

MacLean, Sir Fitzroy. [1949] 1951. *Eastern Approaches.* Edinburgh: J. and J. Gray.

Marley, David F. 1994. *Pirates and Privateers of the Americas.* Santa Barbara, CA: ABC-CLIO.

Mayle, Peter. 1989. *A Year in Provence.* New York: Vintage.

Morgan, E. Delmar. 1886. *Early Voyages and Travels to Russia and Persia by Anthony Jenkinson and Other Englishmen.* London: Hakluyt Society.

Morgan, Susan, ed. 1991. Introduction to *The Romance of the Harem,* by Anna Leonowens. Charlottesville: University of Virginia Press.

Muqi, Che. 1989. *The Silk Road, Past and Present.* Beijing: Foreign Language Press.

Newby, Eric, ed. 1985. *A Book of Travellers' Tales.* New York: Viking Press.

OED (*Oxford English Dictionary*). 1989. Twenty-eighth printing. Oxford: Oxford University Press.

Oxford Atlas of Exploration. 1997. New York: Oxford University Press.

Penzer, N. M., ed. 1926. *The World Encompassed and Analogous Contemporary Documents.* London: Argonaut Press.

Pick, Christopher, ed. 1988. *Embassy to Constantinople: The Travels of Lady Mary Wortley Montagu.* New York: New Amsterdam.

Rice, Edward. 1991. *Captain Sir Richard Francis Burton.* New York: Harper Collins.

Ricks, Christopher, ed. 1987. *The New Oxford Book of Victorian Verse.* New York and Oxford: Oxford University Press.

Robinson, Jane, ed. 1994. *Unsuitable for Ladies: An Anthology of Women Travellers.* Oxford and New York: Oxford University Press.

Rowbotham, Arnold H. 1942. *Missionary and Mandarin: The Jesuits at the Court of China.* Berkeley: University of California Press.

Rugoff, Milton, ed. 1960. *The Great Travelers,* 2 vols. New York: Simon and Schuster.

Schriber, Mary Suzanne, ed. 1995. *Telling Travels: Selected Writings by Nineteenth-Century American Women Abroad.* DeKalb: Northern Illinois University Press.

Scott, Robert F. 1913. *Scott's Last Expedition,* 2 vols. New York: Dodd, Mead, and Co.

Shelley, Mary Wollstonecraft. 1969. *Frankenstein; or, The Modern Prometheus.* London: Oxford University Press.

Stefoff, Rebecca. 1992. *Women of the World.* Oxford and New York: Oxford University Press.

Sterne, Laurence. 1987. *A Sentimental Journey.* London: Penguin.

Swift, Jonathan. 1987. *Gulliver's Travels.* In *The Norton Anthology of English Literature,* 5th ed., vol. 1. Ed. Abrams, Donaldson, et al. New York: W. W. Norton.

Thompson, Hunter S. 1971. *Fear and Loathing in Las Vegas.* New York: Warner Books.

Twain, Mark. 1959. *Adventures of Huckleberry Finn.* New York: Signet Classics.

Voltaire. 1966. *Candide; or, Optimism.* Ed. and trans. Robert M. Adams. New York: W. W. Norton.

Wharton, Edith. 1995. *Edith Wharton Abroad: Selected Travel Writing.* Ed. Sarah Bird Wright. New York: St. Martin's.

Zimmerman, J. E. 1964. *Dictionary of Classical Mythology.* New York: Bantam.

ABOUT THE AUTHOR

Dr. Christopher Brown has degrees from Notre Dame, Northwestern University, and the University of Colorado. He has taught in several humanistic disciplines at colleges and universities in four different countries. Presently he is an assistant professor of English literature at Zayed University in Abu Dhabi. A lifelong love for literature and travel come together in this study.

INDEX